WEST POINT '41

7-30-14

Dear General Lessey,

Your generation was an inspiration ... may you enjoy the stories & experiences of your elders from the Class of '41.

Anne Wilcox

WEST POINT '41

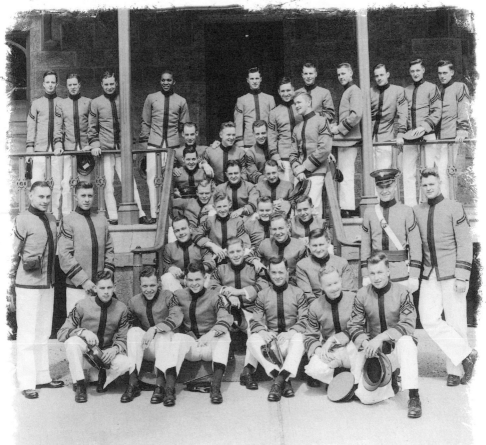

THE CLASS THAT WENT TO WAR AND SHAPED AMERICA

ANNE KAZEL-WILCOX AND PJ WILCOX

With Lt. Gen. (ret.) Edward L. Rowny, U.S. Army

Foreword by Michael J. Meese, Brig. Gen. (ret.), U.S. Army

FORE
EDGE

ForeEdge

An imprint of University Press of New England

www.upne.com

© 2014 Anne Kazel-Wilcox and PJ Wilcox

All rights reserved

Manufactured in the United States of America

Typeset in Charter and Geogrotesque by

Passumpsic Publishing

University Press of New England is a member of the Green Press
Initiative. The paper used in this book meets their minimum
requirement for recycled paper.

For permission to reproduce any of the material in this book, contact
Permissions, University Press of New England, One Court Street,
Suite 250, Lebanon NH 03766; or visit www.upne.com

Cloth ISBN: 978-1-61168-469-8

Ebook ISBN: 978-1-61168-572-5

Library of Congress Control Number: 2013956151

5 4 3 2 1

The authors, and the surviving members of West Point '41 who graciously contributed to this book, dedicate it to class members that made the ultimate sacrifice—killed in action in defense of freedom. Noted is each officer's branch, and place and date where each was killed in action. In the words of the corps, "our hearts are standing at attention."

Capt. Howard F. Adams—Air Corps, over Germany, February 26, 1943

Capt. Emory A. Austin Jr.—Calvary, on Attu, May 15, 1943

Capt. Henry N. Blanchard Jr.—Signal Corps, in Normandy, June 17, 1944

Capt. Edgar C. Boggs—Infantry, on Luzon, February 5, 1945

Capt. Marshall W. Carney—Air Corps, over Italy, October 20, 1943

1st Lt. Ira B. Cheaney Jr.—Infantry, on Bataan, January 30, 1942

Lt. Col. Wadsworth P. Clapp—Combat engineer, in Germany, February 22, 1945

Capt. Lanham C. Connally—Air Corps, over Japan, July 4, 1945

Maj. Thomas R. Cramer—Air Corps, over Italy, July 3, 1943

Capt. Robert L. Cummings—Infantry, over Leyte, November 30, 1944

Capt. James H. Dienelt—Air Corps, over Timor, June 11, 1943

Maj. Donald L. Driscoll—Infantry, in Korea, December 31, 1953

Maj. Paul D. Duke—Combat engineer, in France, August 4, 1944

Maj. Ernest Durr Jr.—Combat engineer, in Northern Italy, April 26, 1945

Maj. Horace G. Foster Jr.—Air Corps, over Hankow, August 24, 1943

Capt. Elkin L. Franklin—Air Corps, over Italy, April 20, 1944

2nd Lt. Herbert W. Frawley Jr.—Air Corps, on subpatrol, May 18, 1942

1st Lt. William Gardner—Infantry, in Normandy, June 6, 1944

Maj. William G. Gillis Jr.—Infantry, in France, October 1, 1944

Lt. Col. Ralph R. Hetherington—Field artillery, in France, December 1, 1944

Maj. Frank B. Howze—Artillery, in Korea, September 15, 1950

Maj. Thomas A. Hume—Field artillery, in Korean prison camp, July 31, 1951

Capt. Harry L. Jarvis Jr.—Air Corps, over Ploesti, August 1, 1943

Capt. Charles E. Jones—Air Corps, over New Guinea, March 16, 1943

Capt. Perry T. Jones—Field artillery, on Luzon, April 12, 1945

Capt. William A. Kromer—Infantry, in the Bulge, December 30, 1944

1st Lt. Paul R. Larson—Air Corps, in the Southwest Pacific, November 17, 1942

Lt. Col. Clarence J. Lokker—Air Corps, over Germany, November 21, 1944

Maj. William T. McDaniel—Infantry, in Korea, June 20, 1950

1st Lt. Alexander R. Nininger Jr.—Infantry, on Bataan, January 12, 1942

Maj. Paul J. O'Brien—Air Corps over Rangoon, December 1, 1943

Capt. Hume Peabody Jr.—Air Corps, over Gibraltar, October 27, 1942

Lt. Col. Charles L. Peirce—Air Corps, over Balikpapan, September 30, 1944

1st Lt. Robert P. Pierpoint—Combat engineer, Japanese POW ship, October 22, 1944

1st Lt. Hector J. Polla—Infantry, Japanese POW ship, January 21, 1945

Capt. Thomas E. Reagan—Infantry, in Normandy, August 1, 1944

Capt. Robert H. Rosen—Infantry, in Holland, September 20, 1944

1st Lt. Maxwell W. Sullivan Jr.—Air Corps, over Holland, January 27, 1943

Capt. David B. Taggart—Air Corps, over Tunisia, January 15, 1943

Lt. Col. Joseph S. Tate Jr.—Air Corps, over Germany, December 22, 1943

Maj. Richard J. Tindall Jr.—Signal Corps, in northern Italy, February 9, 1945

Capt. Francis J. Troy—Infantry, in France, January 25, 1945

Maj. James P. Walker—Air Corps, over Naples, September 7, 1943

Maj. Joseph H. Ward—Anti-Aircraft Artillery, in Germany, April 5, 1945

CONTENTS

FOREWORD

It is now seventy years since World War II and understandable, but unfortunate, that we today forget the magnitude of a world that was truly at war. There was fighting on nearly every continent; over 100 million people served in the military from thirty different countries; there were more than 50 million fatalities; and the results of this cataclysm shaped the fate of the world to this day. In the United States alone over 11 million served from a nation of 132 million. The entire economy was redirected to support the war effort, and virtually everyone personally knew someone who was affected by the war.

By contrast, today instant communication brings us wars from around the world, but they are distant, and relatively few Americans are affected directly. Only about 1.4 million currently serve on active duty from of a nation of over 300 million. Defense represents just 4 percent of the economy, and while Americans have great respect for those who are serving, most Americans don't know anyone in uniform.

Anne Kazel-Wilcox and PJ Wilcox, with General Ed Rowny, have written an important and timely book. With equal parts compelling history, vivid characters, and dramatic stories of war and peace, *West Point '41: The Class That Went to War and Shaped America* is an inspirational book that offers unique insights into key members of America's Greatest Generation. The authors have captured America's military history in World War II, Korea, Vietnam, and the Cold War through the members of the West Point class of 1941 as they entered the United States Military Academy as cadets, graduated into a world at war, and then distinguished themselves during the next several decades serving their nation and growing in their bonds of friendship with one another.

I graduated from West Point in 1981, forty years after the 424 members of the class of 1941, in a very different time and place. But reading *West Point '41* reinforces the continuity of the academy, the importance of high standards, and the anxiety of young cadets, as well as the academic, military, and physical challenges that cadets must overcome. Most important, the book captures the deep bonds of kindred friendship that develop among classmates who endure similar challenges, bonds that then serve them for a lifetime.

Having recently retired as professor and head of the Social Sciences Department there, I found the book not only inspirational but instructive, as it truly brought to life the members of the class and those with whom they worked throughout their military service. As a cadet, I was elected to the Cadet Honor Committee and spent many long hours in honor boards in Nininger Hall—one of the most important rooms at West Point, because it is there that the fate of every cadet who is accused of an honor violation is adjudicated. In spite of all that time in Nininger Hall, until I read the story of Alexander Nininger's heroism as the first recipient of the Medal of Honor in World War II, I had not understood how appropriate and wise the class of 1941 was in dedicating a room, and now an award, in honor of their classmate. Alexander Nininger's name is synonymous with honor at West Point, and this book tells the story of how and why it should be.

The authors' insightful interviews with many members of the class truly bring the drama, courage, serendipity, and sometimes the humor of war to life. The integration of oral history first-person accounts, integrated with official histories and other sources, captivates the reader almost as if this was a novel—but all the stories are true, which is what makes them even more remarkable.

The first part of the mission statement of West Point is "To educate, train, and inspire the core of cadets so that each graduate is a commissioned leader of character committed to the values of Duty, Honor, Country." By chronicling the careers of one of the most significant classes in the history of the U.S. Military Academy, the authors have supported the key verbs in that mission statement and done the academy and the nation a great service. This book *educates* about history, from World War II through the end of the Cold War. It *trains* in leadership, providing examples of success— and failure—and demonstrating the critical attribute of perseverance displayed by those who continue to lead even, and especially, in the face of challenges. And the book can effectively *inspire* not just members of the Long Gray Line, but all those interested in the human drama of individuals faced with challenging, life-changing circumstances.

Finally, *West Point '41* is particularly important today—not just to re- mind us about World War II but to reinforce what the nature of war is. In spite of drones, satellites, and stand-off precision strike weapons, warfare is not some technological abstraction but the ultimate human endeavor with real people making life-or-death decisions on behalf of their units and, ultimately, the nation. *West Point '41* clearly portrays the fog and fric- tion of war through the lives and the eyes of those brave men who fought in it. Every American wanting to learn more about our history and to be in- spired by ordinary men who achieved extraordinary results as they shaped America's future should read this book.

Michael J. Meese, Brigadier General (ret.), U.S. Army

PREFACE

The story of *West Point '41* is seen primarily through the eyes of a dozen or so surviving class members who, following their seventieth reunion in 2011, were able to share personal recollections of their careers from West Point, into war, and beyond. Their stories are based on many hundreds of hours of interviews, after which most officers fastidiously reviewed and corrected the content of their recollections, down to the artillery size, the exact date of a particular battle in the Bulge, the specific canal crossed in the race to the Rhine, the ridge an officer was on in Korea, the conversation with Eisenhower as president, and so on. These officers were trained to be meticulous—there were slim margins for error as commanders in war—and the details of this book are, therefore, believed to be the most accurate representation of historical facts possible.

Contributing officers to these oral interviews are noted following this preface. To those officers, the authors are eternally grateful for their service to our country, their dedication to relaying history for this book—and the honor of the friendship of many of them.

Live interviews for *West Point '41* were supplemented, in a few cases, by military oral histories, personal papers, and accounts provided by family members. *West Point '41* also extracted from various '41 class yearbooks and memorabilia documenting the exploits of the 424 class members. Two autobiographical books that classmates wrote were also relied on to supplement the recollections of their family members. These are noted as *Through Hell and High Water: The Wartime Memories of a Junior Combat Infantry Officer*, by Lt. Colonel (ret.) Leslie W. Bailey, U.S. Army; and *Sub Rosa: The CIA and the Uses of Intelligence*, by Peer de Silva. Furthermore, *West Point '41* shares some recollections also featured in *Smokey Joe & the General*, a biography-autobiography written by Lt. General Edward Rowny and edited by Anne Kazel-Wilcox. General Rowny was the three-star glue that brought classmates together for the remarkable narrative journey portrayed in *West Point '41*. The book relays insight into critical periods, places, and events over the course of nearly half a century in our nation's history.

When the book was begun, a friend of the authors' noted regarding '41 officers: "When these men go, it's like libraries burning down."

Instead, in this book important pieces of history are now preserved. We're honored to be presenting to you *West Point '41*—history in the words of the men who made it.

Anne Kazel-Wilcox and PJ Wilcox

CONTRIBUTORS

The following is a listing of officers interviewed for *West Point '41*, followed by a brief reference to one or two career highlights for each prior to retirement. Below that are officers whose contributions to *West Point '41* were in the form of their oral histories and written recollections along with recollections from their families.

Oral Interview Contributors

Lt. General Edward L. Rowny: Former ambassador, adviser to five presidents, and chief negotiator for nuclear disarmament with the Soviets under President Reagan. Rowny was considered one of the architects of the U.S. policy of "peace through strength." Rowny planned the Inchon Invasion in the Korean War.

Lt. General Walter J. Woolwine: Served as director of logistics for the Joint Chiefs of Staff and was assistant deputy commander, U.S. Army, Vietnam. Earlier, he spearheaded the creation of the Normandy American Cemetery and Memorial on Omaha Beach.

Brigadier General Charles W. Fletcher: Fletcher served as director of Industrial Preparedness Planning for the Department of Defense. Fletcher also developed the Army War College's first course doctrine on military strategy.

Brigadier General Wilson R. "Joe" Reed: Former commanding general charged with establishing the U.S. Army Computer Systems Command. Reed previously served on the U.S. Army Research and Development staff.

Brigadier General Michael J. L. Greene: Greene was deputy commandant of the Army War College and previously commanding general, Headquarters Area Command, Vietnam. Earlier, he closed the "bulge" in the Battle of the Bulge.

Colonel Henry R. Bodson: Served as commander of the Army's first guided-missile program, planned the Nike air defense sites in Alaska, and commanded an atomic-capable Honest John rocket battalion.

Colonel Charles J. Canella: Former chief of the U.S. Army Behavioral Sciences Division. Canella also served as senior adviser to the commanding general of the Army of the Republic of Vietnam at its principal training center.

Colonel Robert H. Edger: Served in Army combat developments, and earlier was commander of the secret Pantex Ordnance Plant, involved in atomic weapons.

Colonel A. G. W. "George" Johnson: Served as deputy chief of staff and comptroller, U.S. Army Area Command Europe, and as a military attaché at the U.S. Embassy in Cairo.

Colonel Gerard A. "Jerry" La Rocca: La Rocca was director of the Apollo Tests and President Kennedy's scientific advisor. He was formerly the director of missile tests at Cape Canaveral Space Center.

Colonel Stanley M. Ramey: Served as chairman of the Department of Military Planning at the Army War College.

Colonel Paul G. Skowronek: Skowronek was chief of the U.S. Military Liaison Mission in the Cold War Soviet Zone of East Germany, and served as military attaché at the U.S. Embassy in Bulgaria

Colonel Herbert I. Stern: Served as Army member of President Eisenhower's four-services Joint Advanced Study Group. Stern was also director of Strategic Studies for the Institute of Advanced Studies at the Army War College

Lt. Colonel Windsor T. Anderson: Served on the NATO staff in Morocco and on the Jupiter missile program.

Lt. Colonel Leslie W. "Ace" Bailey: Bailey was a general staff officer, Fourth Army Headquarters, and served as deputy post commander for the U.S. Army in Heidelberg, Germany.

Lt. Colonel James P. Forsyth: Colonel Forsyth was inspector general at Army Materiel Command, which included investigations into sensitive procurements. Forsyth was a POW in World War II.

Major Jacob H. Towers: Served as artillery battle staff officer at North American Aerospace Defense Command.

Oral History, Written Recollections, and Family Contributions

Lt. General John "Jack" Norton: Formerly deputy commander in chief at NATO's Allied Joint Force Command in southern Europe. Norton also served as commanding general, Combat Development Command, including overseeing development of the Black Hawk helicopter.

Brigadier General Edwin L. "Spec" Powell: Served as deputy commanding general and chief of staff, U.S. Army Test and Evaluation Command. Powell also served as director of Army Aviation, which included instituting trailblazing helicopter air mobility (initiated with classmates Rowny, Norton, and Alfred Moody).

Colonel John F. Harris: Harris oversaw the Department of Defense's Weapons System Management School, and was previously director of the Atlas Missile Program, which sent the world's first communications satellite into space.

Colonel John F. T. "Jack" Murray: Served as commandant, Judge Advocate Generals School. As a JAG officer, Murray represented the U.S. Army in the McCarthy Senate hearings.

Peer de Silva: de Silva served as CIA station chief in Saigon as well as in Hong Kong, Seoul, and Vienna. Earlier, as a lieutenant colonel in the Army, he was security officer for the Manhattan Project.

1

HELL ON THE HUDSON

It was only the fourth day at "Hell on the Hudson," otherwise known as the United States Military Academy at West Point, and already Herb Stern had enough. It was a scorcher, with temperatures hovering around a hundred degrees, but instead of fishing for bass on the Hudson or jumping into a watering hole as any other sane young man might do, Stern was marching in formation dressed in full military gear, lugging forty-plus pounds on his back, plunging, lunging, dropping and dipping to calisthenics, and running until he was ready to drop. And that was just the beginning of the day. As the sweat poured down his earnest eighteen-year-old face that Independence Day of 1937, Stern swore to fellow classmates, "I'm getting out of the Army!" But then, Herb Stern had waited so long to get in.

Stern was nine years old when he knew beyond a doubt that he wanted to be in the United States Army. He'd been captivated by his uncle's tales of terror and triumph of the Americans over the Germans in World War I.

"I ate their eyeballs like grapes," his uncle said of the beastly Germans.

They were the darndest doughboy stories, his uncle's tall tales of heroic Army officers in action. Herb Stern wanted to be one of those men.

A few years after hearing those riveting tales, Herb found out that his uncle had never actually set foot overseas and had certainly never seen a doughboy in combat. But by then it was too late. Herb's mind was set on the Army, so he did what hundreds of other young men did. He planned. He improvised. He coerced. He connived. He got himself an appointment to West Point that hot summer, 135 years after the academy had opened the gates to its gray cloistered walls.

Obtaining an appointment to the academy was no small feat. Each U.S. congressman and senator was permitted a very limited number of seats to give to aspiring young men in their districts; the president of the United States was granted a number more. The slots were coveted and went quickly. And even if some were doled out as favors of sorts, the recipients still had to pass demanding academic tests to gain entry.

Garnering an appointment to the U.S. Military Academy, however, meant so much more than realizing a young boy's dream of becoming a military hero. It was, after all, the height of the Great Depression. Most families had little in the way of funds to place food on the table, let alone pay for college educations. There were no college loan programs, and scholarships were far and few between. West Point offered an education for free—and three meals a day.

That was good enough for Henry Bodson, who knew he couldn't depend on his family for food and support.

I've got to make it on my own, he told himself.

Bodson knew he'd have to be extremely resourceful. He'd gotten by pretty well as a boy on the sometimes-mean streets of Williamsburg in Brooklyn. A whiz in math and science, he'd even skipped a few grades in school, all the while selling newspapers seven days a week for pocket money. When Columbia University invited the sixteen-year-old to a one-day meet and greet to explore attending the university, he was flattered but went primarily because of the free dinner. For all his gumption, Columbia, in Bodson's mind, was way beyond his courageous expectations.

Instead, Bodson opted for a smaller technology institute on the lower east side of Manhattan, Cooper Union, and entered it in the fall of 1934. He did well for a while. Then he faltered. When the dean of academics called him on the carpet, the young Bodson couldn't begin to explain the real problem. He had trouble scrounging up the ten cents for subway fare to reach school. One out of five men in the country were out of work at the time, and subway fares didn't come easy for a seventeen-year-old from Brooklyn with little support.

Bodson, undeterred, moved on to plan B. While Americans were grappling with the Great Depression, across the Atlantic Ocean Germany was arming itself and threatening the rest of Europe. Much of America was in a pacifist mood, still weary of conflict after World War I. But Bodson had always been inclined toward patriotism, and the menace looming overseas ignited that calling. *West Point could be my answer,* he thought.

As Bodson wrote letters to his congressman, Edward Rowny dealt with an altogether different predicament. He too worked odd jobs to squeak by during the Depression, to help the grandmother he lived with put cabbage and potatoes on the table. One positive to Rowny's Spartan life, however, was that his grandmother's Baltimore townhouse was in a district that entitled him to attend a prestigious technical high school, Baltimore Polytechnic Institute. That in turn helped earn him a four-year engineering scholarship to Johns Hopkins University. He excelled in engineering, took ROTC courses, and became president of the college's military honor society.

During those university years, a semester abroad altered Ed Rowny's perception of the world and his lofty ambitions for a career. He'd been awarded a scholarship by the Kosciuszko Foundation to study at Jagiellonian University in Kraków, Poland. The foundation was named after a Polish-born general of the American Revolution who later went on to design and build West Point. One day Rowny spent his small food allowance on entry into the 1936 Berlin Olympics. It was standing room only as he watched Jesse Owens win the hundred-meter race. Rowny was so proud when they hoisted up that American flag. Then his heart sank as he watched Hitler turn his back on the great black athlete.

Germany's relations with the U.S. were already strained, but when he witnessed Hitler's rebuff, Rowny had only one thought.

Things just went from bad to worse. Hitler's headed for war, and he's going to drag us into it.

A fury began boiling within Ed Rowny. Then as dusk fell, that fury turned to spine-tingling fear as Hitler's storm troopers took to the field in a display of terrifying might. There were thousands of them with torchlights, chanting patriotic martial songs to their Nazi leader. The thunder of goose steps nearly caused the stadium to shake, and Hitler's triumphal roars, blaring through speakers around the stadium, whipped the crowd into a frenzy.

Rowny was perspiring; his heart pounding; his mind racing. He scrambled to leave, swearing to himself that he'd better get well prepared for war. He wanted to lead in battle against the goose-stepping Nazis, not follow.

Rowny was already a commissioned Reserve officer after four years of ROTC training at Johns Hopkins, but now that fell far short of his objectives. Though he'd spent four years at Hopkins, he was willing to begin four years anew if it could be at West Point. He had stellar grades, would be armed with an engineering degree from a top university, and was confident he could pass the academic tests. It should be a breeze, he figured. But the West Point creed of "Duty, Honor, Country" didn't necessarily echo into the halls of Congress.

In pursuing a West Point appointment, Rowny discovered something unsettling about his local congressman, whose district included Baltimore. The representative viewed his two allotted seats as his personal bankroll. Grant a seat; pocket the dough. If the new cadets failed out of the academy, that was all the better; it was another opportunity to grant a new seat and pocket more dough. But Rowny had a keen reporter friend at the *Baltimore Sun* who'd gotten wind of the representative's scheme.

"I've got the goods on him," he told Rowny. "For about six years running, he's had no cadet make it past the plebe year. He never picks anyone too bright. He goes for the B-grade, not A—just good enough to get in, but never good enough to make it past the first year. Isn't that convenient? He can get paid off again and again."

The bribes were rumored to range from five hundred to five thousand dollars, hefty payouts even at the lower end of the range, heftier still given students failure rate and the resulting new payouts. Rowny and the reporter concocted a scheme. Under the ruse of reporting on a congressional topic, the reporter obtained a meeting with his representative. He then threatened to blow the lid off the congressman's revolving door of appointments for pay unless he gave Ed Rowny a fair crack at a seat. Rowny breezed through the entrance exams, earning himself a place among the first-year cadets in 1937.

The less-schooled Bodson failed at his first run at the exams. But he'd saved enough money by this point to attend a private high school in Brooklyn that offered prep courses geared toward the academy. He was in good company, as a half dozen other West Point hopefuls attended the school as well. The commitment ultimately paid off as several, including Bodson, made it into West Point.

Still, these cadets had to be near-perfect medical specimens as well. Paul Skowronek reviewed West Point's "Causes for Physical Disqualification" in detail to make sure he passed muster on this front. American cadets couldn't be under five foot six or over six foot six (cadets from the Philippines could be shorter).

Check, thought Skowronek, *I'm good at the lower threshold with two inches to spare*.

For each height, aspiring cadets also had to be a certain weight.

Check, I'm good here too.

There were rules on how many teeth a man had to have, and they had to be in occlusion. There was even a rule that a cadet had to have a penis. It couldn't be mutilated or missing. Skowronek chuckled.

Check. It's all there.

While Wilson "Joe" Reed also had no concerns over the latter, he was missing a tooth. But he wasn't going to let that deter him. No matter that his dentist warned him that the big gap in his smile would be classified as "extreme ugliness," a sure reason for rejection into the academy. For Reed, it was first things first. He finagled his way into the South Side office of Chicago Congressman Arthur Mitchell, the first black Democrat elected to Congress. Reed knew that Mitchell had "four blanks," a reference to unfilled appointments. He also knew that Mitchell probably thought a lily-white boy, originally from South Carolina, would be put off by going to a black congressman. Joe Reed wasn't.

Mitchell ordered in lunch for the two of them, apparently so they wouldn't be seen out in public together. Reed thought that was quite sensitive of the congressman, who probably didn't want his constituents to see him hobnobbing in public with a white boy. Still, Reed got the appointment and then in a dental feat, got a new tooth in three days flat.

Other aspiring cadets hoped their families would carry some weight, with their fathers, and even their grandfathers, having attended the academy. Just in case, families often jockeyed as hard for appointments as did the candidates. The Army dad of Charles Canella lied about his son's age so he could enlist at seventeen to get a leg up on West Point. As though his son being valedictorian at his Honolulu high school wasn't enough: it was an Episcopalian high school, chosen by his *very* Catholic mother because it too would best ready her son for West Point. The conniving for some was all in the family, small details like catechisms tossed aside.

It was tough getting into West Point, no doubt about it. But in doing so, the first-year cadets of 1937 joined an elite lineage of U.S. Army career officers that stretched as far back as Robert E. Lee and Ulysses S. Grant. General Douglas MacArthur had been top of the class at the academy. Generals George Patton and Omar Bradley were West Point graduates, and General Dwight D. Eisenhower called it his alma mater.

If the newcomers were awed by joining the ranks of such military leadership, walking through the gates of West Point that July immediately brought them back to reality. "Beast Barracks," a term dating to when Custer was a cadet, was their rude awakening. Call it training. Call it hazing. Call it torture. Call it all the above. The men hit the ground running in their first six weeks of arduous physical training for plebe year.

Many arrived having no idea what they were in for. But Hell on the Hudson displayed its true colors almost immediately. Within hours the new plebes were ordered on five-mile runs in the summer heat and expected to march in perfect formation armed with rifles. They filed in formation everywhere, from barracks to breakfast, to tactical exercises and to lunch, from classes to dinner, and every foot in between. When not together, they double-timed their step, no strolling permitted. They hustled while they waited. And with the slightest infraction, it was "Drop ten!" For some, those push-ups came several times an hour like clockwork.

The bracings were relentless. So was the nerve-wracking, in-your-face barking from the training officers hell-bent on getting them in shape. "Chin in! Rack back your shoulders! Suck in your gut! Make a nasty motion!" That last order proved especially gruesome for many. To achieve perfect, ramrod officer posture, the lanky Ed Rowny had to make a bump-and-grind motion more like a striptease act than a military maneuver.

Excuses interested no one. So the "resignations" came fast and furious. In those instances plebes were hospitalized overnight, counseled in the morning, and given a chance to rejoin the ranks. Some saw these resignation farces as a cunning way to avoid particularly hot days, but they learned the hard way that with three strikes they were out. What was worse still for those who remained was the five-day plebe hike that included climbing the summit of Crow's Nest. In the steamy summer heat it seemed like Mount Everest. Rowny made it to the top only because a classmate in much better shape carried his pack. Others were not so fortunate. Some keeled over in the final stretches of the hike and were collected by the "meat wagon," as cadets called the ambulance that rushed them off to the West Point hospital for rehydration.

In between the physical "toughening up" the plebes changed clothing several times throughout the day. It was fatigues in the morning, uniform at lunch, fatigues in the afternoon, uniforms again at dinner. Uniforms required a starched white collar beneath the gray, which kept cadets even more ramrod straight than they believed possible. Then the order of the dress code changed chaotically at times with so-called clothing formations. Plebes were given two or three minutes to change from whatever they were wearing at that moment—sometimes pajamas—into full fatigues and packs. More often than not, to save seconds, pj's would stay on underneath the plebes' layers, creating a comical sight for those in need of a good chuckle. Then they might be ordered to "stop sweating!" By the time Charles Canella got through trying to meet the formation deadline, every piece of his clothing was usually on the floor.

Of course, that wasn't allowed either. A cadet earned demerits for so much as a piece of lint on his jacket, let alone an unattended heap. And even when clothing formations were thought complete, a plebe might still encounter a "yearling" classmate—one who'd been a plebe the year before—barking out yet another order to drop ten, with the plebe still wearing all his finery. If the plebe didn't comprehend the barbaric yearling grunts, the winds of war at West Point would seem to descend upon him. When asked what state he came from, newcomer Joe Reed's reply was "the state of confusion." It echoed the feelings of many.

The ordeals were at times so exhausting that some men fell asleep at dinner. The remainder slept in their sweat, too tired to care about the lack of fans that could have brought relief from the heat. Dozens didn't make it through the grueling six-week regimen. They dropped out of their own accord or were simply unable to pass physical muster.

A few cadets arrived with some prior awareness of boot camp, and for them Beast Barracks was slightly less beastly. Jack Norton served two years in the Army as an enlisted man before becoming a West Pointer, something he thought every new cadet should do. Brothers Larry and Michael Greene were third-generation cadets, and Larry had also attended the Army prep school that groomed soldiers for the academy. Other new cadets grew up on Army bases, so they too had an inkling of what to expect from boot camp. A number of these Army brats, in fact, had already known one another for years.

But for every "have" with a hint of experience, there were as many "have-nots" entering West Point. Charlie Fletcher was one of the have-nots. He had spent seventh and eighth grades in a one-room country school in Michigan. When it came time for high school, which was some distance from home, his father went out to an auction and bought him a horse for fifty dollars to ride to school. She was allegedly broken in, but every time Fletcher got on her she bucked him off. Eventually Charlie and "Sally" became friends, and she tolerated the seven-and-a-half-mile daily treks to school.

While Sally's care taught Fletcher about cavalry, it was hardly optimal preparation for entering West Point in 1937. He was a skinny little guy, seventeen years old and right off the farm. Some of his fellow cadets came to West Point with as many as five more years of education than he did. Most came with more life experience as well. What Fletcher did share with so many West Pointers, however, was unbridled determination. But then West Point was about making leaders, not soldiers.

The class at the academy was soon divided by height into Companies A through M, the first and last being the tallest companies, the "flankers." Ed Rowny, Larry Greene, Jack Norton, and John Harris were among those towering over six feet, assigned to the outside right and left of formations for orderly appearances. Shortest were the "runts" like Larry's brother Mike, who upon arrival inevitably wondered about "that other guy in the baggy suit" sharing the same company. Mike was sure he did not resemble those half-pints. In between were middlemen, relieved to have escaped either horrible alternative.

Mike, whose full name was Michael Joseph Lenihan Greene, made the best of being the "little man with the big name," as some quickly dubbed him. One day, a hazing upperclassman put him on the spot.

"Did you know there's another cadet with your name?" asked the upper-classman, clearly itching to dole out abuse.

"No kidding," replied Mike Greene.

The upperclassman introduced the two cadets. "Greene meet Greene. Shake hands."

"What state are you from?" asked Mike of the other cadet.

"Pennsylvania," answered the fellow with the same surname.

"No kidding. So am I," replied Mike Greene. "What city are you from? The other fellow recited his town.

Replied Mike Greene, "No kidding. So am I. You must be my brother!"

The upperclassman was not pleased to have two measly plebes turning the tables on him. "Both of you! Drop for fifty!"

For the Greene brothers, their amusement was worth every painful push.

The class was drilled incessantly, instructed in arms and armor, hand-to-hand combat, mines, maneuvers, and more. "Every man an athlete," was the mantra, as modern warfare was viewed as requiring exceptional physical effort. All cadets were required to participate in sports, which ranged from football to polo and fencing to boxing, the latter two with an appropriately martial flair.

Jim Forsyth, from Kansas, discovered a huge side benefit to joining the football team: the Black Knights dined together in the mess hall and were off-limits to hazing. Then Forsyth was injured in a scrimmage. During a period of rehabilitation, the former high school track captain switched to track and field, intent on regaining his strength. Then he tripped in the high jump and shattered his kneecap.

While Forsyth grappled with disappointment on the sidelines, Paul Skowronek showed the type of industrious nature that had helped so many in the class gain entrance to the academy. The first white flurries of winter gave him a novel idea.

There are ski platoons in war, so why not at West Point?

He got a license to drive a truck, helped clear some trees off a slope, outfitted a Chevy engine to power a towline, and made a ski run at West Point. If there was even a little snow, a few inches at night, he'd sneak down into the basement in his pj's, get out his wooden skis, and head to the hill for a couple of hours. His sleepyhead roommate, Mike Greene, started the rumor that Skowronek was going out to roll around naked in the snow late at night.

It was tennis, however, where sports and religion mixed. Attendance at the nondenominational chapel was mandatory. Catholics, Protestants, and Jewish cadets jockeyed for first use on weekends. But this was not due to earnest worship. "He that prays first is first to the tennis courts on Sundays," quipped Ed Rowny to fellow players.

The gumption of some proved quite inspiring. One Jewish classmate, Joe Gurfein, requested Catholicism instruction from the priest to "make an honest woman" out of his Catholic mother. What he really wanted was to be first to Sunday service, the Catholic, and then first to hit the tennis courts. Later when a rabbi started to conduct a Saturday service, Gurfein insisted that his nose was far too big, so he really must be Jewish and needed to convert back.

That cadet had not yet learned the true meaning of honor. But everyone in the class soon would. The word would be relentlessly driven into their psyches, day in and day out, drilled into them like the steps of their marches till it became a fiber of their being—or such was the intent. "Duty, Honor, Country" was the creed bestowed upon all who entered the gates of the academy. Graduates were expected to carry that creed with them for the rest of their lives.

As General MacArthur said, "Those three hallowed words reverently dictate what you ought to be, what you can be, what you will be. They are your rallying points to build courage when courage seems to fail, to regain faith when there seems to be little cause for faith, to create hope when hope becomes forlorn."[1]

More than anything, the focus was on honor. It was a given that each cadet wasn't supposed to lie, cheat, or steal. The code required that they not tolerate it in others as well. If a cadet saw someone cheating on an exam or violating the code in another manner, even if the guilty party was a roommate, the cadet was expected to report the violation despite the risk of the perpetrator's expulsion. It wasn't about ratting someone out. The code had a far greater purpose. "Some day," the cadets were told by instructors, "you might have your men's lives to account for in battle. Then, the truth will matter."

All in the class would soon have to seek out their personal truths about what it meant to be a leader. Some would rise to the occasion; some would fall. But in the summer of that year 1937, their friendships and their military and lifetime journeys had just begun.

2

UPON THE FIELDS OF FRIENDLY STRIFE

The physical rigors of West Point life were soon matched by academic rigors. At 5:45 a.m. sharp, the bugle reveille and roll of drums began.

Cadet Clarence J. Lokker penned the hazy morning scene: "Like some medieval, walled fortress, the sullen buildings stand out grotesquely in the early morning gloom. . . . There is a flash, a long echoing rumble of sound, the shrill brass of bugles, the reverberating cascade of drum beats in the area. Like the sudden parting of a curtain dawn has flung open a new day."[1]

Cadets dressed quickly. They had five minutes before emerging into the dim light of the area between barracks. Briefly forming ranks, they uttered guttural responses while getting the once-over from a tactical officer searching for the slightest of infractions. Emptying the area, they returned to their rooms to shower, shave, and dress again before the 6:45 bugle playing "Mess Call."

"Then the long lines file into the mess hall," wrote Lokker, "and seethe out again, momentarily lost in other gray buildings now taking shape in the growing daylight. Another bugle—first call for class, and gray ranks again shape themselves and disappear into the yawning portals of stern halls."[2]

The cadets broke off into groups of a dozen to march to their first classes, and for the rest of the day—whether from hall to hall or field to firing range—they were always in marching formation.

In class they began studying the greatest military battles and strategists. They trained in chemistry and physics, studied electric advancements that turned warfare on its head, and began viewing machinery in motion as a multitude of forces acting under natural laws. They were taught to speak and write clear, forceful English and studied constitutional law and foreign languages. And while they received training in complex engineering, they also received instruction in rudimentary topics like military hygiene, the Army not wanting to lose campaigns to disease.

There were few lectures. Instead, cadets were handed reading assignments each night from which they were to determine relevant questions. So overwhelming was the volume that Ed Rowny read with a flashlight past curfew and soon needed glasses nearly as thick as milk bottles. In class cadets had half an hour to ask their questions before being quizzed. Writing answers on the blackboard, each was careful not to glance over a shoulder at an adjacent classmate, lest they commit an honor violation. They were graded every day on every subject and ranked monthly. As the months progressed, top achievers were labeled "starmen," earning gold stars that they wore on their collars. The teaching methods were unorthodox, but then the goal was not to produce ordinary officers.

At times, Charlie Fletcher fretted: *If I don't make it here, I'll be back on the farm looking at the rear end of a horse. I've got to work harder, smarter. Solutions are not enough. I have to understand the approach to the solution.*

Fletcher's great-grandfather had been a pioneer, and young Charlie wanted to be one as well—but not with hay and horses. In 1829 his ancestor built a log cabin in the woods of southwestern Michigan before returning to Detroit, collecting his family, and fording rivers to drive their livestock to the new outpost of opportunity. Charlie's father had been a pioneer as well, earning a degree in electrical engineering when the light bulb was still in its infancy. Fletcher wanted to tread new paths and had good genes to draw on, easily absorbing highly technical issues. He was increasingly drawn to complicated things that flashed—whether electric or explosive. Fletcher, for all his youth, was proving to be an intellect with West Point's grooming. But even average cadets were driven to succeed by an above-average admiration for West Point.

About the only respite from the cadets' grueling regimen was Saturday night hops, when young ladies in gowns flocked from New York City to dance with the men in gray. Others came from states away, from Army posts where their fathers were stationed. Jim Forsyth, considered one of the better-looking elements of the class, with his high forehead and piercing blue eyes, collected female hearts among them. Tall and fair-haired George Johnson filled his dance card as well, fox-trotting his way across the floor or showing off fancy footwork with grapevine and twinkle steps taught by the West Point dance instructor. But even at hops Johnson knew he was being judged; if a cadet didn't dance properly, demerits would be handed out. Johnson gave fair warning to the pretty lasses: "It can't be too wild. No jitterbug allowed."

At one of these early hops, Ed Rowny experienced true classmate loyalty. His prospective date would attend only if her roommate could as well, and that roommate needed a date. The problem for Rowny was that the girl was an "LP," meaning a "lady of the post," a label for a homely girl. A fellow flanker came to his rescue, escorting the girl. Rowny praised the good deed, swearing to friends, "There is no greater love shown than one cadet laying down his life for another by being seen with an LP."

While that seemed humorous enough, the cadets were starting to fully absorb the code of a soldier that included learning to depend on one another, as they might someday need to do in battle. The maturity and integrity of Jack Norton prompted classmates to choose him as their class captain upon whom all could depend. Larry Greene leaned on Ed Rowny to survive academics. The football center's head hung so low with fatigue after field practices that a worried Rowny force-fed him doctrine as he lay falling asleep at night. Then Rowny sacrificed his Christmas break to tutor Mike Greene when that cadet's fate hung on the line.

Even when it came to demerits, '41ers threw lifelines to one another. Like all cadets, Peer de Silva spent hours walking off so-called punishment tours on the area, but in his case the tours were multiplying exponentially. He was a "perpetual area bird." To ease the pain, a classmate put a phonograph on the barracks' windowsill and repeatedly played Tommy Dorsey's orchestra, de Silva's favorite, to help the cadet while away the hours.

De Silva was not alone racking up hefty demerits, and in truth the class was gaining a reputation for its antics. One easygoing Irishman, prone to playing pranks, added shampoo to the mouthwash of an upperclassman—a 250-pound football player—who proceeded to froth at the mouth. So furious was the upperclassman that he tried to throw the young cadet out the second-story window, while others restraining him thought he had gone quite mad.

Mike Greene bore the brunt of jokes between his brother and Rowny. Mike was five foot seven, compared to Larry at six foot one and Rowny at six foot. When Mike visited the roommates, the flankers picked him up and put him on a chair, "so we can speak to you face-to-face," they told him. Little brother got back at big brother by having his whole company of runts stand on chairs to talk to Larry when he visited them.

These endless shenanigans began garnering '41ers the nickname, "the black class." It was anything but. Theirs was a bright class. The spirit of West Point '41 was taking hold. Class members increasingly became extensions of one another, forming what would become lifelong bonds, an indomitable team of future leaders. In a speech to cadets, President Franklin D. Roosevelt reminded them that West Point discipline was not about "unthinking obedience . . ."

"Discipline," said the president, "is the well-tempered working together of many minds and wills . . . all prepared to sink individual differences and egotisms to attain an objective. . . ."[3]

The honor of some, however, was tested when Joe Reed refused to be "silenced" from talking with the only black cadet among them. Like Reed, Jim Fowler had gained an appointment to the academy through Illinois Congressman Mitchell, but conversing with the black cadet was considered a violation of the corps code, a code primarily driven by upperclassmen. Reed didn't buy into it and didn't give a hoot about those who forbid him.

Thought an incensed Reed, *Fowler's not being treated equally; he's not being treated at all. He didn't do anything wrong . . . except wear the wrong skin color.*

Reed got his whole company to back him, and the corps caved in when it became clear that it would have to silence all of that company if Reed could not speak openly with Fowler. Reed wasn't one to fit into molds. Fowler, for his part, didn't easily fit into the archaic white man's world of West Point, but with courage he persevered.

Meanwhile, the field training never ceased. Infantry weapons became less of a mystery. Cadets learned to "drop it and duck" in artillery. They churned waters with mine explosions, strengthened their backs laying pontoon bridges. They got so slippery engaging in hand-to-hand combat in sweltering heat that they felt as though slathered in oil. Cadets spliced wires to connect telephones between companies and platoons, and learned transmission codes for each letter of the alphabet: Able, Baker, Charlie, Dog, and so on, up to X-ray and Zebra.

Daily and nocturnal marches gave them rolling gaits and tough derrieres. With that, however, came bowed legs from playing handmaidens to horses, given the endless hours in the riding hall. Daunting challenges included attempting gymnastic-type maneuvers with cadets jumping on to and over unsaddled mounts, all the while hoping not to be trampled. The exercise was supposed to build cavalry confidence.

Never far from mind in these endeavors was the great physical stamina required in modern-day warfare. The '41ers were reminded of that every time they entered the field stadium, passing under Douglas MacArthur's words etched above them: "Upon the fields of friendly strife are sown the seeds that, upon other days, on other fields will bear the fruits of victory."

Every man continued on as an athlete in some shape or form: Charles Canella, Edwin "Spec" Powell, and Alfred "Ace" Moody with spirited saber encounters in fencing; Skowronek with skiing and horse jumping. Jim Forsyth stayed fit sparring in boxing, after football and track injuries sidelined him. Gangly Robert "Woody" Garrett clinched swimming medals, and Bill

Gillis captained the football team and set hurdling records. Others competed in gymnastics and tennis, in polo and with pistols, and more. A few, like George Johnson, chose gentlemanly pursuits. Johnson brought endless grief upon himself when he'd shown up to Beast Barracks with golf clubs, expecting a country club setting like the one he saw in a West Point picture book at his local Minnesota library. Instead, hazing classmen turned those clubs into an endless ordeal of metal pickup sticks for Johnson. When Johnson found out there was a golf team after all, he was vindicated and joined it.

Johnson also became a member of the choir, more for the group's coveted trips to New York City than interest in chapel singing. The weekend sojourns to perform at cathedrals included free time to explore. Johnson reveled in a diversion to *Faust* at the Metropolitan Opera, piquing his interest in music. Golden-voiced tenor Jim Forsyth, aka "Diamond Jim," was along for these choir trips as well. Each cadet forked over $2 for a Saturday night stay at the Astor Hotel in Times Square. The funds were drawn down from their "boodle books." Cadets received an annual salary of $780, but only $5 a week—in the form of a boodle book—was permitted for personal incidentals. While a couple of dollars for a hotel was a small price to pay to be off the post, cadets thought harder before putting in for a new set of cuffs and starched collar that set each back a penny. Most saved boodles for ice cream and sweets at Boodlers—the little shop at the academy with a big draw—and for corsages for dance dates. Dates were made to understand, however, that if they went to dinner beforehand, the girl had to pick up the tab since boodle books were hardly acceptable at restaurants, and $5 cash a week didn't stretch far enough.

Ed Rowny had plenty of time to save up for his date with beautiful Cheyney MacNabb, an Army brat whose father was a top cavalry commander. Her dance card filled up a half year in advance. She checked Rowny off and said, "You're number 32 on my list."

When Rowny's turn finally came, much to his dismay it coincided with a rare visit from his parents, so he was down and out on his date luck. Not wanting to "disappoint" the girl with a dance card busier than Ginger Rogers, he told Cheyney he'd set her up with a "first-class fellow." Jack Norton was that man, though in the end the girl chose to dance to the tune of Herb Frawley, a fellow classmate and friend.

Even more special than the hops, however, was a special celebration marking one hundred days till summer recess. The '41ers marked the occasion with lots of merriment and hoopla in a "Hundredth Night" theatrical show. Mike Greene went in on the fun, donning lemons in his skimpy top to play a seductive Cleopatra to his brother's strong and handsome Anthony. But even in the lightest of West Point '41 moments, the prospect of war was never far from their minds. In the Hundredth Night, Leslie "Ace" Bailey spoofed Hitler, looking every inch the Nazi, his hair slicked to the side and sporting a toothbrush mustache. The vision, however, looked all too real.

3

AT THE POST

Jim Forsyth was returning from visiting his family at Fort Leavenworth, Kansas, in the summer of 1939, ready to begin his third year at West Point as a "cow." Following the first two years as plebes and then yearlings, and after a sixty-day furlough, cadets were said to be cows returning home from far afield. En route to New York, Forsyth's train pulled into Elgin, Illinois, west of Chicago. As he sat reading, the train whistle blew, indicating his onward journey. Passengers shuffled through the car with suitcases, searching for spare seats on the crowded train. A young lady sat down beside Forsyth, and the pretty sight broke his concentration. She was a girl of medium height with fair skin and gilded-brown hair cascading over her shoulders. Forsyth guessed her to be about twenty.

They began small talk. She told him her name was Ruth Noffs, and her father was a railroad stationmaster in Elgin. She was headed to Maryland to visit relations. Soon, the two were playing cards. Between the heat of the summer and the heat of young adulthood, as the hours passed into the better part of a day, small talk led to amorous talk. By the time the train reached the east coast, James Forsyth had a new girlfriend. Diamond Jim was smitten.

He and Ruth began corresponding, and she became his "OAO," the term for "one and only" girlfriend. The initial bliss of amore, however, did not last long. In September 1939, Hitler's *Wehrmacht*—the Third Reich armed forces—invaded Poland, marking the onset of the war in Europe. For many, the mood at the academy sobered considerably, but Ed Rowny was devastated. Not only did his parents hail from Poland, but he recalled the fright of those terrifying goose steps at the Berlin Olympics. Those boots were now marching across his ancestral homeland.

Upon the invasion news, Peer de Silva and Tom Cleary hoisted a homemade swastika atop a small flagpole as a prank. For days prior there had been talk among friends about how to outprank one another; Walter Woolwine especially egged some cadets on. But this stunt went a little too far. The resulting front-page picture and story in *The New York Times* created an uproar. Rather than face dismissal, de Silva and Cleary were required to respond to every irate letter that poured into the paper—and there were hundreds—with each of the classmates' responses vetted by the academy's English department; out of mischief would come some learning.

In anticipation of a war, lectors including Generals Eisenhower, Patton, and George Marshall began reengineering their talks in tactics to real-time strategies. Many cadets were awestruck to have such men in their midst. When General Omar Bradley stopped George Johnson in training, he nearly froze in astonishment.

I can't believe he's even asking me a question.

Jack Norton struck up a unique relationship with a tactical instructor, Captain Jim Gavin, who was impressed with Germany's pioneering airborne operations. Like another "tac," Lieutenant Jake Waters—the son-in-law of General Patton—Gavin was always seeking ways to improve on the three mainstays of warfare: march, shoot, and communicate. The marching aspect included strategies for tanks, trucks, amphibious units, and other methods of moving forces; shooting involved finessing weapons and firing techniques including those on tanks; and communications on the front lines were enhanced by new twists to radios, signaling, encryption, and so forth.

Gavin and Norton bantered about whether parachutes could enhance the march element. The Soviets jumped out of airplanes into snow banks without the benefit of parachutes. Imagine the possibilities, the two conjectured, if U.S. parachute units could bypass man-made or geographic barriers to combat the German blitzkrieg. The pair deliberated various concepts. During an amphibious landing, parachute units could land behind enemy forces defending a beachhead. They could be inserted at the tail end of a blitzkrieg to destroy refueling tankers or attack supply depots supporting front-line units. Maybe they could bypass mountain obstacles and land on the rooftop of a defended building near the enemy's command headquarters. The opportunities to tactically employ parachute units seemed countless.

While shifting into this war mindset, cadets nonetheless never gave up hope of defeating an adversary closer to home—the Navy. The '41ers rooted themselves silly at the revered annual ritual, the Army-Navy game held in Philadelphia on December 2. As the cadets boarded Philly-bound trains heading down the banks of the Hudson River, flankers chanted to the 2nd Battalion runts, to the tune of the Seven Dwarfs: "They're short and fat and in second bat, high-ho, high-ho." All the cadets felt tall, however, parading through the stadium sally port in their grays and high-choked collars to the roar of approving crowds. While the West Point Black Knights failed to prevail, West Pointers knew that a scoreboard does not gauge defeat; a fighting team or a fighting Army is never licked so long as it keeps trying.

And so the cadets kept trying, on the field and off. In that third cow year, however, tragedy struck at home. The '41 class president, Bill Kelleher, was a varsity football and baseball player, and a boxer ranking in the top third of the class. Before an exhibition baseball game against the New York Giants in the spring of 1940, despite a high fever and bad sore throat, he insisted on soldiering on, playing outfield. He fell deathly ill the next day, was hospitalized, and two days later died from a rare pneumonia against which there were no miracle drugs at the time.

As though that was not freakish enough, Chuck Jobes, a '41 lacrosse player known for an unwavering loyalty to friends, playfully attempted to hoist himself up on to the goal. It collapsed on him, killing him instantly. The two men died within weeks of each other, stunning the class into the realities of mortality. The deaths of young soldiers were anticipated in war, not in peacetime along the beautiful Hudson River.

Yet peacetime, the cadets knew, was fleeting. There were rumors that the class might be graduated early in anticipation of war, but then June Week graduation festivities came and went with no further ado. Members of the class would get to finish out their final year and revel in being "kings of the walk" with rank and privilege.

But first came summer sojourns. They embarked on a trip to the Air Corps at Langley Field, watching bombing and gunnery in action and taking over controls of the B-17 Flying Fortress. They glimpsed developing airplane technology at Wright Field in Ohio. Many, like Gerard "Jerry" La Rocca, became convinced that it was wings they wanted, but then visiting the Signal Corps at Fort Monmouth, New Jersey, gave some a new appreciation for communications as a specialty.

Then there were field artillery exercises in the Pennsylvania Poconos. There in the town of Tobyhanna, many let off steam after long hours of target practice by doing the "Tobyhanna shuffle," heading to Shimko's Tavern to down beers, despite drinking being clearly against regulations. Rowny proceeded to win a polka-dancing contest with the waitress as his partner. He also took his turn, as did classmates, trying to see who could pin down a squealing greased pig, as though they'd not had their fill of slippery wrestling at the academy with hand-to-hand combat in the sweltering heat.

Rowny and Bob Pierpont were the only ones to succeed with the pig. In celebration, the former overindulged and soon passed out. Pierpont came to his rescue—as the cadet had done before when staggering demerits hung in the balance for his friend. Managing to get Rowny back to camp and into a sleeping bag, Pierpont stuffed one of Rowny's greasy, smelly socks into his mouth, knowing full well that Lieutenant Waters would soon arrive for a midnight inspection, which included sniffing cadets' breath for alcohol. Ed Rowny stunk all right, but of sweaty feet rather than beer; Pierpont had his friend's back.

The two survived no worse for wear and at long last became "first classman." It was then, in that final year, that '41ers could let their hair down a bit. George Johnson kidded about the privileges earned over their years at West Point: "I have free reign at the mess hall to sit down on the whole chair, not just the edge."

The first classmen also now knew that screaming at lowly plebes was not nearly as much fun as they first imagined; it was a tremendous amount of work and, in reality, was not about dominance but intended as a lesson in military leadership. More satisfying for first classmen was that they could now more freely express opinions with professors without fear of repercussions. Suddenly, however, many instructors were called up for duty, and twenty from the '41 class were thrust into the role of instructor rather than students, Spec Powell among them. The fast-forward button had been pressed for West Point '41.

Jack Norton, too, was propelled forward, earning the coveted title of "First Captain," making him the top company captain among all companies at the academy, in recognition for his military bearing, professionalism, and charismatic leadership. He was also on the Honor Committee, headed by Powell, which perpetuated the ideals upon which the academy was founded, interpreting questionable moral points and doling out justice to offenders who violated the honor code.

The committee's view: "There is none so honorable as a man of honor, none so despicable as a man of deceit." That meant no sympathy and no second chances for violators. Jack Norton didn't realize that it would apply so personally.

An underclassman came to Norton distressed over an upperclassman lying. The latter had reported all present to protect a friend who was playing hooky, then pressured the younger man to cover up. Norton counseled the young man to divulge the lying upperclassman. It turned out to be Norton's own roommate, who was promptly dismissed from the academy. Then Spec Powell saw his roommate cheating on an exam. That classmate turned in his class ring, resigning from the academy before causing Powell further embarrassment. The '41ers had learned as lowly plebes that as commanders, their soldiers' lives would one day rely on truth. That time was imminent.

There was one bit of mercy in that final year, however. Visiting VIPs at Christmastime were permitted to wipe clean the punishment slates of cadets. Paul Skowronek breathed a sigh of relief as the king of Norway chose to do so for graduating cadets. Skowronek was sure he would otherwise be walking the area long after June Week—probably with Peer de Silva and Joe Reed.

Instead, '41ers temporarily forgot doom and gloom, as the long, hard winters of the Hudson were sometimes known. They reveled in the holiday break—though even once home there were omnipresent reminders of preparations for war, including factories on three shifts gearing up for war. Henry Bodson tried to focus on the day at hand. Attending a holiday party in New Jersey, he mingled with guests, noticing as he did so a pretty, petite girl with dark curls that bounced teasingly. When her brown eyes glanced his way, he detected in her a flicker of recognition. Bodson tried to place her face. He thought back to a summer in his youth, spent near New London, Connecticut, when he was about twelve.

I was visiting Aunt Rose. . . . She used to send me up the hill to the dairy farm to get milk and eggs. That girl always tending the garden . . . it's got to be her.

Bodson found an excuse to talk to the girl, whose gentle voice captivated him. Her name was Belle, she said, and yes, she was that garden girl. Belle explained that she was living and working in New York City. Lucky for Bodson, he was spending his break with family in Brooklyn. The days passed quickly as the two began a whirlwind romance, cavorting about the big city. They strolled along Fifth Avenue, laughed at an off-Broadway comedy, *Hellzapoppin'*, flirted on Central Park benches, and watched the crystal ball drop in Times Square on New Year's Eve. Belle was soon driving her Dodge convertible to West Point for weekend hops, and each week at West Point, Henry Bodson counted the days till he saw his OAO again.

He also counted down the days till graduation—and till he might be called into war.

In those last months, as the gloom gave way to thoughts of graduation, Skowronek participated in the annual horse show on Jerry, his Arabian mount with a platinum blonde mane to match his own. Skowronek won the blue ribbon, making him all the more eager to join the cavalry.

It's going to be big, Skowronek thought of his prospects for advancement on horseback.

Herb Stern, on the other hand, couldn't steer clear of horses fast enough. In fact, many cadets were sure that their legs were permanently bowed from cavalry training—as though the next war was going to be fought like the Civil War, on horseback. They all gladly hung up their spurs for the last hops of their final year.

By then, flanker Ed Rowny had fallen for statuesque Rita, his former polka partner from Baltimore, and Walter Woolwine for Betty Wade, from his hometown of Bluefield, West Virginia. Other '41ers eagerly escorted around campus young ladies who were visiting from Stephens College, an all-women's school in Missouri known for its wealthy, good-looking girls. Herb Stern strolled with his Stephens date along the banks of the Hudson River. The only mandatory protection he carried was a poncho to spread out on "Flirtation Walk" to sit on and take in the glorious views. In many ways, it was an era of innocence for the West Point class of 1941. That innocence would end all too soon.

4

PASS THE AMMUNITION

As they neared graduation, the cadets selected their specialties, with top cadets getting first pick in a manner that reminded some of a football draft. Top graduates like Ed Rowny and Spec Powell grabbed coveted engineering slots. Paul Skowronek opted for spurs, while Henry Bodson, Joe Reed, Herb Stern, and Charlie Fletcher all chose artillery. Jerry La Rocca aimed for the Air Corps but needed a base branch as backup in case he didn't pass flight training; he opted for coast artillery—anti-aircraft artillery. Charles Canella selected infantry, as did Jack Norton, who wanted to pursue infantry jump school.

Having been continually ranked, and in some cases courted by field officers, the cadets' choices were no surprise to most. Only the quartermaster slots, that is, logistics, were shunned, since few wanted to be "supply men." As a result, bottom-ranked cadets were usually relegated to the Quartermaster Corps. The talented flanker, Walter Woolwine, saw it another way. Since the United States was not yet at war, the Army's enlisted soldiers remained mostly ill trained. Many were just farmers doing military drills on the side—not the type of units Woolwine wanted to command after four years of officer training.

What a sad outfit, thought Woolwine of America's Army, *an infantry growing vegetables*.

He saw the Quartermaster Corps in a different light, as a business outfit with money and contracting operations, with transportation and construction corps. Woolwine opted to be part of it. He also knew that an Army marches on its stomach, and the importance of orchestrating food and other supply lines would grow exponentially in wartime.

The day prior to their graduation, '41ers attended a requiem Mass for Kelleher and Jobes. By then, a memorial arch stood for the two, its solid stones and shape signifying the unity, strength, and stability of the corps. The curving arms of the adjacent benches welcomed friends to the site, which had been so carefully chosen—a shady glade at the end of beloved Flirtation Walk.

The class paid homage to those promising lost officers as Europe became ever more embroiled in war, and FDR insisted that America would stand up to Hitler. Class members, in the words of their corps song, began readying to tread where "sons of an earlier day . . . pointed the way," each faced with the possibility of joining the Long Gray Line in war, a reference to men in gray who'd earlier gone to their graves. The '41ers knew the risks, but all had chosen to serve their country.

As the cadets tossed their caps on June 11, 1941, they officially became Regular 2nd Lieutenants in the U.S. Army, expected to help lead their nation in battle. Most were only in their early twenties. Each man filed up to receive his diploma, with the customary ovation greeting the top and bottom graduates of the class, Ace Moody and Earle "Bud" Brown, respectively. Another class member received an ovation as well, a man who for four years had shared a room with no one, had never been welcome on corps squads, and had never been accepted at the hops—Jim Fowler. Now, classmates who had once resented his presence congratulated him with genuine sincerity. He had displayed courage, tenacity, and dignity in bucking efforts to discourage a black man from graduating from West Point. His spirit had not been broken.

The processions to the chapel began the next day, cadets ducking with their brides under the arched sabers of friends, seeking to cement their legacies.

Joe Reed, on the other hand, was packing his bags for Brazil for an extended vacation with a couple of classmates, ready to tango in Rio. There was just one small glitch: the day before leaving, he discovered that his months of language preparation were all for naught. He had been studying Spanish; the girls in Rio spoke Portuguese; Reed's best-laid plans had gone astray.

★ ★ ★

Volunteers and conscripted soldiers on U.S. bases soon swelled into the tens of thousands, but the '41 class was hard hit by a new War Department directive: to capitalize on the training of Regular Army officers, as compared to Reserve officers or conscripted soldiers, Regular officers were to be dispersed throughout the Army to serve as cores around which new units could be built. Class members were disseminated across every specialty and geographic corner, infiltrating about half of all divisions in the U.S. Army. Some felt volleyed between branches with "badminton orders," as commanders tugged at the prospects of obtaining highly trained officers. At times, '41ers felt dazed at the dizzying demands placed on them. Four years earlier, they were lowly plebes. Now they were training volunteers and enlisted men to fight a war.

Joe Reed's commander turned to him, assuming West Pointers had all the answers.

But Reed thought to himself, *I don't even understand the question. . . . I'm a jack-of-all-trades and master of none.*

Such was his rude awakening. He quickly learned a creed to keep out of trouble: "Keep your mouth closed, your bowels open, stay away from headquarters, and never volunteer." West Point had trained him to one day be a general, but first he had to learn to be a 2nd lieutenant. He wasn't given much time.

It would not be long before a colonel grilled Reed's men lined up for inspection. The colonel asked the first man, "Who is your battery commander?"

"Captain Reed, sir!"

The colonel asked the third man down the line, "Who is your battalion commander?"

"Captain Reed, sir!"

Stopping at the sixth man, the colonel asked, "Who is your division artillery commander?"

"Captain Reed, sir!"

Said the colonel to Joe Reed, "Son, I'll say this for you, you certainly have this battery under control."

Classmates were learning early to jockey commands. Scores of them were also involved in the fall Louisiana maneuvers, where more than three hundred thousand troops tested out their mettle under commanders such as Generals Eisenhower, Patton, and Mark Clark. Forces were spread over 3,400 square miles of difficult terrain, however, and supply trucks continually lost their way in unfamiliar territory, failing to deliver rations and sleeping bags to troops. So forlorn were the circumstances that Ed Rowny was forced to lie on the cold ground and go without food for days. He began to hope for real war where conditions might be easier.

Skowronek was not much happier, at times encountering riding conditions that were dicey at best. At one point, he had to slide down a fifty-foot ravine with his horse's hind legs pulled up beneath him.

Cavalry's hell bent for leathers, thought Skowronek, *audacious to the point of recklessness.*

He wondered how cavalry could be effective guarding infantry flanks when they could hardly keep up with truck-mounted troops and tanks.

Cavalry rode all night trying to get into position for morning attacks but ended up so exhausted, they couldn't outflank anyone and instead garnered plenty of saddle sores among them.

Charles Canella got wind of his future in Louisiana as well. Arriving at maneuvers, he was stunned to find that both his company headquarters commandant and commander had been fired. Canella was placed in command, shaking his head at the prospects.

You can put in a thimble what I know.

Other classmates were bomber pilots, fighter pilots—the jockeys of the sky, or paratroopers like Jack Norton who joined the Army's first-ever airborne infantry. Despite chaotic circumstances, '41ers were also already seeking out ways to work harder and smarter. Ed Rowny was given only two days to survey—by personal reconnaissance—a two-hundred-mile stretch of river for optimal crossing points. It was a test by his commander to see how he might tackle what was ostensibly an impossible challenge. Rowny commandeered a Goodyear blimp to do the job by convincing the company's Ohio headquarters office that the endeavor would create an admirable and patriotic public relations spectacle. It did, given a country gearing up for wartime.

Having to improvise also fell to '41er Hugh Foster. Assigned to a signal company, he had to train seventeen Comanches as code talkers for radio and telephone communications. The problem was, there were no Comanche words for many military terms, so Foster had to set about creating them. His vocabulary expanded to include words in Comanche that only he and seventeen Comanches understood.

Despite the challenges of training and maneuvers, for many there was still time for courtships. Henry Bodson proposed to Belle, and they were married at the iconic art deco hotel, the St. George, in Brooklyn. Walter Woolwine's venue of choice was "The Little Church Around the Corner" in New York's Chelsea section, since it could expedite weddings. As commander of his own depot supply company, Woolwine gave himself a three-day weekend leave so that he and Betty Wade could say their "I-do's," embarking upon big dreams in the little church. He also ordered leave for a classmate so that he could serve as witness. The funny thing was that the classmate was not in Woolwine's unit, but the quartermaster was on to something good.

Everyone uses paper for authority. Amazing what you can get done by writing "By order of . . ."

Some of the '41ers were less pleased with a classmate who, after his wife died, married her attractive mother. It was an unsettling concept to '41ers, who scorned that colleague.

Aspiring pilot Jerry La Rocca was more focused on flight. Herb Stern had taken to the air as well. Stern finagled his way into flight-training school in a tricky maneuver to dodge horse-drawn artillery—anything to avoid horses. Joining him at Randolph Field in San Antonio were dozens of West Point classmates, including his friends Duward "Pete" Crow and Paul "Hack" Liles, all there for basic training after finishing primary training elsewhere.

One day between flight lessons the trio cooled their heels pitching pennies on the airstrip, competing to see whose aim was surest by trying to land coins on the runway crack a dozen feet away. For some reason, their flight instructor took offense at their seeming breach of protocol, and though he couldn't pull rank on them as 2nd lieutenants, he could keep them grounded. That's exactly what he did. Herb Stern was flabbergasted. Here they were training for war, a war in which officers would be in short supply, and the training of three well-qualified ones was curtailed over a penny-ante game.

War should have such inoffensive atrocities, thought Stern.

Over the next three weeks, while others in basic training were revving up engines, rolling down runways, and tipping their wings, Stern and company were watching the sky tell time: icy blue at dawn, azure hues past noon, dusty steel foreshadowing twilight. Herb Stern wasn't sure he'd ever glanced at the sky so often, but that was the extent of his airborne views. To pass the time, he played pool at the officers' club. It was there that he heard the news that made his small corner of the world stand still: Pearl Harbor had been bombed. Every pool ball rolled to a stop. Cue sticks stood at attention as though saluting fallen comrades in the cemetery of the Pacific. Silence dropped like a curtain upon the officers' club.

Jack Murray at that same moment was at Fort Lewis in Washington State. His battalion had been scheduled to hold a party when the news broke. The battalion commander, a World War I veteran, insisted the festivities proceed, declaring, "Nothing is going to happen soon. The Japs aren't going to be landing on the shores here before the party."

So there was Murray among the other officers, dancing in tuxedos with their wives in gowns. Then abruptly at 10:30 p.m., an officer stepped into the middle of the dance floor, wearing a steel pot on his head, holding a gas mask, and blasting a shrill whistle. "All officers and men are confined to the post," he announced, "and civilians must leave the post immediately!"

The war was enveloping Washington State sooner than expected, which meant that Murray was immediately confined to barracks in his tuxedo, not exactly fitting attire for war. His wife, Dorothy, headed home to nearby

Olympia to retrieve her husband's footlocker. But while driving, she was pulled over by the police for using her lights—authorities had just initiated a blackout. It subsequently took Dorothy nearly five hours to navigate the hair-raising sixteen miles home and then back to the base in the blackness. She made it, and handed her husband his footlocker for war while he gave her his tuxedo, which was never to be worn again.

Charlie Fletcher, meanwhile, was out in the freezing fields of Wisconsin in the dead of night at artillery practice. He was building fires, attempting to heat the ground so that he could dig in railroad ties against which to brace heavy 155mm howitzer guns—essentially a cannon on armored tracks. It was daylight when his laborious tasks were done and he returned to Camp McCoy. After cleaning his equipment, he crawled wearily into his upper bunk. Then he heard the words, "Pearl Harbor."

★ ★ ★

Nearly halfway around the world, on the island of Oahu, three of his classmates, combat engineers Elmer Yates, Walt Mather, and Curt Chapman, together with their wives, had dined at the Chapmans' rented beach house, close to the Kaneohe Naval Air Station. It was a beautiful, clear night. After taking leave of their hosts around midnight, the Yates and Mathers stopped to soak in stunning vistas at a point overlooking Pearl Harbor. In the distance American ships were festively lit up from bow to stern for the Christmas season. It was December 7, 1941. As the couples basked in the glory of the scene below, Curt Chapman could not have known that his rented beach house belonged to a spy. The owner, a German named Bernard Julius Otto Kuehn, had been relaying details on Pearl Harbor to the Japanese, including the number of U.S. battleships, cruisers, aircraft carriers, submarines, and more.[1]

The Oahu engineers rushed into positions that day as Japanese bombers strafed overhead. Some planes flew so close to the ground that '41ers could see the goggles on the pilots. In every corner of America, there were calls to action, like the sentiments expressed by Navy Chaplain Howell Forgy aboard the heavy cruiser New Orleans in Pearl Harbor: "Praise the Lord, and pass the ammunition, boys." One '41er on the West Coast departed for action so quickly that he unwittingly left his wife a total of two dollars to deal with the national emergency. Meanwhile, on the opposite coast, Ed Rowny's commander offered up his engineering unit to be the first into the war. That shocked his officers nearly as much as the news of Pearl Harbor; many didn't even know where it was.

Herb Stern, however, was still relegated to inaction, feeling mighty useless. The week after the Pearl Harbor bombings, with twenty hours of flight time presumably clocked in the interim, Stern was called up for flight testing. He was soon airborne, at last seeing the skies from a view worthy of a pilot—perhaps, he thought, on his way to someday scuttling the Luftwaffe. Skirting above the clouds, he banked to the left and right, then zoomed in for landing. Rumbling down the airstrip, he ground the plane to a bumpy halt, at which point his testing instructor exhaled a pent-up breath and exclaimed, "That's the roughest ride I've ever had! How long have you been doing acrobatics in this aircraft?"

Replied Stern matter-of-factly, "I've never done acrobatics in this aircraft."

What Stern felt like saying was, *It's not nearly as bumpy as my handling of a horse. Besides, what's the big deal? I've already soloed.*

With restraint, Stern instead explained, "I've done acrobatics in primary training but not in this course."

"Why didn't you tell me?" questioned the instructor.

"You didn't ask."

The testing instructor shook his head. "You're so far behind. . . . I'm going to recommend you get turned back a class."

"I don't want to be turned back," Stern insisted indignantly. "To tell you the truth, I'd rather go back to my basic branch."

Stern had had it with flight instructors, especially given the cold shoulder received after the penny-pitching incident.

Officers should be treated with more dignity, he thought, *let alone be tested on instruction we never received. It's no way to treat officers when there's a war heating up. . . . I wouldn't mind telling the flight trainers to go stick it.*

Wisely, Stern resisted. But he yearned for the familiar feel of a large gun and the comforting sound of deafening artillery blast. The skies, he decided, were far too quiet for his liking anyway. He chose not to contest being washed out of flight training. Pete Crow and Paul Liles didn't fare much better, washing out as well.

Stern was ordered to 8th Division Artillery at Fort Jackson, South Carolina. He reported to duty in early February in boots and britches, appropriately dressed, so he thought, since artillery still remained largely horse drawn. The unit commander, dressed in fatigues, surveyed Stern.

"Well, well, Lieutenant Stern," he said with a smirk, surveying the artilleryman's britches. "A real fine field soldier, I see. . . . Now you've come home. Go and change clothes."

Horses, it turned out, were growing obsolete not just among cavalry units but for hauling artillery as well. Stern gratefully relegated his britches to mothballs while taking his commander's ribbing with a grain of salt; the commander was his old French instructor from West Point.

Stern was in South Carolina not more than a few days when he was ricocheted back to Fort Sill in Oklahoma. He wondered if the personnel officer was having dizzy spells. Adding to Stern's confusion was the fact that the only artillery opening at Fort Sill was in a communications course, a topic with which he had little experience. Yet there he was relegated to becoming an expert in the wiring, equipment, and electronics critical to an artillery headquarters.

As he began grappling with the topics, he received a letter from '41 classmate Irv "Perk" Perkin that read, "My fiancée is attending the University of Oklahoma near you. Why don't you call her and arrange a date with her roommate, Rose?"

Hmm, thought Stern. *Irv's fiancée is beautiful, which means Rose has got to be a looker or Irv wouldn't be making the suggestion.*

He called up Rose, and she readily agreed to double; she'd bring along a friend, as would Stern. When Stern pulled up to Rose's sorority house and set eyes on the nineteen-year-old with smoldering green eyes and cascading brunette waves, he was smitten.

Stern and his friend brought the girls to a fancy restaurant in hopes of impressing them. Oklahoma was a dry state, but Stern had also finagled a bootlegged bottle of gin, which he asked Rose to tuck in her purse before entering the restaurant. Over dinner and laughs, the foursome snuck shots of gin into their glasses, but Rose was in for a rude awakening when she went to retrieve her lipstick.

Her hand shot up to her mouth. "Oh no! My purse is sopping wet!" She peered inside at an empty bottle. "All the gin . . ." Her voice trailed off.

"The whole thing?" asked Stern.

She took another look and nodded dejectedly.

When the pairs left the restaurant with the soggy, gin-laden handbag in tow, it made them reek as though a walking advertisement for Beefeater. It took weeks for Stern to eliminate that odor from his car, though in an odd way he didn't mind. It was a funny reminder of his new girl, whom he began visiting on the weekends. He savored every rendezvous, knowing that each day brought him closer to deployment. Many of his classmates had already been called up into war.

The anticipation of combat was on his mind when Stern opened up his next set of orders. He started at the words. *Fort Jackson?* He reread the words, sure his imagination had the better of him. But there they were.

But I was just there, and they sent me here. And now they want me back there? What the heck?

Yet more badminton orders. Officers back and forth across the plains. Stern resigned himself to readying his footlocker—and bidding adieu to Rose. He had one last precious weekend to share with her, and he wanted it to be memorable.

"What would you like to do, Rose?" he asked. "Just name it."

A feather could have knocked Stern over easier than her response: "I'd love to go horseback riding. What do you think? Wouldn't that be fun?"

Stern swallowed hard and replied to his sweetheart, "Rose, anything for you." Only love could get Herb Stern back in the saddle. Little did he know that Rose was an experienced equestrian. On the couple's outing, much to his surprise, she took off at a gallop as he tried to keep up, making the best of his bumpy ride.

Days later, the pair bid farewell to each other, embracing and whispering words of enduring love. Then the Army officer drove off, glancing in the rearview mirror at Rose's waving hand slowly fading out of sight like a slow-motion film. And so began Stern's long ride back east—a ride that seemed longer due to his very sore bottom.

But, thought Stern, *Horses and all, it was worth it.*

Upon arriving at Fort Jackson, he immediately perked up after discovering that Joe Reed was there as well. The two initially shared a tent till realizing the stupidity of their housing arrangement. Since the government was "furnishing" their quarters, they were each foregoing a housing allowance of forty-two dollars per month, not an insignificant sum of money for each.

"This is ridiculous," said Reed. "We're giving up our allowances to live in a tent. For that amount, we could get rooms in Columbia."

They did just that, finding a one-bedroom rental. Then Joe Reed met a wealthy college student who thought it would be a hoot to live with the West Point pair. For fifteen dollars a month, he offered each a bedroom in his posh penthouse apartment, which boasted one of the finest addresses in Columbia. The penthouse had sweeping views and came complete with a manservant.

The weeks started flying by as the two officers shuttled back and forth to Fort Jackson, returning to their penthouse each evening. That is, until Stern broke the news to Reed: "I proposed to Rose and she's accepted."

"You're kidding me, right?"

"I'm afraid not, Joe. We're getting married, very soon."

When Rose soon arrived to Columbia for the wedding, Joe Reed scolded her: "You're breaking up our happy home."

Behind the humor were more than words. Herb Stern was "home" to Reed in every sense of the word. He was Reed's best friend, fellow artillery-man, a classmate sharing indestructible cadet bonds. And for Reed, whose mother years earlier had reluctantly given him up for adoption, unable to care for him at the time, Stern had become a true brother. Reed lost his happy home—but the bonds that tied Stern and him together would stand the test of time, like that of so many '41ers.

There were many more ties enveloping class members at this point as a baby boom burst upon them. One after another the "juniors" were born. Between flight training Jerry La Rocca juggled a bouncing bundle named Andre.

Paul Skowronek, meanwhile, had been at Camp Bowie in Texas, where on weekends in the summer the magnanimous ladies from adjacent Brown-wood hosted dances at the officers' club. Twenty-year-old Virginia Lyle, crowned "Miss Brownwood," attended. She was a petite, flame-haired beauty with a fiery spirit to match and had brown eyes as wide as the Texas skies. Those eyes fixed upon the dashing image of Skowronek in summer formal uniform—black trousers topped with a white cropped-jacket with gold-braided epaulets. Skowronek was sure it was the flashy uniform that drew the flame to him. After a dance, he invited Miss Brownwood to his table to share in his private stock, Brownwood being a dry town. His Old Forester bourbon had a gold label inscribed with "Lieutenant Skowronek" as though from his personal distillery.

The next day, he drove up to Virginia's home in a white convertible with red leather seats, wearing cavalry boots and britches. Miss Brownwood was hooked, and the glamorous duo quickly became an item.

Outside of Skowronek's training, the pair became inseparable. Most eve-nings they'd head out for milkshakes at the soda fountain or take romantic rides to the lake with the convertible top down. Weekends were filled with horseback riding or sailing. It was the beginning of a glorious summer filled with budding dreams for the future. But as the days shortened, the time drew near for Skowronek's regiment to participate in more months-long maneuvers. The evening before his departure, on July 23, 1942, the pair knocked on the door of the military chaplain's quarters at Camp Bowie. Skowronek held up his marriage license obtained hours earlier and asked, "Can you marry us? I'm leaving tomorrow."

The chaplain took it in stride, apparently used to urgency in this time of war.

"I'll marry you right now," he declared. The chaplain's wife stood in as witness.

Paul Skowronek got the girl; she got the car. Then he was gone, carried away by the winds of war.

★ ★ ★

By the time Skowronek returned from maneuvers a couple of months later, Virginia had taken up with a new companion—a towering Russian wolfhound almost as big as she. She had named the dog Khorki, after huntsmen stories from the Russian poet and author Ivan Turgenev, who also wrote about upheaval in turbulent times, like those Virginia was tumbling into given newly married life with an officer in wartime. Virginia had chosen the wolfhound as a graceful match for horses, and her cavalryman husband couldn't agree more. Perhaps Virginia glimpsed a bit of his future, as she could not have chosen a more fitting breed for her spouse.

Skowronek was then transferred from one base to the next, first to the newly formed 2nd Cavalry Division at Fort Clark, Texas, where he trained new recruits from dawn till dusk, then to Fort Riley, Kansas, for officers' advanced cavalry training. To avoid long-distance separations, Virginia rented a room in the nearby towns. Rooms were in ample supply at the time, from families with men training for war and from those capitalizing on renting to soldiers called up. War cut in places, boosted in others.

At Fort Riley, Paul finagled a place for Khorki in the post's kennel, leaving Virginia space to spread out in her rented room. From there she went to work. Realizing that Paul was soon slated to head overseas, she set her sights on joining the newly formed Women's Auxiliary Ferrying Squadron, or WAFS. She'd do her part in the war effort, she told Paul, piloting military aircraft from factories to U.S. air bases to have them ready for Air Corps officers heading into war. She needed to earn a private pilot's license, and knowledge of Morse code was also a plus.

So, Paul borrowed a student telegraphing instrument from the Cavalry School, and in her room Virginia began tapping away practicing Morse code, sometimes long into the night. Her elderly landlady was not attuned, however, to spirited young ladies delving into wartime occupations. The noises coming from Virginia's room sounded so strange to the prying landlady that she was convinced something illegal was going on. She handed the fiery redhead her walking papers.

Virginia, her spirit far from broken, planned a move to Abilene, Kansas, to begin flying lessons while Paul was ordered back to Fort Clark to ready troops for deployment. Before they parted, the pair scoured over matching pocket dictionaries, marking several hundred frequently used words with two letters each. These were to be their private codes, which when strung together, would be shorthand to save on pricey Western Union telegrams—for the Skowroneks it would be love on the cheap.

The creative concept worked swimmingly till the coded messages came to the attention of the Fort Clark security officer, who took Captain Skowronek to task. The latter explained away the pair's budget-cutting love letters.

"Innocent enough," agreed the security officer. "But it looks bad; you're going to have to stop."

Though Skowronek obeyed orders, working beneath the radar seemed to be in his blood.

By this time, Virginia could solo a Piper Cub plane, and she graduated to cross-country flying lessons, though that took her about a hundred miles away from Fort Clark. To make up for the distance, she grew ever more enterprising. There was no landing strip near Fort Clark so Virginia and Paul requested, and got approval, for her to land a plane on the base's polo fields; it would be a way for the pair to rendezvous for brief but blissful evenings. But there was one more hurdle. Given Fort Clark's proximity to the Mexican border, for security reasons no aircraft could be left unattended on the base. Captain Skowronek erected a tent in the polo field beside Virginia's Piper Cub, outfitted a trooper for a restful evening there, and the plane became "legal" for the night.

Virginia's dreams of a flying career were dashed when the WAFS adopted a new set of rules requiring female pilots to be at least five foot six and weigh 135 pounds. The slight Virginia, standing two inches shy of that and tipping the scales at only 110 pounds, was a lightweight. Her WAFS career was over before it started.

Discouraged but undaunted, on her last trip to Fort Clark she took Paul for a flight over troop training areas. As the captain waved to his cavalrymen, she dove the mono-wing Luscombe down and then pulled up its nose as though giving the Luftwaffe a taste of what American girl power could do.

It was but a short time later that Paul Skowronek received his marching orders. Russian novelist Ivan Turgenev wrote, "If we wait for the moment when everything, absolutely everything is ready, we shall never begin." Ready or not, Skowronek and his troops were headed to North Africa.

5

HUMBLE HONOR

Ed Rowny's roommate in his last year at West Point had been Ira Cheaney, a pleasant fellow who, together with his best friend and fellow cadet Alexander "Sandy" Nininger, were labeled "the quiet ones." The two shared a love of classical music, romance languages, and tales of exotic places. Rowny often heard the two sharing their opinions on Beethoven, Tchaikovsky, and Brahms or speaking together in French. Rudyard Kipling was a favorite of Cheaney's, but more than anything the pair loved reading about the bold soldiering exploits of Philippine Scouts—elite Filipino soldiers serving with the U.S. Army in the Philippines.

Nininger had ample inspiration for such grand exploits. His grandfather, Alexander R. Nininger, an infantryman, fought the Indians in the Old West. His great-grand uncle, Alexander Ramsey, was the first governor of Minnesota and secretary of war under President Rutherford B. Hayes. What the allure of the frontier was to them, the Philippines seemed to be to Nininger and Cheaney. Perhaps no one should have been very surprised, therefore, that the two requested assignments to the Philippines in anticipation of being called into war. It was also inevitable that while many in the class were gearing up for fronts in Europe, the two would receive ribbings for heading to the balmy Philippines. Classmates labeled Nininger and Cheaney as "running from the war," though Rowny couldn't imagine the two mild-mannered guys killing anyone anyway.

Nininger saw it another way, saying, "I would not kill out of hate, but I would kill out of love for my country."

"You're going to end up sitting out the war," Rowny told the pair, "roaming the country with Philippine Scouts. You're letting your romantic notions get the better of you."

"This is what we want to do," insisted Cheaney.

Cheaney and Nininger were deployed to the Philippines in the late fall of 1941, among the first from the class dispatched overseas. Only a few classmates joined them in that theater, fellow infantryman Hector Polla and engineers Bob Pierpont and Bob Kramer. They were part of a Philippine division composed of two Philippine Scout regiments, the 57th and 45th Infantry Regiments, and one American regiment, the 31st Infantry Regiment—dubbed the "Polar Bear regiment" due to its previous service in Siberia in World War I—plus supporting units. All were ultimately under the command of General MacArthur. The general had been recalled from retirement by the War Department, charged with defending the Philippines, a U.S. territory.

The Philippines was a key target for the Japanese since the islands formed a natural barrier between Japan and the rich resources of East and Southeast Asia. Coinciding closely with the attack on Pearl Harbor, Japan bombed key airbases in the Philippines on December 8, 1941. In the process they decimated the U.S. Army Far East Air Force, which had the largest concentration of planes outside of the continental U.S. and lost half of the planes stationed in the Philippines in the attacks.[1] Amphibious landings by the Japanese followed.

Subsequently, General MacArthur's troops were the first U.S. soldiers to face the enemy on the ground, but they were up against tens of thousands of Japanese forces. The Japanese, in addition to capturing key naval bases and airstrips, occupied the Philippine capital of Manila, on the island of Luzon, on January 2, 1942.

As that was occurring, MacArthur's troops retreated to the Bataan peninsula, across Manila Bay, waiting on reinforcements, and MacArthur established his headquarters on the small island of Corregidor at the entrance to the bay. General MacArthur's strategy was to trade terrain for time—to slow the enemy's momentum while inflicting damage—or in MacArthur's words, "Stand and fight, slip back and dynamite."[2]

While his forces battled for Bataan, regiments of the Philippine Scout division had the mission to plug breakthroughs and deter Japanese landings behind the Abucay Line, which was the main line of resistance. The line ran roughly east-west from Mabatang, north of the city of Abucay on Manila Bay, inland toward Mount Natib, a dormant volcano. The 57th Infantry Regiment defended the majority of the southern side of this line, with the terrain between it and the enemy to the north—Japan's 65th Brigade—dominated by fishponds, a sugar cane plantation, and grassy areas. The headquarters of the 57th was in Abucay, within a sixteenth-century Catholic church, and the aid station was in the adjacent *convento*, or convent. The regiment was operating under the command of Major General George M. Parker's II Corps, which occupied the east side of the peninsula next to Manila Bay, while Major General Jonathan M. Wainwright's I Corps occupied the west side of the peninsula along the South China Sea.[3]

Second Lieutenant Sandy Nininger was in Company A of the 57th Infantry's 1st Battalion, situated along the eastern edge of the line by a key road leading south. The company, in early January, was anticipating an imminent enemy attack and intensified efforts to shore up its defensive position by developing a "defense in depth." Troops burned down empty houses along the road that led west out of Mabatang. They cut down trees and mangroves in the swamps to improve their fields of fire from which they could engage the Japanese. In the absence of steel poles, they sharpened bamboo poles to fashion a barbed wire fence strung out along the line of resistance. In front of that barrier were planted triple lines of land mines, which they could cover from firing positions. They planned to heavily defend the highway on their right, eastern side of the line, since the Japanese were known to prefer movement along hard-surface roads. If the enemy broke through Philippine defensive positions by the main road, they might steamroll through the 57th Infantry's 1st Battalion.[4]

To the left along the Abucay Line, flanking Company A's position, was Company K of the 3rd Battalion, and to its left was Company I. Both had drastically different terrain to deal with than Company A. There were dikes with water so deep and fishponds with walls so steep that it would be impossible for the enemy to penetrate, except with dismounted ground forces moving treacherously through the terrain. What posed a far greater threat was the sugar cane plantation along portions of Company K's sector. For Nininger, it was cause for concern, and he and Manuel "Manny" Mabunga, a highly skilled Scout in Company A, talked of how it should be plowed to detect advancing enemy troops. The cane field also seemed a perfect approach for enemy tanks.[5] Colonel George S. Clarke, commander of the 57th Regiment, disagreed because he was concerned that plowing the field would expose 57th positions to the enemy.

As all this was playing out—the positioning and preparing—one day Sandy Nininger took off the money belt he was wearing and handed it to his Company Commander Frederick Yeager, a 1940 West Point graduate. Nininger insisted that Yeager take the belt since the company's fund—a few hundred Philippine pesos—would be more secure in it than in the commander's wallet. In one of the belt pockets was also a small crucifix.

Explained Nininger, "My father wore the same money belt in World War I and considered the crucifix as his good luck charm."

Yeager took the belt.

The Battle of Bataan soon began. On January 9, the Imperial Japanese

Army began unleashing heavy artillery into the 57th Infantry's eastern sector. Their main attack ensued on January 11. The Japanese secretly made their way through the dense sugar cane fields, emerging from the shadows in the direction of the Abucay Line and Company K and I positions. An enemy suicide squad approached a mined area, its soldiers standing erect before shouting, "*Tenno heika banzai!*" which meant, "Long live the Emperor, ten thousand years." Then soldiers threw themselves on buried charges to explode them, thereby degrading the obstacles so their fellow soldiers could continue the attack.

Japanese artillery began to pound Company I on the left side of the line. Waves of enemy troops climbed over the barbed wire barricades, which ensnared and entangled many, but the dead were no deterrent to the Japanese, instead serving as human bridges over which the living could cross. The enemy defeated Company I's defenses and took aim at Company K.

At one point Major Harold K. Johnson, executive officer of the 57th Infantry (later chief of staff of the Army, 1964–68), called in a reserve battalion that seemed to slow the enemy's advance.[6] By dawn, however, it became apparent to Fred Yeager that his flank, Company K, had been hard hit by the night attack. The magnitude of the setback was unknown. Yeager thought it critical to determine the situation, for the protection of not only his company but for the entire regiment, so corrective action might be taken.[7] Having infiltrated the 3rd Battalion, the Japanese seriously threatened the entire regiment's rear positions.

Army troops were retreating, but Sandy Nininger wanted to do the opposite—detach himself from his company to aid the stricken battalion. He told Yeager, "Fred, give me some good men for a reconnaissance patrol, and I'll try to establish just what the situation is."

Nininger explained that he knew the terrain and general area where Company K was in trouble. He reminded Yeager that he had once set up defenses there during training maneuvers.

"I know a good approach, an irrigation ditch into the area," said Nininger. "I need a squad of good men, and I will try to pick up enough information so we can figure out some kind of counterattack."

Yeager agreed to the plan.

A team of ten Philippine Scouts, Manny Mabunga among them, was selected to join Lieutenant Nininger. They moved out on the mission. Nininger had on him an M1 rifle, a load of hand grenades, and his pistol. His plan was to sneak down the dry ditch and take the enemy by surprise where it had infiltrated Company K. His strategy worked, and among an area of mango groves he began to rush through the dense foliage from one position cover to another. As he did so, he was shooting snipers out of trees, hurling grenades into foxholes, and engaging in hand-to-hand combat.

When his makeshift patrol ran low on ammunition, it returned to headquarters to report and resupply. Then Nininger and three Scouts, including Mabunga, returned to the Company K sector to continue the offensive, battling on. Again, they later had to return to headquarters, and although Nininger at this point had been wounded three times, he proceeded back to enemy territory—this time on his own.

Philippine Scouts from the patrols commented to Commander Yeager, "Lieutenant Nininger . . . very brave, very brave."

Inserting himself into the hostile positions yet again, Nininger pushed on far into enemy territory.

His body was later found lying by a tree, after the position was recaptured. The bodies of an enemy officer and two soldiers lay dead around him. Far from running from war—Sandy Nininger had run into it. It was January 12, 1942.

Alexander R. "Sandy" Nininger was the first man in World War II awarded the Medal of Honor, America's highest military honor.

Read words in General Orders No. 9, U.S. War Department, 5 February, 1942:

> The President of the United States of America, in the name of Congress, takes pride in presenting the Medal of Honor (Posthumously) to 2nd Lieutenant Alexander Ramsey Nininger, Jr., United States Army, for conspicuous gallantry and intrepidity above and beyond the call of duty while serving with Company A, 1st Battalion, 57th Infantry Regiment, Philippine Scouts in action with the enemy near Abucay, Bataan, Philippine Islands, on 12 January 1942.[8]

The exact cause of Nininger's death was uncertain, but years later former Rhode Island state senator John A. Patterson, the nephew of Nininger, spoke to an intelligence officer and a dentist who also served in the 57th Regiment. The two men helped the Catholic chaplain at the Abucay church bury five dead men. The dentist recalled that among the deceased was an American, possibly Sandy Nininger. He had been shot in the head, was brought to the aid station, and died shortly thereafter.

"The deed that Sandy Nininger did," wrote *Time* magazine shortly after Nininger's death, "was beautiful only in its violence; it was dedicated to the hope that other American boys might enjoy the beautiful things for which Sandy Nininger never seemed to have enough time."[9]

(Nininger's body was never recovered after the war, and Patterson continues to search for its whereabouts to bring Alexander R. Nininger home. In an interview in late 2013, he expressed hope that renewed congressional efforts to recover veteran remains, together with DNA advancements, might make that a reality.)

The day after Nininger was killed, Ira Cheaney was near to where his best friend had perished. Cheaney, who was also with the 57th Infantry, was organizing and leading a charge to drive away hostile snipers delivering deadly fire from concealed positions in the trees. The snipers had caused many U.S. casualties, which lowered the morale of Cheaney's battalion. Cheaney, in response, led charges to neutralize hostile positions and in doing so relieved considerable pressure on his unit.

In the days to follow the battles continued, and Cheaney spurred his platoon on, trying not to give up one grain of sand, repeatedly repelling the Japanese. Soon, his small, beleaguered group was occupying a strip of beach that represented the only untaken enclave in their sector of Bataan. The men were up against insurmountable odds, but Cheaney fought on, trying to buy time for other U.S. units to withdraw to nearby Corregidor. He went down firing his last remaining rounds, joining the Long Gray Line on January 30, eighteen days after his best friend. For his extraordinary heroism in action, Ira Cheaney was posthumously awarded the nation's second-highest award, the Distinguished Service Cross.

West Point classmates were stunned by these losses so early in the war, let alone hearing of the remarkable guts and grit of two thought to be so gentle. None would soon forget the roaring clamor of the quiet ones. Later, Fred Yeager would insist that the Bataan campaign would have ended in January 1942 rather than three months later, had Nininger not obtained information in his offensives that proved critical to regimental counterattacks.[10]

In the meantime, the fate of Hector Polla remained unclear. He was among seventy-thousand-plus American and Filipino forces on Bataan that surrendered on April 9 and became prisoners of the Japanese. The Japanese forced them on the sixty-mile "Bataan Death March," a scorching trek out of Bataan. The prisoners were beaten, bayoneted, beheaded, and shot. Others were deprived of food and water. Thousands died along the way.[11]

Lieutenants Kramer and Pierpont evaded capture as Bataan fell by making their way from the east side of Bataan to the west. Returning to their former engineer battalion headquarters, together with nine fellow officers, they were surprised to find that it had not been infiltrated. They replenished their ammunition, maps, water-purifying tablets, and quinine, then carried an eight-man plywood assault boat three miles to the coast and pushed off into the China Sea. The small group paddled furiously across Manila Bay, trying to outwit the enemy. They had only one revolver and one M1 rifle among them. Enemy searchlights swept the waters but failed to detect their small boat. The group passed Corregidor, which was still in U.S. hands, but didn't stop, instead continuing their southern crossing. All the while, they battled spasms of seasickness.

The boat landed in Cavite, a province to the south of Manila. There, Kramer and Pierpont helped destroy an enemy outpost before taking to the jungles, improvising to live off the land with the help of natives, any of which they knew might turn them in for a reward. When two among their group failed to return from a reconnaissance trip for water, they decided it best to split into two groups to lessen the burden on locals. Kramer went in one direction, Pierpont the other.

In August 1942, four months after their odyssey began, Pierpont's group surrendered to a Japanese detachment due to severe reprisals against Filipinos aiding them. Pierpont was sent to the POW camps of Cabanatuan and Bilibid.

Kramer remained on the lam, losing his shoes to a raid. He continued trekking through the wilds of the islands, mostly in his bare feet, remaining elusive and using guerilla tactics to harass the enemy. Two of his colleagues were quickly lost to pneumonia, a third to an enemy raid. Kramer and one remaining companion managed to avoid the enemy by the slimmest of margins. Suffering dysentery, Kramer lost forty pounds, but still he and his colleague kept on, organizing natives into guerilla units and training them to fight. They built their troop numbers up into the hundreds.

Then one day, Kramer and his colleague were away from their camp when the Japanese discovered it and burned it down. The pair fled. They heard of an American outpost on Mindoro Island to the south, and with the help of natives were ferried there. Within a week, however, the Japanese discovered that outpost as well, and the Americans were ambushed. Only Bob Kramer evaded death. His jungle saga—on the run—continued.

★ ★ ★

As all this was happening in the Philippines, combat for other '41ers at this early stage in the war was primarily limited to the airmen. West Point had trained some of the best pilots in an era when the Army Air Corps ruled the skies and there was not yet an Air Force. Jack Norton's classmate and friend, Herb Frawley, was among those best.

Frawley was a happy-go-lucky young man who'd easily made friends back at West Point. He had a knack for sports and was generous and handsome as well. Those were plenty enough reasons for Cheyney MacNabb to fall for him. He was also the first '41er at the controls of a heavy B-24 bomber. As squadron commander, he took off from Barksdale Field in Louisiana early on May 18, 1942. It was to be a momentous day, his wedding day to Cheyney. But first he had some German U-boats to tend to, enemy subs knocking out U.S. shipping efforts in the Caribbean.

As Frawley arrived at the target area a storm moved in, the ceiling dropped, and there was little visibility. He kept the squadron in the area till he was down to just enough fuel to get home. Heading back to Barksdale, he found the weather was not much better, with heavy thunderstorms cloaking the area. Frawley didn't have sophisticated landing equipment to give position and bearing, such as a very high-frequency Omni range (VOR) system, developed later and decreasing the need for navigators.[12]

Frawley took the lead heading into Barksdale so others might follow safely. On his approach his plane hit a high-power tension line.

Cheyney was waiting at the church with her wedding party when she got the news: her husband-to-be had been killed in a fiery explosion, her dreams for a beautiful future with the '41er gone up in smoke.

The war, meanwhile, was still in its infancy. Others among the '41 class were designated to areas of shipping and coastal importance like the Panama Canal Zone and Iceland, or Burma or India where road infrastructure was being established for supply lines into China for future offensives. Pete Crow was among those in the China-Burma-India Theater.

Crow had washed out of flight school and ended up at Air Corps depots in India as part of the Quartermaster Corps. There he oversaw a crew charged with gathering up and rebuilding planes that crashed on route to China, which got him to thinking that he might have a future in the Air Corps after all. Perhaps he was swayed by the plushness of his assignment. At times he lived like a king as the guest of the maharaja of Bikaner or the maharaja of Bharatpur, princely figures that oversaw states within India. Their liveried servants would collect Crow and his crew at train stations and escort them via horse-drawn carriages, called *tongas*, to air-conditioned hotels. They were offered cigarettes on diamond-studded gold trays, taken on sightseeing tours by elephant, and went hunting for panthers, pythons, and tigers. Crow's conquests included a tiger over eight feet long. Added to that were dancing girls for entertainment and gifts to Crow of pearls and a star ruby.

Crow's days were in sharp contrast to other members of the '41 class. Confusion seemed to prevail not only in training but often in deployments as well. Perplexed as to his fate was '41er Jerry La Rocca, who walked the beaches of San Diego wondering what he was supposed to be doing. He had been in San Francisco when Pearl Harbor was attacked. Right after the attack, he opened up new orders, but it turned out those orders, deploying him to the Philippines, had been issued prior to the Japanese attack—before America and its military had been turned upside down. The orders were immediately withdrawn since the U.S. needed forces protecting the West Coast in anticipation of further attacks. Fighter pilots would be key and Jerry La Rocca—who'd been more than successful at flight school—was one. He was assigned to the flight control center in San Diego. It ended up being a case of hurry up and wait with no sign of the enemy in sight. La Rocca had twelve hours on and twelve hours off. For him, tedium grew in those off hours.

La Rocca had always been a particularly inquisitive person; he'd taken apart his mother's Singer sewing machine as a young boy just to figure out how it worked, then rebuilt it based on drawings he made of its configuration. Now to pass the time, he began studying documents describing Japanese equipment and tactics. He pored over their fleet structures, armaments and range, ship speeds, and fleet tactics.

They always turn to the left when attacked . . . in a big circle.

He learned the tables of organization so that he knew the number of guns that, say, an anti-aircraft battery might have and how it was typically deployed. He scoured reports, analyzing anything he could put his hands on, disgusted with what he saw as a lack of intelligence among members of U.S. intelligence at the San Diego flight control center.

They've never flown . . . mostly lawyers and schoolteachers who think you can get intelligence by looking at photos or talking to pilots after they land. Are the pilots going to tell the truth about whether they hit their targets? How can they even know for sure when they don't have enough altitude to see beyond the dust and smoke? How many pilots have come back and said, "I missed my target?" Not a lot that I can think of.

La Rocca's input ruffled the feathers of intelligence officers rather than pleasing them. But before he knew it he'd been appointed operational analyst for the XIII Bomber Command—in a nutshell, La Rocca became the chief intelligence analyst.

Little did La Rocca know, but a naval officer he met in his youth had docked in San Diego. As a young boy in the 1920s, La Rocca had often accompanied his father to work at the Philadelphia Naval Shipyard. His father, born in Marseilles, was always around boats and as a civil service worker had become a brilliant chief machinist. He was now helping to design an air-pressure catapult that might help boost a plane off the end of a carrier's deck by adding to its velocity. His work was on the USS *Saratoga*, the first U.S. vessel to serve as an aircraft carrier. In the process of this work, the senior La Rocca had become good friends with a naval air officer, Marc Mitscher. The officer, who in World War I was awarded the Navy's highest award for valor, the Navy Cross, had also experimented with catapults and was involved with fitting out the *Saratoga*.[13]

Since the days of the *Saratoga* work, Mitscher had been promoted to captain and taken command of the *Hornet*, a newly commissioned aircraft carrier. It was March 1942, as the ship docked in San Diego. It was fitted with catapults, which by now had been refined. Their design consisted of enormous cylinders, held below deck, containing pistons. The cylinders were connected by cable to an airplane on deck, and when the pressure in the cylinders was released, it pulled the cable with such force that it flung a plane on deck forward at high speed, helping it to quickly get airborne.[14] Over the course of ten days in San Diego, these catapults were aiding pilots undergoing qualifying tests for carrier takeoffs from the *Hornet*.

It was from that ship, 650 nautical miles off the coast of Japan, that sixteen twin-engine B-25 bombers took off on April 18, 1942. They were the first-ever bombers launched from an aircraft carrier—though they were 150 nautical miles farther from Japan than originally planned. It was the famous "Doolittle Raid," so called after its commander, Lieutenant Colonel James Doolittle. The raiders bombed military objectives in Tokyo and four other Japanese cities before most of the pilots were forced to crashland along the Chinese coast as they ran low on fuel.[15] Still, the success of striking at the supposedly impenetrable Japanese mainland buoyed Allied morale.

Mitscher was then detached from the *Hornet*, which became a key target of the Japanese and was sunk. In the spring of 1943, as a rear admiral, he became Commander Air, Solomons, or "ComAirSols," headquartered on the island of Guadalcanal. La Rocca arrived to the island as well.

Guadalcanal, situated to the northeast of approaches to Australia, had strategic importance. Whoever controlled Guadalcanal could control sea routes between the U.S. and Australia. The Japanese had tried to sever those routes by establishing forces on the island in May 1942, after which they began building an airfield. In response, the U.S. landed Marines on Guadalcanal in August; the country wanted to safeguard Australia from an invasion and protect the buildup of Allied troops there since they might serve as a springboard for a major assault on Japan.[16] The U.S. quickly captured Guadalcanal unopposed as the Japanese retreated into the jungles.

The enemy retreat, however, was brief, and months of battling followed for control of the strategic island. The Japanese were entrenched on the northwestern end of the island, the U.S. toward the southeast at Henderson Field—the airfield begun by the Japanese but which had since been captured by the U.S and renamed.

In between enemy positions lay an inhospitable jungle. That jungle proved more challenging than the Japanese expected, as their soldiers fought terrain nearly as much as the enemy and were forced to leave behind heavy artillery during offensives. Both sides called in reinforcements on numerous occasions, but U.S. air and sea forces prevailed and secured the island in February 1943. Still, when Mitscher arrived to Guadalcanal in April, Japanese forces occupying northern islands in the Solomons remained a threat, and Guadalcanal was under constant fire.

La Rocca, who was on the staff at Henderson Field, was asked to report to Admiral Mitscher one day. It was the first time Jerry La Rocca had seen Mitscher in about fifteen years, but the admiral remembered the inquisitive young boy from the naval yards. Mitscher asked, "What are you doing here, son?"

"Sir, I'm a fighter pilot," replied La Rocca. With a touch of humor he added, "The Air Corps sent me over here so that the Navy could teach me how to fly combat."

With a smile, Admiral Mitscher said, "That was the right answer."

Mitscher instructed La Rocca to report to the Marine colonel in charge of operations, and before he knew it Army Air Corps officer La Rocca was flying Navy and Marine air combat missions. He was also involved in intelligence operations, remaining ever the student and still studying Japanese tactics and formations. He noted that in Japanese troop convoys, destroyers were always far out in front, trying to spot U.S. submarines. Cruisers and additional destroyers ran adjacent to the troop transport ships, which were always in the center of formations, and battleships with long-range guns were usually on the outer flanks. The U.S. kept going after the battleships. Bombing squadrons would fly very low, below the range of the enemy's naval guns, the angles of which U.S. pilots knew could not be depressed enough to hit them. In that way U.S. squadrons avoided the big guns, while the enemy resorted to machine guns to try and hit the planes. The enemy had ample success, but more often than not it resulted in downed planes but not necessarily killed pilots; pilots were plucked from the sea by U.S. float planes.

Jerry La Rocca considered a different approach to these offensives and one day presented his concept to Admiral Mitscher.

"We're losing airplanes; we're not losing pilots," he pointed out.

"Yes, they have a lot of guns on those battleships," agreed the admiral.

"I have an idea," suggested La Rocca. "The Japanese destroyers are always alone out in front, trying to detect submarines. The cruisers and battleships are slow, going only about fifteen knots, and it takes them several miles to turn. So if you bomb the destroyers, the battleships and the rest of the flanks will need to turn out of the way to avoid them, and that will leave the troop ships exposed."

Mitscher thanked La Rocca for his input but said little more.

La Rocca wondered if he'd spoken out of line. *He's probably saying to himself, "Who's this 1st lieutenant with the Air Corps telling me as an admiral what to do?"*

A couple of weeks passed. Then word came in that a Japanese convoy was spotted churning across the seas. A briefing was called in the operations center to discuss knowledge of its size, makeup, location, aircraft cover, and more. During the briefing, the chief operations officer announced, "Today's mission is as follows. . . . The admiral has a new idea. We're going after the destroyers that are submarine chasing out in front of the convoys."

U.S. pilots, flying the Douglas SDB Dauntless—a two-crew scout plane and dive-bomber—soon aimed their torpedoes for the lead destroyers. Diving in for the kill, they began dropping their bombs vertically, hitting their marks. As they pulled up and out of their dives, the tail gunners—extensions of the pilots—blared away at the destroyers with machine guns.

The ships following in the path of the destroyers began slowing down, eventually trying to make sharp turns—to the left—to avoid the lamed destroyers. Amid the mayhem, however, the fleet became scattered into a haphazard pattern. As that occurred, enemy troop ships—open and exposed—were attacked broadside by U.S. dive-bombers. It was a scene of mayhem as hundreds upon hundreds of enemy troops were blasted overboard or forced to jump from burning ships.

Following the great success of this offensive, Admiral Mitscher received considerable kudos from General MacArthur.

La Rocca, on the other hand, remained mum. *I'm not going to say anything to anyone; people will think I'm an idiot if I run around saying "I told the admiral to do that."*

A few weeks later Admiral Mitscher called La Rocca into his office. "Congratulations, Major," said the admiral.

"Thank you, sir. May I ask what the congratulations are for? And I believe you made a mistake with major, sir."

"No, it was not a mistake. You are now a major," explained Mitscher. "That was a brilliant idea you had, brilliant. I'm giving you a case of liquor, and I want you to celebrate with my staff, Major La Rocca."

La Rocca was stunned, less so over the liquor—though like most troops on the island, he hadn't seen any in months—more so because he jumped over the rank of captain directly to major. (He later discovered that Mitscher had, in fact, quietly given him a field promotion to captain after the destroyer incident and in quick succession followed it with the promotion to major.)

La Rocca held his party, ostensibly to celebrate his promotion, though in his mind he was celebrating much more. Navy officers on Guadalcanal had frequently kidded the Army Air Corps officer, asking him, "Are you learning anything from us?" Now, as those same officers entered the party, it was to see La Rocca's 1st lieutenant silver bar insignia replaced by the gold leaf of a major. And he had "learned" plenty.

Navy intelligence, meanwhile, had broken the code of Japanese radio intercepts and in doing so revealed that Admiral Yamamoto Isoroku—the mastermind behind the attack on Pearl Harbor—was planning to fly to an island in the north Solomons accompanied by fighter escorts. On April 18, 1943, U.S. P-39 fighter planes taking off from Guadalcanal shot down his plane near an island called Bougainville. It crashed into the jungle, killing Yamamoto.

The morale of American troops soared, though Japanese bombings still rarely let up. La Rocca became accustomed to sleepless nights. With his bayonet, he carved a foxhole amid coral rock, a feat in and of itself. He frequently used that foxhole in the middle of the night as Japanese planes—usually one or two at a time—bombed from overhead. Much worse, however, were Japanese battleships that bombed the island's shore, trying to decimate territory and push Allied Forces into the sea. It was at times like that when La Rocca, from his foxhole, could see the sky saturated with coral dust from the bombings. Blankets of the thick dust would settle down on him in his foxhole, as he gagged and clamored for clean air. Even his ears would be caked with coral as the battleships churned up the coastline. Troops began branding the enemy tactics as "washing machine Charlie."

U.S. counterattacks, like Japanese attacks, rarely ceased. Toward the end of spring, La Rocca was sent on a mission to knock out enemy anti-aircraft guns on the island of Munda, a Japanese stronghold and base of operations. It was late in the day, near dusk, and he was piloting a Dauntless when he came in visual contact with his target. He dove in and dropped his two-thousand-pound bomb, confident that he made a hit that obliterated guns and crew. Usually protocol was to dive and "get the hell out of there," but La Rocca wanted to see the damage inflicted. He navigated toward the water before circling back to see the expected ruins. Unbeknown to him, however, the Japanese had dug an escape tunnel leading away from the anti-aircraft gun, and they had taken refuge there during his attack. They were not only alive, but aiming at his low-flying plane.

They scored a hit.

La Rocca tried to skirt enemy fire and head back out to sea. *I need to gain ground . . . to reach the water.*

He got a thousand or so yards out over the water when he realized his plane was on fire. "Prepare to bail out!" he yelled to his tail gunner.

Both did, quickly losing sight of each other.

La Rocca's parachute was now a bright, billowy target, and the Japanese began shooting at it from shore. La Rocca yanked hard on his cords, trying to rock his chute back and forth to become a more difficult target for the enemy, thankful that dusk provided some cover. But bullets struck his chute. La Rocca started losing air, plunging toward the water. A parachute landing into water was difficult enough, given no reference points regarding altitude. Now La Rocca had no idea if he'd be able to land with his shoot trailing behind him so it would not smother and tangle him in a watery grave; the aim was to slide into a water entry like sliding into first base.

La Rocca was lucky in that respect, landing safely and inflating his "Mae West," as soldiers called their puffed-up inflatable life preservers. His luck was less so with his inflatable rubber dinghy, which La Rocca discovered had become detached from him in the fall. If rescue pilots were to come in search of him, without the dinghy, he was little more than a small head bobbing in a vast ocean with rough seas.

At least I'm not bleeding, he thought.

He tried to settle down. Then it occurred to him.

Sharks. They're probably circling me. No . . . I can't let my imagination run away from me. They're not circling. And I have shark repellent.

La Rocca's shark repellent was in the form of a blue powder, which when released into the water turned iridescent and was supposed to ward off species in the area like Tiger sharks.

But if I use it now, the Japanese might spot it . . . and then in the morning, no one will be able to find me with this current. I'll be miles away from where I was shot down.

Jerry La Rocca settled into his watery bed, drifting with the waves as blackness settled in. He prayed. And he prayed some more.

The sun rose early the next morning. As the dusty yellow ball lifted in the sky, La Rocca scattered the contents of his small container of shark repellent around him. An enormous, bright azure circle began to form and, like escalating ripples in a pond, grew larger and larger.

La Rocca continued to float, staring out at the horizon. Then he saw it. *A beautiful float plane. Oh my God! It's heading for me.*

U.S. pilots had spotted La Rocca's telltale azure trail and located his tail gunner as well. As the float plane came in for landing, retrieving both, accompanying U.S. fighter planes strafed the Japanese onshore.

Jerry La Rocca's Pacific prayers had been answered.

6

BAPTISM INTO WAR

Ace Bailey reported to the 34th Infantry Division headquarters at Fort Dix, New Jersey, on a cold, blustery morning in February 1942. Checking in, he was asked by a captain if he knew anything about 81mm mortars. He answered that he had only seen a wooden type on the Carolina maneuvers; given an Army short on supplies, it had improvised with makeshift mortars to simulate real combat.

"You'll be just right," the captain told Bailey of his mortar experience. "You've got yourself a job." With that, the recent West Point graduate became an 81mm-mortar platoon leader.

Bailey was notified that he had but a short time before his unit was to sail. To prepare for battle, the training was to be a grueling sunup-till-sundown regime under the watchful eyes of a post commander who was convinced the men were subpar soldiers. A few weeks into their ordeal, Bailey felt the commander's wrath one weekend morning when the commander showed up to inspect the officers' quarters, only to find barracks filled with unkempt beds. He put officers on notice that they had until 2 p.m. to turn the place spotless, or he would cite them for dereliction of duty.

The cleaning task was easier said than done since most officers were on leave for the weekend, many visiting their new brides. A recall went out but there were far too few housekeeping hands to go around. In desperation, Bailey asked Sarah, his wife of just four weeks, to help scrub the barrack floors. She raced from the pair's nearby apartment to attack the floors like she was at war with them.

Just shy of the appointed inspection time, she heard, "Here he comes!" With only seconds to spare, she exited out one set of barrack doors before the inspecting officer swung in through the others.

The Baileys' was not a typical newlywed moment, but then nothing was typical three months following Pearl Harbor. America needed to retool, and it was being driven into a tailspin as the gears of productivity shifted. Industrial factories used for civilian purposes were converting to military production, but as that effort geared up, material shortages began strangling output. Every American was urged to pitch in to help. Kids ran metal and scrap drives; young women patriotically gave up stockings to conserve on nylon; families became subject to ration books dictating how much they could buy of scarce items; auto assembly lines halted consumer production to make way for Army vehicles. As fuel grew scarce under rationing, Virginia Skowronek was forced to sell Paul's precious convertible. Everyone felt the pinch.

Even broadcasters were squeezed as the government censored news to keep a positive spin on the war effort. Nearly every aspect of life, as Americans knew it, was altered. None felt the upheaval more than mothers who sent their boys off to war, in the flash of an eye, their sons catapulted into becoming men. Women moved into the workplace to replace those called into action. Sarah Bailey scrubbing barrack floors was but a small contribution.

Sarah was at least thankful that the 34th Division's deployment was delayed until April. Then the countdown began. On April 28 troops at Fort Dix were placed on twenty-four-hour alert and embargoed from communicating with the outside world. Regardless, Ace Bailey, like other enterprising officers, managed to sneak his wife into his room for one last evening of passion. The next day, he boarded a train headed for the shipyards of New York City. He stared blankly out the window as the locomotive pulled out of the Fort Dix railway station.

What lies ahead? When will I see Sarah again . . . or will I?

The bells of the gate crossing clanged like a boxing bell, breaking his daze. He glanced at the tracks, noticing a lone blue Chevy at the crossing gate. It jogged his memory. He did a double take.

That's my car. And that's Sarah . . . How did she get past the post guards and on to this back road?

The petite blond sat behind the steering wheel as though hugging it for consolation, looking frail and forlorn. She was yearning for one more glimpse of her new husband, not knowing if it might be her last. Sarah Bailey had all of twenty years behind her—and no idea what now lay ahead.

The train lurched forward and her image disappeared from Ace Bailey's view, as fleeting, it seemed, as their weeks together as husband and wife. His transport ship was soon churning across the Atlantic, bound for Londonderry, Northern Ireland.

★ ★ ★

Ed Rowny's regiment, under the command of Colonel John "Joe" Wood, had traveled on a more southerly transatlantic journey than Bailey six weeks prior. Wood, Rowny, and other white officers commanded the 41st "Singing Engineers," a regiment that consisted entirely of black soldiers, given the Army's segregation policy. The soldiers, all from the South, were renowned for their awe-inspiring singing of Negro spirituals while performing drill parades—parades so dazzling that *Life* featured the Singing Engineers in their twelve-page spread on Fort Bragg in the June 1941 issue.[1] The regiment now became the first U.S. unit dispatched overseas. It went out in style from Charleston aboard a luxury cruise liner that had been called into wartime service because transport ships, like most everything else, were in short supply. At Rowny's first glance at the stateroom style, his recollections of the cold, hard ground of the Louisiana maneuvers faded into distant memory.

The converted cruise ship was among a fleet transporting the 41st Engineer Regiment to Liberia, on the west coast of Africa, where the regiment was to build an airbase. The base was to serve as a midway point for ferrying U.S. supplies to the Soviets as part of a lend-lease agreement between the two powers. It was part of FDR's effort to appease the Soviets since they complained they were doing all the fighting while the U.S. was still mobilizing. Once the airbase was built, equipment and supplies, such as jeeps and ammunition, would be flown from Florida to Brazil then onward to Liberia, followed by a stop in Sudan, before ultimately reaching the Russians in Yalta on the Black Sea. Arranging to build the airbase had required delicate diplomacy since Liberia declared its neutrality in the war, but the country would benefit greatly from an international airport. Liberia's heritage was also tied to the U.S.; it had been founded with freed American slaves in 1822 during President James Monroe's tenure, thus prompting Washington to decide that sending a black unit to the country, the 41st Engineers, would be symbolic.

Sending American forces to Liberia, however, was about far more than satisfying the Soviets. Liberia was one of the few rubber-producing areas of the world, its thick, lush jungles filled with trees that oozed latex used to make plane wheels, tank treads, lifeboats, jeep tires, and more, a virtual wartime wonder product. The Allies needed to tap into this key rubber source, cultivated on the vast Firestone rubber plantation in Liberia. At the same time, it was imperative for the Allies to keep those resources from falling into enemy hands. There was a worldwide shortage of rubber with the situation becoming so dire that Germans, in some cases, were resorting to making vehicle wheels out of metal instead of using tires. The Japanese, meanwhile, had captured key rubber plantations in Southeast Asia. So the U.S. turned its sights on Liberia. U.S. planes ferrying supplies to the Russians could, on return trips, carry latex back for use in American factories.

As the 41st Engineers headed to Liberia, all was smooth sailing for the fleet until April 3, eight days out. On that day one of the supply ships, *West Irmo*, failed to zigzag as ordered by its escort, a Royal Navy destroyer. Captains and crews often got tired of this zigzagging because it slowed voyages down considerably. *West Irmo* was about two miles away from its escort, which was off its starboard quarter, when a torpedo from German U-boat *U-505* struck the supply ship, blowing its bow off and creating a gaping hole nearly twenty square feet in size. Men and metal went hurtling skyward, and ten stevedores who had been sitting on a hatch were killed.[2]

Rowny could see the blazing figures of fellow soldiers plunging into the sea. He scanned the horizon, wondering, *Who's next?*

Survivors took to lifeboats, but the seas were rough and debris was scattered about. It took two hours for the escort to retrieve all ninety-nine survivors.[3] The 41st Singing Engineers quickly came to the somber realization that war was not a three-letter word but a stark reality. It turned out to be a lone torpedo, which puzzled the troops, but they thanked God for that incongruous blessing. The remainder of the fleet sailed on unscathed.

Two days later, as the 41st fleet approached Liberia's shores, Rowny gazed at the glorious beaches that lay ahead. Palm trees bent in the breeze as though beckoning from a scene out of *South Pacific*. Bare-breasted women in colorful skirts waved and jiggled their wares, which lit a fire under soldiers ready to let loose after ocean confinement. Among the crowd lining the shore was a dignitary who stood out as a paradox, meticulously clad in a finely tailored suit. He officially greeted America to Liberia's shores as though a master of ceremonies running a three-ring circus. In fact, Rowny would soon find out that the Army's time in Liberia would, in many ways, be just that.

Talk about a welcoming committee, thought Rowny. *This is going to be interesting.*

He glanced around at the half-naked women and the eyes of wide-eyed troops.

Just how much work are we going to get done?

The women proved to be only the half of it. Colonel Wood and 1st Lieutenant Rowny had their work cut out for them. First, they had to convince Firestone executives to cooperate with the military. U.S. troops had been trying to unload materials from their ships on to rectangular barges to bring them ashore, but the flat barges proved ill equipped for the rolling surf. Firestone, on the other hand, had about forty to fifty seaworthy vessels, lighters with hulled bows and flat bottoms. Colonel Wood went to Mr. Firestone's office and requested their use, but Firestone, saying he needed them and that his company was not a "charitable organization," refused.

That prompted one of Wood's senior officers to put his hand on his revolver and announce, "In the name of the United States, I hereby commandeer Firestone's lighters." Wood then proceeded to borrow Firestone's phone. He asked the operator to put him through to the White House, at which point Firestone grew visibly paler. The colonel asked for the president, but was informed that FDR was not available. Wood requested that this message be forwarded: "Please deliver this message to the president. The 41st Engineers arrived off the shore of Liberia minus one supply ship, which was torpedoed in the Atlantic. In the interest of U.S. security, the Firestone Rubber Company has agreed to let us use its lighters. Respectfully, Colonel J. E. Wood."

Firestone was visibly relieved, given Wood's face-saving choice of words.

The 41st Engineers soon began tackling the monumental challenge of building an airbase amid termite hills—and jungle terrain. On top of it all, they had to cope with a mountain of beer. Someone in D.C., it seems, decided that a beer a day per soldier might help moral among the all-black regiment. But they had miscalculated and sent a *case* per man, per day. For a ninety-day supply, that amounted to about six million cans of beer, all in cardboard cartons and with the rainy season fast approaching.

"Pretty soon, we're going to have three thousand soldiers sliding and tumbling on rivers of rolling beer cans," griped Ed Rowny.

Two guards were assigned to protect the beer bounty, but the troops quickly lost interest in warm beer in an even warmer climate. The guards stood down, letting the natives have a heyday with the jungle brewery, which resulted in a free-for-all as though golden riches had been heaped upon the people.

While a can crisis was averted, there was less success with the more serious problems of malaria and venereal disease. Both began to run rampant among the troops. Mosquito nets and quinine pills helped to a degree in combating the malaria, but it was critical that troops keep themselves covered as they toiled in the jungles. With temperatures soaring above a hundred degrees, rarely were shirts kept on, and sunstroke was added to the list of soldiers' woes.

Averting a plague of venereal disease was trickier. It was hard to reign in men when hundreds of naked women were roaming about. Add in the threat of battle and possible mortality in the not-too-distant future, and it made for decisions born of spontaneity rather than foresight. In Colonel Wood's view, however, losing men to battle would be bad enough; losing them to disease before even entering combat was unconscionable. In a pre-emptive strike, the colonel charged Rowny with constructing an "official" Army brothel, one that would have a schedule of time slots as well as a physician to dispense penicillin regimens to keep the ladies clean. Wood figured better to reign in the chaos than leave things to chance. Needless to say, when word filtered up to Army brass, they were not amused. The brothel was short-lived.

Somehow, despite it all—the plethora of obstacles and torrents of rain that pounded on the tin roofs like machine-gun fire—Ed Rowny's engineers completed the airfield on time. The runway was an engineering marvel, constructed on an elevated slice of land with six-foot concrete wall sidings protecting it from flooding. It would stand the test of time, serving as the country's main airfield for decades to follow.

With the job complete, a spate of new orders came in from Washington. Wood was promoted to brigadier general and ordered to Alabama to head a cadre in the newly formed 92nd Infantry Division. Rowny was promoted to captain, and Wood assigned him to the same division. The rest of the 41st troops stayed on in Liberia to continue airfield work such as adding a control tower. Later, the troops would move north to the Mediterranean coast.

But things were only beginning to heat up in Africa.

★ ★ ★

Ace Bailey, with the 135th Infantry Regiment of the 34th Infantry Division, sailed from Belfast in late October. He was aboard a British cruiser, the *Sheffield*. Together with other American and British officers, he assembled in the ship's wardroom, where each officer was handed a large-scale map of a city with intricate details of its harbor and port installations—a city with no name. The men were to etch every aspect of the nameless location into their memories.

Not until a week out did they discover the objective: French North Africa, which remained largely loyal to Vichy France, the French state—named after its administrative headquarters in Vichy—that was collaborating with Nazi Germany. In opposition to Vichy France was the Free French, a resistance organization led by General Charles de Gaulle. President Roosevelt and Prime Minister Churchill had agreed on an Allied invasion—Operation Torch—to clear the North Africa region of the enemy so that the

Allies could move freely about the Mediterranean and ultimately invade the "soft underbelly" of Axis power—Italy. Securing North Africa would also prevent the Germans from leapfrogging across the Strait of Gibraltar from Morocco into Spain, in effect, neutralizing the risk of a southern invasion by the Axis into Europe.

More than one hundred thousand Allied troops, under the command of General Eisenhower, were to strike at three North African port cities: a western task force would strike the important naval base of Casablanca in Morocco; a central force would hit adjacent Algeria, in Oran, to capture its port as well as airfields on the Mediterranean coast; the mission of the eastern task force was to seize Algeria's capital, Algiers. Targeting the latter were forty-two thousand troops including U.S. infantry, Army Rangers and British commandos. Ace Bailey was among them. He was aboard the *Malcolm*, one of two destroyers—the other was the *Broke*—steaming toward the capital on a dark and moonless night, November 8, 1942.

As the *Malcolm* approached Algiers, Bailey could discern the incandescent outline of the city. Then abruptly, the city lights were extinguished, its residents apparently alerted to monstrous shadows approaching from the sea. Enormous searchlights ashore began scanning the waters, crisscrossing in frantic motions, trying to pinpoint the invaders. The destroyers eluded the beams at first, keeping course for the break in the jetty and the boom they were to ram through. Then the blinding glare of lights struck them, throwing them off course, causing them to veer north. Missing the break, the destroyers were forced to head seaward for roundabouts. They made a second attempt at plunging through the boom, but artillery shells began blasting down on the destroyers, causing both to again miss their marks.

Ace Bailey was packed on to the crowded deck of the *Malcolm* as an artillery shell exploded its smokestack, hurling fragments in every direction. Another shell hit, and then another. The ship listed violently. Bodies fell. The deck became slippery with blood. Holes were ripped into the sides of the ship, and water began pouring in. Bailey, trying to keep his balance, was ordered to move his platoon from the ship's port side to starboard to avoid the artillery storm. But as he scrambled past the middle island, a large pile of mortar containers ignited, causing the *Malcolm* to turn into a floating fireworks display. Shrapnel began rattling off Bailey's helmet. His mind raced.

Do I stay here or jump overboard and take my chances at being rescued from the Mediterranean?

Before he could dive into the black abyss, in a daring maneuver Lieutenant William Muir rushed at the mortar containers and began hurtling them overboard, his actions invigorating others to jump in and help. Within seconds, all the burning material was overboard. By now, however, the ship was so disabled that it was forced to hobble seaward to get beyond range of the firestorm. Only then did Ace Bailey discover that another platoon leader, one who had assumed the port spot abandoned by Bailey's platoon, was killed there.

Had we stayed there, thought Bailey, *so many more of us would be dead.*

Daylight soon broke and with it came the grim task of a mass burial at sea. Bailey watched as those killed aboard the *Malcolm* were encased in mattress covers and in a solemn ceremony hoisted overboard to an eternal resting place in the sea.

While the *Malcolm* remained at sea, the *Broke* persevered, making it into port on its fourth try. Troops debarked with minimal difficulty, seizing key objectives such as a power station and oil depot, but the promising outlook for capturing Algiers grew dim as enemy artillery pounded shore and ships, inflicting heavy casualties. Foot-wide holes in the *Broke* caused water to pour in. In a desperate attempt to save it, a British destroyer forged into port and began towing the *Broke* out to sea. Despite the salvage attempt, the ship was claimed by the Mediterranean Sea. With it went sorely needed ammunition and supplies.

Despite Allied planes dive-bombing in support of landing efforts, the situation grew still worse. Troops ashore found ammunition running low, no artillery support, no sign of help from an expected Allied eastern contingency—and no way of digging foxholes into concrete city streets.

With dire prospects, American forces surrendered to the French just past noon on November 8. Their imprisonment was short-lived. Two days later, the French were overwhelmed by the Allied eastern task force, and the city of Algiers fell. The *Malcolm* then hobbled into the port, on the last of its engines, and Ace Bailey stepped on to the shores of Africa on November 10, 1942.

Bailey was soon toiling along the docks of Algiers, unloading ships as forces hurried to establish supply lines for Allied troops racing to capture additional North African objectives. When that job was done, his duties became that of sentry—helping to guard the division headquarters, light duty that left ample time for him to explore his surroundings. Bailey became enraptured with the sights and sounds of a city that was even more colorful than the myriad of vibrant spices lining its market stalls. He walked along broad, fashionable streets in the French section, lined with palm trees and modern buildings. The streets were frequented by smartly clad residents that lived in terraced villas with orange and lemon trees on perfectly manicured lawns. The Arab section revolved around the ancient Kasbah, a walled citadel surrounded by narrow, mazelike streets lined with run-down buildings, scenes of poverty, and throngs of men either in fezzes or wrapped in hooded cloaks that to Bailey resembled sheets.

What a city of contrasts . . . a fascinating metropolis.

He became acclimated to the contrasts as well as the local mobs, both Arab and French, which clamored and clawed for cigarettes he threw their way. When not subsisting on Army beans, hash, and stew, Bailey savored the figs and tangerines fresh off Algiers's trees, along with local mutton and good wines at French cafés.

Before long, Christmas had come and gone for the 34th Infantry in Algiers, and word had come down that the Germans were making inroads to the east in Tunisia.

It won't be long, surmised Bailey, *before our company takes its place on the front lines.*

On New Year's Day 1943, regiments with the division were ordered to bus out. Ace Bailey heard the last cries from children yelling, "Chowing gum! Bonbon!" He was off.

His unit traveled beyond the foothills of the Atlas Mountains, past nomadic villages. It trekked toward the second-largest city in Algeria, Oran, and continued far beyond into rock-strewn hillsides filled with olive trees that wept droplets on Ace Bailey's face as he bivouacked. The lieutenant listened intently as a radio brought news that British Field Marshal Bernard Montgomery had crossed into Tunisia in pursuit of *Wehrmacht* Field Marshal Erwin Rommel; the latter had raced to control Tunis, the capital of Tunisia, to deny the Allies that North African foothold that pointed like a finger toward Sicily and the Italian boot.

As the weeks went by, Bailey watched the sky increasingly streaked with both German aircraft and Allied anti-aircraft fire as his unit drew closer to the front in Tunisia. He heard word that German tanks were approaching that front while enemy paratroopers were landing to the rear. All the while, the drizzle was so constant that even when a farmer tried to flood Bailey's men out of the drain ditches in the fields, the mud-soaked soldiers were unfazed. This was the glory of war—the monotonous hiding, repositioning, trudging, waiting, worrying, and patrolling.

It was on one of those trudging days, a day filled with ten muddy miles of slipping and sliding, that Ace Bailey received a cablegram. His son, Leslie W. Bailey Jr., had been born to him thirty-one days earlier. It was almost nine months to the day since Sarah had snuck into his barracks for one last night together before his deployment.

Now, for just a moment, the proud new father got to revel in warm reflection. It was a fleeting moment. Then the war in Africa resumed for Ace
Bailey.

★ ★ ★

Cleo Pez arrived in North Africa on November 21, D-Day + 13, as part of the
Army Nurse Corps, which she had volunteered to join after Pearl Harbor.
Already she'd served in England, and now she was in Africa working seven
days a week helping with combat injuries, from 7 a.m. till the last operation of the day was complete, often going without a meal break. Her only
"rest" was the occasional short tour of ward duty. But she didn't mind. And
she didn't complain that while her officer rank was equivalent to many of
those she treated, she was paid a mere seventy-five dollars a month. Such
was the glory of trying to save those who gave much more than she—their
limbs and lives.

It was through a ward assignment that Cleo was introduced to a quiet,
thoughtful man. His name was Spec Powell. Among the best and brightest
of the class of '41, he had graduated number five in rank. He was nicknamed for the cadet term "specoid" since he was gifted with a remarkable
memory able to reproduce, verbatim, nearly every speck of a textbook page
a month later.

Powell had left Fort Dix for the port of New York, and there boarded
the *Queen Mary* for his voyage into war. It had been the ship's first trip
with troops not from the British Empire, though upper-crust touches remained aboard. There were drawing rooms with sofas and cocktail tables.
Beautiful menus lavishly described meals, and waiters served tables of ten
or more. What was all too "Army," however, was that most food tasted to
Powell like sawdust. Eating sawdust would soon be the least of his worries.

After stints in England and Ireland, Powell arrived in North Africa on
December 20, six weeks after the assault landings. He was commanding
a company of combat engineers in the 1st Armored Division with the mission of providing support mobility for front-line infantry, such as clearing
minefields and building bridges, as well as counter-mobility—preventing
the enemy from being mobile. This compared to general support engineers
without front-line duties whose tasks included building headquarters,
maintaining roads, and other construction tasks.

The division made its way into central Tunisia to join Allied Forces that
stretched about halfway down the elongated country to a place called El
Guettar. Powell's unit was on that southern front, after which there was
a gap in Allied Forces. There were more southern forces in the vicinity of

the Mareth Line, a long Axis line of fortification to the southeast of the city of Mareth with forts, cement-reinforced tank barriers, artillery casemates, deep trenches, and more. British Field Marshal Montgomery's Eighth Army was moving up from Libya toward that line, having captured Tripoli on January 23. The Eighth Army was opposed in its efforts by Field Marshal Rommel and his Afrika Korps. Additional German troops had come over from Sicily to counter the U.S. invasion of western North Africa with hopes of linking up with Rommel's troops withdrawing from Libya into Tunisia. Powell's division was among the U.S. II Corps and British First Army forces up against these additional German forces.

During the last week of January, Powell made long-range reconnaissance patrols of terrain, bridges, and ravines. He marched his company up and down a north-south road by the small city of Gafsa, a tactic intended to confuse the enemy as to Allied intentions. To the north, on January 30, the Germans captured the town of Faid, along the Faid Pass. Within the Atlas chain of mountains, Tunisia has Western and Eastern Dorsal portions that run roughly parallel to the coast. These were all but impassible but for a series of passes that cut through their mountainous terrain.[4] The Faid Pass was a broad opening that sliced through the Eastern Dorsal, whereas two other eastern passes had inferior roads or trails, making the Faid Pass the most important in the area. Were the Germans to control the pass, it would provide an avenue for their forces, advancing from the Mediterranean, to infiltrate west toward Allied Forces.

In the middle of the night on January 30, Powell was awakened and told to report to the division's artillery command post near Gafsa for a meeting to put together a task force, labeled Combat Command D (CCD), which would include Powell's engineer company. The task force was to advance east and seize high ground. The 168th Infantry component of CCD was still hundreds of miles away, somewhere between Gafsa and Algiers to the west.

The task force, minus the infantry, moved out at dawn with Powell's engineer company following behind a tank battalion. Powell thought it such a peaceful morning that he could almost picture a Sunday picnic, except there was little more than thin grass and cactus as he traversed the wide-open terrain. His visions of leisurely pastimes were soon shattered as he experienced his first encounter with the terror of a German air attack.

It occurred about 1 p.m., when a single-file column of 2½-ton trucks carrying a battalion of the 168th Infantry, which had caught up with the formation, began to pass the engineers. They were close together, moving fairly slowly. The canvas tops of their trucks were still up, shielding them from the bright, blinding sun—and obscuring from their sights the air attack descending upon them. But Powell saw it. Just before the tail of the infantry column passed, he heard a droning in the sky and saw a tight column of Stuka dive-bombers, Ju-87s, which at first had been hidden by the glare of the midday sun. They were to the south, descending fast and beginning to make a wide 180-degree turn, heading in the direction of the infantry trucks.

Where's the fire against them? Where?

Powell grabbed his radio microphone and screamed, "Air attack! Air attack!"

His two machine gunners opened fire. They were out of range but hoped the noise might alert those ahead.

Powell watched the Stukas begin diving, one after another, eleven of them in a row, plunging so low their tires were barely missing the tops of the targeted infantry trucks. They dropped their long, cigar-shaped bombs with deadly accuracy, the explosions creating a whistling unlike anything Powell had ever heard.

The Stukas disappeared as quickly as they appeared, while Powell's truck lurched forward, proceeding up the road to help infantry. But it was too late. Looking around, Powell couldn't believe the carnage.

Bodies blown to pieces . . . human pieces all over the place.

Every truck had been hit. And the anti-aircraft teams . . . they had not gotten into position in time; their gun platforms were open with no protective armor plate. The crews were lying dead on their half-tracks or beside them.

This was Powell's baptism into war, the bloodiest scene he had ever seen.

What a picnic—for the Germans.

Powell didn't have time to discover the fate of the bodies. His unit had to move on. The tragedy, however, made him more convinced than ever that he needed to be a rigid company commander, insisting on combat discipline and standards to protect soldiers' lives. He always made his men wear helmets, put camouflage nets over their vehicles, and dig slit trenches— narrow trenches just big enough to fit one man or a few; such trenches could protect against bodily injury, though a concussion from the powerful Stuka bombs could kill a man even if his body looked otherwise unscathed.

Powell's engineer unit traveled east five miles, taking position on high ground past a rail town called Sened Station.

★ ★ ★

Two weeks later German panzer divisions, structured around armored vehicles, launched attacks west in efforts to link up with Rommel. Despite scouting reports of a glut of German armored vehicles east of Faid Pass, on February 13, II Corps commander General Lloyd Fredendall issued spot orders—as was his habit—to the 1st Armored Division commander, General Orlando Ward. Fredendall wanted a task force heading toward the Faid Pass. Hastily assembled, the task force was to help the Free French should they need it. It consisted of infantry and armored and artillery units as well as combat engineers.

The task force, which was almost entirely new to combat, moved out early the next day. When it reached an area dubbed the Kasserine Pass, amid the Western Dorsal, it was almost immediately surrounded. (Kasserine, in fact, was a town and not a pass. Various passes funneled into and out of the town including one heading west into a long, flat valley—the so-called Kasserine Pass.) Within hours, fifty-four of the task force's fifty-seven M3 medium tanks were knocked out, its cavalry-era howitzers—75mm and short-barreled—little match for the modern, high-velocity guns of the German Mark IV Panzers. Scores of U.S. troops were killed or captured.

Fredendall dispatched another task force the day following to restore the situation. Again, it had little combat experience, though it was equipped with more modern M4 tanks with 360-degree rotatable turrets. Still, all fifty-seven tanks belonging to that task force were destroyed by day's end. The 1st Armored Division and support troops, centered around Sidi Bou Zid, withdrew east. By the night of the fifteenth, the area to the west was strongly in enemy hands.

Upon hearing about the task force losses, Powell didn't understand how unseasoned and underequipped U.S. troops could have been effective against Rommel's panzers.

Fredendall used green troops. Troops were too hastily assembled, unready in experience and arms . . . too many men lost, a lot of obsolete equipment destroyed . . . miles of barren open land abandoned.

Fredendall, needing drastic action, ordered Combat Command B (CCB) within the 1st Armored Division into action. The cohesive task force, which had been fighting together for months, moved down from the north to attempt to block the German advance eastward. It succeeded in establishing positions in the rolling terrain south of Kasserine, east of the north-south highway. The effective combat team inflicted significant damage on the enemy while sustaining limited damage itself.

Despite that success, Fredendall still was convinced that a main enemy attack would occur farther south. He ordered CCB to withdraw west, through the Kasserine Pass and Valley. CCB was to establish itself farther south in anticipation of the enemy attack and protect corps supply and support areas from being captured, which in turn would also safeguard corps headquarters farther west in Tebessa, Algeria. CCB's move, however, left the Faid Pass practically undefended but for combat engineers—men who had little choice but to run for their lives when the Germans infiltrated their positions in the middle of the night.

Over the next few days, CCB was ordered to retrace its steps to the west.

Spec Powell, meanwhile, had been busy at Thelepte Airfield south of Kasserine. It was a large airfield, measuring ten miles by five in Powell's estimation, with Allied planes scattered about for protection. In the wake of advancing Germans, the airfield was evacuating squadrons on February 16–17.[5] Some of the planes, however, were in no condition to be flown, so Powell was ordered to destroy them—and everything else at the airfield including gasoline, so none of it would fall into German hands. The only exception to his purge was aircraft ordnance, bombs, and ammunition, which were left for other teams to destroy.

Powell and his men began using picks to puncture gas tanks and set them afire. In other cases they put thermite grenades on airplane engines, which set some on fire, while others carrying bombs, like a twin-engine Douglas A-20, exploded. Powell thought it all such a shame, all the valuable equipment going up in smoke.

Amid the mayhem, he received an order from an Air Corps colonel: "Don't destroy any gasoline, because I am going to be out with my squadron, and I need to refuel."

Asked Powell, "When will you be back here?"

The '41er was not pleased with the answer, since the hour noted was when the covering force was supposed to leave.

The colonel dismissed Powell's concerns, insisting, "I'm coming back anyway."

Powell continued on with his work. Even if he saved some fuel for the Air Corps colonel, there remained enormous amounts to discard. Looking around, he saw a hundred-plus stockpile of fifty-five-gallon drums, added to which were hundreds of five-gallon tins. A similar pile was a mere five hundred yards away, then another and another. Logistically, it was an enormous task, eliminating pile after pile, puncturing everything and setting it all aflame.

By the time Powell was nearing the completion of his work, the Germans were closing in, his covering force was leaving, and the colonel and his fighter planes were showing up to refuel. They did so, but as the fighter planes were taking off, Powell was still at the airfield, and the Germans were beginning to fire at him. Powell was grateful for all the smoke; he knew the Germans had trouble seeing him, and they were also a fair distance away. Spec Powell safely withdrew with his engineer company before the Germans seized the smoldering airfield.

Powell's engineer company was then attached to CCB as it headed back to the Kasserine Valley, charged with blocking paths and passes from enemy penetration. All through the night—and the rain—the combat team marched. As daylight broke Powell began digging craters to lay minefields, attempting novel mine patterns since he'd heard the Germans had gotten wind of the standard ones. In some cases the enemy, recognizing the U.S. Army's doctrinal ways of planting mines, could easily clear them out. To get around this, Powell created new patterns, keeping a record of each through an ingenious knotted-cord pattern—rather than in writing—and he adapted each minefield scheme for the varied terrain.

A steep path: *twenty or so mines could blast the whole ravine.*

A wider path: *we need flanking mortars and tank destroyers for a good defensive position.*

Other CCB units, meanwhile, were dispatched on reconnaissance to observe the Germans, with the mission of making contact without becoming decisively engaged. While doing so they were also to collect Allied stragglers and help reform units. The bulk of Allied troops were then organized at the west end of the valley to take on Rommel when he attacked. Rommel did order his troops to attack on February 22, but these experienced CCB troops beat him off in fierce firefights. Rommel withdrew a few miles south to reinforce the Mareth Line and awaited an anticipated offensive by elements of Montgomery's Eighth Army as it arrived to reinforce the Allied effort.

An Allied counterattack began early the next morning with B-17s skimming low over the valley to "skip-bomb" areas of the passes and paths, so called for the way bombs skipped across the ground, bouncing toward their targets. At the same time, Allied artillery began a massive offensive, the biggest Powell had ever seen, while a tank battalion was positioned to watch over the pass. But no enemy appeared. When the smoke from the artillery preparation cleared, all Powell saw was artillery-pocked terrain.

It was then that Spec Powell got orders to report to the tank battalion commander, Lieutenant Colonel Gardner. Powell had to remove a dozen anti-tank mines just to reach the lieutenant.

Gardner had but one request for his engineer commander: "Get me through the pass as *fast* as possible."

He wanted to capitalize on what appeared to be a window of opportunity.

Powell forged ahead on foot through the pass, trying to spot German mines in the road as the rest of his company followed with mine-clearing equipment. The clay was hard packed, allowing Powell to make out most mines pretty easily since the chopped-up dirt covering them was a dead giveaway. Each "Teller" anti-tank mine was about a foot in diameter and had a handle on the side of it so that the mine resembled an upside-down pan. To remove the mines Powell had his men wrap wire around the handle, then back off and pull the mine out of the ground. But many mines were interconnected like mousetraps with springs. He had to position his forces so that a man disabling one mine did not inadvertently set off a booby trap that might kill another soldier toiling nearby.

Powell kept at this laborious task, as did his troops, forging ahead a mile into the critical pass. Then Powell traveled another mile and still another till the maze of mines he had encountered grew to number in the several hundreds.

He heard shots in the distance and halted. They stopped after four or five rounds. *Probably some nervous GI*, thought Powell.

By then, he had walked four miles—through the entire pass—and still no sign of the enemy. Powell was surprised but encouraged. The mine-clearing team had made it, and the terrain was all clear.

He radioed Combat Command B headquarters, announcing, "The enemy has abandoned the pass."

With those words, the Allied tank column victoriously began moving single file through the contentious pass, heading back west and reaching the objective of Kasserine about six hours later. Never did the tanks encounter Rommel's troops, the general apparently choosing not to grapple with these more experienced Allied Forces.

The Battle of the Kasserine Pass was over, having stretched nearly one hundred miles over ten days. Many in the upper echelons of Allied command, however, had by now lost confidence in Fredendall. General Eisenhower relieved him of his command in early March and replaced him with General George Patton.

In the meantime, there was a lull in Allied-Axis contact, during which time Patton reorganized II Corps. In Powell's view, Patton was "unscrambling" the mixture of troops and giving divisions sectors of responsibility and missions, a level of order that Powell had not seen under Fredendall. The corps again began concerted attacks, taking back control of Gafsa. Powell was with the 1st Armored Division when it took Sened Station for the fourth time, and Patton attempted to attack through El Guettar. By then, in late March, Montgomery and the Eighth Army had succeeded in an assault on the Mareth Line. Rommel fled toward the mountains, and the Eighth Army headed north into Tunisia.

By early April the Eighth was in front of II Corps. Axis resistance collapsed, and its forces surrendered on May 13. The war in North Africa was over.

Spec Powell was then tasked by the Army with writing after-action reports for each of the major combat actions of the 1st Armored Division and its elements throughout the North Africa campaign. He had at his disposal all orders issued by division headquarters. He had a continuous operations journal and daily operations reports made to corps headquarters. He had records of all division radio traffic and all telephone calls. He had access to every transcribed word of the corps commander and his staff. With all this at his disposal, Powell figured he was arguably the most knowledgeable person in the Army on the 1st Armored Division's operations in North Africa—and in the Kasserine Pass. And of course, he had commanded boots on the ground during critical aspects of the battle. But he saw a disconnect with press reports touting the "defeat" of Allied Forces at the Kasserine Pass. Powell didn't get it.

What defeat?

Sure, figured Spec Powell, the battles gave General Eisenhower a wake-up call as to the incompetence of his field commander Fredendall, but better to discover that early in the war.

But the press?

Half-informed and dead wrong, thought Powell. *We regained real estate lost in less than two weeks. Rommel's all-out efforts to seize badly needed supplies failed, and he didn't discredit all U.S. troops. . . . Rommel didn't buy much time before his ultimate failure.*

While there had been devastating losses, in Powell's view, Allied troops had learned and gained confidence for the battles ahead. Other factors that influenced Rommel's failure were, wrote Powell,

1 Montgomery's readiness to resume the British Eighth Army offensive up through Tunisia from the Mareth Line.
2 The increasing effectiveness of Allied air power especially in isolating Tunisia from its re-supply sources in Europe.
3 The British arrived in the north fork of the Bahira-Foussana (Kasserine) Valley.[6]

Spec Powell, meanwhile, had been charged with the operational aspects of moving all 1st Armored Division units out of Africa. He was preparing to send them to a place called Anzio.

7

JUMP TIME IN SICILY

The ultimate success of the North African campaign cleared the way for Allied Forces to aim for the stepping-stone leading to Italy—the enemy-held island of Sicily. Securing Sicily would not only eliminate an Axis stronghold but open up Allied routes to the eastern Mediterranean and help destabilize Benito Mussolini's fascist regime. From the shores of Sicily, mainland Italy was a stone's throw away, only a couple of miles distance.

The Allied invasion of Sicily, labeled Operation Husky, was to include the first large-scale airborne invasion in history. General "Jumpin' Jim" Gavin's protégé, paratrooper Jack Norton, was front and center in that effort, serving as a battalion executive with the 505th Parachute Infantry Regiment of the 82nd Airborne. The goal was for airborne forces to drop behind the beaches near the city of Gela, on Sicily's southern shore, where General Patton's Seventh Army was to land. Airborne forces were to knock out enemy pillboxes and communications, confuse the enemy as to the location of landing forces, and block the roads into Gela to protect the beachhead. At the same time the British would prepare for Field Marshal Montgomery's Eighth Army to land to the east, around the southern tip of the island from Seventh Army objectives.

There was ample moonlight on the night of July 9, 1943, as planes from the 82nd Airborne took off from Algeria at approximately 10 p.m. They were heading three hours east toward Sicily, embarking on a complex airborne route to avoid friendly fire from Allied ships in the Mediterranean. But the winds were picking up as they took off, "Mussolini winds" as some dubbed them.[1] By the time Norton's plane reached Sicilian air space, he had to contend with gale force winds whipping up to forty knots.

Norton was serving as jumpmaster, responsible for combat jump procedures, proper rigging, plane exits, and more. The enemy fire began as his men were preparing to jump.

These are dangerous conditions, he worried, *high winds and enemy fire.*

But the paratroopers were out the door. What happened next was out of Norton's control.

Almost as soon as his chute opened, Norton hit the ground. He was stunned. He looked around. *This doesn't look anything like what we studied on the maps.*

He scanned the scenery, noticing high rock walls. No one in their right mind would plan a drop by walls. Realized Norton: *We've been dropped in the wrong place!*

The planes had either been blown off course or been outright erroneous in their navigation. Norton quickly discovered that many men had landed directly on the walls, suffering broken necks, legs, and arms upon impact. Only a fraction survived the jump. Those who survived now had to contend with the enemy.

Norton and other officers quickly established a temporary command post. From there, Sergeant Freeland, a linguist who spoke Italian, headed off on reconnaissance to scope out where they were. Within thirty minutes, he and Norton took to a road they thought resembled one on the maps they had studied. Norton crept along one side of the road, Freeland the other. They moved methodically, carefully, till they heard voices. Norton thought he could make out some of the words.

He whispered, "Get down!" to Freeland.

The two men got down on their knees.

Then Norton attempted a sign-countersign to determine if the voices were those of Allied Forces: "George."

He hoped for the reply, "Marshall."

Instead came, "Marshall, hell!"

A stream of machine-gun tracer bullets tore through the night skies. Bullets clipped the strap of Norton's helmet; more bullets knocked the epaulets off his shoulder. Norton and Freeland grabbed hand grenades, each lobbing one about fifty feet in the direction of the enemy. The resulting pyrotechnics unveiled the enemy in pillboxes. The whole area was surrounded by barbed wire. Norton and Freeland were trapped.

They each unloaded a second hand grenade into the pillbox area. Then they ran, hurdling the barbed wire in a race for their lives. They didn't stop running till they got back to their command post.

Despite the fiasco, Norton and other airborne forces took on the enemy from wherever they had landed. The enemy was even more confused than the Americans, with forces coming at them from all directions. It gained U.S. forces time.

The British, meanwhile, were encountering their own aerial difficulties.

The goal of the British 1st Airlanding Brigade was to land south of the city of Syracuse, on the southeast coast, and seize the Ponte Grande Bridge that spanned the Anapo River. Forces would then move into Syracuse and secure its docks for use in Eighth Army disembarkation. Of 144 British gliders in the brigade that took off from Tunisia, however, nearly half crashed into the sea, drowning many of the crews. Dozens more landed in the wrong areas. Only twelve gliders reached their targeted sectors.[2] Nonetheless, British forces encountered only light Italian resistance and took the bridge.

The amphibious landings that followed were supported by heavy fire from offshore warships. By the end of that first day, July 10, the British had seized Syracuse, and Montgomery began pushing northeast toward the strategic port of Messina, across the straits from the Italian mainland. U.S. forces encountered greater difficulties around Gela from Italian forces, a panzer division, and German air attacks. The Italians, however, were woefully deficient in equipment, training, and morale.[3] Furthermore, the German defensive strength was not properly allocated since they expected a main assault aimed at Corsica or Sardinia, based on disinformation—from a corpse. British intelligence had dressed a dead body as a major in the Royal Marines, given him "top-secret" papers pertaining to a Greek invasion—with those papers locked and bound to his wrist—then dropped the body into waters off southern Spain, where it conveniently washed ashore for the Germans to find.

The ruse, Operation Mincemeat, was unheralded in its success, resulting in German forces being far outnumbered in Sicily. U.S. forces were able to break out from the Gela beachhead and began heading north and west toward the port city of Palermo, the Sicilian capital. U.S. forces had captured the capital by July 23.

Over the course of the next month, despite some lack of coordination between the Allied Forces—Patton claimed orders from the British to halt his advance were "garbled"—U.S. and British forces squeezed the Germans into the northeast corner of Sicily in the region from Catania, about midway up the east coast, to Messina. British forces punched through the former.

The Italian government, jarred by Allied success, arrested Mussolini in late July 1943 and set up a provisional government, which would soon begin negotiations with the Allies for an armistice.

While the British were then preparing to take Messina, Patton, who was in a horse race against Montgomery to win respect for U.S. troops—and glory—closed in and captured the city on August 17, just hours after the last Axis forces exited the island.[4] The campaign was complete. The Allies owned Sicily.

With success, however, had come hard lessons, especially given the havoc of airborne portions of the invasion. General Gavin, discontented with the invasion jump that had proved fatal to so many, immediately pushed for improvements to airborne doctrine. He assigned Norton to experiment with the concept of "Pathfinders"—advance teams that would go in ahead of airborne forces to plant radar-navigational beacons to improve future airborne assaults. Norton began developing the "table of organization equipment," or TOE, to prescribe the wartime organization, capabilities, tactics, staffing, and equipment requirements of the proposed Pathfinder units. Over the course of thirty days, working with the Army Air Corps, troop carrier pilots, and some of his officers from the 505th Regiment, Norton and his group created and finessed the Pathfinder doctrine.

The doctrine, Norton believed, would correct future jumps so that, in his words, troops could "arrive at the right place at the right time and be heavily concentrated so they could take on the enemy at full force."

It would not be long before Norton would get to test his theories.

★ ★ ★

While most U.S. and British forces, like Norton, had moved on from North Africa, Paul Skowronek was languishing in Oran. The 2nd Cavalry Division, to which he belonged, had arrived in the Algerian port city only to be disbanded. Skowronek was stunned. He'd seen the signs back on the Louisiana maneuvers—that horses were giving way to tanks—but still he'd hoped that hooves might prevail, that there was some role for them in war. The powers that be decided there wasn't. His cavalry division would be broken up into truck and port battalions.

Great . . . a future as a freight stevedore, thought Skowronek. *All those cavalry drills at West Point. The jumping, charging, mounted firing. Cadet legs forever bowed. And for what? What's next for me?*

As the unwitting captain of a port battalion, Skowronek was forced to wait on equipment for the division to make its switchover from cavalry to stevedores. He tried, in the meantime, to keep his soldiers busy. Skowronek was training. Marching. Waiting for something to happen. At times, he felt like the desert sands saw more action than he did.

There was a glimmer of hope on the horizon, however, as General Willis Crittenberger arrived in Africa to interview officers leaving the 2nd Cavalry Division. Crittenberger was a former West Pointer with a soft spot for cavalrymen, having been one. He was in the midst of reorganizing the

IV Corps, which he was to command as part of the Fifth Army in the Italian Campaign, and was culling officers for his corps headquarters. In the process, Crittenberger hoped to "rescue" a few cavalrymen.

Skowronek was surprised to be called in for an interview with the esteemed general, not just because of Crittenberger's presence but because he was accompanied by Massachusetts senator Henry Cabot Lodge Jr., who was serving as the general's senior aide. Lodge had a previous World War II tour cut short when FDR ordered state representatives who were simultaneously serving in the military to resign from one of their two positions. Admirably, Lodge decided that combat duty ranked higher than rotunda duty and had just resigned his Senate seat to return to active duty as a lieutenant colonel.

Skowronek adeptly answered questions from the two, apparently impressing them.

"Do you want to join us?" asked Crittenberger.

The younger man's heart skipped a beat. "Sir," he answered, "I'd be honored." *Maybe,* Skowronek thought to himself, *I have a future after all.*

Skowronek was the only 2nd Division cavalryman to make Crittenberger's cut, though for the time being, IV Corps remained in reserve for the Italian Campaign. Skowronek's temporary residence became a midway stop to the Italian mainland—Sicily—and his ship pulled into the port of Catania, on the eastern shore.

Catania was an ancient city seated at the foot of Mount Etna, which over the centuries had rocked the region with its seismic fury, spewing forth rivers of lava that buried parts of the city. Catania had had to be rebuilt seven times, but the resilient city always rose again, as it did after countless invasions—and would again after the recent Allied one.

In Catania, Skowronek passed the days waiting on orders. He strolled the blacked-out city streets, past eighteenth-century baroque buildings built of volcanic gray stone. The structures loomed ominously, as though gargoyles might lurch from their shadows. The threats, of course, remained more imminent from the Nazis, who were still within bombing range. But explosions were not on Skowronek's mind, or at least not that kind. He continued to stew over his cavalry unit imploding, and at times his chin hung a tad lower than usual. His step lacked its usual swagger.

As a diversion, he explored the capital of Palermo, a few hours drive to the northwest. Like Catania, the city was steeped in history, ruled centuries earlier by the Phoenicians, the Byzantines, and the Arabs and then bounced between the Normans, Spaniards, Austrians, and Bourbons before its annexation to Italy. The recent invasion, however, had taken a rabid bite out of the city. It had been heavily bombed. The port was virtually destroyed. Grand palazzos stood empty. Craters marked where the villas of nobility once stood. But leave it to a resourceful General Patton to find one grand villa that retained all its frescoed glory. From there, Patton planned aspects of the Italian invasion.

Skowronek took it all in, the medieval and modern ruins presenting a striking urban paradox. He roamed the city, breathing in the scents of citrus and olive that lingered despite the residue of gunpowder. He walked Palermo till his feet grew weary and his throat parched, till he noticed a bar with darkened windows, blacked out like the rest of wartime Palermo.

I could use a drink.

Wandering in to the establishment, he sat down on a stool and ordered a glass of red wine and rested his hand on the bar, waiting. An American officer sitting on the adjacent stool pointed to the burly ring on Skowronek's finger, emblazoned with a gold eagle and the letters USMA.

"What class are you?" asked the stranger.

"Class of 1941."

"Jesus, you've got to be kidding me. So am I." The man held out a hand and introduced himself. "Joe Gurfein, Company B."

"Unbelievable," replied Skowronek, shaking the hand with a firm grasp. "Paul Skowronek, Company G. Joe Gurfein . . . I know the name, but I guess we never really came across each other."

"Until the invasion of Sicily," replied Gurfein wryly.

Skowronek smiled and the two began a warm exchange of where-I-came-from and what-I'm-doing-here, intermixed with "Remember when at West Point . . ." and "Did you know so and so?" With cavalry momentarily forgotten, the glimmer returned to Skowronek's eyes as the two talked first over one drink and then another. It was as though they had horsed around since the first days of Beast Barracks.

Joe Gurfein was now a commander with the 82nd Airborne, having traded in his West Point tennis shenanigans—volleying religions for court access—for engineering and parachuting. He explained that he was running a parachute training school in the area for French forces, in the event of an air assault into France. Skowronek explained his predicament, waiting for orders to be sent to IV Corps Headquarters, following the cavalry's demise.

"Come over tomorrow," Gurfein offered Skowronek, "and I'll show you my outfit."

"I might just do that," replied Skowronek. "I've got nowhere in particular to be till I get new orders."

Gurfein scribbled down information for his classmate and they parted.

The arid sun was gleaming early the next morning when Paul Skowronek showed up at the 82nd Airborne jump-training school, decked in his usual britches and boots.

"Hey, I'm glad you came," said Gurfein, greeting his classmate with a friendly slap on the back. "But I'm busy at the moment with a USO group that showed up unexpectedly."

Skowronek couldn't help but notice the woman waiting beside Gurfein. *He's smart enough to pick the prettiest one*, he thought.

"I'll be going up for a training jump in a little while," Gurfein continued, "taking up French soldiers in a C-47. Why don't you jump with us? I'll have you fixed up with a jumpsuit and parachutes."

"I've never jumped before," replied Skowronek.

"You don't need an awful lot of instruction. You can just watch them and do the same thing. And I'll jump with you."

"Sure," replied Skowronek, not one to resist adventure.

Next thing he knew, while Gurfein was showing the beautiful USO entertainer around, he was donning a jumpsuit over his cavalry britches. Not long afterward, he was airborne with just under twenty aspiring French paratroopers.

Over the roar of the engines, Gurfein instructed his classmate. "Okay, here's what you've got to do. When you stand in the door, push yourself out with your hands. Keep your head down. Put your hands over your chest reserve chute. Keep your knees loose and when you land, do a PLF."

Gurfein bent at the hip, rounded a shoulder, and twisted in mock demonstration of the five-point parachute landing fall that was meant to disperse a jumper's weight—in a rolling maneuver onto one side of the body—from the balls of his feet to his calf, thigh, buttock, and then side of the back. In fact, '41 classmate James "Butch" Kaiser was the one that developed the landing method.

Skowronek nodded. *Doesn't sound too complicated. Just stay loose.*

That was the extent of Skowronek's "lesson." Gurfein scrambled back and forth between the canvas benches flanking the plane's interior, doling out instructions to his French students. Then the instructor took a seat in the forward section of the plane, farthest from the door, beside Skowronek. The two would be the last to jump.

As the warning lights moved in sequence from red to yellow, Gurfein yelled, "Stand up!" The men, laden in their clumsy gear, hoisted themselves up. Gurfein yelled, "Hook up!"

Each of the jumpers hooked his static line to the cable above, which ran the length of the plane. Each static line was linked to the jumper's parachute backpack so that when he jumped, the line would become taut, its force yanking open the chute and causing the static line to break off, thereby freeing the jumper to fall.

The green light flashed. The husky sergeant jumpmaster, towering by the door, began hustling the waiting paratroopers forward, tapping each on the back and yelling, "Go!" One by one the men hurtled out.

Skowronek awaited his turn, next to last. But as the line of froggies dwindled to the final jumpers, there was an unnerving thud against the plane. A parachutist's static line got snagged, and he was bouncing unmercifully against the bird like a human yo-yo. Gurfein bolted to the door alongside the jumpmaster. They struggled against the wind velocity to haul the man in, laboring to pull in his static line, hand over hand. Successfully retrieving him, Gurfein swiftly undid the line caught under the man's arm and in the blink of an eye, pushed the jumper right back out.

Gosh, Gurfein's good, thought Skowronek. *Guess I don't have to worry.*

With his human cargo redeposited out the plane's door, Gurfein, catching his breath, turned to Skowronek. "We'll have to go around a second time to get back to the drop zone."

As they waited on the jump color sequence to repeat, Gurfein explained the tricky snag experienced by the Frenchman—his arms had gotten in the way.

"The metal fastener at the end of the static line comes up rather rapidly when it pulls out the chute. You have to hold your head down or it can stun you. And you need to have your hands over your reserve chute, so they don't get in the way. That way, you can also pull your reserve rip cord if your main chute doesn't open."

Skowronek now stood at the door, looking out at the world from a new altitude—and new attitude. The go signal flashed and with a deep breath, he jumped. Out of the bird, into the blue. Gurfein was on his tail.

Skowronek plummeted. He felt the hard pull of the static line and the chute release. He felt a sharp jerk upward as a billowy white canopy unfurled above him. He began floating toward the drop zone.

"Keep your knees bent and feet together!" he heard a voice yell from somewhere above.

Instinctively, Skowronek flexed his knees, as though preparing to urge his Arabian horse, Jerry, over a hurdle. The ground zoomed closer, images appearing to Skowronek like through a fly's eye. The ground came at him faster and faster.

Just stay loose and roll. Loose and roll. Loose and roll.

Skowronek hit the ground. With scant equipment, his 125 pounds landed lightly, and he immediately rolled to redistribute the impact from his feet to his legs, butt, and back. He'd made it in one piece.

"Wow!" he exclaimed out loud. "I've *got* to do that again."

Paul Skowronek was antsy to jump the next day—and the next. But almost immediately after his exhilarating initiation, he got orders to ship back to Africa, back to Algeria. He read the orders with consternation.

What the heck . . . have the plans for IV Corps been screwed up? Did Crittenberger change his mind?

As it turned out, a transportation officer charged with logistically moving troops around the Mediterranean had Skowronek's last known address as Oran. So Skowronek went back to move forward, returning to Oran while his orders to join IV Corps caught up with him. And so it was from Oran that he was shipped to Italy in early spring of 1944.

My roundabout tour of the Mediterranean, Skowronek figured.

His next stop was Salerno, south of Naples, where there was more time to hurry-up and wait till the Anzio breakout was achieved and Rome secured. To occupy idle minds in the downtime and be productive, Fifth Army officers and 15th Air Force bomber personnel showed each other the ropes under an "exchange program." Army officers sat in on Air Force briefings on bombing missions, observed flight patterns, and attended debriefings. In return, pilots got a taste of infantry, including visiting regimental headquarters and at times getting so close to artillery operations that foxholes quickly became their friends. Paul Skowronek leapt at the chance to see the Air Force side of the exchange, heading to wing headquarters in Foggia, on the eastern shore of Italy, almost directly opposite Naples.

The wing commander in Foggia, recognizing Skowronek as a West Point '41er, dispatched him to the 32nd Bombardment Squadron. The squadron commander turned out to be Edwin "Bud" Harding, a flamboyant, fiercely dedicated Air Corps officer who was one part W. C. Fields, the other part daredevil—and he was a fellow '41er from Skowronek's West Point class. Skowronek knew Harding well, having been in the same company. It didn't surprise Skowronek that a cadet known for fancy springboard diving had taken to new heights.

Bud Harding, in turn, wasted no time in trusting Skowronek: "I'll put you on my B-17 as a waist gunner." Typically a waist gunner was an enlisted man, but a command pilot could usually do as he saw fit, and Skowronek fit the bill to be part of Harding's trusted team.

In short order, Skowronek was donning a heavy, fur-lined jacket, and with britches on, stepped into fur-lined trousers necessary to endure the icy chills of bombing missions at twenty thousand feet. He topped off his outfit with a flight helmet and amusingly glanced down at his crazy getup.

I wonder what'll happen if the Germans shoot me down over Yugoslavia? They'll think something really crazy is going on. I can just see them: "A bomber in britches... Vat could it mean? Vat are they planning?" Skowronek chuckled.

His amusement was short-lived, as his first bombing run began on June 5. The target: Voda Railroad Bridge in Italy. Harding and his copilot were accompanied in their forward positions by the navigator, bombardier, and flight engineer. Toward the middle of the plane were the radio operator and ball-turret gunner. Skowronek took his station beyond by the "waist" of the plane, manning a gun aimed out a window to defend his side of the aircraft while another waist gunner was positioned opposite. Behind them was the single tail gunner. There was a crew of nine in total, all connected by intercoms located in the ear cups of their flight helmets.

The mission was to be the proverbial "milk run," a straightforward bombing mission on a bright, clear day. The main challenge would be the mountains surrounding the target, which was tucked into a valley.

As the plane rose to fifteen thousand feet, the crew donned oxygen masks, snaking hoses dangling from their faces. When the plane pierced higher altitudes, Skowronek encountered his first taste of enemy anti-aircraft fire. Unimpressed, he called Bud on the intercom. "This flak doesn't seem so bad."

Moments later, enemy fire hit Harding's wingman, causing that plane to erupt in a fiery trail headed earthward from twenty thousand feet. "Forget that last transmission!" Skowronek's voice crackled over the intercom.

Harding's crew lost sight of the downed plane as intense, accurate fire began to tear through the squadron's ranks. The milk run turned into a fireworks display. How the squadron didn't lose more of the fleet was anyone's guess. But the squadron plowed through, achieving its ultimate objective—the bridge.

Announced Bud Harding, "Target is destroyed."

Then the squadron scrambled, with Harding skillfully veering off toward home base, the bombing mission complete. By that point, the downed plane was long gone, perhaps into oblivion, or maybe the crew miraculously survived and bailed out. Harding and his crew had no way of knowing.

The following morning, Skowronek was back up in waist-gunner position. This time the objective was a power station in Turnu Severin, Romania. The facility was in the "Iron Gate" gorge region, where the Danube River narrows and cuts through towering limestone cliffs along the border of Yugoslavia. Harding's squadron was part of a hundred-plus force of bombers on a double mission, dubbed so because it would endure from dawn till nearly dusk, far beyond the usual stint of three to four hours. The squadrons—nine B-17s apiece—soon began thundering down the runway of Foggia, taking off nearly every sixty seconds from the main airstrips and satellite airfields nearby. The goal was to saturate the target area since bombing from twenty thousand feet was an inexact science—let alone trying to get a bull's-eye between cliffs—but if hundreds of bombs were dropped, some might find their mark.

The squadrons crossed the Adriatic Sea, invading Yugoslav air space and continuing east toward Romania. The formations swept toward the Iron Gate like the wall of an approaching hurricane. The eye hit as the bomb run commenced. Harding's plane was straight and level, while the bombardier took his readings with the Norden bombsight, the ultrasecret analog computer that determined the trajectory of a payload, factoring in winds and the plane's direction, speed, and altitude. So priceless was this military asset, which resembled a bulky, complicated camera with a myriad of lenses, mirrors, knobs, and measuring devices, that the bombardier was supposed to protect its secrets with his life.

Harding's bombardier did his Norden business and then uttered the edict, "Bombs away."

Up to ten bombs apiece were released from one B-17 after another, with each then making a quick turn after release to make room for subsequent squadrons and avoid any anti-aircraft fire. When the last planes unleashed their fury, the gray curtain lifted and the bombers scattered to make their way home. No fighter opposition was encountered.

"Good bombing job!" said Harding, congratulating his crew.

Harding's squadron was soon flying back over the Adriatic Sea. Skowronek took off his oxygen mask as the plane descended to about six thousand feet. Then one of the squadron's B-17s faltered. It was in distress, sputtering and tilting from side to side, though it was unclear whether due to engine trouble or enemy fire. The pilot was obviously trying to regain control, but his efforts were futile. The bomber crashed into the Adriatic.

Harding yanked on his throttle and veered back toward the crash area. His team scanned the waters for survivors, trying to discern bobbing heads amid the cresting waves. Not long after, they spotted two drifting rafts—filled with the crew.

"Thank God," someone uttered.

"Let's get them our rafts," Harding ordered. "We don't know what kind of shape theirs are in after getting hit. Ready or not, we're going down there."

He circled back and began rapidly descending. When the plane reached about five hundred feet, in a daring maneuver with no wing cover for protection, the crew dropped two life rafts out of the plane. The rafts, each equipped with supplies including radios and beacons, landed close enough to the drifting men for retrieval.

Satisfied, Harding announced over the intercom, "Now they'll have a chance. Let's hope some partisans help them onshore."

There was little more the Air Corps officers could do except take heart that partisans opposed to the Nazi regime, perhaps those loyal to the Yugoslav monarch, King Peter, might aid the crew when it reached shore. They'd all heard crazy stories about downed crews straggling back to base a month after being shot down. In fact, a '41 classmate, Bruce Cator, who had been in the same West Point company as Harding and Skowronek, would soon find himself in that predicament. He was piloting a B-24 in an attack on the Ploesti oil fields in Romania—refineries fueling the Nazi war machine—when he lost an engine from a direct flak hit. He lost a second engine and could not maintain altitude. The crew of ten had to bail out over Yugoslavia and were then on the run, hiding by day, hiking over rugged terrain by night, not knowing whom—whether partisan, Communist, Chetnick, or Bulgar—they could trust. After twenty-seven days on the lam, aided by loyalists to the king, they made it back to Italy. Cator's classmate, Fred Ascani, meanwhile, was trying to land piloting missions in inclement weather behind enemy lines in Yugoslavia to rescue evadees like his classmate.

For their part, Harding and Skowronek continued their air raids over the days that followed, alternating them on days off with escapades to a local bar in Foggia that Harding had adopted as his own. West Point '41ers fought hard, and they played hard.

After four missions, Skowronek was anxious to get one more under his belt. If he survived five, he would be eligible for the coveted Air Medal.

I bet I'd be the only cavalryman in the Army to have an Air Medal. Got to get in one more mission.

The Allies, however, had by now broken through Anzio and captured Rome, and the Italian Campaign, including IV Corps, was advancing along the west coast. Skowronek got his marching orders to join headquarters. Bud Harding flew his classmate to Anzio, landing his B-17 on a short runway intended for supply and fighter planes, not heavy bombers. Officers looked on with piqued interest, wondering who dared to land a bomber on the abbreviated runway and curious as to what bigwig would disembark. Captain Paul Skowronek emerged in boots and britches to rather puzzled looks.

Shortly afterward, Skowronek was in IV Corps headquarters, assigned to the intelligence G-2, Colonel Thomas Wells, who had been a tactical officer, or tac, at West Point when Skowronek was a cadet. Skowronek recounted to Wells his bomber missions as well as dismay at having fallen short of enough missions to qualify for the Air Medal.

"I'm one short," he said. "I needed five missions to get the medal, but I completed only four."

"You can fly ten hours of our spotter missions," suggested Wells. "We have supporting artillery, and ten observation missions in the light aircraft is the equivalent of one bomber mission."

Skowronek was soon aboard a Piper Cub two-seater, field glasses in hand. But it turned out he need not have fretted; his classmate had his back. Bud Harding got wind that Colonel Elliot Roosevelt, FDR's son who was in the 15th Air Force, had been in a similar predicament to Skowronek. Roosevelt was one shy of winning the Air Medal for completing photo intelligence missions. The colonel, however, had done some aerial tap dancing—counting a double mission as two to help stretch four missions into five.

"If Roosevelt can get the medal that way," Harding told Skowronek, "I'm putting you in for it, for the double mission to the Iron Gate. If they give me crap, we can claim nepotism."

Skowronek was thankful but didn't put too much faith in the plan. He continued on with his observation missions—over Orbetello and Grosseto, Campagnatico and Fornia, Montorsai, Buriano, and so on, trying to accumulate his ten spotting hours.

One day soon after, General Crittenberger held a presentation formation at command post. Officers were lined up, all spit and polish. Some were to receive promotions, others awards. Skowronek stood expectantly, about due for his promotion to major. Crittenberger ceremoniously made his way down the line of officers. When he got to Skowronek, he took out a small box and from within pulled out a bronze medal in the shape of a compass rose, engraved with an eagle carrying two lightening bolts in its talons—the coveted Air Medal. Skowronek stood stunned. He didn't need the spotter missions after all. Harding's plan had worked.

The cavalryman's face lit up in a broad grin as Crittenberger pinned the medal on his chest while pronouncing, "For meritorious achievement while participating in aerial flight." Crittenberger then read off the successful bombing missions of waist-gunner Paul Skowronek.

At that moment, Skowronek knew beyond a doubt that cavalry or not, he still had a future in the Army.

DAWN AND DUSK

Before the break of dawn on June 6, 1944, Jack Norton, with the 82nd Airborne, was in a C-47 transport plane headed for Normandy. More than two-dozen men in full paratrooper gear lined the plane's benches. Their objectives: drop behind the beaches, knock out pillboxes, block German approaches to beaches designated as Allied entry points.

As they neared the coastline, Norton glanced out the window at a sky lit with tracers and illuminating devices. It was the work of the Pathfinders, who had infiltrated the ground thirty minutes earlier. After the debacle in Sicily, Norton had spearheaded developing the doctrine, which involved sending in an elite force prior to the main assault to set up signaling devices to guide aircraft to drop zones. This included radar homing devices modeled on British equipment, along with colored panels and smoke grenades for daytime recognition and marking-lamps for night, among other Pathfinder protocols. The straightforward goal: to make it possible for troops to arrive at the right place at the right time and be heavily concentrated so they could take on the enemy at full force.

Seeing the Pathfinder handiwork in the night skies over Normandy, Norton's anticipation grew.

It looks like the Fourth of July times ten, he thought. *I can't wait to get out of this aircraft—can't wait to get to the ground.*

Norton was forced to hang fire. The 82nd Airborne pilots were having trouble holding formations, given the heavy cloudbanks. As many as 450 airplanes trying to stay tip to tip in V's was a feat under the best of circumstances. Add in the clouds and fifty-knot winds, and the planes had to scramble to avoid collision.

The pilot of Norton's plane accelerated in attempt to rise above the gray blanket. But the move brought the plane up to an altitude untenable for the jump, and the pilot was a mere ten minutes from the drop zone. He pushed his luck. Then the red light went on, a four-minute warning.

With just two minutes to go, the pilot was running out of time. He began rapidly descending, screaming toward the zone at a speed greater than usual for a drop.

The green light went off. It was jump time.

Norton hurled himself out the plane's door, but given its speed, the air hit him with such force that he blacked out. His automatic pistol and the World War I revolver that once belonged to his father burst through their holsters and hurtled into the dark beyond. The ammunition in his pockets pierced through his fatigues, raining onto the fields of France as though warning the enemy that the 82nd was on its way.

Norton was still unconscious when he tumbled to the ground in a heap, the folds of his chute surrounding him like a blanket of snow. About ten minutes elapsed until slowly he came to. He looked around, shook off his daze and surveyed the damages. No broken bones. He counted himself lucky that he had not been pierced by a "Rommel asparagus," one of the hundreds of thousands of spikes installed in possible Allied drop zones by German Field Marshal Rommel; if the spikes didn't nab a jumper, the barbed wire connecting them easily could.

Norton knew he was off target, like so many other paratroopers who had scattered over a fifty-mile line from east to west. His first thoughts were that he needed to connect with others in his stick—the group with whom he'd jumped—but they were scattered about in the dark. He reached into his pocket and pulled out a toy metal clicker that made a noise like a cricket. After clicking it, he waited to hear if any paratroopers within earshot heard him and clicked back. Hearing nothing, he moved cautiously about ten yards and clicked again. Silence. He repeated this several times before he heard the magic sound. Click. He had connected. He and another paratrooper sounded their way toward each other and then advanced together. Moving undetected by the Germans in this manner, they soon assembled a group of about twelve troopers. The group slinked among the shadows till they spotted some farmers toiling in the predawn hours. Once Norton was certain they were locals, he put his French lessons from West Point to good use, asking as to German whereabouts.

"*Où sont les Allemands?*"

The farmers pointed in the direction Norton was *not* to go. Then the farmers resumed their work, as did Norton.

He figured out that he had landed north of Sainte-Mère-Église, a key Allied objective. Like others in his stick, he weaved his way around obstacles in search of the marker light identifying the group's assembly point. He had been versed on beach fortifications, and the spikes, booby traps, and machine-gun positions Rommel had covering the landing zones; the field marshal had anticipated where paratroopers and gliders would land and prepared well. Given the situation, Norton didn't quite see how the Normandy strategy was going to win the war and like others in his division, saw the division's role as desperate—but there was no time for second-guessing on D-Day. The 82nd had to get forces out on the roads to block German armor and infantry that would be coming out of the northwest, from Cherbourg and Valognes toward Sainte-Mère-Église, and moving up from Carentan in the south.

As it turned out, with the help of the Pathfinder doctrine that General Gavin had directed Norton to develop, it seemed that about three-quarters of the troops, including Norton, had landed within a mile of their targeted drop zone. They had enough mass to take on the Germans.

Word soon filtered in to command posts, however, about the less fortunate. Paratroopers illuminated by a farmhouse fire in Sainte-Mère-Église—perhaps sparked by tracer fire—were plucked from the sky like ducks, shot on the way down. Several hundred men drowned in the marshes, while others were caught with broken legs and killed. Some bounced off the rooftops of Sainte-Mère-Église. One private, John Steele of the 82nd Airborne, got his chute hung up on a steeple. There he dangled, thirty or so feet off the ground in his harness, shot through the foot and playing dead so as not to be further target practice for the Germans.

The invasion had not even hit H-Hour, the official time of commencement, and already the first into the fight, the parachute infantry at "H-Minus" had suffered devastating losses. However, the 505th Regiment to which Norton belonged still had enough mass between three battalions to put a dent in German plans. And they had combat experience, which went a long way in battling bedlam. They'd had their shakedowns in Sicily and Italy, the only D-Day regiment in General Matthew Ridgway's 82nd Airborne Division—or the 101st Airborne for that matter—that had tested their mettle in combat. Norton, who was the operation's planning chief for the 1st Battalion, considered the 505th lucky in that regard; it was led by commanders who'd had experience reacting to enemy maneuvers on the battlefield and had seasoned young lieutenants who could take over in the event of a commander's death. "If they don't die," Norton said at one point, "they'll get promoted." Not meant to be glib, the statement was the stark reality for those in at H-Minus.

Needless to say, the battle-hardened 505th was tasked with tough directives. They were to block enemy forces poised to attack Allied troops coming across the beaches. Norton's battalion peeled off west, blocking the Germans from crossing a causeway. The 2nd Battalion jockeyed north, holding off the enemy from moving south with their flat wagons, tanks, and infantry. Within about four hours, the 3rd took the town of Sainte-Mère-Église, which sat along a key route that the Allies feared could have been used in a German counterattack. The town, the first liberated in France, was also to be the defense fallback for the division if seaborne forces failed in their advances. The 3rd Battalion then headed south to ward off a German parachute unit.

Whenever Norton had any doubts about survival, he remembered the Ninety-First Psalm his teacher, Miss Douglas, had taught him growing up in Norfolk, Virginia: "He who dwells in the shelter of the most high . . . you will not fear the terror of the night, nor the arrow that flies by day."

Around D-Day+3, Norton's units became stalled. There were three battalions trying to attack north toward Cherbourg, in the direction of advancing German armor and infantry. Artillery support from the division was critical to success, but just as the artillery storm was set to begin, Norton heard bad news: the division forward artillery observer—the sole person tasked with control of the planned barrage—had been killed. He had been up on a hill with a clear view of the battlefield and was charged with calling in artillery and make firing adjustments. Then under his direction, all three battalions were to let loose, bombarding the enemy at the same time.

Urgent word came from the front that a replacement observer was needed. The regimental commander, Colonel William Ekman, gave orders to Norton: "Get in my jeep and take over!"

Norton sped up the road to the hill where the forward observer had last been seen. Observers, who were always officers, worked in teams that usually included two enlisted soldiers, one serving as radio operator and the other as telephone wireman. In this case, Norton found only the radio operator, but he was safe and sound. Norton got into position on high ground and then called in for artillery fire. It was a strange situation to be in, thought Norton, but not out of the realm of prior training. He mentally reassured himself: *Great. Everything's going fine.*

Jack Norton was ready to direct fire, when the radio operator on the other end stumped him with a challenge. "What's the verification?"

Norton needed a password of some kind so Allied artillery knew he was one of theirs. For a moment, he froze.

Oh my god . . . it has to be a code. What is it? I can't remember.

But there was no time. Enemy fire was raining down. "God damn it!" he bellowed into the radio. "We're all getting killed up here! Fire the barrage!"

They did.

The Germans responded by plastering the hill where Norton stood with a mortar bombardment. He and the radioman ran like blazes as the maelstrom rained down around them, but at least Allied artillery had been let loose—and the three to four days of blocking had succeeded; ground forces were ashore.

The division moved on, attacking to the north and west, clearing the way for other Allied troops. As they did so, the days turned into weeks on the front lines . . . and the losses mounted.

★ ★ ★

In late June Captain Jim Forsyth, or "Diamond Jim" back at West Point, was gearing up for the next Allied wave. He commanded the headquarters company of the 320th Regiment within the 35th Infantry Division.

In the U.S. Army, there was usually, though not uniformly, a "triangular structure" to infantry organizations. Three squads typically made up a platoon commanded by a 2nd lieutenant. Three platoons combined to make a company, with each company containing about 100–150 soldiers commanded by a captain. Three companies constituted a battalion, typically commanded by a lieutenant colonel, and in turn three battalions combined to make a regiment 1,000-plus in size, commanded by a colonel. Added to these units—and adding to the strength of each in size—were add-ons such as machine-gun squads, anti-tank platoons, and so on.

At the next level, a division had three to five regiments with approximately 10,000–15,000 in infantry troops, plus organic units such as artillery, commanded by a brigadier general, plus supporting units such as ordnance, medical, engineering, and more. A two-star major general was in overall command of a division with a brigadier general serving as assistant division commander. All told, a division could reach up to 25,000 in strength.

Two to three divisions made up a corps of about 20,000–50,000, under the domain of a three-star lieutenant general. Two to four corps made up an army, such as General Patton's Third Army with 50,000-plus troops, while an army group had two-plus armies.

In terms of the 35th Infantry Division to which Forsyth belonged, it had been culled from the National Guards of Kansas, Missouri, and Nebraska, which had been mobilized to fight in the war. Regular Army officers like Forsyth had been added to the division's ranks, among whose notable alumni included a former Missouri National Guardsman and World War I commander named Harry S. Truman; talk back in Washington was that Truman was FDR's pick for a vice presidential running mate in the upcoming election.

The 35th Division was in southwest England preparing to ship out for France following the Normandy invasion. As the 320th Regiment lined up for inspection on June 25, there were mixed emotions among the troops. They knew how treacherous the beachheads had been on D-Day, the staggering casualties, and the sacrifices made. But on this particular day, there was also a buzz in the air. The commander reviewing the lines was none other than the Supreme Allied Commander, Europe, General Dwight D. Eisenhower, accompanied by his son, John, a lieutenant recently graduated from West Point. Joining them was General Patton and division commander General Paul Baade. It was a galvanizing send-off for the three-thousand-strong troops of the regiment. Less than a week later, they pushed out.

Forsyth landed along the Normandy beaches not far from where some of his classmates had a few weeks earlier. His regiment immediately joined the front lines heading in the direction of Saint-Lô, a key city on the northern peninsula of France that some called "hedgerow hell" for the area's maze of towering hedges. Thousands of oddly shaped farm plots were surrounded by these dense hedges, some as high as thirty feet, making it impossible for soldiers to predict who lurked behind the next corner or for forward artillery observers to see anything worth a damn to their firing centers. Worse still, hedgerows were typically alongside dirt roads sunken below field level from centuries of use; they were ideal ready-made trenches for the enemy to hide machine-gun nests, snipers, and mortar.

For commanders like Forsyth expecting a breakout, the geography was extraordinarily frustrating. Units would sometimes take an entire day to progress through just two hedgerows, making the scale of territory claimed more befitting hedgehogs than an army of tanks—tanks had as much trouble piercing through the thickets as troops. But slowly, tens of yards at a time, Allied Forces progressed and soon took Saint-Lô, though at a high cost. The 35th Infantry Division lost 2,500 men in their first ten days of combat, among them some of their most seasoned officers. Units had to regroup, and commanders moved up to fill the vacancies, including Forsyth's classmate, Major William "Bill" Gillis. The former West Point football captain and hurdler was charged with the 1st Battalion of the 320th Regiment, a command usually reserved for an officer of lieutenant colonel rank or higher.

Yet with the breakthrough at Saint-Lô came an air of optimism; the peninsula was firmly in Allied hands. General Patton's Third Army tank columns roared deeper into France, while the First Army took the key cities of Avranches and Mortain along an axis to the south, opening up a wide route into Brittany.

It was then that the Germans realized that if they did not halt the break-out, it could portend their downfall, and they might be pushed back to fight the war on their own soil.

On August 7, German Field Marshal Günther von Kluge launched a massive counterattack aimed at splitting the First and Third Armies; Hitler was more ambitious, hoping to push the Allies back into the sea. At one point during the panzer tank offensive, an American battalion from the 30th Infantry Division became surrounded on high ground east of Mortain on "Hill 317." The battalion managed to hold that critical observation point for five days, though troops were severely wounded by the constant panzer attacks. The battalion was also running low on ammunition, food, water, and medical supplies despite attempted airdrops. The 35th Division, it was determined, was the only one in a position to try to rescue the "lost battalion."

The 320th Regiment's 1st Battalion, under twenty-six-year-old Gillis, was assigned the task. Supported by a tank battalion fifty-four strong and a barrage of advance artillery, the battalion raced toward enemy lines, penetrating a mile into their midst by nightfall. As the sun rose the next morning, so too did the battalion—up the hill. With cover fire from tanks, they took the last five hundred yards in hand-to-hand battle. A 2½-ton truck and tanks then bolted up the hill to retrieve the most seriously wounded.

At the end of the day, casualties among Gillis's 1st Battalion were heavy, and thirty out of fifty-four tanks were destroyed. But at least the lost battalion had not become the deserted battalion; one battalion saved the other, making its own sacrifices in the process. For their bold heroics at Mortain, the 1st Battalion earned the Presidential Unit Citation, the equivalent of a Medal of Honor at the unit level, and from the country of France, the Croix de Guerre with a Silver Star.

Hitler, meanwhile, was denied victory. He disengaged from the Battle of Mortain on August 11, and the Germans began retreating toward their northern border.

The U.S. Army's 35th Division started quickly advancing east, hot on Patton's tail. Forsyth, joined by his adjutant and driver, went reconnoitering the next morning in search of a new forward site for their regimental headquarters. As they set out, their jeep rumbled along country roads, passing a few abandoned tanks that had been knocked out. Otherwise, compared to the frantic scurrying of soldiers and barbarous exchanges of the prior week, the roads were silent. It was like the howling winds of a hurricane had given way to the surreal stillness of the storm's eye. There was not a soul in sight, as expected. The enemy was long gone, and almost all of the division had proceeded forth. Forsyth's mind wandered. It was his sister's birthday, August 12, and he reminded himself to write her once the new command post was set up.

Forsyth scanned the horizon in search of a fitting location. To the left were flat plains and to the right rolling hills in swirling hues resembling a Van Gogh painting. Forsyth was spread out in the backseat of the jeep with a map while his adjutant, Captain Davis, was in the passenger seat beside Corporal Jerry McCarthy, the driver. They bantered about, reveling in the calm summer day. As they proceeded, they debated over good, worse, and totally unsuitable options for places to pitch command-post tents.

Then suddenly out of nowhere: *Bam-Bam-Bam-Bam. Bam-Bam-Bam. B-Ba-Bam.* A spray of machine-gun fire hit the jeep.

What the hell!

Forsyth instinctively ducked.

So did McCarthy. But the jeep kept going without his foot on the gas. After about ten seconds, the jeep slowed enough for Forsyth to leap out. He rolled into a ditch to the left and found the driver had mirrored his actions. Their survival instincts had kicked in at the exact same moment, dive or die.

Like a spooked horse that had bucked off its passenger, the driverless jeep kept going, except it still had Captain Davis in it. Forsyth knew beyond a doubt, however, that Davis had taken bullets to the head. Only two of them now had a chance of survival. Neither Forsyth nor the driver said a word as each rolled onto his belly. They played dead, lying parallel to the road, while the whizzing machine-gun fire quieted down.

Forsyth went over the options in his head: *There's nothing but open fields on this side. I could try darting across the road and running into the woods for cover . . . but the chances of making it without being killed are slim. Jerry is probably thinking the same thing. Damn . . . and the carbine's still in the jeep; we've got no weapon. Best keep playing dead.*

A minute passed. Then two. Forsyth's senses were on high alert as he listened for the slightest hint of enemy position—a twig breaking, the rustle of feet. Nothing. He knew the direction the gunfire had come from, but it could have been from twenty yards away or a hundred. The enemy could still be approaching.

With each minute of waiting, Forsyth became more hopeful. But he soon felt a painful throbbing in his head. He'd been hit, and he could feel a trickle of blood dripping down his temple. He remained motionless, not daring to put his hand up to gauge the extent of the injury.

I'm breathing, and I can think straight. Or at least I think I'm thinking straight. It can't be that bad.

The pair continued to lie there as the minutes passed. First ten. Then twenty. Thoughts of mortality raced through Forsyth's mind. So did thoughts of Ruth, his wife.

God, I pray I can see her beautiful face again—those smiling blue eyes that laugh. If I don't make it out, I wonder if she'll ever know what happened to me. I wonder what'll happen to her . . . another war widow. But I might make it. Maybe we'll still have a family. I don't hear anything.

Then all hell broke loose. At the same moment that vehicles could be heard motoring in from the west, blasts of gunfire erupted and fire was returned.

Damn, thought Forsyth. *The Germans are still here and someone else got caught in the ambush.*

He remained frozen as the firefight raged, then slowed, then stopped. Forsyth now heard German voices. Then he heard boots. He felt a nudge on his back. Then another. The German officer hovered above. He said nothing. But one thing was clear: Captain James Forsyth and Corporal Jerry McCarthy were now prisoners of war.

Their captor wore all black, signifying that he was with the SS, or Schutzstaffel, Hitler's dreaded paramilitary security force. In his hands he held Forsyth's helmet, which had been knocked off. The officer smugly pointed to three bullet holes in it, as though saying, "We've got good aim, so beware. Don't do anything stupid." He pivoted the helmet in his hands and inspected the lining, which still had two bullets in it. The third bullet had apparently been the one that exited and grazed Forsyth, who was now feeling strong divine intervention, even if the German officer was the unlikely messenger.

The sergeant—Forsyth could tell his rank by the collar markings—gestured for the two men to get up. With his gun aimed on them, he directed them to start walking. Using his two prisoners for cover, he paced them down the road to where the second ambush had occurred, about a quarter mile away. There on the ground next to a jeep was the corpse of Lieutenant Prescott, a platoon leader from Forsyth's regiment. Several others had been killed as well. Apparently, the remainder of the platoon had fled to the rear and disappeared out of sight.

The SS officer surveyed the German handiwork, confident that not a rasp of breath remained among the disfigured. The captor then forced the pair a short distance away, past what he described, in broken English, was a German artillery position shrouded among the trees.

"Seventy-five millimeter," he said, referring to an anti-tank cannon. "You lucky we no use on you. We do not want to reveal location."

Forsyth immediately understood. Three men were a waste of valuable artillery; the SS had been interested in bigger prey—like a platoon. The Germans, however, had not gone unscathed. A German soldier lay on the ground moaning, badly wounded in the shoot-out and unable to walk.

"*Tragen sie ihn!*" the SS sergeant ordered.

From the gestures it was clear that he and McCarthy were to carry the wounded man. The two formed a two-handed seat carry, each grabbing the other's wrist with one hand to form a seat, while reaching for the other's shoulder with the other arm to form a seat back. Their passenger in tow, they were then herded back down the road, passing the sheared-off head of their comrade, Captain Davis, along the way. The two sides of the human chair tried not to gag, lest they lose their grip and get shot for dropping their passenger. Soon, they reached a headquarters outpost in the woods. A couple dozen SS sentinels were spread among the trees while high-ranking officers congregated near the center, talking in animated tones as they glanced over at the prisoners. The pair was permitted to sit down as the SS officers went about their business.

Forsyth had the chance to ask McCarthy, "How does my wound look?" He bent his head down for inspection.

McCarthy peered at the laceration closely. "Looks like you got grazed, but it doesn't seem deep. Does it hurt a lot?"

"No, not real bad, could be a lot worse."

"That's an understatement. You were a lot closer to joining Davis than you realized," commented McCarthy.

Forsyth nodded. "Were you thinking the same thing as I was back there, that we'd get killed if we made a run for it?"

"Yeah, I didn't see any way out except to play dead and hope maybe they went away."

"That's what I figured," replied Forsyth. "I'm surprised the sergeant didn't stick his rifle in us and shoot us dead in the ditch."

"You're an officer," replied McCarthy. "You're worth more to them alive. Or at least they'll want to find out what you know."

"I'll just pretend I don't understand anything. *Ich spreche nicht Deutsch*; I speak no German."

"I don't speak any either," concurred McCarthy.

Slightly before dusk, the two men were ordered up and directed to begin walking. Carrying the wounded German, they traversed three or four miles before their hands began to slip and their knees buckled. It became apparent that they could carry the SS officer no longer.

The march was halted and the group got ready to bed down for the night. The prisoners had the cold ground, though they had no complaints; better to be on top of it rather than six feet underneath. Forsyth drifted in and out of sleep, wanting to keep an eye open for a gun aimed at him—or an opportunity to escape. But he caved in to sporadic slumber.

The next morning was the same routine, treading for miles through forested terrain with their heavy human burden. Forsyth thought it impossible that his muscles could burn more than they did, as though it was the hundred-mile hike at Beast Barracks multiplied exponentially. As the pair fought to put one foot ahead of the other, Forsyth overheard a top commander talking to other officers. He knew that he was the topic of conversation and wondered about his fate.

Are they talking about killing me? Torturing me? Sending me to a concentration camp?

He had to wait on the verdict because they soon arrived at yet another headquarters post. Forsyth was separated from McCarthy and immediately turned over to intelligence officers for interrogation. This time, the SS officer spoke English quite well.

"What is your name, rank, and number?"

"Captain James Forsyth, 24038." U.S. Army protocol allowed that information to be given—no more.

"What organization are you with and what regiment?"

No answer.

"Where were you going?" questioned the SS officer.

Forsyth stared straight ahead.

Undeterred, the SS officer continued. "Where was the rest of your regiment coming from, that other platoon?"

Forsyth remained silent, wondering at what point he'd be subjected to torture, given the infamy of SS death squads. But the interrogator simply took a different tact.

"How far away was your old post, and how many kilometers did you travel today?"

The interrogator was obviously experienced and knew U.S. Army protocol. Regiments usually spaced two battalions on the front about a half mile apart, holding one in reserve a half mile to the rear. Command posts were typically another half mile farther behind, maybe a little more.

He's trying to back in to positions, Forsyth figured. *Trying to calculate where our artillery and forward infantry positions are moving today. Like hell I'm going to tell him.*

The prisoner gave no hint of acknowledgement, and the SS officer, surprisingly, showed little frustration. It was as though the prisoner was a pesky bee that he wanted to swat away. Forsyth got the impression that he'd been through this before and was not interested in wasting further breath.

Maybe they plan on chaining me up at the next command post. Or maybe, just maybe, they realize they're beginning to lose the war and want to hedge their bets. . . . The captors could soon be the captives.

The following morning, the two POWs were set to head off in different directions. They shared a sidelong glance—and a nod—as though saying, "Good luck and Godspeed," then departed with their respective captors. It was to be the last Forsyth ever saw of McCarthy.

With that, Forsyth began walking . . . and walking . . . first through northern France, then eastward across Germany. He was herded with other POWs at various points along the way, and at times the prisoners had to shield themselves from the friendly fire of Allied air attacks. Once, marching through an orchard for cover, Forsyth had to duck for shelter, not just from the spray of bullets but from a hail of apples as well. In another instance, a German ambulance was bombarded from overhead, inflicting injuries on the medics. The incensed survivors were prepared to take their anger out on the American POWs passing by, but the SS made it quite clear that officers like Forsyth were off limits. The SS had their orders, whatever those were.

As Forsyth marched, one thought kept nagging at him. *I should not have got caught; I wasn't supposed to let that happen.*

Forsyth beat himself up over what he could have done differently; POWs were not viewed as heroes of any sort in this war, and twice he tried to escape. In the first case, he was among five or six prisoners holed up in a barn for the night. In the early morning hours he hid in the loft. The SS officers were none the wiser when they departed on their journey later that morning. Forsyth remained under cover, considering his alternatives.

Should I go now or wait for nightfall? And how on earth am I supposed to become invisible dressed in an American uniform in the heart of Nazi-land?

While he was still formulating a plan, about an hour later, the SS returned to scour the premises. Forsyth need plan no longer. They quickly discovered him.

A second time, he managed to slip out from the group's encampment after dark. The former West Point hurdler raced down the road into the woods but was immediately missed, and a search was ordered. He crouched behind shrubs along a stream, hoping against hope that he would not be discovered. But the search party's flashlights lit him up like a Broadway marquee. Still, despite his attempted escapes, he was not mistreated.

By the time Forsyth had traversed the four-hundred-mile width of Germany, the bulk of it on foot, it was mid-September, a month after his capture. The lush greens of Normandy in summer had been traded for the sunset hues of autumn. And the sun was about to set on Forsyth's journey. In its last leg, he was packed into a railway boxcar on its way to Poland. It was headed to Szubin (also *Schubin*), east of Berlin in northern Poland. His final destination: Oflag 64, a Nazi POW camp for American officers.

Ruth soon received the dreadful news of her husband's fate. Captain James Forsyth, she was informed by the War Department, had been killed in action. She collapsed in sobs.

9

GOTHIC FRONTS

In March 1944, Captain Henry Bodson sailed from Norfolk, Virginia, into Oran, Algeria, which remained a point of debarkation for many Allied troops heading toward the Mediterranean Theater of operations. With its heavy naval traffic and submarine-infested depths, however, the Mediterranean was like a cauldron kept at a boil by the Germans. Allied commanders were hesitant to risk moving transport ships through its troubled waters, so troops had to bide their time in North Africa till the tide of power changed. Toward early April that occurred, allowing ships to press onward, which for Bodson meant squeezing aboard a crowded British transport ship. The final destination was undisclosed, but Bodson was tired of the stifling heat and swirling dust of North Africa.

As long as I'm going somewhere, he thought, *I don't care who takes me there.*

The guns of the 39th Field Artillery Battalion, part of the 3rd Infantry Division, were waiting for him—wherever that might be. His orders were to report to the battalion's commanding officer. He was replacing an outgoing captain who had either been killed or perhaps reached the end of his rope with combat fatigue; at this stage of the war combat veterans were permitted to return home in some of those cases.

In a matter of days the skyline of Naples was within Bodson's sight. It was the most bombed-out city in Italy, with close to two hundred Allied air raids having wreaked havoc for nearly a year in attempts to destroy Axis supply lines that originated from the port and led north to Rome and beyond. The raids succeeded, and the 82nd Airborne, including Jack Norton, helped take Naples in the fall of 1943, marking the first major European city to be captured by the Allies.

Arriving in Naples in April 1944, Bodson saw the blunt impact of the prolonged air raids on the civilian population. There were charred storefronts and crumbling homes at every turn. As he dined at the Army base, just beyond the fencing he spotted a boy, a mere five or six years of age, ducking his head face-first into a garbage can in search of food. The bin seemed to swallow the little boy, who undoubtedly competed with rats and mice for morsels. Bodson lost his appetite and wondered how to aid the hungry child, but the boy scampered off as quickly as he appeared.

From Naples, Captain Bodson boarded an amphibious troop transport headed north, which landed infantry on the beaches of Anzio. Anzio was a region about halfway between Naples and Rome that had been captured in late January. In that operation the Allies succeeded in diverting German defenses south so that the enemy only loosely defended a fifteen-mile stretch of beachhead, enabling the 3rd Infantry Division and other Allied units to seize it. The region was key because it was within striking distance of the Allied objective of Rome, yet near to Allied airbases and military depots in Naples to the south.

Onshore a lieutenant met Bodson, and the two drove several kilometers inland. Bodson scanned the gently rolling hills of lightly wooded farmlands as they went. The Anzio region had been part of an ambitious land reclamation program launched by Mussolini, whose projects included turning swampland into fertile agricultural land to increase Italy's self-sufficiency. The fields were now dotted with brick farmhouses and barns that were built under the program in the previous decade. They offered sturdy, well-built structures for Allied troops to house headquarters. Most of the local population, in fact, remained in their homes and were even occasionally forced to share accommodations with Allied officers. But more often than not, officers tried to leave the Italians some semblance of normalcy, instead taking to bunkers or other structures.

Henry Bodson found the headquarters of his fire direction center in a large, brick barn, where it had been established shortly after the Anzio invasion. As he entered, he noticed the lingering smell of cattle, despite the farm's few surviving cows—those not slaughtered for food—being relegated to the fields. Officers and enlisted men sat in the barn where the cattle once fed, hay still coated sections of the floor, and farm equipment stood idle; the locals could manage only small plots of acreage amid a war, just enough to raise crops for sustenance.

Artillerymen were busy, poring over map coordinates, yelling into telephones, and hurriedly jotting down target information. These were seasoned troops, Bodson knew. Most had entered the war in North Africa, in the vicinity of Casablanca in November 1942.

On Bodson's first night at the center, he scouted out the corners of the barn for a secluded corner in which to lay his head. But among the crew of fifteen or so, the prime real estate had long before been claimed. He saw limited options.

That concrete feeding trough, that manger. Maybe it would work . . . just slightly wider than me. Then I wouldn't have to worry about boots kicking me in the middle of the night.

He laid his thick bedroll down and settled within. Exhausted, he quickly drifted off to sleep, snuggled within the trough as though swaddled.

When a fellow officer spotted the sleeping Bodson a while later, he kidded, "Well, if it isn't Little Jesus." There was a good laugh among those awake, and the nocturnal name stuck. By day: Captain Bodson. By night: Little Jesus.

Captain Bodson promptly adapted to the frenetic pace within the fire direction center, which operated 24-7 and had maniacal bursts of activity followed by lulls before the next storm. As enemy targets or troop movement were spotted, requests for concentrations of artillery firepower were called in over the radio, quick and staccato messages such as: "Fire mission. Pillbox. Crossroads 285. Northwest 315. Precision. Single gun. HE. Delay. Will adjust!"

This meant that a pillbox had been spotted near crossroads. Artillery was to destroy it with a single gun using high-explosive shells. The observer requested a delayed fuse to allow shells to penetrate the pillbox before detonating, and each round was to be adjusted depending on the success of the prior one.

At night, a request might include: "Fire mission. Tank column. Destruction. High angle. Battalion and all additional fire. HE. Cannot observe."

Translation: We believe there is a column of tanks, but there are hills blocking observation, so we need high-angle shells to soar over the hills. Call in all artillery available. Use high-explosive rounds that will explode on impact. But since we cannot clearly observe the target, it's blind fire.

Artillery, simply put, was far from aim and fire.

The 3rd Division infantry had by then settled into a routine. The troops patrolled north and south of the Anzio and Nettuno beachheads—a stretch of about fifteen miles—as well as inland about ten miles. But the Germans had superior positions on high ground to the north in the Alban Hills on the approach to Rome. They had clear views southward, so the Allies had to dig in for better protection.

And dig they did. While stagnant trench warfare had become largely obsolete in World War II due to greater armor and air mobility, small portions of the active Anzio beachhead were a throwback to World War I. There was a honeycomb of trenches along parts of the front lines on both sides, primarily large foxholes connected by small pathways. These footholds led into little in the way of gained ground for either Allies or enemy. After almost four months of bitter combat, the expedient liberation of Rome, to which Churchill aspired, seemed a prospect as laboriously slow as Michelangelo's painting of the Sistine Chapel. The 3rd Division bided its time, waiting on reinforcements for a planned breakout in May.

Between intermittent battles, Bodson's artillery battalion used the lulls to prepare for the upcoming offensive. In the ink-black night, troops moved forward to the Mussolini Canal—part of a spidery network of canals that spanned the region. The canal flowed from the Apennine Mountains situated inland and down over low, flat plains and swampy marshes until it poured into the sea near Anzio. While the canal protected the right, southern flank of the Allied beachhead line, the treeless expanse on the northern side offered little cover for a breakout. Artillery had to make up for what nature failed to provide.

Over the course of three weeks, 39th artillerymen descended several dozen at a time down the banks of the canal, which were about twenty feet in height. There, by flashlight or moonlight, they slaved for hours with shovels and picks like railroad workers. A scoop of Italian soil at a time, they slowly dug semicircular excavations into the sides of the canal, throwing away the mucky evidence into the water below. When one recess was complete, they moved on to the next, ultimately excavating twelve caves—enough to house each of the battalion's guns.

Hours before the Allies were to start their offensive breakout, the troops lowered their dozen 105mm howitzers into the prepared firing positions, using trucks outfitted with A-frames that served as arms to lower the monstrous guns. Finally, they covered the artillery with camouflage netting. From the air, all looked quiet on the Mussolini Canal.

The Allies, reinforced by additional divisions, were ready to launch the breakout. In the predawn hours of May 22, the heavy pounding commenced, with every artillery piece of every division letting rip as though the skies over Anzio were raining meteorites. Within two days the 39th alone bombarded enemy infantry and armor with some ten thousand rounds, and the Allies pierced the beachhead perimeter. The retaliatory march on Mussolini's former seat of dictatorship, Rome, could begin.

The offensive line slowly snaked its way through the hills toward the capital city, but near the town of Cori an infantry bottleneck occurred on a narrow, twisted road. The spigot of advancing troops drew to a slow trickle. Rather than dueling it out, Henry Bodson stopped his command car and got out. He lackadaisically leaned against his car, figuring he'd read letters from home until the traffic jam eased.

Suddenly overhead, a scene began to play out as though in slow motion. An approaching plane. Lower and lower. It was zeroing in on the column of infantry troops about a hundred yards ahead. It swooped like a falcon, diving almost vertically. It was so close that Bodson could see the bomb dropping from the undercarriage.

The letters in his hands scattered to the ground. He slid down the road's embankment, jolting to a halt aside a stream.

Ahead on the road, there was a horrifying, snarling anarchy of metal, bodies, and shrapnel hurled into the air as the bomb hit.

Then came a second plane, and a third. Bodson crouched behind thickets of brush, watching the sky hail bombs, wondering if he was next. At moments, he instinctively held his breath, but curiosity prodded him to peer upward at the parade of planes.

They look vaguely familiar. From where? What type? I can't quite tell.

Still they came on. A fourth plane. A fifth. A ghastly procession of dive-bombers.

Someone's thrown a yellow smoke grenade. What's going on? No, no . . .

A sixth plane approached. It dipped its wings from side to side—a sign of recognition. The Allied plane was acknowledging the swirls of yellow smoke, the agreed-on sign noting Allied troops.

Bodson gaped in realization. *Oh my goodness. It was friendly fire. . . . Oh my god.*

Momentarily, Bodson stood stunned, shaken. He thought his legs might give way. Recollecting his wits, he scrambled out of his sanctuary as the roar of planes ceased. But the screams and turmoil Bodson heard up the road were nearly as deafening. Wailing sirens of misery pierced the air. Dozens of soldiers lay dead or wounded. Medics raced to administer to those for whom there was hope, skirting from one to the next in a form of triage dodgeball. It was utter chaos, utter anarchy.

The smoky, gruesome scene seared into Bodson's mind like a snapshot frozen in time, never to be forgotten. The victorious march on Rome, minutes before seeming imminent, had turned into devastation.

Later, Bodson would learn one of the pilots of the attack planes, realizing his grave error, had committed suicide.

In the days following that bombing incident, there were heavy casualties on both sides as the Allies doggedly persisted in their push north. They were relentless, as though all roads did lead to Rome, and they had the sacrifices to show for it. In the first five days of the offensive alone, more than four thousand Allied lives were lost. But less than two weeks later the prize city finally fell to the Allies. It was June 4, 1944, two days before the Normandy invasion.

The 3rd Infantry Division was assigned to occupy Rome and stabilize the Eternal City before the division reverted a few weeks later to familiar staging grounds near Naples. There, with time on their hands, officers regrouped. It began a period of healing for the wounded and for the remainder, training. The drills never ceased, even along battlefronts.

With training directives on his mind, Henry Bodson brought a group of noncommissioned officers to sand dunes along the coast. He began instructing them in calling for artillery firepower. After covering the basics, he got down to methods for artillery adjustment, using a large cotton ball to represent an artillery shell burst in mock scenarios. A day later it was showtime. The captain set up an improvised firing range: the guns were positioned a few miles inland, and the observer post was stationed on a sand dune looking out to sea. The "enemy" was a large anchored raft floating offshore.

Captain Bodson stood before his observer students, ready for action. "Now," he asked, "who wants to volunteer to direct artillery fire?"

A number of hands popped up among the couple dozen men. Bodson scanned the crowd. One volunteer was a redheaded, freckled-faced sergeant.

He can't be more than eighteen years old, thought Bodson.

"Young man," he asked, "what's your name?"

"Sergeant Audie Murphy, sir," the soldier replied.

"Okay, Sergeant Murphy. Let's see how you shape up. Come on up." Bodson handed the young soldier field glasses.

Murphy held the glasses to his eyes and made some observations and calculations. He then spouted off firing orders to a nearby radio operator. As the orders were transmitted to the fire direction center inland, a wag in the group remarked, "Let's dig some foxholes fast! That first shot will be in our laps."

The laughs were plentiful. Bodson gave a stern look in response, and the boisterous soldiers quieted down. After a few anxious moments, they heard the whine of an artillery shell above. Heads quickly dipped into their collars like ostriches, but then far in the distance they saw the sea surge and rippling circles swell outward in waves. The shot had landed in the water, directly in line between the shoreline observation post and the objective—but it was short.

Murphy yelled to the radio operator. "Short! Add one hundred!"

Good grief, marveled Bodson. *He's making a jump in range, just enough to get over the target. He's trying to bracket it. Genius.*

Moments later a shell whined again.

"Over! Drop fifty. Fire for effect," ordered the freckle-faced soldier.

This time, there were no ostriches in the sand. The mission clobbered the target three miles out at sea.

Audie Murphy smiled, pleased with himself, and slowly sat down. The rest of the crowd sat stunned, with the exception of Henry Bodson, who felt like a proud father whose son had just won first prize; Audie Murphy, after just a few hours of artillery instruction, had fired the perfect round, an artilleryman's dream.

Shortly afterward, the 3rd Infantry Division was put on notice that it would be pulled out of Italy. In mid-August, in the port of Naples, officers began preparations. Bodson was in command of six amphibious transport trucks, named DUKWs for the model type, though troops referred to them simply as "ducks," an apt description for an amphibious vehicle that swam in the water and walked on the land. Bodson's DUKWs, with names like Beachcomber, Beer Barrel, and Bottom's Up, were to be loaded on to larger transport ships, landing ship tanks or "LSTs." The massive preparation behind it all was mind-boggling.

Henry Bodson mused, *What do my troops need for an invasion when I don't know where we're invading?*

He had to consider an enormous range of possibilities. He neatly wrote out a cargo manifest on the back of a map of Naples; it was the largest piece of writing material he could find for his rather elaborate needs. Aboard the six DUKWs would be four 105mm howitzers, eight bazookas, two heavy machine guns, and ammunition for the weapons. They collectively accounted for the bulk of the weight aboard the DUKWs, each of which had a capacity of eight thousand pounds. Added to those loads were rammer staffs, aiming circles, mine detectors, shovels, picks and axes, camouflage nets, tarps, and more than a thousand sandbags. There were telephones, radios, a switchboard, and near endless reels of wire, plus rations, and of course, personnel.

But the logistics puzzle didn't end there. In addition to the DUKWs, there were trucks and trailers with kitchen apparatuses to load onto the LSTs, as well as bedding rolls, baggage, and executive equipment. At times, moving a small army was like moving heaven and earth.

On August 14, 1944, after Bodson's inventory had been loaded down to the last can of water, he boarded his ship, part of a vast armada of 885 ships in total. The sea surrounding Naples resembled a miniature board game in a war room where commanders jockey battleships in military chess. But this was no game. It was Operation Dragoon.

As the armada set sail for "destination unknown," Bodson went up on deck. It was a glorious, sunny morning on the Mediterranean as he scanned the spectacle unfolding before him. It was hard to tell where the sea began and the ships ended. Vessels blended into the horizon or appeared swallowed by the sea.

Closer in, Bodson noticed a speedboat whizzing between ships, heading in the direction of his LST. Among the group on the foredeck was a portly man waving wildly to those aboard the transports, and they, in return, waved back with exuberant enthusiasm. As the speedboat drew nearer, a wry smile appeared on Bodson's face as he discerned the image of the waving man.

Darn if isn't Winston Churchill, stogie and all, wishing the troops good luck.

The Allies were about to invade southern France.

The invasion had been bandied about among the Allies for the better part of a year. Plans were drawn up, plans canceled, and the merits of an invasion hotly debated. On one hand, a southern onslaught was viewed as a complement to the attack on Normandy; it would weaken the overall defenses of the enemy in France, and similar to Italy, prevent German forces in the south from reinforcing the north. On the other hand, that strategy in Italy had brought on a wearisome, uphill battle against an enemy entrenched in superior positions on mountainous high ground. In addition, amphibious vessels needed for a southern French offensive were in short supply between the grueling demands of the Pacific and D-Day in Normandy.

But as the Allies got bogged down in northern France, a southern invasion changed from a concept with possibilities to that of critical necessity. As a result, in the same week that Bill Gillis and Jim Forsyth grappled with hell among the hedgerows, their classmate, Henry Bodson, was nearing the shores of the French Riviera. He was part of a 150,000-strong force — close to the 160,000 that stormed Normandy. The armada of 885 ships and landing vessels carried nearly 1,400 smaller landing craft and about 21,400 trucks, tanks, tank destroyers, bulldozers, and vehicles. It was not the way Bodson envisioned visiting the glamorous seaside resort of Saint-Tropez. But there it was.

The Riviera was not an obvious place to battle a war, but to the west, the ports of Marseilles — France's largest — and Toulon were clear targets. The Germans, aware of the Allied naval buildup from their Luftwaffe reconnaissance, had fortified those areas. In turn, those fortifications left them challenged to defend the rest of the long coastline, leaving German forces spread thin.

The Allies planned to capitalize on weak links in German defenses and to confuse the enemy had bombarded all along the coast leading up to the invasion, including raids on the Italian Riviera far to the east. The night prior to the onslaught, dummy paratroopers were also dropped in, while small boat fleets simulated amphibious landings, both as diversionary tactics far from the true objectives. Adding to the bedlam were Pathfinders unintentionally dropped in the wrong places due to low cloud cover, which in turn caused subsequent paratrooper jumps to be widely scattered, baffling the enemy still further.

Despite the chaos, both intended and unintended as Operation Dragoon unfolded, the Riviera was the epitome of splendor with brilliant sunshine and calm, azure seas. Only the sooty, lingering haze from the last of Allied bombings divulged that the sunny playgrounds had been traded in for war—for Seventh Army division landings on Alpha, Delta, and Camel Beaches, code names respectively for the locales of the 3rd, 45th and 36th Infantry Divisions landings.

Henry Bodson had studied the terrain model of Alpha Beach until he knew its curves almost as well as those of his wife. He and his troops from a 3rd Infantry artillery unit off-loaded the LSTs in their DUKWs, assembling in a circular pattern about three miles offshore. At the scheduled time they formed a wave about two hundred yards wide and headed for the objective. Troops spotted the breach in offshore obstacles where division engineers had blasted a passage and easily forged their way through. Resistance was light, allowing the unit, one of many troop waves that morning, to drive directly across the beaches.

As the unit reached the cover of woods, Bodson's thoughts were triumphant. *No casualties!*

About a mile inland, he ordered his men to unload the howitzers. They placed them into firing positions to protect advancing infantry, which sought to move rapidly before enemy forces could organize a coherent defense. Together with armored units, the infantry and artillery aggressively pushed east and west along the coastal road and into the interior, as did the French First Army that followed in subsequent waves. Casualties were minimal in the initial onslaught, and the Allied offensive established a second enormous combat front in France. The Allies were now squeezing the Nazis from the west and south, trying to put the genie back in its bottle, and it appeared to be working.

The failure of the Germans to stave off the southern France invasion, combined with their foiled attempt to retake Mortain in the north, prompted the Nazi high command to reevaluate its French strategy. The Germans began to withdraw from the country. Except for defending the key ports of Marseilles and Toulon—which within weeks would be taken by the French—Germany's southern troops retreated north up the Rhône River valley. Allied Forces, in close pursuit, kept up the pressure, all the while heeding an important French edict: don't crush the vineyards!

While vines may have survived, as enemy troops fled they left behind destroyed and abandoned tanks, vehicles and horse-drawn supply wagons at every turn. Henry Bodson was stunned to stumble upon a field where hundreds of horses lay dead, as though it was a colossal cavalry morgue. Having seen so many soldiers' corpses, he didn't know why the scene was so unsettling.

Perhaps I have grown far too accustomed to dead men—but not dead animals.

The body count continued to rise over the ensuing months as the 3rd Division began "mopping up" the German pocket around Colmar in northeast France. While dents were at first inflicted into the pockets, the cold, snow, battle weariness, and German armor began to take its toll. Bodson was the officer in charge of the fire direction center for the 39th Field Artillery Battalion headquarters when, one day in late January 1945, forces were in the midst of an Allied thrust near the village of Holtzwihr. Bodson halted at the sound of an incoming radio transmission. An infantry officer was desperately calling for artillery fire support, and in the background Bodson could hear the deafening blasts of a firestorm.

What he didn't know was that the infantry officer had assumed command of his company only that morning after its commander was badly wounded. As heavy enemy tanks and infantry were overtaking his position, the officer ordered his troops to the safety of the nearby woods. He now stood alone atop his company's burning tank destroyer with no fire support. A portable phone connecting him to artillery headquarters—and to Bodson—was his only hope.

Upon getting the officer's transmission and data, Bodson immediately relayed the information to those he was supervising in the fire directions center, yelling, "Pour it on!" Artillery was carefully rationed, given intense demands in the Battle of the Bulge, but this was not a moment for frugality.

As the artillery roared, the infantry officer, shrouded in smoke, grabbed the tank destroyer's single machine gun, firing it in between transmissions to Bodson to adjust artillery fire. The lone commander held off the

Germans for an hour while well-placed artillery bombarded their infantry and destroyed a number of tanks. The Germans retreated, their casualties heavy.

The officer phoning Henry Bodson had been Audie Murphy, the freckled-faced kid he instructed in artillery adjustments six months prior. Murphy's actions earned him the Medal of Honor. When Bodson heard about that, he felt humbled, realizing that his lessons may have played a part.

★ ★ ★

While Bodson pushed north in France, fellow '41 officers were trying to scale mountains of obstacles in northern Italy. The Italians had surrendered on September 8, 1943, but German troops still dominated the landscape, refusing to relinquish Italy to the Allies.

Hills gave the Germans superior positions in southern Italy, while to the north they were firmly entrenched along a line of imposing mountain summits that stretched east to west, bisecting the north from its boot. Labeled the "Gothic Line," this natural barrier of defense was situated within Italy's vast Apennine mountain range and ran from the Adriatic coastal city of Pesaro inland to just north of Florence, ending at Pisa on the Mediterranean coast. Natural approaches to the Gothic Line, which ran several miles deep in places, were fortified by the Germans with pillboxes, gun bunkers, and connecting trenches, all of which were protected by wide bands of barbed wire entanglements, mine fields, and anti-tank ditches. The Germans also had excellent vantage points for interlocking fields of fire covering wide areas of its terrain.[1]

Hitler's dictate was to defend the Gothic Line at all costs; it was the last significant barrier of defense separating Allied Forces in Italy from mainland Europe. If the Germans defended the line, it would prevent the Allies from entering the broad Po Valley, as well as the main industrial and agricultural areas of northern Italy, including Bologna. For the Allies, on the other hand, the Po Valley represented a route for potentially advancing into the Alps, the Balkans, and perhaps Austria before winter arrived.[2]

Not long after Bodson departed Italy in August 1944, Lieutenant Colonel Ed Rowny arrived in Pisa with the 92nd Infantry Division, part of General Mark Clark's Fifth Army. The 92nd was under the command of General Edward "Ned" Almond, as well as the assistant division commander, General John Wood, who had been in Liberia with Rowny. The 92nd Division was another all-black unit, dubbed the "Buffalo" Division, a term that some said was coined by American Indians who, in earlier times on the prairies, saw black Army soldiers clothing themselves with buffalo hides to keep warm during the cold winter months.[3] Others thought it had to do with the soldiers' dark curly hair.

Rowny's combat engineer battalion within the 92nd was dispatched to a large courtyard in Pisa that surrounded the Leaning Tower. The unit was to temporarily camp there while waiting for further instructions. It was then that Rowny learned of the provincial knowledge of his soldiers. He ordered his troops in Company A to spread out on one side of the tower while Companies B and C were to camp opposite. But Company A refused to put down their bedrolls. The soldiers froze.

Rowny walked up to a group of them and, with a puzzled look, asked, "What's the problem here?"

"Sir, that tower's about to topple," insisted a concerned soldier. "We can't sleep on this side 'cause we'll all be killed. We better get on the other side and fast, sir."

The usually serious countenance of Rowny held back a chuckle. "Didn't you ever hear the story of the Leaning Tower of Pisa?"

Foreheads creased and heads nodded in the negative. Rowny explained that the bell tower was unlikely to fall overnight, given that it had been leaning for hundreds of years. Despite his proclamations of safety, however, it became apparent that his men would be up all night in fear if relegated to the sinking side. So all three of his companies—about nine hundred men in total—squeezed in on the "safe side," lying shoulder to shoulder like sardines. Rowny took his chances and, together with his officers, spread out on the opposite side.

The main mission of the 92nd Infantry Division then commenced. It was to pin down German forces to deter them from being redeployed to the western front as the Allies pressed east on the Continent toward the Nazi homeland. But rough terrain posed a logistical nightmare. How to transport supplies and equipment from cavernous gorges up to mountains with peaks soaring to six thousand feet?

Ed Rowny's engineer battalion built a "skyway," similar to a ski lift, to reach high-altitude posts. Additionally, over 350 mules and 150 horses were purchased from locals to create a supply convoy. Caretakers of the animals were recruited to assist the 92nd as well, and they in turn enlisted additional friends to join the caravan till the ranks of Italians grew to about six hundred men. A cavalry officer—one of the best polo players in the Army—was ordered to the area to command these forces. The officer's visions of gallant galloping on horseback in battle were quickly dashed when he discovered that his cavalry was a mule-pack battalion. Such were the glories of war. Men and mules alike began training in combat-like conditions.

While supply routes got sorted out, little headway was made against the enemy. One of the main Allied objectives was a general offensive toward Bologna along the entire front. A 92nd task force became responsible for the Ligurian Sea coastal sector. The task force, which included one of the division's finest regiments, the 370th Infantry, sought to capture the city of Massa. Success with that objective might open up the chance for advancing along the main highway toward the former Italian naval base at La Spezia. Just as Henry Bodson had experienced in southern Italy, however, for every yard of Allied ground claimed, counterattacks set troops back. It was yet another tug-of-war progressing with minimal gains. In six days of attacks in October 1944, the 92nd task force netted only two thousand yards and failed to capture its objectives, and some of its best infantry and noncommissioned officers were killed. In total, the task force suffered over four hundred casualties, and troops became disheartened at the inability to seize and hold objectives.[4]

Still, Generals Almond and Wood were anxious to keep the Germans engaged, as was the Fifth Army commander, General Mark Clark. Offensives continued over the following months in efforts to prevent the Germans from thinning out their units and sending men to the western front. The 92nd Division planned and executed attacks along the high ground parallel to the Ligurian Sea. For every Allied kilometer gained, however, they were often pushed back severalfold. When that happened, the Germans would return to their well-entrenched positions on the Gothic Line.

The days grew colder. Ammunition grew shorter. Christmas came and went, though a bright spot occurred after Congresswoman Clare Boothe Luce—a former *Life* war correspondent—visited the 92nd Division over the holidays. She returned to the States, publicly arguing that the Italian front was the "forgotten front." She appealed to the War Department for more funds, petitioned Congress to approve such funds, and swayed the press to pressure Congress. More supplies and air support were soon dispatched to the 92nd Division. The support hardly came soon enough.

General Wood concocted a scheme to add new elements of surprise to the battle equation. Ed Rowny agreed it was an ingenious idea. It involved the 10th Mountain Division, which was located in reserve to the rear of the 92nd. The 10th Mountain Division was composed of elite forces trained to fight on skis that had been culled from ski patrols, schools, and colleges in the United States. Wood didn't need skis to execute his scheme, but he knew the division's members, such as young lieutenant Robert S. Dole (later a U.S. senator), would be an asset. Wood planned to have 92nd Division infantrymen move forward in an attack, and as they did so, 10th Mountain soldiers would occupy the infantry's vacated foxholes.

A 92nd Division attack soon ensued and, as expected, the usual volley of yardage commenced. In the difficult mountain terrain, the Allied line advanced marginally and was followed by an enemy counterattack that forced the boundary back—and then some.

The Germans, overconfident, chased the Allies as they scampered in retreat past the shelter of even their own foxholes. As the Germans charged past those dugouts, the 10th Mountain Division forces popped up from the foxholes in white camouflage fatigues, appearing like armed ghosts delivering a solid wall of fire.

For a change, the Allied line held.[5]

The 92nd Division, meanwhile, was under immense pressure from the Fifth Army to successfully penetrate the Gothic Line. The Allied combined chiefs of staff remained convinced that the Germans would thin forces in Italy to reinforce their forces in northern Europe. They pressured General Lucian Truscott, the new Fifth Army commander, to launch an offensive against the Gothic Line; General Clark had moved on to command the 15th Army Group.

Truscott pinpointed early February for the intended attack. The Fifth Army was to attack the Gothic Line north of Florence with the objective of capturing Bologna. The plan called for the 92nd Division to first launch an all-attack along the high ground inland, halfway between the coast and the Serchio Valley. The Serchio is the third longest river in Tuscany, its valley situated between the Apennines to the north and rock quarries of the Carrara region to the south. The plan was to have two regiments of the division launch the attack while a third would defend the northern end of the valley, which had been the site of a prior German assault.

General Wood suggested that a task force make an offensive along the coast to make the Germans believe that was the main attack. The idea was that by drawing German reserves to the coast, it would weaken their defenses on high ground. That would enable the main attack—with the help of extra firepower and air support—to penetrate the enemy's front lines. The Germans might then be unable to conduct their usual counterattack, since their reserves designated for that purpose would be fighting the task force.

General Almond agreed and designated Task Force One for the offensive. The task force would consist of the 366th Infantry Regiment, dubbed the "blue stocking" regiment since, as civilians, many of its officers occupied high positions. Added to that would be artillery support, engineers, chemical warfare experts, signalmen, and medics. The task force would have 1,220 total soldiers in total. Ed Rowny was stunned to be selected to command Task Force One. His offensive would be along what were once heavenly beaches in Viareggio, north of Pisa, though sand castles and lollipop-colored umbrellas had given way to the buried treasures of the enemy—mines. The Germans had booby-trapped the beaches and area waters with explosives to ward off another potential amphibious landing like the debacle in southern France. The diversion had all the makings of a suicide mission, and General Wood made that clear to Rowny.

"It's a hair-brained idea, going around the flank," admitted Wood. "You're certain to be surrounded and lose a lot of men, yourself included."

"Will it help the division?" asked Rowny.

"Sure it will. I mean, look, we're faced with a problematic situation," explained Wood. "We need to prevent a counterattack to our attack. We've failed in previous attacks, and I don't see any way to advance unless we can somehow divert enemy reserves so we can punch through this time to capture our objective."

"Then I'll do it. . . . Try to keep the reserves bottled up."

"That's very brave of you, Ed," replied Wood.

"You're my commander," Rowny assured Wood. "If it'll help the division succeed, then I'm at your command."

"It'll be brilliant if it works." Wood paused. "It'll be disastrous if it fails. Either way, it will be costly."

For extra support for Rowny's mission, Wood sought to enlist the help of a Fifth Army tank battalion, which fortuitously was commanded by Rowny's West Point roommate, the flanker half of the Greene brothers, Larry, brother of '41er Mike Greene.

"Colonel Greene," Wood succinctly announced over the phone. "I need you to send me twenty-five of your best tanks for your buddy here, Ed Rowny. He's about to embark on a major offensive, and he'll need all the help he can get."

Wood outlined the dicey circumstances and the odds stacked against the task force.

Unflinchingly, Greene responded, "I'll do you one better. I'll pick the twenty-five best commanders in my battalion and twenty-five of their best crews, and if I have to reassign teams to make sure Ed gets the best third of my battalion, I'll do that too." Emphatically, he added, "I'll deliver the tanks to Ed myself, and I'll help him go through a dry run."

Greene was giving his old roommate a fighting chance, knowing full well that Rowny's success—and possibly his life—might depend on tank support.

Rowny's task force soon began its offensive. Morning dew lingered on the ground as artillery fired concentrations, beginning at 0545 hours, to cover the noise of tanks preparing to rev up and move to the launching point. The goal was to reach the Cinquale Canal where it met the sea, cross it undetected, and then turn inland ninety degrees and dig into position. The central forces, meanwhile, had the objective of capturing Bologna, a critical juncture inland that was the nerve center of northern Italy's transportation system.

General Wood, not knowing if he would see his protégée again, bid Rowny off with four simple words: "God be with you."

Rowny was ready to proceed, though concerns about mines in the area lingered in his mind. He planned his maneuvers for low tide, betting the Germans were unlikely to have laid mines in an area usually submerged. Two nights earlier his engineers had done their best to clear the beaches above the tide line. But Rowny knew some mines probably went undetected, and he wasn't a big fan of soldiers using bayonets to discover them as a last resort, a precarious proposition at best.

He had an alternative. "Let's form a single-file daisy chain," he suggested to his deputy, Captain William Holbrook. "Better one of us gets blown up advancing rather than a whole line."

"You got it," replied Holbrook. "How do you want it to work?"

"I'll take the lead to start, while you hold up the rear. I'll move about a hundred men up, then after say, fifteen minutes, we'll switch off. I'll go back for the next hundred while you take the lead of the first group."

There were close to seven hundred infantrymen moving up in total, two of the three battalions in the 366th Regiment, while tanks took up the rear. After the first two battalions advanced, the third was to follow.

The long, winding human chain began its march forward, with each man hooking either a hand or his belt to the soldier in front. It was a weary, snaillike process made slower by a beach that acted like quicksand under the weight of the heavily laden men. Sand engulfed legs nearly up to their knees. Men stumbled, needing to be helped up by a hand in front or in back of them.

Then came the whizzing of gunfire overhead, followed by mortar fire. Soldiers froze at this first encounter with the enemy. Some shielded themselves by digging in behind tanks, while others tried to crawl inside the tanks. Rowny and Holbrook encouraged troops onward, forming them into small groups; although there was no safety in numbers, there was comfort.

When it was Holbrook's turn to the lead the daisy chain, he was struck by enemy fire. The wound was not critical, so he bandaged it up as Rowny resumed the lead. The next time they alternated, Holbrook got hit yet again. Still, he insisted on persevering. This happened a third and a fourth time.

"Damn. Every time you take the lead," Rowny said, "you get hit. Why not just stick to the rear and I'll keep the lead, give you a break."

Holbrook shook his head. "No way I'm giving up. They're small wounds, and I'll be fine. Nothing I can't handle. As long as I can still move, I'm gonna keep going." He resumed the lead once again. This time the bullet hit its mark. Holbrook crumpled to the ground—he was dead.

Rowny agonized over the loss. *My God, why am I still standing, unscathed. Why him? Why not me? Why?*

But Rowny had more than a thousand men relying on his command, so while stunned at the hand of fate, he couldn't dwell on it. War did not wait on the wounded or dead. Ed Rowny had to keep on.

About six hours into the task force's ordeal, the troops reached the Cinquale Canal, twenty kilometers south of the Gothic Line. At that point, far in the distance—from enormous, sixteen-inch barrel naval battleship guns abandoned by the Italians near La Spezia—the enemy fired a shell nearly two thousand pounds in size. It landed like a bull's-eye directly in the middle of Rowny's command group.

As the smoke cleared from the thunderous blast, Rowny found himself looking at the bloodied face of one of his officers.

Oh Lord, there's no body attached to it.

Rowny looked away from the head's unbatting eyes. Then he glanced around, dazed. Dismembered arms and legs were strewn everywhere, some atop officers still alive but moaning. Rowny felt for his own extremities.

Are my arms still here? Maybe I'm in shock and I don't have them. What about my legs?

Disoriented and confused, he patted himself down. But he was all there.

Unharmed and collecting his wits, he quickly applied a tourniquet to a wounded officer and fumbled to provide the man a morphine syrette. He radioed for help, only to discover that his communication lines were severed. As stretcher bearers began hauling survivors to the rear, he was further unnerved to discover that seven out of ten in his command group had been killed. He was devastated—yet elated that he survived.

I shouldn't be thrilled, he scolded himself. *I'm not supposed to feel this way when my officers—my friends—are dead.*

Despite his colliding emotions, there was no going back. So Rowny took his next steps forward. His task force reached the mouth of the Cinquale Canal, and the tanks lurched forward, prepared to enter enemy territory.

Another deafening blast struck, and the world seemed to come to a standstill. The lead tank had hit a mine on the delta. A second tank tried to circumvent the disabled one by taking to the seaside, but its engine flooded in the water. A third tank hit a mine trying to bypass the disabled tank land-side. To deactivate more possible mines, Rowny reverted to using snakes—fire hoses laden with explosives that were detonated along the ground at intervals to clear paths. But the exploding snakes, in turn, created huge, impassible mounds of earth.

"Damn it!" Rowny griped. "Every obstacle we overcome creates a new one. What the hell do we do now?"

No one had a good answer.

Stressed by an offensive plummeting from bad to worse, Rowny radioed his former roommate. Larry Greene immediately set forth north, rumbling toward Cinquale. He arrived an hour or so later with a bulldozer to smooth out the mounds and a tank retriever to serve as a tow truck for armor. While the mounds were flattened, each disabled tank, one by one, was ferried to the rear so that Rowny's task force could progress forward. Before he advanced, he was the beneficiary of one more voluminous act of goodwill from Greene; the latter dipped further into his reserves to help his West Point friend, giving Rowny three new tanks to replace those lost.

It was many hours and bullets later that demoralized troops finally prepared to bunker down for the night. Rowny set up a command post in the lull before dark. Only half of his infantry troops had survived the debacle, and the division's main attack on high ground was not faring any better. Rowny learned about that attack when the division's signal commander, a '41 classmate, Major Richard Tindall, restored his communications. "Ace," as he was known, had garnered his nickname as one of the country's top-ranked tennis players, but Rowny felt he deserved the label more for what he could do with a little wire and ingenuity. Ace supervised the Signal Corps work to get Rowny's unit back in working order.

With his communications restored, Colonel William McCaffrey, at division headquarters, updated Rowny on the main attack. It had been launched half an hour after Rowny's. The division's leading troops penetrated the enemy's forward line but ran into heavy machine-gun fire from concrete pillboxes. The enemy then counterattacked and U.S. troops fell back to their original line of departure. The division launched a second attack mid-morning, after a fifteen-minute artillery preparation, but they were again met with heavy machine-gun fire from heavily fortified German positions. Yet again the enemy counterattacked and the division assault was thrown back.

McCaffrey relayed that General Almond planned to reinforce infantry regiments, move them to new jump-off positions, and attack again the next day. He asked Rowny whether his position was tenable or if he wanted to request that Task Force One be withdrawn.

"The decision to stay or withdraw isn't up to me," replied Rowny, "but up to General Almond."

Rowny explained the heavy casualties but said he still had a full company of twenty-four tanks, disabled ones having been replaced, and he thought he could hold his position, albeit not knowing the extent of enemy forces.

"I'll relay our conversation to General Almond," replied McCaffrey. "Stay in position unless you hear otherwise."

Darkness soon descended on the seemingly cursed task force as General Wood's words—suicide mission—rang in Rowny ears. As though the Germans read his mind, another enemy barrage ensued.

In the midst of continuing bombardments, nearing midnight, Rowny was astonished to see a Red Cross courier arriving to his command post. The courier handed Rowny a message.

"Dearest," it read. "You are the proud father of a handsome baby boy. What shall I name him? Love, Rita."

With word of a new life amid such tragic losses, the new father was overcome with emotion. He offered up a prayer of thanks and then reflected.

I probably won't make it through this battle, and I want my son to know where I took my last breath for freedom.

He quickly penned a reply and handed it to the courier. "Wonderful. Call him CINQUALE. I'll explain later. All my love, Ed."

Attacks and counterattacks persisted through the remainder of the night with the worst of enemy offensives coming from portable "flamethrowers." Soldiers had backpacks containing two cylinders, with the hydrogen in one igniting the fuel and compressed nitrogen in the second, spewing forth, through a soldier's handheld hose, long streams of fire. When the devastating flames hit American tanks, they spiked the temperatures within to about five hundred degrees. Men inside were baked to death.

At one point, Rowny wondered, *Will daylight ever come?*

Apparently not if the Germans had it their way. Around 2 a.m. Ed Rowny heard voices. German voices. Extraordinarily close voices. There was an exchange of fire burst outside, and Rowny heard grenades exploding against the cement building housing his headquarters.

What the hell . . .

Then all went quiet, and Rowny was left to wonder what had happened.

When rays of sunrise later peeked through the cracks in the bunker, he and other officers cautiously set forth to take an inventory of their surroundings. They opened the door to find two dead Germans in the doorway. They had been a sliver away from destroying the command post.

While the bunker withstood the night onslaughts, most of the task force's twenty-five tanks were destroyed in the maelstrom. Troop losses had also climbed higher. Rowny stood by Ace, surveying the hellish aftermath. As they debated their next moves—how to salvage what remained of their crippled operation—the Germans began one last finale. The next events were a blur as Ace crumpled to the ground inches away from Rowny, struck by an artillery fragment that pierced his chest near the heart.

Ace Tindall died the next day. To Rowny, the unfathomable randomness of war became even more immeasurable.

By now, his ranks were so seriously depleted that a new task force commander, heading a battalion, was sent in to relieve him. Rowny thought it made sense since in addition to his staff, the new task force commander, Colonel Harold Everman, was bringing with him two infantry companies. With the colonel's entire battalion plus the remnants of Rowny's task force north of the canal, Everman could establish a defensive position twice as large as the one Rowny was turning over. Rowny spent the rest of the day helping the colonel establish his new defense position north of the canal, then he returned to the division headquarters.

Overcome with weariness, he was about to collapse on a cot when the Red Cross courier reappeared. Rowny couldn't have been more surprised if an archangel stood before him. The courier handed him another message.

"Dearest, Your message garbled. Our son has been named Peter Edward. Love, Rita."

Peter Edward, pondered Rowny.

He repeated the name aloud. "Peter Edward." He thought of his prior message to Rita and reflected on it.

Now I've kind of taken to the ring of Cinq.

The nickname for his son would stick, forever a reminder of life and death at Cinquale.

The 92nd Division, meanwhile, failed to penetrate the Gothic Line. For the next six weeks, neither side conducted any major offensives.

10

THE NOSE OF THE BULGE

The Siegfried Line, Hitler's defensive line to protect Germany, was a barrier consisting of 390 miles of bunkers, tunnels, and tank traps, stretching from the Netherlands in the north down along the borders of Belgium, Luxembourg, and France until the line reached Switzerland in the south. Operation Market Garden was an Allied plan to circumvent the northern end of that line. "Market" was code name for the airborne side of the equation, which would be the largest airborne operation in history, while "Garden" represented the ground portion. The plan was for Allied Forces to jump into Holland over the course of several days in September and seize key bridges and canals leading to the Rhine. As airborne forces secured those sites in the vicinity of Arnhem, Allied ground forces would then rapidly advance. From Arnhem, Field Marshal Montgomery believed the Allies could sweep into western Germany, a stone's throw away, and by doing so win the war in Europe by Christmas.

Already, on September 4, the Allies had overtaken Antwerp, Belgium, to the south near the Dutch border. Operation Market Garden would cork up remaining resistance in that area, including clearing approaches to the deep-water port of Antwerp to secure it for Allied use. The capture of Antwerp had shocked Hitler and caused disorganization among German forces. Montgomery was keen to act rapidly and capitalize on the disorder, and in his view, each day meant that advantage slipping away as the enemy reorganized.

General Eisenhower was unconvinced as to the overall plan and at first opposed the operation. He did not believe a "single thrust," as Montgomery proposed, through Belgium and Holland toward the heartland of industrial Germany, the Ruhr Valley, was optimal. Instead, he preferred to continue a broad-front attack to keep the Germans guessing. This approach had been pursued following the Normandy breakout and included Montgomery's 21st British Army Group moving east to recapture Belgium and advance into the Ruhr Valley and General Omar Bradley's U.S. 12th Army Group heading south then east through the Ardennes Forest of Belgium into Luxembourg and on to the Saar River Valley, Germany's second most important industrial region. The 12th Army Group included the U.S. First, Third, Ninth, and Fifteenth Armies. General Patton's Third Army was advancing on the southern flank to eventually meet up with Bradley.

Adding to his qualms about Operation Market Garden, Eisenhower was also concerned about a shortage of supplies to support the Allies' rapid advance, and he was not keen on diverting supplies away from Generals Bradley and Patton.[1]

General "Jumpin' Jim" Gavin also expressed reservations. The commander of the 82nd Airborne disagreed with landing sites chosen by British Brigadier General Robert Urquhart because some of the insertions would place paratroopers six miles away from their objectives. The British Airborne Corps headquarters, on the other hand, generally viewed the considerable dispersion as an acceptable risk given the element of surprise and extreme depth of airborne penetration.[2]

Six miles, however, left time for the enemy to detect and reduce that Allied element of surprise. Gavin griped to his operations chief, Jack Norton, about Urquhart's choices: "My God, he can't mean it."

"He does," replied Norton. "But I wouldn't care to try it."[3]

Field Marshal Montgomery, with the support of Churchill, soon swayed President Roosevelt and Eisenhower to go forward. There were only seven days to plan and prepare for the operation, which would combine forces of the U.S. 82nd Airborne Division, the U.S. 101st Airborne Division, and the British 1st Airborne, collectively becoming the First Allied Airborne Army under the command of U.S. General Lewis Brereton.

Operation Market Garden was scheduled to launch on September 17, 1944. Norton would have to "try it" after all. Norton was going to be one of the few paratroopers to make all four major combat jumps of the war—the invasion into Sicily; the Oil Drum Drop two months later onto the beaches of Salerno, Italy, so-called for ignited drums serving as beacons for pilots; D-Day into Normandy; and now the Netherlands. The mission of the 82nd Airborne Division:

> Land by parachute and glider, commencing D-Day, south of Nijmegen; seize and hold the highway bridges across the Maas River at Grave and the Waal River at Nijmegen; seize, organize, and hold the high grounds between Nijmegen and Groesbeek; deny the roads in the Division area to the enemy; and dominate the area bounded North by a line running

from Beek West thru Hatert, thence Southwest to Eindschestraat, South by River Maas and the Mook-Riethorst highway, East by Cleve-Nijmegen highway and Forst Reichswald, and West by a line running North and South thru Eindschestraat.[4]

The skies were sunny and clear on the designated day with the baby-blue horizon giving no inkling of what was to come. By around midday planes carrying the U.S. 82nd and 101st Airborne Divisions and the British 1st Airborne Division began disrupting that heavenly serenity, buzzing across the sky almost wingtip to wingtip in near-perfect formations.

Like V's of ducks in a very tight pattern, thought Norton.

The plane he was on began descending gradually, lower and lower. It was a far cry from the rapid descent his plane had been on heading into Normandy. This time, Norton figured, he might actually be able to hold on to his equipment, though he knew full well that his landing still might be potluck. Maybe he'd land on a road, a hilltop, in the woods or water, perhaps in a village. Wherever it was, he hoped it was not with everybody shooting at him. And he hoped the division had more exacting drops than in Sicily where men plummeted into rock walls.

Soon, paratroopers began forming an aerial carpet over eastern Holland. The 101st was dropped southernmost, near the town of Eindhoven, which meant they would be the first to benefit from advancing British ground forces, 30 Corps, coming up from the south. The British 1st Airborne jumped to the north in an attempt to secure the bridge over the Rhine by Arnhem; since they would have to hold their position the longest before 30 Corps could reach them, they were allocated the most men on the initial drop. The 82nd Airborne was relegated to the no-man's-land in between; the unit had fewer men than the northern faction and, unlike units dropped to the south, would not quickly benefit from advancing ground forces. Artillery was to help tide the 82nd over—that and perhaps a degree of insanity. Paratroopers were, after all, no ordinary breed.

Norton wondered, *What kind of men want to go forth to war and jump out of airplanes?*

Not sane ones, perhaps. There were some who questioned why, given a perfectly good airplane, a person would want to jump out of it? But Jack Norton felt in his element when hitting that rush of air.

Norton landed forty miles behind enemy lines without incident. There was limited flak, and 1,150 U.S. planes along with 106 gliders penetrated and made it through enemy territory, while 331 British planes and 319 gliders succeeded. In fact, all airborne division landings were exceptional in terms of precision, and within one hour and twenty minutes, twenty thousand American and British troops were far behind enemy lines.[5]

Among those troops, in the same 82nd Division as Jack Norton, were his '41 classmates Butch Kaiser, a battalion commander; Jock Adams and Bob Rosen, both company commanders; and Francis "Joe" Myers. Also jumping in was '41er John C. H. Lee Jr., son of General John C. H. Lee—the latter dubbed by some as "Jesus Christ Himself" due to his initials; General Lee was second in command to General Eisenhower, the Supreme Allied Commander, Europe.

The 82nd Division All-Americans were to seize a seven-section bridge, described as bigger than the Brooklyn Bridge, along with another immense bridge span at Nijmegen, in addition to four canal bridges. The belief was that as soon as division forces grabbed those bridges and area roads, British forces would steam up the road in support of them in the two to three days following.

But this was war. Not much ever went according to plan in war, though the mission started out well enough.

Within two hours of landing, the 82nd Division secured Groesbeek and rapidly occupied its defense position in and around the town, including seizing critical high ground. With only so many troops at hand, General Gavin deemed it a priority to seize that high ground and two bridges that would ensure a smooth link up with the ground column. Then the 82nd could focus on Nijmegen. If the 82nd took only the bridges, such as that at Nijmegen, high ground would be difficult to hold; if it only took high ground and some bridge objectives, the 30 Corps ground column—trying to link up with the 1st Airborne at Arnhem—would be unable to access other key bridges necessary for an advance. He was not alone in his thinking.

Deputy commander of the First Allied Airborne Army, British General Frederick Browning, personally gave an order to Gavin that, although every effort should be exerted to capture the Nijmegen Bridge as soon as possible, the high ground ridge was essential to gain and hold for "painfully obvious reasons." If that ground was lost to the enemy, Allied ground units would be immediately outflanked.[6]

But a speedy capture of the Nijmegen highway bridge was not in the cards. The 82nd was short on infantry in relation to its widely dispersed objectives.

Still, division troops attacked the city in attempts to open a path for oncoming British armored units. The All-Americans, Jock Adams and Bob Rosen among them, began making relentless attacks against the enemy in Nijmegen, but they came under furious enemy fire and were unsuccessful.

U.S. forces kept at it into the next day and the following one, until it came down to fierce house-to-house fighting as troops tried to eradicate the Germans from the streets, rooftops, and alleys of the city. They proved to be a slippery enemy with combatants popping out like armed jack-in-the-boxes at every turn. The 82nd Division forces were increasingly surrounded.

On the fourth day came a glimmer of hope for the U.S. forces as a detachment of British tanks appeared through the haze of smoke and debris. Bob Rosen, on foot, started guiding the tanks into positions. He zigzagged and sprinted across the streets of Nijmegen, from one tank to the next, bending low and dashing quickly to avoid being hit. A constant spray of bullets whizzed overhead as he nimbly darted and ducked, making runs for it. But it was too many runs amid too many enemy snipers. Rosen was hit. Fellow soldiers urged that he be evacuated. He refused. With blood seeping down his uniform, he kept directing British tanks into strategic positions even as his breaths came shorter. Then Captain Robert H. Rosen took his last gasp and collapsed. He joined the Long Gray Line, making the ultimate sacrifice. He followed more than two dozen officers from his West Point class who had already given their lives in the war.

Wrote General Gavin to Rosen's wife, Marjorie: "During his last action he led a portion of his Company in a charge into enemy positions. He paused in the middle of a bullet-swept street to direct his men and exposed himself to continuous sniper fire as he moved back and forth through the lines with snipers less than seventy-five yards away." Rosen's, actions, added Gavin, "drove the enemy back and made it possible for the subsequent attack to succeed."[7]

On the same day that Rosen was killed, the 82nd Airborne took the bridge at Nijmegen—on September 20. It proved not soon enough.

Despite some successes, Operation Market Garden proved a debacle. Initial elements of surprise rapidly subsided in the wake of the slow advance of Allied ground troops. In the days to follow the Allies failed miserably to achieve or retain their objectives, and losses were heavy—more than seventeen thousand casualties among air and ground forces. Arnhem was never reached. The Allies grasped for it, like an outreached hand grasping for a drowning swimmer, only to have the swimmer, so close, slip away. Arnhem was, as General Browning projected, "a bridge too far."

The supposed shortcut to the Rhine instead became like the longest day. Dreams of Christmas homecomings faded away. Mothers, wives, and girlfriends would instead have to await those much-delayed letters from the front, hoping beyond hope that it was not *the* dreaded letter from the War Department.

Allied Forces pressed on toward Germany. The long way. The hard way. The rumble of Patton's tank drive continued to roll across the western front toward the Rhine, toward the heart of Hitler's empire.

Norton and his troops, in the meantime, kept on with their daily combat struggles in Holland. They were in, with no easy way out. They persevered over the days—and the weeks—till one month drew into two. The days grew shorter and colder. Jack Norton had little more to wear than the summer garb he'd jumped in with. No one had imagined the need for snow-packs back on that bright blue September day. They had imagined victory.

★ ★ ★

South of Norton's location, the Allies persevered in their attempts to penetrate the Siegfried Line. A technology breakthrough was the extra kick intended to make the difference. Cloaked in secrecy, it was the radio-proximity fuse, code-named "Peanuts." Herb Stern was among gunnery officers directed to a remote location, a broad treeless expanse outside of Cologne, to witness its demonstration in the late fall of 1944.

Originally intended for anti-aircraft use, the proximity fuse had been adapted for field artillery. Also called the variable time (VT) fuse, it relied on miniaturized radio electronics in the nose of a shell. The electronics were activated when the shell was fired, sending out sensitive beams that prompted the shell to detonate when a target entered its zone, like a two-way radio sending and receiving messages. In contrast to the older-style mechanical time fuse, which often resulted in burst irregularities, the explosion from this new fuse was intended to hurtle thousands of shell fragments downward in a meteoric shower, making artillery significantly more potent than when a shell exploded into the ground.

Stern anxiously waited Peanuts's demonstration as a battery of guns prepared to demonstrate the new technology. The deafening blasts went off, then the bursts. Stern's eyes tried to track the shells hurtling skyward. Watching in awe, he witnessed explosions appearing like a battlefield of asteroids. Shrapnel hurled in every direction.

Stern was dumbstruck, glad that he was not in the path of Peanuts's fury. "I just can't believe it," he muttered to fellow officers. "Astounding."

Then to himself, he added, *This will be the turning point in the war*.

The fireworks display was like nirvana for the artilleryman, sentiments echoed among the spectators, provoking endless speculation of the fuse's possibilities. It was made clear to officers, however, that quantities were limited, and they would have to temper their enthusiasm till manufacturers could rev up production; the calm before the hoped-for storm.

A storm soon hit but it was of a much different nature—a tempest instigated by the Nazis. In mid-December the enemy began a counteroffensive that put a large geographic dent in the Allied line of incursion, a "bulge" as the press called it because the enemy's encroachment area slightly resembled a U-shape. The bulge was an attempt to split the Allies in two in the Ardennes region of Belgium, along its border with Germany. The Ardennes, a low-lying mountain range accentuated by rolling hills and dense forests, had been called the "ghost front" up until then due to its lack of combat activity. Not anymore. The Battle of the Bulge, the largest battle of World War II, subsequently raged in its cold, snowy forests.

Jack Norton had barely fought his way out of Holland when, still in summer duds and light boots, he was sent to the front lines of the bulge. Other officers from his West Point class descended on the Ardennes as well— Charlie Fletcher, Jack Murray, and Joe Reed among them.

Herb Stern was up north along the Siegfried Line when his 84th Division was ordered south to the Ardennes. It was not logistically simple to move twenty-five thousand men and equipment but move they did, nearly overnight. They were relocating to the nose of the bulge by the town of Marche, which was a major German objective. The division began heading south on December 18. Despite some rerouting to avoid enemy roadblocks, Stern's unit established positions around Marche late the following afternoon. The move, however, caused utter chaos, and Stern was convinced that he had never seen so much confusion in his life. No one had any idea where other 84th units were, so no one knew where to lay lines of communications, whether coming or going.

Still, the unit to which Stern belonged took its preordained position. But once there, Stern couldn't shake an uneasy feeling over the lack of contact with units supposedly flanking him. Adding to his woes was that fact that his unit commander, Lieutenant Colonel Harry Hubbard, had seemingly vanished. Grappling for more direction, Herb Stern decided to take a walk to see if he might come across other troops, anyone, anything that could clue him in. About a quarter mile down the road, an agitated Belgian woman passed him striding at a brisk pace, looking spooked like she'd seen the devil. Her hands waved frantically in the air, warning, *"Les Boches! Les Boches!"* a derogatory term for Germans. The enemy was not far off, Stern knew, and his worries grew.

Our battalion position is completely unprotected. I've got to get behind protection.

Weighing on his mind was also the tragic Malmédy massacre, named after a Belgian town where the SS had captured more than a hundred U.S.

soldiers on December 17. Rather than hold the troops as POWs, the Nazis had shot the Americans execution-style in a field. Soldiers that appeared to cling to life were executed at close range or clubbed until their last gasp expired. A few faked death and survived. The rest were left for the icy tentacles of winter to claim as frozen corpses.

Word of the incident, just a couple of days earlier, spread like wildfire among the 84th. Asked Stern's troops, "Is that what we have to look forward to if we're captured?"

Thinking of those German claws, Stern decided to hell with his dictated position. He was supposed to be behind infantry, in support of them, but there were no indications whatsoever of any U.S. infantry ahead of him. Stern ordered his artillery unit to pick up and relocate to what he hoped was a safer haven. The unit moved to the northeast till they came across infantry positions that were forming the shoulder of the bulge.

Hours later, Stern's troops were hunkering down in bunkers for the night, tucked into their bedrolls to await the fate of daylight. It was then that they received word from another unit that a lookout spotted a German column rolling through the artillery unit's previous setting.

An eerie chill went through Stern. *If we were still there, our whole battalion would be dead.*

In the Ardennes, he quickly discovered, mere meters dictated destinies.

In the days that followed, Stern set up headquarters in a grand chateau whose count had fled to Brussels. The comely countess and her teenage daughter remained on, residing in the chateau's top floor while Stern and his men took to the more secure basement.

She's got more guts than the count, figured Stern. *Hell, she's got more guts than us.*

The stoned-in basement soon grew to be like an icebox, as weather conditions rapidly deteriorated. It was among the worst of winters, descending like a freezing blanket over the Ardennes. Wretched cold was accompanied by howling winds that shook shivering soldiers to the core. Icy roads sent jeeps and half-tracks sliding into ditches, and the fury of blizzards began impeding tank movement far more than the enemy. When it was not snowing, the fog was often so dense that it was impossible to determine if the enemy lie ahead or behind.

Where is the front? At times, Herb Stern couldn't see his hands in front of his face.

He also did not see much of his commanding officer, not because of the fog but because Colonel Hubbard kept abdicating his headquarters for that of the infantry regiment. Doctrine stated that an artillery commander needed to establish command liaison with the infantry counterpart that he supported; Hubbard took that concept to a whole new level. Stern, as a result, was increasingly in charge of the artillery unit.

On one such occasion, it was early in the morning, and the gray veil outside was as thick as ever when Hubbard called to inquire about the unit registering. Registering was an essential task when a new position was established and involved firing artillery to collect data for the purpose of making adjustments to ensure that subsequent volleys were accurate. The task involved firing a round at a specific target that could be identified on a map, with forward observers then confirming whether those rounds accurately hit. If the rounds missed, any errant data in mapping or equipment was corrected. Exposing chart, weapon, ammunition, or weather errors by registering determined whether artillery needed to be adjusted in range and bearing, say, to the left or right.

"Have you registered yet?" Colonel Hubbard asked Stern.

"No, none of our observers can identify a base point because of the weather."

Hubbard called back five minutes later and repeated the question. He got a similar answer.

Five or ten minutes later, Hubbard pestered again.

Stern was becoming incensed. *It's not like he can't see the damn pea soup outside.*

When Hubbard rang again, Herb Stern had just about had it."No, we have *not* registered," a vexed Stern retorted. "Our observers still cannot see anything. I tell you what, I am going to go register myself!"

"Don't you dare leave the CP," warned Hubbard.

Stern hung up the phone and said, "To hell with orders." He calmly told his driver, "Let's go," and walked out of the command post.

He was soon on high ground and through the gray clouds of mist, could barely make out a crossroads in the valley below. It coincided with what he saw on his map, which had north-south and east-west grid lines and was drawn on the typical one/twenty-five-thousand scale, that is, depending on the circumstances, one inch might represent twenty-five thousand inches, one foot represent twenty-five thousand feet, and so forth. Stern radioed the grid data of the crossroads to an assistant, ordering artillery fire. A few minutes later Stern was rattled, feeling the earth shake behind him from a shell exploding to the rear.

What the hell! That round is supposed to be down in the valley. He quickly realized an omission in his transmission. *I forgot to say that I was on a high elevation.*

"Convert to high-angle fire," he radioed.

That added information—taking into account the contour of the land so that shells could soar above the hills—could dictate the difference between life and death. The firing data was adjusted, the artillery reaimed. Bull's-eye. The battalion had an accurate point of reference for its computations.

That night, as darkness swung over the Ardennes, Stern's forward observer spotted black figures moving in the valley. It was a German armored column—hordes of half-tracks filled with troops, approaching the exact crossroads that had been registered earlier that day. Roused with excitement, the observer immediately called in artillery fire with the exacting data from the day's registration. Almost instantaneously, Stern relayed the same to division artillery headquarters, requesting emphatically, "All available guns!"

There were eleven other battalions in addition to Stern's within about a twelve-mile radius. All dozen battalions aimed their guns—collectively 144 strong—at the enemy column. They let go, raining on the Nazi parade, firing nearly every type of cannon at U.S. disposal. The 84th Division stopped the Germans cold, blunting a major enemy offensive to take Marche.

It was but a small respite for the Allies.

Soon, it was Christmas Eve. Stern didn't observe the holiday, but he couldn't help but inhale the mood of his men who did. There was a palpable melancholy. In the middle of war, they were far from loved ones, an ocean apart from new wives and in some cases, expectant ones. They mulled over family memories and whether they'd live to see the next generation.

Stern peered out the window at the blanket on the earth. He wondered, *What's so special about a white Christmas anyway?* Irving Berlin's melody had little place in Belgium, where men hoped beyond hope to see any of Mother Nature's colors besides white.

A knock on the cellar door interrupted his train of thought. It was the countess, carrying a steaming bowl of mulled wine. Looking angelic, smiling broadly, she held the bowl up to Herb Stern. He inhaled the heavenly, warm aromas of red wine, cinnamon, and cloves.

"Happy birthday," the countess said to the astounded officer.

How did she know?

She handed the mulled wine to Stern, and as he savored a glorious sip, she told him, "You must come with me. I have something upstairs for you."

Herb Stern followed the countess, half expecting a prank—perhaps fellow officers jumping out from behind dark stairwells. He ascended the stairs while carefully balancing his wine, lest he spill a single drop of the nectar. The countess led him, of all places, to a gilded bathroom on the top floor of the chateau. There, a steaming hot tub beckoned Herb Stern like a siren's song. Stern could not remember the last time he'd had a bath or when he'd even come across working plumbing in this war. Like so many soldiers, he'd grown accustomed to a "whore's bath" poured from steel helmets.

He soon sank into the tub, the rippling warmth encircling him, his bowl of mulled wine beside him. Herb Stern was sure that this birthday, his twenty-sixth, was the most glorious he'd ever had. It was but a brief respite, during which Stern was oblivious to the winds of war howling outside.

He was also oblivious to the message transmitted from the chief of staff of the German 19th Army to the G-3 of the Army group, the former asking, "Is it psychologically appropriate to continue to fight into the evening of 24 December, Christmas Eve?"

Came the G-3 answer: "The Reichsführer," referring to Heinrich Himmler, the highest-ranking SS officer, "believes this moment to be of no particular importance."[8]

Christmas came and went without Stern's unit encountering the 19th Army, the Reichsführer, or any enemy forces for that matter. But he was soon rubbing his hands in anticipation of the next rendezvous with the devil, the reason being that proximity fuses, at long last, were rolling off Allied assembly lines. When Stern's unit finally got its share, it was as though the officers had found a pot of gold at the end of the rainbow.

Sure the fuse had its hiccups, like when Stern and his artillerymen shot it off from positions behind trees and the shells detonated far too early.

"Hell, we're blowing up more trees than soldiers," quipped Stern.

The fuse, it seemed, detected foliage as the enemy and needed fine-tuning so that it would not detonate so early in its trajectory path. Stern and his officers were relentless, searching for the answer key and altering their positions, but what needed altering was the fuse setback. While Stern and his colleagues kept experimenting, word got back to armory manufacturers, and the fuse models began improving at a rapid rate; hard-pressed to win the war, they quickly churned out Allied enhancements to designs. Whereas initial rounds burst over trees, later models had setbacks adjusted so that they detonated at the desired twenty yards above ground.

It was with that setback modification that Herb Stern felt like the Allies hit pay dirt. *This really is going to change the face of the war*, Herb Stern swore. *I'll place my bets on it.*

11

CONTACT AT HOUFFALIZE

As Herb Stern kept at his artillery meteor showers, Major Charlie Fletcher grappled with chaos farther east as S-2 intelligence officer of the 174th Field Artillery Group, a heavy artillery unit within the VIII Corps of the U.S. First Army. Fletcher was gathering intelligence on the enemy, including where they were and what they were doing, as well as his unit's own area of operations. He was also identifying artillery targets so his unit could make tactical decisions on the battlefield. At one point, caught in an endless bottleneck of jeeps, he lost patience with vehicles maneuvering to get ahead of him.

"Is your job more important than mine!" he yelled to an officer. He didn't notice the man's rank and didn't care; they were all fighting the same war.

Soon after, he witnessed the opposite problem, a caravan of men all headed in one direction—away from the sound of guns. Fletcher shook his head.

Unbelievable. They're tucking their tails between their legs and running. How the heck are we supposed to win a war this way?

Fletcher swore that some day, he would train men to do differently. But for the time being, he struck out to the front along Belgium's northern border with Germany. There, the Allied front line protruded east, on a map resembling a crescent moon that stretched for about twenty miles. South of that span, the enemy had pushed into American lines and was trying to broaden its indentation. General Bradley, on the other hand, wanted to "straighten out" his wall and move its edges two hundred yards forward.

A U.S. armored unit along with two regiments of the 106th Infantry sparsely protected the American wall. Fletcher's unit, the 174th Field Artillery Group, supported the southernmost of those 106th regiments, while the 28th Infantry protected his artillery unit's right flank. Fletcher was unimpressed, however, with these positions assigned by Bradley. Infantry had few places to retreat if attacked, since they were backed up against a wall of woods in the Ardennes.

We've got indefensible positions, thought Fletcher as he scoured situation maps. *Bradley's so interested in holding on to a few acres, but all he's put there are scattered outposts. And they're motley crews, nothing more than recon-naissance and cannon companies with no real infantry capability. How are they supposed to engage in any serious combat?*

Fletcher concluded that American troops were merely occupying ground, little more. Despite this abysmal assessment, he had orders to push east and in mid-December was prowling in that direction in his command jeep south of Saint Vith with his driver, Sergeant Labadie. They had a ten-minute head start on artillery vehicles, which was Fletcher's usual routine, advancing first so he could alert the column behind him of any obstacles in its path.

The weather was cold, the skies cloudy and threatening as they traveled along the tortuously narrow, muddy roads surrounded by rocky and for-ested terrain. They rolled through one small blink-and-you-miss-it town. Exiting out its other side, Fletcher noticed a scene of domesticity that hinted little of the battles waging about. A woman had just finished hanging clothes out to dry, and the freshly laundered whites flapped in the breeze like flags of surrender.

But surrender was hardly on Fletcher's mind, as his attention was drawn to a light tank that stood idle near the clothesline, alongside a wooded area.

7th Armored Division. But what is it doing here?

He abruptly ordered Labadie to stop and darted over to the tank. "What's going on?" he shouted up to the man in the turret.

"We just . . . we just got ambushed by infantry," sputtered the sergeant, appearing visibly shaken. "My lieutenant commander was riding with his head and shoulders out the turret, and they shot and killed him." He pointed, "Just east of here; I'm heading back west."

"I've got an artillery column right behind me," said Fletcher. "Can you buy us some time to get through? If you position the tank to protect our left flank, then the Germans won't attack if they come through the woods here."

The sergeant barely finished saying yes when Fletcher spotted enemy foot soldiers crossing a road due east. They were heading toward the wooded yard with the clothesline, and only a hundred yards separated them from Fletcher and the tank sergeant.

"Turn around and point the tank toward the infantry!" yelled Fletcher. "Stop them from crossing the field!"

The sergeant's survival instincts kicked in as he swirled the turret around and began firing at the approaching infantry. The enemy troops scrambled to become shadows among the trees. But Fletcher didn't know how many more were behind that first wave. Next thing he knew, a shell pierced the tree trunk right beside him, a near hit so close it could have been an arrow slicing an apple on top of his head. Fletcher could even see the 30-caliber shell. But the 7th Armored light-tank barrage was working its wonders. The enemy troops backed off in retreat, leaving the tidy line of hanging clothes riddled with holes—domesticity turned collateral damage.

With the gunfire subsided, Fletcher and the tank sergeant hollered back and forth, debating their next moves while Fletcher's eyes scanned the horizon for more shadows. He heard the rumbling before he saw it—a column of German tanks, heading directly toward them, approaching from the south.

"Turn south!" he yelled to the sergeant. "Tank column!"

This could be the end, thought Fletcher.

But in a matter of minutes, the light tank's gunfire had disabled the lead enemy tank, causing the procession behind it to temporarily halt in its tracks.

Fletcher shouted up to the sergeant, "Let's get out of here! That's as much of a delay as we're gonna get."

Without waiting for an answer, Fletcher dashed back down the road to Labadie, who was nervously waiting in the jeep. Fletcher jumped in and Labadie hit the gas, heading in a northwesterly direction. The light tank retreated as well, in the same general direction.

As they tore down the road, Fletcher told Labadie, "That's the closest I've ever been to getting killed. A shell missed me by inches—so close I could see the cartridge."

"I'm sure the Germans will get another crack at you."

"Of that, I have no doubt. But at least we bought some minutes, and it probably saved a lot of guys. The Germans must have broken through the 28th. We just don't have the right defenses. This is crazy."

Fifteen minutes or so later, Fletcher's command jeep passed over the crest of a high hill. His unit's artillery column was to the rear in the distance, zigzagging up the same incline. Fletcher scanned the clusters of trees on the horizon, searching for enemy movement behind the wooded smokescreens. Then he spotted it, another German tank unit drawing toward him like a magnet drawn to its match.

Fletcher blanched. He grabbed his radio and called back to the group commander. "German tank unit approaching from the south. Turn around and get back down the hill! I will try to buy time."

The artillery battalion could take on the tanks, but they needed at least ten minutes, maybe more, to position their 155mm howitzers. And the German tank column was too close—and closing in. There was no time.

The devil's trying to overrun us, thought Fletcher. *Totally broken through the 28th, coming at us like water through a faucet.*

He glanced behind the jeep, back down the hill to his unit. There was chaos as artillery vehicles took to the sides of the winding road, trying to turn around their enormous guns in an area that left little room for maneuvering.

We've got no chance, Fletcher worried, his eyes darting around for a way out.

Then he detected an anti-aircraft gun—an American one—a few dozen yards away, beyond a small field and up an embankment.

"See that sunken road," Fletcher said to Labadie, pointing to their rear. "You get there! I'm going for the gun."

Charlie Fletcher bolted out the jeep and sprinted across the open field. Miraculously he was not fired on. He ran up the six-foot embankment to the anti-aircraft gun, which was well concealed from the enemy's southern perspective, tucked into a ditch behind some reeds. It was a powerful gun, capable of firing hundreds of rounds of 1½-inch shells a minute and self-propelled atop a light tank. But the voice inside Fletcher was wary of its shortcomings.

Great for hitting a plane. Not a tank.

The German tanks were closing the gap; they were a mere hundred yards away. Not bothering to ask for opinions, Charlie Fletcher started doling out orders to the gun crew. "Aim at the lead tank," he told them, "the hot zone; we're going for the hot zone. Let's heat 'em up."

The crew obliged. A round of shells. Then more. And still more. Fletcher directed the fire, continually in the same spot—on the left side of the lead tank. The Germans were firing back, but with the American position shrouded in the reeds, they kept overshooting the mark.

Then Fletcher saw it, on the left side of the tank, the red glow indicating that the energy transfer from the incessant anti-aircraft rounds had heated the tank's interior.

"Just what I wanted," he told the gun crew. "Right next to the gunners. They can't last long now. They've got to be baking."

Within seconds, the armored crew, about to get fried, scrambled out of the tank. With the lead tank immobilized, the remainder of the column sat frozen.

Enemy downtime, Fletcher knew, was limited. He congratulated the anti-aircraft crew and then ran back across the field to Labadie. As the two sped off, there was a glint in Charlie Fletcher's eyes.

I'm probably the only person in the world to defeat a German panzer with a 40mm gun.

U.S. forces needed every stroke of good fortune they could get. For his part, Charlie Fletcher was awarded a Silver Star for valor in action against the enemy, the third-highest combat award after the Medal of Honor and the Distinguished Service Cross. "For immobilizing one tank and holding others at bay while highly outnumbered forces could retreat," the citation read.

The German's aim of expanding the dent in their bulge would have to wait another day.

★ ★ ★

The long winter dragged on. For the Allies, however, the tide was not turning fast enough. So there was soon to be a concerted surge by the U.S. First and Third Armies toward the key town of Houffalize, a central point in the enemy's bulge, ten miles north of Bastogne. The First Army was to sweep down from the northern edge of the bulge near Marche, while the Third Army would head up from Bastogne in the south. Major Mike Greene was with the latter as executive officer of the 41st Cavalry Reconnaissance Squadron of the 11th Armored Division.

Greene was not far from Bastogne late on the afternoon of January 15 when a command jeep pulled up to his unit's headquarters carrying Brigadier General Willard A. Holbrook Jr. Daylight was fast fading as the general informed Greene that Patton wanted to immediately "close" the bulge—beginning that very night. It would be achieved by a contingency from the Third Army heading north to Houffalize in haste to make contact with the First Army as it headed south to reach the same. Mike Greene, the runt half of the Greene brothers, would lead the mission.

Greene pored over maps to determine what the mission entailed: Houffalize was ten miles behind enemy lines and on dominant high ground. Other than entering it from a main highway—a sure death sentence—the only routes of approach to maintain a level of surprise were through snow-covered trails in the woods. But dusk was approaching. The odds were stacked against him between the fading light, the weather, the geography, and the timeline. But Mike Greene couldn't focus on why the mission would *not* work, but instead on how it could, and every minute counted.

He hastily organized a task force that would include his reconnaissance cavalry unit, added to which would be assault-gun troops, a light-tank company and reconnaissance platoons that would rendezvous with him in Rastadt to the northeast. Within the hour Greene's cavalry unit was off. On the departure route, however, he intercepted an incoming jeep carrying

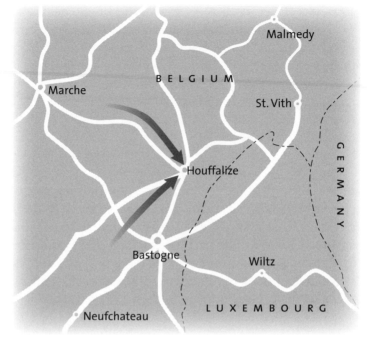

First Army advances from Marche; Third Army advances north from Bastogne.
Based on circa 1949 rendering by Major Michael J. L. Greene.

an injured officer who warned of minefields in the direction the task force was heading.

Great, thought Greene. *Low light, snow, and mines. But there's no choice, no other way to go.*

His unit rumbled forward with their senses extra-honed, like mental sonar, on the lookout for the minefield. They soon spotted mines just under the snow to the right and left of their intended path. Amid the tripwires, they deciphered tire tracks indicating vehicles had somehow made it through; Greene's task force had a chance. The first of the jeeps inched forward along the trodden path as their commander anxiously watched. The jeep made it. Another vehicle advanced, then another, till six had successfully traversed the field. Greene was elated and jumped on the battery box of his half-track, motioning his driver forward with the wave of an arm.

The driver stepped on the gas. There was an enormous blinding explosion. Mike Greene's world went black.

He quickly came to, wondering, *Where am I?* He was alive—but badly shaken. Glancing around, it dawned on him that he was lying in the snow, about ten feet from his half-track, and the vehicle looked seriously damaged. It all came back, the minefield, the explosion. He moved his joints and limbs. Nothing seemed broken. He saw that his driver had survived as well. Greene rose to his feet.

Just then, a vehicle from another American unit spotted the task force column and its disabled half-track. The vehicle pulled up and the soldier within explained that there was a route around the mines. He pointed in the right direction.

Rerouted, minus one half-track, Greene's task force successfully proceeded on to Rastadt. The town was veiled in complete darkness as the forces entered, but for the glow of buildings burning from fighting mere hours earlier. The enemy, evidently, lurked close by. The blazes proved an odd blessing since the flickering flames provided the only illumination Greene had as he gathered elements of his task force together to strategize. Their best intelligence, gleaned from actions earlier that day, was that the Germans had withdrawn in the direction of Houffalize, or perhaps slightly west. Greene took in the information with skepticism.

Who knows where the enemy troops really are, or their strength? Combat elements tend to have colored imaginations.

Soldiers could weave grand tales, he knew. Battles became bigger, troop sizes more formidable, enemy weapons grew alive. Yet Greene didn't doubt the Germans were near.

Greene, proceeding on foot, led the task force out of Rastadt, trying to decipher trail maps as they tread through dense forests. The maps were only marginally helpful since they didn't account for Mother Nature's wrath —or the enemy's. He had to continually alter the group's planned course to account for unexpected obstacles. The woods in one area had been so heavily bombed that large craters blocked the way, while in an area of open terrain, the snow was so thick that it masked trails altogether. The night and weather became the group's main foes.

As the weary miles went on, Greene grew even more frustrated with the maps.

They don't match the visuals in front of us. Are there illusions because of the drifting snow, or is it the dark, or do we all have jittery nerves? Maybe, thought Greene, *it's all of that.*

His troops knew that the enemy might appear at any moment and from any possible direction, and their nervous tension hung as thick as the woods. Greene began to wonder if encountering the real enemy might be more bearable. The darkness, however, remained hauntingly silent of gunfire.

By 3 a.m. the column was on the outskirts of Houffalize, just two miles from the city. Greene was astounded that the Germans missed a prime opportunity to thwart the Allies—a bridge remained in place over the Rau de Suhet River. The smirk on his face faded to a frown as he saw what lay opposite—a steep slope of about forty degrees, covered in pure ice. No wonder. The Germans didn't figure Americans to be experts at ice climbing.

The task force tried to forge ahead, rushing vehicles up the frozen incline. One after another, each skidded backward. Troops fitted extra treads to the tanks, harnessed vehicles to them, and resorted to pulling them up one by one, tow truck style. It was a slow and arduous process up the hundred-yard hill in the blackness, a battle against the ice, the night, and fatigue. Despite the frigid air prickling at their faces, men started falling asleep from sheer exhaustion. By 5:30 a.m., however, most of the column had reached the top of the ridge, and the task force was able to proceed. Hints of the steely morning light were appearing as the task force closed in on its objective, Houffalize—once a resort town, now the focal point of the Allied effort to crush the German offensive.

As the task force advanced, suddenly the lead armored car was swallowed into the earth, sucked into a huge sinkhole. In fact, it was a well-concealed tank trap. Greene had no doubt it was one of many such booby traps, so again he set out on foot, along with his lieutenant, Eugene Ellenson, to investigate the surroundings. The pair walked about two hundred yards to a sign indicating Houffalize's city limits. Given their treacherous journey, the two congratulated each other on having gotten that far, then scrutinizing the scenery, began sizing up possible routes into town. With some ideas in mind, they turned back toward their column.

As they did so, they noticed a head in a foxhole up a hill, probably a U.S. patrol. Ellenson suggested making contact, and the two started up the hill. It proved to be yet one more German jack-in-the-box as a head popped up with a machine gun trained on them, shouting, "Hands up!"

In desperation, Greene yelled down to colleagues for fire; all he had on him was a pistol while Ellenson carried only a flashlight.

Immediately, American forces responded with a barrage of anti-aircraft fire. The gunfire diverted the jack-in-the-box's attention long enough for Greene to jump behind a log and Ellenson to slide down the hill. The enemy in the foxhole jumped out of his safe haven and fled in retreat. The commotion, however, alerted other enemy forces to the Allied presence. Small arms, anti-tank, and mortar fire began to hail down on the task force in a maelstrom.

Undeterred, Greene set troops into combat position. He ordered observers to the high ground to report on enemy movement; assault gun platoons, which were highly mobile with short cannons, were placed into firing positions; light tanks were prepared to maneuver. But as they stood armed and readied, not only did the small-arms fire of the Germans steadily increase but also heavy mortar fire began to fall on the assault-gun platoon, seriously wounding the platoon leader and several others. Greene ordered the gunners to retreat.

At the same time artillery fire began to pummel the high-ground observers. Greene commanded them out of the direct-impact area but ordered them to remain in a position where they could observe to the north, south, and east.

It was just before 9 a.m. when Ellenson reported that his platoon could see troop movement on the opposite side of the river, to the north. Greene turned his head and saw streams of green fatigues about 1,500 yards away.

They've got to be the First Army! His heart pounded.

He held his men back from barreling out to establish contact. There'd been enough surprises already, and there was a chance the troops were retreating Germans. Greene dispatched a patrol to gauge the situation, warning to "proceed with caution." He also directed tanks to traverse the high ground to the south of Houffalize, telling them to enter the town and conduct a "lightening harassing raid."

The tanks advanced, proceeding on a high elevation, which reduced the enemy to limited fields of fire. It allowed U.S. forces to burst into Houffalize with machine guns roaring, igniting parts of the town ablaze.

As that action was going down, Greene stood like a sentry, watching, waiting, wondering about the increasing procession of troops trudging though the snow on the far side of the river.

Then it was all a fast blur of events. His patrol returned minutes prior to 10 a.m. Yes, they reported to Major Greene, it was the U.S. First Army, the 41st Armored Infantry, 2nd Armored Division. And yes, the patrol had made contact.

It didn't take long before a victorious Mike Greene, with the Third Army, was shaking hands with the First Army commander in charge. The two United States Armies began joining forces along the river. They closed the bulge in a tour de force for the Allies.

The impact of the achievement hit Mike Greene, reverberating deep within. It was a humbling moment. The worst battle of the war to date, with more than eighty thousand American lives lost, was drawing to a close, and the chance to invade the German homeland and defeat the Nazi empire was drawing near. Hopes of a Christmas homecoming could now bloom into one in spring, when America's boys might finally be brought home.

Patton, in his notes on the Bastogne Operation, marked the stupendous milestone in a much more perfunctory manner: "16 January 1945—At 0905, 41st Cavalry of the 11th Armored Division made contact with the 41st Infantry of the 2nd Armored Division in Houffalize, thus terminating the Bastogne Operation so far as the 3rd Army is concerned."[1]

12

THE EMPIRE IS UNSEATED

As the Battle of the Bulge drew to a close, the race toward the Rhine intensified. Herb Stern, as part of the 84th Division in the Ninth Army, had a forward observer team near the Rhine's west bank. The observers were holed up in an abandoned flak tower, about ten-stories high, formerly used by the Germans to defend against air attacks. Now it was an ideal lookout from which the 84th artillery observers could call in targets. Every five to ten minutes, the fire missions were radioed in to Stern's headquarters and one after another, the shells were reported to have landed like bull's-eyes, hitting pay dirt. Such preciseness gave Herb Stern an uneasy feeling.

There's something funny going on. We're not that good. What the hell are they shooting at?

Stern requested that the division's military police visit the flak tower that evening to check on observer activity. He couldn't make a surprise visit himself, since the observers would be alerted to his presence upon first sight of his approaching jeep. The military police, on the other hand, could be there for any number of reasons, maybe just trying to scrounge up smokes.

Stern received the unsettling MP call: his team of lieutenant and two enlisted men were shacked up, fraternizing and procreating with three German girls—a wartime harem in a flak tower. Not only had Eisenhower expressly forbidden fraternization with German civilians but worse still, the artillery targets the observers had been calling in were fictitious.

A furious Stern suffered no fools. He dispatched a replacement team and recalled the derelict ones. He busted the sergeant and radioman, reducing them to privates and warning the lieutenant to prepare for a court martial. Then he expediently filed formal charges against the latter, forwarding them to the division's artillery headquarters, commanded by Colonel Charles J. Barrett, West Point class of 1922.

Upon receiving the charge sheets, Barrett phoned Stern. "You don't want to really court martial the lieutenant," he suggested. "How about we remove the charges?"

"General, it's your prerogative, but I will *not* remove the charges. My charges stand."

Two weeks later, Stern opened up an official letter addressed to him. Seeing the signature of General Eisenhower made him bolt upright. Reading the contents within made him turn red. Herb Stern was in "dereliction of duty" for failing to court martial the lieutenant observer.

Good god, thought Stern. *Barrett removed the charges, and now I'm to blame.*

Stern phoned his commander. "Sir, have you seen this letter to me from General Eisenhower?"

"Major," answered Barrett, "I'm sorry about that. You insisted that the charges stand, and I removed them. It's my fault. I'll advise headquarters and have the letter removed from your files."

While Stern hardly contemplated his long-term career at that moment, Barrett knew it would be a dim one if the letter from the supreme commander remained in his files. Barrett got it expunged, and he wrote to Eisenhower admitting that it was he who removed the charges. Barrett was none the worse for it, and in fact in the interim had been promoted to brigadier general.

★ ★ ★

Like Stern, Charlie Fletcher was heading toward the Rhine while grappling with conflicting directives. The 174th Field Artillery Group, for which he was intelligence officer, was positioned among the most forward in Patton's drive east. On March 16, the unit, which had been supporting Mike Greene's division, reached the confluence of the Mosel and Rhine Rivers, distinguished by a spit of land that juts out where the rivers meet. On that spit in the city of Koblenz stood an enormous monument as the centerpiece. Fletcher took out his field glasses to view the imposing copper statue.

Emperor Wilhelm in all his glory . . . almost as big as the Statue of Liberty, thought Fletcher.

The German emperor was astride his horse in full regalia with a flowing cape, a plumed helmet, and an angel protectively standing beside him. The statue sat atop a massive rectangular pedestal, on which were inscribed the words: "*Nimmer wird das Reich zerstöret.*" It meant, "Never will the empire be destroyed."

Fletcher's radio buzzed.

"Munitions 2?" asked the voice.

THE EMPIRE IS UNSEATED ★ 135

"Yes, sir," confirmed Fletcher of his code name, referring to the 174th Group and he as S-2.

"This is Lucky 3." That was the moniker for the operations officer, G-3, of Third Army headquarters. "Do you have observation of the intersection of the Mosel and Rhine?"

"Yes, sir, I do."

"Do you have any guns targeting that area?"

"Yes, sir."

"Lucky 3 is ordering you to destroy the statue."

Replied Fletcher, "Yes, sir." Fletcher put the receiver down.

That's one heck of a statue. More like a fortress. It's going to take a lot of fire to knock it down.

He reflected on which gun was best put to use. *Precision fire. Probably an 8-inch howitzer.*

The massive, self-propelled gun weighed more than thirty thousand pounds and had a seventeen-foot barrel. Fletcher radioed his firing unit to ready it. He then began a series of complicated formulas to determine the firing data, preparing to handle the firing directly rather than going through a fire direction center; his orders were coming from Army headquarters, and there was no room for error.

But something nagged in the back of Fletcher's mind.

That list of protected monuments. Did I see the statue on it?

He searched for the manifest and quickly scanned it. Wilhelm was on it. He needed to contact Lucky 3 to inform him.

Proceeding through the chain of command, from regimental headquarters, Fletcher aka Munitions 2, telephoned through to the switch that was code-named "Mogul" for VIII Corps Artillery headquarters. From there, he got lobbed to the next level of command, switch "Monarch," for VIII Corps Headquarters.

From Monarch, the line went right through to Lucky 3.

"Sir," said Fletcher. "I don't mean to question orders, but the monument of Emperor Wilhelm is in the book as protected."

"Wait a minute," responded Lucky 3.

After a brief pause the next voice Fletcher heard was a high-pitched one, a voice he'd heard before. "Are you questioning me?" General Patton bellowed into the phone. "People of the Third Army don't question Lucky 6!"

Fletcher had been bandied about from regimental to artillery headquarters to corps and then Army headquarters—Munitions to Mogul to Monarch to the top of the military food chain, Lucky, and its commander, Lucky 6.

"Sir, I'm not questioning you," explained Fletcher. "Not at all. I'm simply ensuring that all the facts are known before taking action."

"Destroy it!"

"Yes, sir," responded Fletcher. "I intend to do just that."

What Patton wants, thought Fletcher, *Patton gets. Wilhelm has seen the last of the Rhine.*

Fletcher was soon ready to let loose with precision fire. One after another, two-hundred-pound shells began to pummel the fortresslike pedestal supporting the emperor. Lobbing shells in a 10-kilometer trajectory, expecting them to hit the prancing hooves of a horse, proved a vexing proposition. Wilhelm was immovable and obstinate, but Fletcher was bullheaded and persistent. Under the horse. Over the horse. He adjusted the fire again and again. It took about twenty rounds, but finally Charlie Fletcher kicked the emperor off his horse. And there Wilhelm hung, caught in the Allied noose, dangling from his pedestal—till Fletcher's rounds blasted yet again, reducing most of the symbolic monument to smoldering rubble.

The sun was setting on the Nazi empire.

Very near to Fletcher's location, West Point '41er Jack Murray was also advancing on Koblenz. As a fellow intelligence officer, Murray had been collaborating with Fletcher every few days as they advanced east. Now he was in a command jeep with his driver, carrying with him a large box that had been given to him by a flashy officer from Washington on behalf of General Frank L. Culin.

The latter had announced to Murray: "This is the last flag that was flown on the last day of the American occupation in World War I, and it was flown over a certain building in Koblenz."

Ordered the general, "You will take this flag and see that it gets put back on that same building when we take Koblenz."

After scouring maps, Murray was able to pinpoint the building, which was within sneezing distance of the remains of Wilhelm. Jack Murray soon stood before that building, near the smoldering emperor's rubble. He opened the large box and carefully unfolded the enormous flag. One West Point '41er had helped take the "empire" down, and now in the aftermath another would get to hoist the stars and stripes up. The flag soon waved triumphantly, a message that the United States would not stand down. Murray snapped a photo of the flag and called General Culin to share the news.

"Murray, good job," Culin said approvingly. "Listen," he added, "you have been working pretty hard. How would you like a little leave?"

"That would be great, General."

"General Patton's dog has to go back to England for some shots, and if you can get down to Trier before five o'clock this afternoon, you can ride on the plane."

"That's swell," replied Murray.

Murray and his driver sped from Koblenz, trying to make the eighty miles to Trier in time. Fortunately, the English bulldog was waiting. Murray was sure it was the ugliest dog he'd ever seen, muddy-colored and scrunched up in the face like it had been rammed into a steel wall. The beloved bulldog, however, got the privilege of sitting up front with the pilots on the flight to London, while Murray and his driver sat in the back between the mailbags. But Jack Murray had no complaints. The bulldog got its shots, he got a week's vacation, and within that week Patton's army victoriously crossed the Rhine.

★ ★ ★

The 84th Division, including Major Herb Stern, soon reached the Weser-Elbe Canal, over which a treadway bridge had been erected for crossings, though far too many troops had arrived all at once, creating yet one more bottleneck in a war fraught with traffic jams. There were dozens of trucks and vehicles lined up along the riverbank from north to south for as far as the eye could see. Each was waiting to make a right turn on to the bridge, including the 333rd Combat Team. The team consisted of an artillery battalion, including the one for which Stern was operation's officer, along with an infantry regiment and supporting units.

Stern, exasperated at the crossing logjam, bolted out of his jeep and walked toward Colonel Lou Truman, the president's cousin and chief of staff of the 84th Division. Truman was attempting to direct traffic, apparently with little success.

"Colonel," said Stern, "General Bolling wants our combat team to cross the canal in a hurry to get to Hanover."

"Can't you see traffic is all backed up?" Truman replied in annoyance. "You can't get across now."

"Yes I can," declared Stern.

"If you're so smart," retorted Truman, "then do it!"

Stern nodded. He strode a few hundred yards up to the front of the long column. Jumping atop the running board of the first truck, he shouted, "Move up! Move the whole column up!"

As soon as Stern got down, the driver stepped on the gas, heading north past the bridge crossing. Stern waved on the next trucks to follow, and the whole line cranked up and began moving beyond the bridge.

Watching his handiwork in action, reflected Stern, *I don't know how they're going to turn themselves around on this narrow road to get back to the bridge, but that's not my problem. Let Truman figure it out.* He chuckled.

When the entrance to the bridge cleared, Stern jumped back into his jeep and began motoring forward to cross the bridge with his team.

As he was passing Truman, the president's cousin hollered, "You think you're so smart!"

"If you weren't so stupid, you would've done the same thing," retorted Stern. With that, Stern stepped on the gas, not wanting to press his luck by sticking around, given that he was only a major compared to Truman's colonel rank.

The 333rd Combat Team pressed on toward the Elbe River, the next major north-south river in Germany after the Rhine. If the Allies could cross it, Berlin was possibly theirs for the taking. But first came the large city of Hanover, population 475,000, which the Allies wanted to seize before the Germans destroyed it in retreat.

Six miles west of the city, however, the division had a major loss. Lieutenant Colonel David Jones, the right-hand man and operations officer for General Barrett, had been on an advance reconnaissance mission on April 10 when a sniper, in the small village of Northen, shot and killed him. A livid General Barrett rushed to that area, coming upon an American artillery battalion along the way that was from the 102nd Ozark Division. He stopped the operations' officer leading the artillery column, explained the situation, and said, "Turn your guns on that village and destroy it!"

The officer was West Point '41er Joe Reed, who was happy to oblige. Reed unlimbered his battalion guns and direct-fired at the village, leveling most of it. Reed went on his way, unaware that his best friend and fellow artilleryman, Herb Stern, was just ahead of him. Though scattered across the vast expanse of war, '41ers often seemed a stone's throw from one another—working toward the common goal.

To fill Jones's position, the next senior lieutenant colonel, Harry Hubbard, was moved up to Bolling's headquarters, leaving Hubbard's former battalion leaderless. Herb Stern hated to profit from a fine officer's death, but the dominoes in the chain of leadership had fallen. He wrote an executive order.

"I, Herbert I. Stern, hereby assume command of the 325th Field Artillery Battalion."

General Barrett, getting wind of the self-appointment, appeared at 325th battalion headquarters.

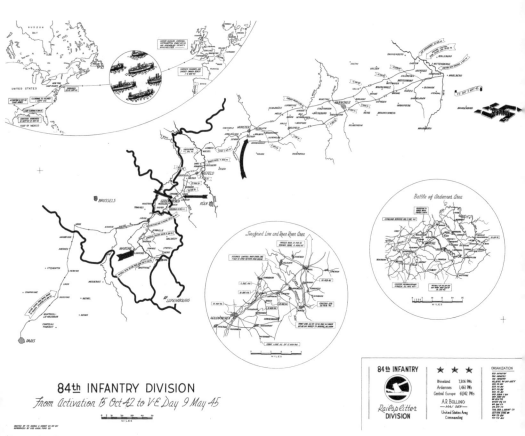

The 84th Infantry Division's sweep across the Western front, highlighting Brussels to Berlin, Dec. 1944–May 1945.

"I see you have assumed command of the battalion," he said to Stern. "You know you are *not* the senior major in the division artillery."

"General, until you assign someone senior to me, I'm going to command the battalion."

Barrett eyed the West Pointer, all twenty-six-years young. The 84th had moved at breakneck speed—150 miles in nine days—and combing Army ranks for a more senior artillery commander at that point would be like searching for a one-horned steer on a cattle drive. Besides, Barrett had long had his sights on Stern, having singled him out for his division three years earlier. In truth, Stern also had more experience than the executive next in line in the battalion's hierarchy; Stern could have been in that executive's position but had shunned its paperwork role, preferring combat operations. Stern taking over command was fine with the general.

Barrett laughed. "Well if that's the way you feel, then you can have the battalion. Congratulations."

With that, Stern became responsible for some thousand troops, charged with supporting infantry regiments as well as division-level artillery units. He was also expected to come to the aid of any other unit in the 84th Division needing fire support in the field.

Stern's unit immediately proceeded to Hanover and, together with the rest of the 333rd Combat Team, was the first to infiltrate the city. The element of surprise was severely demoralizing to the enemy, and after seeing the strength of the entire 84th Division descending on the city—about twenty-five thousand troops in total—the Germans put up minimal resistance and fled in retreat. The Allies quickly took the city.

From there, the 333rd Combat Team headed northeast. Nearing the town of Salzwedel, Stern's column was held up in traffic, stalled beside entrance gates to a facility enclosed with a long and high barbed wire fence. Stern cringed at the putrid smell permeating the air. Then he saw them—a mob of gaunt faces on skeletal frames. All female.

This can't be real, thought a shocked Stern.

But it was. More than three thousand emaciated women were confined within a Jewish labor camp like rats in a cage. Stern saw bones protruding from sickly bodies. They were scantily clad in tattered rags. Most looked aged well beyond their years, with lots of ghostly white hair. There were teenagers among them, clinging to women—perhaps their mothers. Evidently, the Nazi captors had abandoned the laborers in the wake of advancing American troops.

Stern, like other soldiers, bounded out of his vehicle and attacked the entrance gates. It took but a short time for bolt and wire cutters to disengage the main gates. Then the men dodged to allow the flood of emaciated women their freedom.

Some women lunged at soldiers who were offering up their K-rations. Others begged for a cigarette. Still others began ransacking the nearby stores, devouring handfuls of grain forthwith, driven by starvation.

Stern's battalion could do little to help. It was not prepared; he had orders to keep moving. He prayed that liberation for the women was a start. Before moving on, the 84th troops torched the concentration camp.

Twenty-five miles south, in the medieval town of Gardelegen, the commandant of the Luftwaffe garrison was ceremoniously surrendering to U.S. forces. He was in a sedan decked with waving white flags, led by a motorcycle escort. But unlike the timely liberation of some laborer camps, like that in Salzwedel, time in Gardelegen had proved to be a poison. As the Luftwaffe commandant was leading American officers to his troops, neatly drawn-up for surrender, other Luftwaffe and SS officers were on the outskirts of town by a grain barn, overseeing the digging of mass graves. The day prior, they had herded more than a thousand military and political prisoners into the barn, where straw had been doused with gasoline. SS and Luftwaffe officers, some said to look all of sixteen, laughingly then lit matches. The roasted bodies were still smoking when the Ozark Division, Joe Reed among them, stumbled on the ghoulish scene—a day too late. They could smell death before seeing it. Heads and hands still stuck out from beneath the doors, where they had been clawing for survival, before apparently being killed with a hail of bullets while trying to escape the blaze.

While the Ozarks were setting up a memorial cemetery for the victims, Stern and the 333rd Combat Team continued its thrust toward Berlin. As forces steamed ahead, they cleared the roads of enemy pockets, usually ordering enemy troops to simply drop their weapons and march to the rear, where the military police could mop them up. If soldiers surrendered, American troops didn't chase them; there was no time.

But that was not the case with the British 30 Corps. It was operating just north of the Ninth Army, and on occasion the 84th Division became attached to the British, with the latter then doling out assignments. Usually the first thing U.S. troops did in such cases was send in water cans to draw rum rations; in that regard many troops considered the Brits far superior to the American. But where the Brits were viewed inferior by some American troops was in their methodical movement: the British were deliberate in not leaving behind a broken cracker—let alone an enemy. What resulted was that as the 84th Division rushed east, it often got far ahead of the 30 Corps, leaving the U.S. division's left, northern flank exposed.

A German armored column in that northern swath tried to skirt the oncoming 30 Corps by heading south, which brought it directly in contact with Stern's artillery units; he'd acquired command of yet another battalion by this point. Though the Germans were trying to escape U.S. forces, they were instead presented with the perfect setup to conduct a surprise attack.

Stern's executive, Jervis "Dutch" Janney, urgently radioed his boss, who was four or five miles ahead with the combat team's lead elements, trying to dodge a torrent of enemy fire.

"We're being attacked!" he yelled. "A whole column of tanks!"

"My god," replied Stern. "Where are you? Where's the hostile position?"

Dutch relayed his location. "We've swung around and dropped the guns. We're direct firing."

Stern's eyes widened. Back in Louisiana, he taught his men direct firing against moving targets, one of the few officers in the Army to drill units in that technique, which involved unhitching howitzers from their carriages and dropping the noses of the enormous guns to point them straight ahead. The maneuver was like shooting canons as though pistols, rather than lobbing artillery high in its typical arc.

"Keep the tanks engaged with the direct fire," said Stern of the dozen artillery guns. "Hold tight and let me get help."

He instantly radioed General Bolling. He spat out the brief engagement details: "My battalion's been ambushed. A German armored column. We need infantry to defeat the tanks. I can't do it with just artillery. Can't leave my men there."

"I'll get an infantry unit back there as soon as I can."

Stern radioed back to Janney. "Help is on the way. Infantry."

"Okay, we've got them backed up in the woods, about a dozen tanks and armored infantry."

"Retain one battery to keep the Germans there," ordered Stern. "Displace two forward to support our forward infantry; I can't leave infantry exposed. And I'm on my way back."

Just then, the Germans hit the battalion's ammunition trailers, setting them ablaze. A few quick-thinking officers unhooked the burning trailers and, with only seconds to spare, gave a huge heave-ho with the trucks to which they had been attached, shoving the trailers into the adjacent river before they could explode and create a towering inferno.

As the firefight continued, Stern's operations officer, Gordon Foster, was in a nearby house that was serving as temporary headquarters. Foster sat on a bed, peering through the windows with binoculars, watching the firestorm outside. Suddenly, an enemy tank round pierced a wall of the house, blasted directly between his legs, and shot under the bed and out the opposite wall. Foster's long, horselike chin nearly hit his stomach. The shells were not high-explosive ones, so Foster still had his balls, but by the time Stern arrived on the scene and surveyed the ongoing mayhem, it was clear that his unit would have been massacred had the Germans employed HE shells. Apparently they had run out.

While that was some consolation, three of Stern's soldiers had been captured while returning from a routine mail run. They had driven directly into German sentries serving as peripheral defenses. The situation remained grim.

Here I am now a battalion commander, worried Stern, *and I might lose my whole battalion.*

But Bolling's promised infantry unit arrived, and it was more than

Stern had hoped for. It was a battalion of nearly one thousand troops as reinforcement, much to the chagrin of its commander, who was irritated at having to come to the aid of an artillery unit that was supposed to be supporting him.

I don't give a rat's ass about his gripes, swore Stern to himself.

He left to rejoin the lead infantry unit, which was still on the move. For Stern, it was like helter-skelter, back and forth from one maelstrom to another.

Reinforced with the infantry, the units holding back the Germans in the woods quickly overpowered them without a single American fatality. When the last of enemy elements fled, Stern was ecstatic to hear that they left behind their American POWs—Stern's three men. All in all, he was jubilant over the battle's success as well as the cunning and courage his unit had displayed.

As the firing ceased, his remaining artillery battery in the forest could at long last proceed forward. The commander called Stern to inquire about a rendezvous. "How do I find you?" he asked.

"Just follow the K-ration boxes." When Stern had been told to accelerate toward Berlin, he had taken the order quite literally, taking no time to stop and chow down. The road was littered with the remains of his units' meals-to-go. The trailing battery commander had no problem tracking Herb Stern.

Though his artillery units prevailed, Stern's supply lines had been severed. To replenish ammunition would mean 250 miles of round-trip travel to reach the ammunition dumps, a circuitous route south then back west, followed by north, before reversing the route in return. Wisely, before crossing the Rhine, Stern had stocked his vehicles with triple the usual allocation of ammunition, strapping crates atop every square inch of vehicle. As a result, he determined that his troops could survive with the remaining fire. But aside from K-rations, they had no food. What Stern did have was a kitchen trailer his troops had stolen from another American unit along their journey. He put it to good use.

While traveling through farm country, along the way Stern situated a command post in an abandoned farmhouse whose evacuees happened to have left behind dozens of chickens. Stern was fighting a war, his officers were famished, and in the abandoned henhouse, he saw a solution.

"Let's round up those chickens," he directed a few officers. "Put them in the kitchen trailer. We'll have eggs any way you like 'em."

There were resounding whoops at the idea, and the men eagerly scrambled to catch chickens. In war, anything goes. As they continued advancing over the ensuing weeks, every time they set up command at an abandoned farm, they rested the chickens on roosts so that headquarters had fresh eggs daily.

They also had wine, thanks to a Princeton-educated captain by the name of John Navarre de Macomb, who, due to his lofty upbringing, recognized the value of fine wine when troops stumbled upon a huge cellar.

"Major, I'm in a building full of tremendous casks," he radioed Stern. "But some dumb doughboys shot the darn casks and the wine's pouring out; it's almost up to the top of stairs. If you can send all the water cans from the battalion that you can round up, I'll fill them with wine and send them back."

Stern promptly dispatched a truck with every single canister his men could put their hands on, which became a considerable amount when troops heard of the bounty involved. Upon delivery of the canisters, Macomb and a few others sat there in the soggy cellar, like fishermen wading in a river, but instead they were fishing for Rhine wine. It was a good harvest, and for the next few days the entire battalion enjoyed the vintage with their meals.

On about the third day, Macomb radioed to Stern again. "Major, about that wine I sent you . . ."

"Yes, Mac."

"Something's happened. I went back to that cellar, and it turns out that the wine we were drinking . . . well . . . it had a dead German in it."

Herb Stern gulped. But by that point all the wine had been consumed— fermented by a Nazi corpse.

There were no ill effects, and the 333rd Combat Team continued on. It finally hit the Elbe in late April, at which point General Bolling called Stern. "I want the combat team to cross the river as soon as we can put up bridging. Head to Berlin as fast as you can."

Engineers immediately began arranging pontoons across the river, on which they set tracks for the makeshift bridge. Stern began assembling the artillery procession that would cross, a motorcade of over 100 vehicles including howitzer prime-movers, motor carriages, trucks carrying ammunition, fuel trucks, mess-unit trailers, command cars, and more. Everything they needed to bear down on Berlin.

As the teams turned on their engines, the roar of the motors was deafening.

There's nothing between us and Berlin, thought Stern triumphantly. *Just fifty-one miles. We can be there in twenty-four hours, ours for the taking*.

All Stern needed was the command to lurch forward. He quickly grabbed the radio when Bolling called.

"Stand down!" commanded Bolling. "It's off. Crossing's off."

"Yes, sir."

Stern hung up the radio, taken aback but not prepared to question a command. He ordered his artillery procession halted and his troops to return to tactical positions in the event the Germans crossed back over the Elbe in retreat.

And there the combat team sat battle-ready for nearly two weeks. They still had no replenished food rations. The unit, however, was in the middle of cattle country, so Stern looked the other way when his men returned to headquarters with slaughtered cattle for meals, telling them, "If anyone asks, I'll just say they were killed by German shells from across the river."

Troops didn't expected to devour steak in the midst of war, but they did just that. They also devoured local venison and used concussion grenades to cull fresh fish from streams, which worked like a charm.

Stern, meanwhile, had chosen a well-kept, tidy house for his artillery headquarters. It belonged to a physician, as evidenced by the paraphernalia scattered about. As usual, one of the first things his officers did was to look around for "goodies" like beer, wine, pistols—anything that might offer small comforts or be of practical use.

"Take a look at this, Major," said an officer carrying a beautifully engraved wooden box, about eighteen square inches in size.

He set it down before Stern, who opened it to see an interior filled with velvet trays and small compartments. Each was filled with sparkling stones.

Stern let out a low whistle. "I'm no gemologist, but these look like diamonds. And looks like there's all kinds of other precious stones in here . . . rubies, emeralds . . . all sorts of precious and semiprecious stones."

"What do we do with it?"

"Tie it up and send it to corps headquarters."

Stern shut the lid and the officer sent it on to artillery headquarters, which, following protocol, would then forward it to corps headquarters.

General Barrett unexpectedly appeared the next day around lunchtime and sat down to join Stern and his officers in their meal.

I hope steak isn't on the menu, mused Stern. *I could get hell for pilfering German property.*

As the chef put down steaming bowls, Stern exhaled. Lunch was stew.

"Guess the rations came through!" said Barrett with delight.

Stern smiled, his tenderloin secret safe.

That evening Barrett called Stern. "Major, do you know what I had when I got back to headquarters tonight?"

"No, sir. What might that be?"

146 ★ WEST POINT '41

"They put down a nice white plate in front of me, and on it was K-rations! Can I come back to your place for lunch tomorrow?" Barrett let out a hearty laugh.

Though Barrett could joke, it was no farce when Stern got an angry call from the corps G-2 a day or so later. Questioned the intelligence officer, "Major Stern, why the hell did you send this empty chest to us?"

"Empty?"

Stern was ready to kick himself. *What an idiot I am. An honest, stupid idiot.*

As the days wore on, boredom took its toll. Like many soldiers, Stern's long-term radio operator, Anthony Golembeski, roamed the countryside scattered with stone farmhouses. But unlike others, Golembeski peeped into a window and set his sights on the German girl within. He attempted to rape her but the scrawny radioman proved no match for the husky German girl, who practically washed the floors with his head before throwing him out the door.

Another enlisted man witnessed the aftermath—Golembeski with his eyes turning shades of purple and blood oozing from his head—and brought the offender back to headquarters.

"What do we do with him?" asked an officer.

The radioman had served with Stern throughout the war, but now Stern could barely look at him. "I'm going to prefer charges against him for attempted rape," he announced.

Looking at the battered man, he also thought, *He got what he deserved.*

The man would later be sentenced to twenty years.

While Stern put Golembeski out of his mind, he had trouble blocking out horrifying images of the bony women at that labor camp back in Salzwedel. It gnawed at him.

What happened to them when we left on the road? Have they found food, shelter? It's not that far. I could be there in a couple of hours. I could find out.

Before long Stern was at a former military hospital that the Allies had overtaken. They'd renamed it "Camp Vassar" and were using it to house the concentration camp survivors. It was a mere month since Herb Stern's jeep had been parked outside those gates. But now he saw women that appeared to be entirely different specimens. They appeared happy and recovering their health. Stern could hardly believe they were the same women.

He returned to the combat team along the Elbe River, which continued its vigil. Waiting and watching. So flat was the land on the opposite bank that he could view the approaching Russians through field glasses. He could see the silhouettes of Germans falling to enemy shells and observe the clockwork-like maneuvers of Russian armor advancing. The armor was followed by troops on horseback, which snared enemy stragglers. As that occurred, the armor would advance yet again, and so on continued the armor and cavalry leapfrogging. Stern was mesmerized by the methodical precision of the Russians. And he soon began watching the aftereffect of their handiwork—the gray-clad corpses of Nazi soldiers floating down the Elbe, both men and women, bobbing up and down in the swift current.

As Stern's battalion sat watching the surreal spectacle, they played cards, smoked cigarettes, and waited for the Soviet Army.

As they bided their time, and the Germans appeared increasingly unlikely to retreat west—the scant forces that were left of them—the Americans were free to do most anything they wanted. Anything but cross the river. Orders were clear. A crossing would be left for ceremonious bigwigs at a later date. But as time dragged on, Stern felt like he was watching sand sift through an hourglass.

"I'm bored out of my damn mind," he said one day to his S-2, Fred Steffins, and the assistant S-2, Bob Wuerfle. "Why not grab one of those rowboats and cross the river? See what these tough Russians are like?"

"We'll be up a creek if anyone finds out," replied one of his colleagues.

"Who over there's gonna tell on us?" cracked Stern.

The three men laughed. They were soon in a rowboat.

The Russians saw the three Allies approaching and quickly welcomed them into their camp enclosure. Many of the Russians towered over the Americans, appearing like burly bears that might eat their cubs.

"I'm glad they're on our side," whispered Stern to his colleagues.

He then gaped at the Russians imbibing from huge gallon-sized jugs. *What the heck is it? Purplish in color . . . almost looks like gasoline.*

Just then, one of the burly officers gave him a friendly slap on the back. Handing Stern a mug, he poured some of the concoction and indicated with hand gestures that Stern must try it. Stern was ready to gag but he lifted the jug and pretended to swallow, letting most of the ghoulish liquid drool down his chin and on to his tan-colored tank jacket. The drunk Russian took little notice.

About four days later, Stern noticed something odd when he went to put on his tank jacket—the nap had been eaten away where the Russian drink had dribbled.

Holy smokes. Imagine what it would have done to my insides!

Meanwhile, the erudite verdict came down: The Allies would not march on Berlin. Instead, General Eisenhower and Prime Minister Winston Churchill had agreed to let Stalin capture the long-coveted prize. History was made—or lost—depending on the point of view.

BITTERSWEET FREEDOM

As Jim Forsyth passed the time at Oflag 64, he was permitted to write home one postcard and one letter weekly. He previously used up his quota writing to his wife, so in the dim light, on the thin burlap mattress in his barracks' cell, he sat to pen a card to his parents and sister.

Where can I even begin? Forsyth wondered. *How do you boil your life down to three by five?* Jim Forsyth longed for his words to be in person.

> Dear Mom, Dad, and Mary,
> I am in the best of health and spirits. Was thinking of you on your birthday, Dad. May we have happier ones to come. Keep Ruth's chin up for me as well as your own. . . . Have faith and write.
> Love, Jim.

A few days later, he tried to be upbeat in his allotted letter, not uncharacteristic of his strong spirit—and academy training.

> I have been reading some good books from an excellent library. I've been playing quite a bit of basketball and seen two movies and a play. Our officers organize all our activities. . . . All in all, the time passes a lot faster than I would have thought. We even have a monthly paper and other local news from time to time. Well, the year is going into its last quarter, and it can't go any too fast for me. Most of all, I miss you all. Good-bye.
> Love, Jim.

His parents were skeptical as to ball games and movies at a prisoner of war camp. Was it misinformation and censorship? Or did German officers have some incongruous sense of civility? With the enemy beginning to falter on fronts, it was hard to distinguish truth from fiction. Forsyth's parents just hoped there was a semblance of fact in what their son wrote. For that bit of truth, they prayed.

In actuality, Forsyth had not been mistreated since arriving at Oflag 64, which was a former boys' school with barracks annexed to it—and an inordinate amount of barbed wire. Like most officers, he slept six to a room on a double-tiered cot. His mattress, filled with wood shavings, was flimsy at best, but then there was less of Jim Forsyth to bear down on it. Subsisting on potatoes and turnips had caused his five-foot-eight frame to plummet from about 150 pounds to below 120, and for the first time in his life Jim Forsyth knew what it meant to go hungry.

The occasional cigarette did little to stave off hunger pains. Tobacco received in Red Cross parcels was, more often than not, swapped in exchange for morsels of food from the prison guards. Forsyth usually retained just a small wad of tobacco, enough to roll a handful of cigarettes that he smoked a third at a time. What the Germans didn't ration, he rationed himself.

His prison garb nearly resembled his bedding, a heavy burlap shirt that scratched his skin, together with nondescript pants, and the boots in which he'd arrived. The clothes reeked of sweat since he was rarely permitted a shower, only about once every couple of weeks. Still, Jim Forsyth drove himself to exercise, usually three times a day. He knew that if he did not keep his strength, his body could easily succumb to the many illnesses that ran rampant within the camp. And if there were a chance to escape, he might then not have the power even if he had the will.

There was, in fact, an "escape committee" among American officers, the most senior of whom were a World War I veteran, Colonel Thomas Drake, and Patton's son-in-law, Lieutenant Colonel Jake Waters. Both were West Point alumni, and as an instructor Waters had overseen the '41 flankers of Company A, including Ed Rowny and Walter Woolwine.

Those senior officers kept order among the prisoners along with an agenda of activities, which for months had included surreptitious digging of tunnels exiting the prison grounds. It was generally understood that officers had a duty to attempt escapes, not just for their own freedom, but because successful breakouts and the ensuing confusion diverted German military and intelligence units away from the fighting front.[1] The problem of where to hide extracted dirt had been solved by putting it into used Red Cross boxes and piling the boxes into ceiling rafters. The rafters, in turn, were buttressed by slats of wood from prisoners' cot frames. Like on the battlefield, the solution for every problem seemed to create new challenges needing new solutions. But this was an enterprising bunch. Among them was Tuck Brown.

Brown was Forsyth's classmate, though the two had not encountered each other at Oflag. Brown was captured in Salerno, Italy, in September

1943, in a firefight that left one of his friends dead from a gunshot wound and another dead from a grenade explosion that rendered Brown unconscious. And so Brown ended up at Oflag 64 where Waters assigned him as "officer in charge of dirt disposal" for the largest of the escape tunnels. His human chain worked in the predawn hours each night till Brown estimated they had removed more than sixty cubic yards of dirt, and the tunnel reached beyond the barbed wire barricade.

Then came a radio intercept from Eisenhower warning officers to cease and desist from all attempts at breakouts given the slew of British officers executed following their attempt to escape a POW camp in Sagan, southeast of Berlin.[2] The tunnel exit was sealed off. So Jim Forsyth, along with the 1,400 other officers at Oflag 64, kept on keeping on, busying themselves and trying to create clever forms of entertainment.

The YMCA and Salvation Army had donated countless items for the prisoners so the camp was not without small comforts, including a library. Forsyth was particularly amused to find *The Forsyte Saga* among its shelves.

Can't be a more fitting title for me to read, he thought.

So Jim Forsyth whiled away the hours with his nose in a book or in the Bible. He walked the prison grounds, which while highly guarded, remained relatively free for prisoners to roam. Or he played endless games of poker and bridge, more often than not with a winning hand. Fellow prisoners were enterprising in their endeavors: One studied Russian because he said, "You can't ever tell." Another began a collection of every cigarette cover to hit Oflag. Still another embroidered division insignias, while a comrade spent time whittling wooden chains. Anything to pass the minutes, the hours, and the days. But the weariness of it clawed at others, testing their mental mettle. Some sat dazed with far-away looks as though willing themselves to different lands, imaginary worlds where phonographs drowned out the clicking of Nazi heels and fireplaces roared to warm chilled spirits.

The monthly paper, the *Item*—made by prisoners for prisoners—duly noted the ticking passage of time. Highlights of the paper included photos of pretty wives and girlfriends from back stateside, smiling from the paper's pages, Oflag's pin-up girls with requisite come-hither looks and tousled curls. But when a grandfather clock was installed in the main building of the POW camp, the newspaper turned its focus to the sands of time. The response was hardly enthusiastic. Griped the *Item* on October 1, 1944:

> To begin with, we pre-expended Olfagites already have entirely too much time on our hands. For instance, we've already served collectively

something like 500 years in this glorified hoosegow, and we don't like being reminded of it so much. . . . Grandfather ticks away deliberately in a hushed tone of voice that says: 'No rush, no rush.' . . . We think it's high time we got back to the young ladies on the front and back pages of this issue, who are doing a little clock-watching of their own.[3]

Grandfather time, however, continued to put officers' lives on hold. The days grew shorter. The nights, colder. And the shadows of the men on the stone walls of their cells grew fainter and ever humbler.

Then the Red Cross parcels, which were lifelines for prisoners at Oflag, began to dry up as the rails between Germany and Poland fell under a barrage of Allied air raids. Forsyth and other "Kriegies," short for *Kriegsgefangenen*, or prisoner of war, took to cooking packets of instant soup on makeshift stoves in the hallways of their barracks. They'd stack a used food tin on top of another, stuff the bottom one with newspaper and twigs and fire it up, while the upper tin held water for heating. The hallways would become so hazy with smoke that it sometimes looked like a battlefield, and in a way it was—a battle for sustenance. Prisoners complained that they would next have to boil their shoes for soup. On the rare day when men were provided bread, it was hardly worth risking molars on the loaves that sometimes had expiration dates two months prior.

But one day, the Red Cross pulled through. Trumpeted the *Item*:

> It came to pass in the years of the great war that a shortage descended upon the people of Schubin. And many Kriegies did weep and wail and there was great gnashing of teeth. For, lo, there were no more red-cross [sic] boxes. . . . Then there came to the people a great noise and a roaring of wind. The people did get hope, for their longing was indeed great. . . . And the parcels arrived and the people rejoiced.[4]

It was Christmas 1944, and each prisoner received a Red Cross parcel funded by the U.S. government. Jim Forsyth opened his and bowed his head.

Thank you, God. I pray that next Christmas, I might be home with Ruth.

Then Forsyth, ravenous, indulged in turkey and plum pudding, nuts and dates, tea, honey and strawberry jam, chewing gum, candy, and more. It was all the fixin's, plus tobacco and playing cards. Later, he attended Christmas service led by military chaplains—they too were prisoners—and together they rejoiced at Jesus's birth and at being alive.

In no time at all, however, their futures looked much less certain.

On January 20, 1945, just days after Mike Greene helped close the bulge, the 1,471 prisoners at Oflag were informed that they would be moving out the next day. The guards were tight-lipped beyond that, but prisoners knew that their captors' days were numbered with the Russians fast approaching Szubin.

Forsyth rolled up his meager belongings and prison-issued clothing within a bedroll as he pondered what lay ahead.

They must be bringing us back to some point still under German control. We're probably bargaining chips to trade for POWs held by the Allies.

The following day, the sky was gray, like dark slate, as the men departed. Only those too sick to walk were left behind, together with a few troop doctors and a number of prisoners who took their chances by hiding in the unfinished tunnels. Most, like Forsyth, chose the departing enemy over the approaching ally, the latter in the opinion of some, wolves in the guise of friends.

White flurries were falling on the plains as the columns of prisoners began trudging in a winding labyrinth nearly a mile long. Forsyth was among the luckier ones, positioned somewhere in the middle of the pack. There had been a blizzard the night prior, and those in the lead had to plow through snow up to several feet deep. By the time Forsyth reached where they had been, he walked a path well trodden. Still, the winds howled, bending his frail figure.

The prisoners were mostly silent as they walked, each man seemingly lost in thought as to what the future held. Only briefly did they stop to rest, but they were provided little in the way of rations to keep them going. They trekked for miles till darkness. By that point the columns had separated into smaller clusters, with the guards for Forsyth's group of about fifty indicating that they were to seek refuge in a barn for the night.

The men entered to find a modern building with endless rows of hogs, probably a farmers' co-op, as was typical of the region. As Forsyth glanced around at well-nourished animals, he couldn't help thinking, *The hogs get better treated than us. . . . They have heat and plenty of food.*

It was a hard pill to swallow for a man, any man, to see pigs treated better than men fighting a war for liberties. Forsyth thought back to an earlier time, another barn, another march.

Did I make the right decision that day not to risk fleeing in my fatigues? Would I have made it? Where would I be now, or would I be dead?

Those thoughts had been jamming his mind since earlier that day, when some prisoners had broken from the lines and slipped into the shadows of the forest. Between the receding Germans and the advancing Russians, Forsyth doubted they would get very far unnoticed, even if those who fled could survive the elements. A healthy degree of caution up to that point, Forsyth decided, had kept him alive. Comforted by the thought, he lay down in an aisle amid the hogs. And he slept.

Not all the nights were so comfortable. The group took to ditches, haystacks, unheated barns, and sheds. The days of traipsing led into a week, and then another. More prisoners wandered off the beaten track, some on purpose, some because their weary, frozen feet could tread no farther. Guards also went missing, defecting in the wake of Russian artillery booming and growing ominously closer.

One day along the route of the march, Forsyth and some fellow prisoners were ushered into a house to be interrogated.

Wondered Forsyth, *What do they expect to get from me at this point? Do they think they've broken me?*

He found himself looking up at a bulky, handsome man with dark, wavy hair and deep-set eyes. Rather than trying to intimidate, the German officer seemed quite affable. It appeared that he was trying the "good cop" routine—befriend the enemy in hopes that they lower their guard.

After the man greeted Forsyth and welcomed him to a chair, he introduced himself, speaking in good English. "I'm Maximillian Schmeling."

Forsyth's eyes widened. "The boxer?" he asked. "Former heavyweight champion?"

The man smiled. "Yes, one and the same."

"The first to ever slam Joe Louis, the Brown Bomber, to the floor, fourth round in 1936, one of the biggest upsets in boxing history? Lost in the rematch at Yankee Stadium a year later, in the 'Battle of the Century.'"

Max Schmeling chuckled. "So you're a boxing fan?"

"My West Point coach refereed some of your matches! Billy Cavanaugh."

Now, suddenly, it was Max who was excited. "Cavanaugh! You went to West Point? You know Cavanaugh?"

The two men suddenly lost track of all others in the house. And in their small corner of Poland, with the snow, wind, and war raging outside, the two also forgot that they were on opposing sides of one of the greatest conflicts in history. They were just two men, with a few degrees of separation, able to share a passion for times and events before the world went to war.

Little did Forsyth know that while Schmeling put on a bold front, playing his dutiful German role in the war, in truth, he had not only refused Hitler's request that he join the Nazi Party but also refused to stop associating with German Jews and had risked his life to save two young Jewish boys. Jim Forsyth and Max Schmeling had more in common that just boxing—they each retained their honor.

A few days later, Forsyth's group and another column of prisoners who had followed a similar route came upon two railroad boxcars, slatted cars likely used for cattle. The guards commandeered the boxcars and began herding the hundred or so men within. As they did so, Forsyth, out of the corner of his eye, saw a face among the crowd that rang a slight bell in his mind.

The voice belonging to the face boomed out like reveille, "Jim Forsyth. Is that you?"

As the man pushed near, Forsyth looked closer at the scraggly, unshaven image under the hat.

"It's me, Tuck Brown," said the man, a West Point classmate, a flanker from Company A. World War II had come full circle for two prisoners of war, to their beginnings.

"Tuck Brown!" Forsyth's shock gave way to a grin. "I can't believe it. Damn, it's good to see you, Tuck."

The two grasped each other in a quick embrace. "What the hell are you doing here?" asked Forsyth.

"Same thing as you, I guess. Trying to stay alive," answered Brown. "I was at Oflag 64. You too?"

"Yeah, got there in September. Captured in Normandy."

"I was there fifteen months, since after the Italy invasion, unconscious from an explosion when they got me. But I can't believe we never saw each other at the camp."

Their conversation was cut short as guards hustled prisoners outside the boxcars to move within, though many were confused and agitated given that the boxcars were already overflowing with passengers. So Brown and Forsyth did what their academy beginnings had taught them to do—command. Tuck Brown took control of one boxcar and Jim Forsyth the other.

The latches of the boxcar doors swung closed and the men became locked within a new, dark prison. Only a few slivers of daylight crept through the cracks of Forsyth's boxcar as it rumbled forward. It proved to be every bit the cattle car, the prisoners its herd. There was so little room to spare that Forsyth organized the passengers in his car into two groups: one sat, warmed by a small fire in the center, while the other stood along the walls of the car, often shivering. At intervals, they switched. A couple of times a day, the guards halted the rail procession so the men could disembark to go about their business. Then the train continued on, heading northwest till it reached the rail yards of Berlin a few days later.

There, the Allied air raids began. In the gloomy confines of his makeshift cell, Forsyth heard the roar of engines and then the explosions. His boxcar rattled under the blasts, the Allies unaware of the human cargo in the yards. The raids continued relentlessly, the Americans bombing by day, the British by night.

Somehow, miraculously, the boxcars remained intact and moved on the next day. But soon the journey on wheels halted and the grueling marching on foot began anew. Forsyth and Tuck Brown were relegated to different paths.

On Forsyth trudged. Right, left. Right, left. Reliving moments with Ruth to keep his feet moving, to keep them heading toward her. Then at long last, he and the column of stragglers reached a POW camp in Germany, where they were detained among other Allied officers.

Passing some days there, Forsyth played cards with some foreigners, including one from Holland. The Dutchman shared recollections of a young girl that lived down the block from him in Amsterdam. The girl and her family, who were Jewish, had resorted to living for two years in hidden passages of a building to escape the wrath of Hitler's regime. Then a neighbor betrayed them, said the Dutchman, turning them in to the Nazis to face certain death.

"Her name was Anne Frank," added the Dutchman. "I don't know what happened to her after that; she's probably dead. She was just maybe thirteen or fourteen years old."

The simple story about a girl and her family, the compassion of some—and the vile betrayal of others—brought home to Forsyth why he had been fighting a war. His thoughts ran back to West Point, where he had been taught to trust comrades with his life and to never accept cheating, a betrayal of trust. The moral code of West Point took on new meaning for Jim Forsyth.

Other prisoners from Oflag 64, meanwhile, were scattered among POW camps, including one in Hammelburg, which Patton's forces tried to storm to save his son-in-law, Colonel Jake Waters. Not only did Patton not gain Water's freedom, but more than thirty American troops died in the rescue operation while others were taken prisoner.

Soon, however, liberty would come for Jim Forsyth. After he had been transferred to yet one more POW camp, Russian victory appeared imminent and Forsyth's German captors fled in the wake of the advancing Red Army. It had been more than seven months since he had been captured, since he had traipsed across three countries and then back across two—Jim Forsyth's walking tour of Europe.

But at long last came his taste of freedom. And it was sweet.

Not so for some fellow prisoners. The Russians had no food for the internees, so troops were dispatched to search the surrounding area for food. They returned with a cow that was carved up, thanks to a POW who had a knack for knives and butchering. Starving prisoners were so overwhelmed when presented with plentiful, palatable food that a few overindulged. In their emaciated states, with stomachs severely shrunken from the deprivation of food, their insides ruptured, killing them in a dreadful manner.

Forsyth's saga, however, drew to a close.

Henry Bodson, farther south in Germany, was beginning one anew.

★ ★ ★

Henry Bodson was heading toward Munich and encountering broadening chaos at every turn. Some areas resembled the Wild West, filled with celebrants, pilferers, or those trying to slink undetected into the shadows of defeat. American officers were tasked with trying to restore order when encountering lawlessness, which happened time and again as Bodson's battalion made its way across the miles. Approaching Augsburg, in the Bavaria area north of Munich, the unit came upon a riot in full swing beyond the gates of a factory. Gangs, apparently mostly displaced Russians and Poles, were looting like barbarians. Bodson raised his pistol and fired several shots into the air.

Suddenly, shoes in the hands of looters dropped to the ground, sounding like a massive clattering of hooves. Others froze with absconded leather jackets or belts in their hands. Bodson's men moved in to disperse the crowd, forcing the people—men, women, and children alike—to return their stolen bounty, piling the goods into heaps that became massive as the thieving crowds exited the gates.

So overjoyed was the factory manager with his American savior that he tried to blanket Bodson with a long, gray leather jacket as a gift of appreciation.

Handsome, thought Bodson. *But the man shouldn't have to reward me for stopping robbery. And the color of an SS officer's uniform.* Bodson held back a chuckle. *Won't exactly win me a popularity contest at the moment.*

Wisely, he declined the gift.

His battalion continued on in support of an infantry regiment, reaching Munich, where there was a changing of the guard among the governors and those governed. Luftwaffe officers, on one hand, were spotted trying to flee into the woods, but American infantry rounded them up and declared them prisoners of war. At the same time emaciated survivors of Dachau were stumbling in the streets, in their freedom not knowing which way to turn. American soldiers used transport vehicles to deliver them to makeshift humanitarian stations, though the newly liberated were too delirious to appreciate that their German captors had become the captives.

In truth, at times it was hard for American soldiers to tell the difference between the enemy and the innocent, as Nazi officers and sympathizers took to disguises. U.S. forces could only do so much as units dashed across Germany to secure key enemy objectives.

VICTORY EUROPE

In the first week of May, Allied units raced toward the Bavarian city of Berchtesgaden, not far from the German border with Austria. The alpine city was a coveted prize since it was a key outpost for senior members of the Third Reich (including Hitler, who maintained a luxurious home there for years). The residence had also served as a headquarters for planning Nazi victory. While much in Berchtesgaden was destroyed from Allied bombing, within the walls of Hitler's fine abode, the wine cellar stood intact—an oasis amid the smoldering rubble, stocked with fine vintages pilfered from the French. It would not remain that way for long with the thirsty 3rd Infantry Division fast approaching. Berchtesgaden had, in fact, been slated as a prize for the 101st Airborne till that division got delayed in its advance due to blown-out bridges. The 3rd Division had the glorious task of capturing the town on May 4, 1945, with little resistance.

Despite Berchtesgaden's capture, the ultimate objective was broaching the nearby Eagle's Nest. The capture of Berlin had been a strategic Allied objective, but the Eagle's Nest, Hitler's mountaintop retreat a few miles from Berchtesgaden, was a symbolic one. Ostensibly a teahouse built for Adolf Hitler's fiftieth birthday in 1939, it served as a more sumptuous retreat than the moniker "teahouse" implied. It was outfitted with a brass-lined elevator shaft that whisked dignitaries up a sheer mountain face to the six-thousand-foot summit where the enclave was perched. There, sun terraces framed with enormous arches overlooked stunning vistas. A circular great hall was laid with exquisite rugs. Tapestries hung above a burgundy-colored Italian marble fireplace—supposedly a gift from Mussolini. And there was a large reception room that hosted special events like the wedding of Gretl Braun, the sister of Hitler's companion, Eva. The führer and thirty-three-year-old Eva, meanwhile, after being newlyweds for just forty hours, committed suicide on April 30—she with a cyanide capsule, he with a bullet to the head.

Henry Bodson and others in the 3rd Division scaled on foot the steep summit road of the Eagle's Nest, cursing out the gilded elevator that had ceased functioning. The troops ventured off-road and around obstacles on the rocky climb, panting in the thin mountain air, the sweat pouring down many an earnest young face. From a distance the troops appeared like ants frenetically swarming up a hill—till their winding paths converged at the shrine of the devil.

Bodson entered the Eagle's Nest and scanned its surroundings.

I expected more . . . grandeur, maybe gold . . . but it's pretty austere.

Everything of value had been stripped long before, leaving the Eagle's Nest resembling little more than a typical mountain chalet with simple country furnishings. Still, plenty remained for American troops to nab as proof of their conquest, whether the corner of a leather chair, a scrap of a loveseat, or a fork that Hitler might have used to stab a filet mignon. Souvenirs came in all shapes and sizes as pocketknives sliced and diced. Flatware was tucked into pockets, dishes into backpacks. Anything movable was "liberated" in the name of Allied Forces.

Henry Bodson was a little late to the free-for-all, but in the pantry, he spotted linen hand and dishtowels.

So much for clinching the grand prize, he thought, *but it's something*.

He held up the fine linens, noting the cream-colored herringbone stripes embroidered with "Der Platterhof," a choice hotel turned military retreat that had serviced the Eagle's Nest. Bodson tucked the linens into his backpack.

Someday these towels will have a story to tell for my children and grandchildren about the 3rd Division capturing the Eagle's Nest.

It was perhaps fitting that, in the end, that victory was left for the 3rd Infantry Division, the only Allied division to have fought Germany on all fronts—beginning in North Africa, from Casablanca on to Tunisia, then proceeding into Sicily. The division then breached the Anzio beachhead before invading southern France and marching on to the Nazi homeland. And the war wasn't over. Austria lay ahead. All told, the division would have 531 consecutive days in combat along a twisted path so treacherous that its losses would tally up higher than any other U.S. division in the war: 4,922 killed in action; plus the wounded, many of whom would later die from their injuries; plus troops captured, interned, and missing. Collectively, it amounted to nearly 26,000 soldier "casualties" by Army definition.[1]

The 3rd Infantry Division dearly knew the cost of freedom, of fellow soldiers giving their lives for one another, and they knew the dire duty of digging makeshift graves. Yes, airborne divisions had leapt into glory in a war increasingly fought in the skies, but ultimately boots on the ground paid the dearest price. The Eagle's Nest belonged to the 3rd Infantry Division.

While the 3rd Division claimed its just due, farther north the 87th Division, with Jack Murray, sped across Germany. After breaching the Rhine, the division clocked a brisk eight to ten miles a day. Traversing the country, it soon reached the Czech border and entered the bombed-out city of Plauen. There, the division was halted for several weeks as its troops waited on the lagging Russians so that the spoils of war, in terms of occupation, could be divvied up.

Before that occurred, on May 7, General Culin informed three of his officers, including Murray, that the Germans agreed to surrender. It was to be the end of the war in Europe, a war that had taken an unimaginable toll on soldiers, on civilians, on the fabric of European life. Once grand cities now lay smoldering; swaths of countryside were barren wastelands; small villages—the soul of Europe—remained hauntingly quiet. Murray was told, however, that the following morning the Axis and Allies were to stop shooting. The curtain on the European Theater was to drop, and Murray was assigned to help notify Allied units that it was finished.

"I'm giving it to you orally," explained General Culin. "We are not going to have anything in writing."

Jack Murray was dispatched to carry the momentous news to the regimental headquarters of the 347th Infantry, positioned about fifteen miles away, over the mountains marking the dividing line between Germany and Czechoslovakia. Traveling along, his jeep reached a wooded area along a mountain pass. A scant twenty-five yards ahead, he saw three Germans venturing across the road carrying machine guns; the soldiers didn't appear to be hunting rabbits.

Murray's driver quickly jerked the jeep back around a bend to get the two out of sight. Jumping out, the two hid in a ditch, waiting motionless—their only movement, shallow breathing. All they had between them was a pistol and two carbines. Not a heady arsenal. Murray could hear the rustling of the Germans not far away.

What are they doing? Probably trying to figure out what we're doing. Could they be an advance party for an entire division?

He and the driver lay in wait. Five minutes. Ten minutes.

Now this is ironic, thought Murray. *The war is over. I know it's over. But my driver doesn't even know it's over. Do these Germans know it's over?*

Murray contemplated his options. *What am I supposed to do? Go up and say, "Look fellows, the war is over?"* Someone, thought Murray, is going to be the last man killed in World Word II. *I'd rather it not be me.*

After about twenty minutes the rustling faded, and Murray and his driver grabbed their chance and sprinted back to the jeep, hoping this German patrol was an anomaly. Hitting the gas, the two made it safely to the 347th Infantry. There, Jack Murray delivered the astounding news to American troops: World War II in Europe was to end just past daybreak. The final bows had been taken. Enemy troops would surrender.

It turned out, however, that the Germans wanted to surrender to someone important, a name they'd heard, like someone in Patton's army. No Lucky 6 was in sight, so Murray took charge. He ordered a young American officer, fluent in German, to reach out to a German commanding general, using the Czech phone lines. Murray, through his interpreter, got the general to agree to surrender his troops; the West Pointer, the Germans discovered, was as good as they were going to get.

Jack Murray soon crossed behind enemy lines, rumbling along in his jeep with a white flag flying from it, denoting that hostilities had ended. He passed rows of curious enemy troops, who appeared welcoming but remained fully armed. Their guns were at their sides, waiting . . . watching . . . for that moment in time when their saga in history would end. Like when the last page of an epic novel is turned to disclose a blank page, a page that speaks of finality and, for some, endings of discontent.

Earlier, Murray had spotted in the area a long swath of a plain that stretched on for about five miles. He ordered the Germans to march to that plain and line up. There, the West Pointer from the class of '41, who just four years earlier had hurled his cap in the air to celebrate his commission as a new Army officer, now accepted the surrender of forty thousand Germans—in the largest conflict in history.

Once the official surrender was complete, the Germans began returning up the road from whence they'd come. Overjoyed local residents streamed out of their homes, offering the soldiers drinks, breaking into song, and pinning lilacs on soldiers' uniforms—flowers picked from the blooming fields where hope springs eternal. Murray sat in his jeep, taking in the spectacle.

I wish I had a camera, he thought in disbelief. *I'm the chief honcho of forty thousand German prisoners, including about forty generals.*

One of those generals wore four stars, General Kruger. He swiftly advised Murray that he had a cousin in the U.S. Army, as though six degrees of separation might protect him from future war crime tribunals. Murray was hardly moved. He and his officers had the Germans dump all their weapons into huge piles and then, in a fitting move, used German tanks to flatten the piles into metal pancakes—German armor destroying a German arsenal.

They look ready to cry, Murray thought as he scanned the German troops.

For several weeks, Murray remained in command of those troops until word came down that they were to be discharged. The German soldiers would be permitted to return to their farms, to sow crops, to breathe life back into the fields of war. Orders came from Eisenhower's headquarters that upon discharge every German officer was to receive twenty marks and every soldier ten, so the enemy's military payroll ledgers could be closed out; the bean counters wanted the beans accounted for, even when ending a war.

"Where do the marks come from?" asked Murray.

The answer from command central: "That's your problem."

Murray turned to one of his prisoners for counsel, asking the finance officer, "How do you pay your troops?"

Replied the major matter-of-factly, "We go down to the nearest bank and we draw the money."

Murray enlisted the man's services, and the two were soon at a bank. That the bank remained standing amid the rubble was fortuitous—both for the Germans needing pay and Murray who needed to pay them. Murray signed for a few million marks, thinking in the back of his head: *Somehow or other, this isn't going to cost me anything.*

In all likelihood, his million marks' heist was taking from those who had robbed to pay off others who had *been* robbed. His banking scheme became a model for other American units. Jack Murray received a Legion of Merit for his ingenuity.

It would be many years later—and many law courses later—when Jack Murray awoke with pangs of guilt in the middle of the night, wondering, *Oh my God, how did I happen to do that?* But at the time, aside from the clear victory of the Allies in Europe, there was little about ending a war that was black and white. Most was gray, as gray as the last of the smoldering rubble.

★ ★ ★

As Murray grappled with finance, other officers from West Point '41 raised glasses in celebration of Victory-Europe Day, "V-E Day." Henry Bodson sipped champagne confiscated from Hitler's chalet together with Audie Murphy, who was by now the most decorated soldier of World War II.

Jack Norton, with the 82nd Airborne, was celebrating with General Gavin near Berlin. Like Herb Stern, after battling in the Bulge, his division had been ordered to the Elbe River. From there, that division attacked across the river, reaching Mecklenburg, where General Gavin usurped a castle belonging to the crown prince of the town. In the ancient structure, he set up a division command post. He also accepted the surrender of 150,000 Germans who preferred to bow to the 82nd rather than face the wrath of the oncoming Russians.

The Russians arrived at Mecklenburg in due time, and Norton was among the 82nd officers receiving the corps commander. That happened to be General Smirnoff, the same name as that behind the vodka dynasty. Smirnoff was duly impressed by the 82nd Airborne's majestic take on an army command post. In turn, the Russian commander decided to host a V-E celebration party for 82nd officers in the ornate building he'd chosen for headquarters.

The Americans, well aware of the Russian reputation for drinking—let alone a host named Smirnoff—prepared themselves. Among the twenty or so 82nd Division headquarters' officers, word spread: "Drink a quart of milk before you go!" Jack Norton obliged, wondering what was in store.

It became immediately clear upon his arrival to Smirnoff's headquarters, at about 8 p.m., that it was to be no brief cocktail reception. Thought Norton: *This is a party set up for the rest of the night.*

The Russians were in it for the long haul, but damned if Norton and other All-Americans weren't determined to keep up. First, however, there was an "entrance fee," that is, the requirement that each U.S. officer drink an ice tea–size glass full of vodka before admittance. Once within, they were treated to only small morsels of food. It was hardly enough to blanket their stomachs, and most were thankful for downing milk aperitifs prior to arriving.

Two kinds of vodka were offered, one clear—undoubtedly Smirnoff—the other a heavy amber-colored vodka, described as a hunting vodka. Whatever the type, all Norton knew was that the Russians wanted their allies to get "floppy." Far be it for the All-Americans to disappoint. The 82nd officers, however, quickly caught on to Russian maneuvering off field: they had an A team and a B team. When the Russian A team got soused, it left the party rooms to sober up in the showers, while the B team came in as a replacement. Jack Norton had no replacements but carried on like a trooper in the drink fest. Before long he and others in the crowd were breaking into laughter and song, belting out a boisterous rendition of the "Song of the Volga Boatman," accompanied by some rousing accordion playing.

"*Ey, ukhnem! Ey, ukhnem!*" came the sounds of the words in deep baritone. "*Yeshcho razik, yeshcho da raz. Ey, ukhnem. Ey, ukhnem.*"

The English translation: "Yo, heave ho! Yo, heave ho! Once more, once again, still once more more." The song's words were more than fitting for the party at hand. Norton soon whipped out his harmonica to add in some red-white-and-blue nostalgia.

The officers, meanwhile, were oblivious to the fact that across the street, up on the roof of another building, their military drivers—Russian and American alike—were stationed with binoculars. There they sat with an oversized slate board, tallying up the officers too drunk to leave the party of their own accord. Each time a Russian officer was carried out, a big X was marked on the slate; likewise for the Americans.

As the drivers were guffawing, inside the party Jack Norton looked on perplexed at an old-fashioned washtub brought into the party room.

There's water in the tub . . . and little white herring. They seem to be lying on their sides. I think one of them is winking at me.

Food had finally arrived. It was pickled herring. Added to that was a live white goose making an entrance toward midnight, one so big that its beak seemed swallowed within the endless folds of its neck.

"If you see this goose again," announced a Russian officer, "You'll know that you survived the party!"

It reappeared to Jack Norton, cooked and ready to be devoured an hour or so later. Not only had he survived the Russian offensive, but General Gavin and he were among the last officers standing. The next day, however, the fine officers of the 82nd Airborne were undoubtedly questioning, "At what cost victory?"

While V-E celebrations abounded in Europe, the mood was more somber from Charles Canella's point of view. Canella had been relegated stateside for most of the war, much to his chagrin. He was still yearning for combat—and the promotions that only it could bring—and his younger brother, a West Point "starman," had been killed over France in the D-Day invasion.

The loss was devastating enough, made worse still by Charles Canella's realization of his father's next likely action:

He's heartbroken, and he'll probably pull the sole survivor son act. I knew he knows about it . . . the act. I got hell from him for choosing infantry, and I got hell from him for being a paratrooper. Now, with Keith gone, he'll want to keep me out.

Technically, such an act had not been officially passed in Congress, but as an Army veteran, the senior Canella knew he could put in to protect his sole surviving son from being called into combat, given that he had already given up his only other son. The War Department had received far too much poor publicity over brothers perishing together in tragic war incidents. Charles Sr. had a right to claim that his family had given enough.

Still, the junior Canella kept requesting combat, and in the end his father did not stand in his way. So now Charles Canella found himself along the roads nearing Pilsen, having fought his way across a good part of Czechoslovakia to get to that point.

"Canella," an officer shouted to him. "If you're gonna make yourself a hero, look down the road. There are thousands of Germans ready to surrender to you."

Canella looked, then halted, stunned at the apparition.

They're not Germans. They're Russian POWs . . . walking skeletons.

To Canella, it was a haunting scene. *They're human shields to clog the roads; the Germans released them to stop us. . . . But I have no facilities to handle them, no rations.*

The sea of victims grew worse still. He encountered hundreds of desperate Czech refugees trying to flee west, trying to evade the advancing Russians, whom they abhorred. The Czechs feared their fates, and Canella didn't blame them. He heard the shrill of the refugees, wailing men, women, and children begging, "Don't leave us to the Russkies!"

Canella was ordered to turn them back, to erect blockades to retain the refugees in Russian domain. He was to stop them cold in an order that shook him to the core—an order he considered disobeying. The refugees, he knew, might be headed back to a living hell.

Who, he wondered, *could have dispensed such an order? How heartless can they be?*

It was not the type of "combat" that Charles Canella had so long craved. But if he disobeyed orders, he'd face a court martial and chances were, the end of his career. So Charles Canella did as was commanded.

It was under those circumstances, in his small corner of Czechoslovakia, that Canella got wind of Allied victory. It was bittersweet, like James Forsyth's long march to freedom, and Charles Canella would forever live with the haunting memory of that refugee blockade.

But for the moment, time marched on. Canella got orders to take the city of Pilsen. It was dark and his men were near exhaustion when the orders came down, so he decided to first proceed into the city with a task force of about forty troops to scout out the situation. Reaching Pilsen's outskirts, he had trouble detecting a radio signal amid the tall buildings.

"Wait here," he ordered his assistant. "You keep charge, while I run up into this building to try to get a signal."

He returned not long after to a scene of stillness. His unit's tank sat in the square—empty. He scanned the streets for movement. No sign of life. Charles Canella did not see anyone in his task force that day, or the next, or the next. It was as though his men had disappeared into thin air. He found no answers as to their whereabouts.

★ ★ ★

While Charles Canella was grappling with the silence, it was a boisterous scene for James Forsyth upon his release. He was sent to campgrounds in the vicinity of Le Havre in preparation for a return to the States. There, tens of thousands of men were within a tented camp, which was divided into four sections. When transport ships arrived to ferry troops home from the first section, then the number four section got moved to three position, three to two, and two to one, with the cycle repeating as troops were rotated home.

During the wait, soldiers initially had some leeway to travel about. Far too many, however, went AWOL in "*gai*" Paris, presumably succumbing to women and wine. By the time Forsyth arrived at Le Havre, the lax latitude had stiffened, but he cared little. His thoughts were on Ruth, on weaving his hands through her dark wavy locks and smothering her with kisses— one to make up for each day he'd been gone.

He had to bide his time, however, while the sweltering days of summer wore on. Finally, in mid-June, the newly christened Coast Guard ship, *Admiral H. T. Mayo*, pulled into Le Havre. It had Forsyth's name written on it; he and more than 5,800 other freed POWs and soldiers headed for home.

The enlisted soldiers were the first to board the *Mayo*, followed the next day by POWs. Forsyth had a few dozen of the latter under his control, but in the boarding crush, his group was dispersed aboard the 608-foot ship. It was as though the men had gone into hiding and sure enough, it quickly became apparent that among the war-weary troops, no one wanted to work, let alone show up for kitchen duty. There were blank looks among soldiers in the mess hall when the ship sailed, and they discovered that meals were not forthcoming; it seemed like getting a job in the Great Depression was easier than getting grub aboard the *H. T. Mayo*.

Forsyth, who'd taken an officer's berth, bandied about the issue with one of his cabinmates, the chief boatswain mate on the *H. T. Mayo*. He was a handsome, strapping man that Forsyth might have instantly recognized under different circumstances, but after months in a prison camp Forsyth hardly expected to encounter a Hollywood movie star on a POW ship.

The chief boatswain introduced himself. "Victor Mature," he said, holding out a hand.

Forsyth did a double take as he shook the hand. "The Hollywood actor?" he asked.

"I'm not much of an actor," replied the self-deprecating Mature. "But yes, that's me."

Mature explained to Forsyth that when he tried to enlist in the Navy early in the war, he'd been turned down due to color blindness, but he'd found a home in the Coast Guard. In truth, the thirty-two-year-old with smoldering dark looks was better known as the "beautiful hunk-of-a-man" in Hollywood, having appeared in films such as *My Gal Sal* with Rita Hayworth, *Song of the Islands* with Betty Grable, and *The Shanghai Gesture* with Gene Tierney. After he'd joined the Coast Guard, he'd worked his way up through the ranks while good-naturedly being relabeled by his cohorts as the "hunk of junk."

While Mature was more used to bunking down with starlets than sharing quarters with former POWs, in Forsyth he found another officer hellbent on restoring order to the ship. The two decided to team up to corral kitchen police.

"We need about 20 men," said Forsyth. "How about I take starboard and round up 10? You take port."

"Am I looking for a certain rank?" asked Mature.

"Round up some privates if you see them, but if you can't find any then grab the first 10 men you see and put them to work."

And so began their daily teamwork to keep 5,819 passengers fed as the ship churned across the Atlantic, heading toward Boston. Aside from complaining over KP—kitchen patrol—and a few random fistfights, it was smooth sailing. The weather was fair and many former POWs, having been relegated to dim cells for so long, slept on deck, basking in their newfound freedom and relishing views of the starry constellations.

The *H. T. Mayo* pulled into Boston harbor June 21, 1945, and James Forsyth set foot on American soil again, a thin man, a weary man, but a free man. He was just in time to celebrate his fourth wedding anniversary. James Forsyth was soon on a train headed for Kansas to be reunited with his wife.

It was there that he heard about the letter from his classmate Bill Gillis, sent to Ruth:

> Somewhere in France, September 26, 1944
> My dear Ruth,
> By lucky coincidence your letter arrived the same day that I received definite information that Jim has been captured unhurt, and is not killed. I'll tell you as much of the details as censorship will allow because I know how much you love him, and you know how much you both mean to me.

According to the best information I can get from several sources, Jim was captured by a German ambush patrol, behind our lines. . . . This information came to me from the platoon leader of the man who was captured with Jim and escaped some days later. He said he had seen Jim and that he was all right and in the hands of the Germans.

I know how much you have worried, Ruth, God bless you, and I'm so very thankful that I can report this much optimistic news as being a certainty according to eye witnesses. From all accounts we have had from men who have been captured and have escaped or have written back to their outfits, the Germans abide strictly by the Geneva Conference rulings on handling of prisoners, and in no cases have been known to physically mistreat prisoners. . . . That's why I have faith, Ruth, that Jim is okay and will be coming home to you with the rest of us when this war business is finished. . . .

Sincerely,

Billy

It was upon Forsyth's warm welcome home that he discovered that Bill Gillis would have no similar homecoming. Gillis was killed in France five days after he wrote the letter to Ruth—words of hope and optimism laid to waste in war.

By now, the West Point class of '41 had lost more than 10 percent of its ranks to World War II. Victory, indeed, had come at a steep price to the class of 1941.

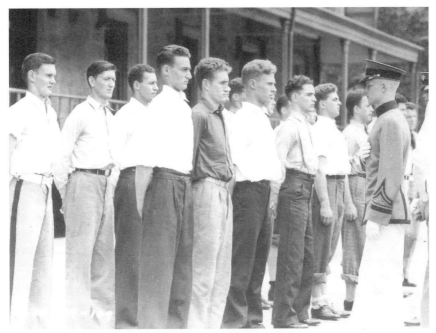

Plebes' first day. *Top left*: Robert Pierpont, Ed Rowny, and Irv Perkin; *front left*: Vincent Carlson and George Stillson. Courtesy of the Greenes.

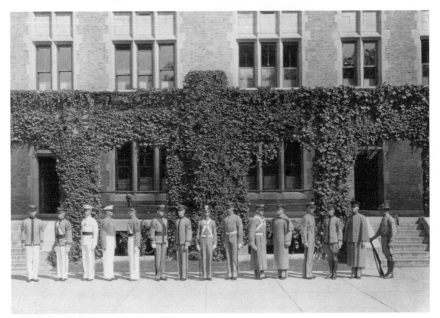

A uniform review demonstrates the plethora of cadet uniforms to new cadets. Courtesy of the Fletchers.

Nicknamed "Diamond Jim," James Forsyth played football, ran track, and was said to collect female hearts. He twice escaped the Germans in World War II only to be recaptured. Courtesy of the Forsyths.

West Point ski team and captain, Paul Skowronek (*right*), 1941. Skowronek helped clear academy slopes to make a ski run and outfitted a Chevy engine to power a towline. Courtesy of Paul Skowronek.

As a cadet, Herb Stern despised horses and did everything possible to avoid cavalry, instead becoming an ace artilleryman. Courtesy of Herb Stern.

Like so many '41ers, Charles Canella said his "I do's" before being shipped off to war. Charles and Evelyn Canella wed at Camp Walters, Texas, on February 27, 1943. Courtesy of the Canellas.

Alexander "Sandy" Nininger was posthumously awarded the first Medal of Honor in World War II for heroics that cost him his life in the Battle of Bataan on January 12, 1942. Courtesy of John Patterson.

Jack Norton, with the 82nd All-American Airborne Division, is presented the Legion of Merit by his mentor, Commanding General "Jumpin' Jim" Gavin (USMA '29), for exemplary service during World War II. Norton was among the first to jump into Normandy on D-Day. Courtesy of the Nortons.

Following World War II, Walter Woolwine was key in shaping the vision for the Normandy American Cemetery and Memorial, overlooking Omaha Beach, to honor those lost in the Normandy invasion. Courtesy of American Battle Monuments Commission.

Henry Bodson (*forefront*) commands a Corporal missile test, the Army's first surface-to-surface tactical missile, at White Sands Proving Grounds, New Mexico, 1953. Courtesy of Henry Bodson.

Jack Murray, photographed teaching at the Army's Infantry School, went on to recognition as a JAG officer representing the U.S. Army in the McCarthy hearings. Courtesy of the Murrays.

Oversees assignments for Jim Forsyth included serving in Heidelberg (*pictured*), Korea, Japan, and Turkey and advising the Jordanian army at the request of King Hussein. Courtesy of the Forsyths.

Ed Rowny (*left*) planning the Inchon Invasion into Korea in 1950, which included grappling with thirty-two-foot tides and typhoon season. Courtesy of Ed Rowny.

As the enemy advanced, Ed Rowny oversaw the destruction of Port Hungnam in Korea on Christmas Eve, 1950, then helped rescue a hundred thousand fleeing civilians by putting them on evacuating U.S. ships. Courtesy of Ed Rowny.

Leslie "Ace" Bailey, commanding officer, 2nd Battalion of the 25th Infantry Regiment in Korea, 1951–52. Courtesy of the Baileys.

George Johnson (*center*), military attaché to the U.S. Embassy in Cairo, presides over a lunch honoring Egyptian military attaché Colonel Ghaleb (*left*). The '41ers influenced the geopolitical balance of power around the world. Courtesy of the Johnsons.

Jerry La Rocca (*second from left*) commemorates the completion of a U.S. Air Force satellite rocket testing facility at Arnold Engineering Development Center, Tennessee, together with General Bernard Schriever (*left*). Courtesy of Jerry La Rocca.

(*above left*) Henry Bodson, at Martin-Marietta in 1959, served as technical adviser for the U.S. Army's orientation film on the Pershing surface-to-surface missile. Courtesy of Henry Bodson.

(*above right*) In the early '60s Edwin "Spec" Powell wrote an Army memorandum calling for "bold new approaches to mobility," which helped lead to combat helicopters and air cavalry divisions. Courtesy of the Powells.

(*left*) Ed Rowny testing out armed helicopter concepts in Vietnam, 1963. Courtesy of Ed Rowny.

Herb Stern at Fort Carson, Colorado, in 1962. He trained six thousand soldiers in the snow, only to be told they were being deployed to the tropics of Southeast Asia. Courtesy of Herb Stern.

Paul Skowronek, chief of the U.S. Military Liaison Mission in the Soviet Zone, salutes (*on left*) a flag that was the only American flag to fly in Communist East Germany. It previously flew over the U.S. capital. Courtesy of Paul Skowronek.

Paul and Virginia Skowronek hosted lavish parties at the U.S. mission at Potsdam House, inviting Soviet officials to maintain a rapport with the enemy during the Cold War. Courtesy of Paul Skowronek.

Jerry La Rocca is promoted to colonel by Col. Bud Sands at Cape Canaveral Missile Center, while his wife, Elaine, attends to the pins. Courtesy of Jerry La Rocca.

Peer de Silva Jr. sits on a hospital bed at Clark Field in the Philippines after his father, Peer de Silva Sr., CIA station chief in Saigon, was wounded in the bombing of the Saigon headquarters in March 1965. Courtesy of Peer de Silva Jr.

Charlie Fletcher, commander of I Corps artillery in South Korea, put his unit on red alert when North Korean commandos infiltrated the South trying to assassinate its president. Courtesy of the Fletchers.

Wilson "Joe" Reed (*right*), commanding general of the U.S. Army Computer Systems Command, helped usher in the computer age. Pictured with General William DePuy, Army assistant vice chief of staff. Courtesy of the Reeds.

Jack Norton (*in helmet*), commanding general of the 1st Cavalry Division (Airmobile), shows off captured enemy weapons in 1966 to South Vietnamese Prime Minister Nguyen Cao Ky, General Stanley Larsen (USMA '39), and General John Heintges (USMA '36), deputy commander, Military Assistance Command, Vietnam. Courtesy of the Nortons.

Air Force General George Brown (*right*) went on to become Chairman of the Joint Chiefs of Staff. Pictured with General Creighton Abrams (USMA '36). Courtesy of Walter Woolwine.

U.S. logistics command in Vietnam is handed over to General Walter Woolwine (two stars) in ceremony with General William Rosson (four stars) in 1969. Courtesy of Walter Woolwine.

Walter Woolwine's challenging logistics: a CH 46B Chinook heavy-lift helicopter delivers a 155mm cannon with a double package of ammo below. Possibly Hill 847 NNE of Khe Sanh. Courtesy of Walter Woolwine.

'41ers in Vietnam, *left to right*: Walter Woolwine, Roy Atteberry, Jack Norton, Mike Greene, Harry Besancon, Robert Tarbox, Larry Greene, and Hugh Foster. Courtesy of the Greenes.

President Ronald Reagan and Ed Rowny in 1982. Rowny was chief U.S. negotiator for nuclear disarmament with the Soviets and one of the chief architects of the U.S. policy of "peace through strength." Courtesy of Ed Rowny.

For years '41 classmates had a "supper club" in the DC area and rotated it among their homes. *Top left to right*: Herb and Rose Stern, Johnnie Fletcher, Mike Greene, Charlie Fletcher, and Eileen Greene; *bottom left to right*: Maureen and Joe Reed and Marka and Burnside Huffman. Courtesy of the Greenes.

Henry Bodson displays his bounty from Hitler's Eagle's Nest, which the 3rd Infantry Division captured in May 1945. Courtesy of Anne Kazel-Wilcox.

The imposing statue of Emperor Wilhelm, which Charlie Fletcher destroyed in World War II, was reconstructed after Germany was reunified in the early '90s. Courtesy of Anne Kazel-Wilcox.

BOMBS AWAY

V-E Day was behind the officers, but not necessarily combat. Many '41 officers, such as Joe Reed, were put on notice to be ready for yet another deployment—to Okinawa—as the war still raged with Japan. Before shipping out, and thinking, *use it or lose it,* Reed set up an artillery range in the fields of Germany to fire off ammunition still on hand. A local burgermeister, similar to an American mayor, protested that the war was over.

"That's true here, but not over there," Reed responded.

But the complaints continued.

Then Reed got to the root of the problem. Nearby was a so-called mother-home, or *Lebensborn,* where women had been impregnated to do their part in producing a superior Aryan race.

"You scared everyone," the burgermeister explained to Reed, "and in one day, we had twenty-seven births."

Not one to get in the way of a woman's business, Joe Reed moved on.

Bodson also moved on. While the 3rd Infantry Division remained in Austria and enjoyed a massive victory parade near Salzburg, Bodson was relishing a brief respite on the French Riviera. He strolled along the ocean promenade in Cannes, reflecting on his surroundings compared to the Riviera he'd observed nine months earlier. Then, smoke from artillery hung over the beaches in dusty gray clouds, and infantry boots beat the streets. Bodson could still hear the ringing in his ears from gunfire like it was yesterday. Now, the scene was one of tranquil, tropical splendor with palm trees swaying in the summer breeze and pretty ladies prancing down the street in oversized sunglasses that hid laughing eyes. It was night and day between war and peace.

Rambling along, Bodson nearly collided with Audie Murphy. An unexpected happenstance, and for both, a welcome reunion. Murphy, like Bodson, was on a short leave for R & R. The two began walking together and chatting carelessly, reminiscing about the 3rd Infantry, about people they knew in common from their months serving at 15th Infantry Regiment headquarters. When the pair tired of walking, Murphy invited Bodson to his hotel for a drink. There, the conversation took a more personal turn toward Audie's past—and his dreams for the future.

Audie shared with Bodson his upbringing: one of twelve children, the son of poor sharecroppers, from a small town in Texas. He spoke with candor of how he and his older siblings struggled, prompting Audie to cut short his education to help support the family. His honesty impressed Bodson.

There's not a phony bone in his body, he thought.

Talk turned to the future. Senior officers of the division had suggested that Audie consider attending West Point to pursue an Army career. "What do you think, Henry?"

"Well, there are no real military requirements or qualifications to attend the academy," answered Bodson. "But certainly, your reputation would be well known, and it would be honored there." Bodson hesitated. "You're what, twenty years old now?"

"Going to be twenty-one in June."

Bodson nodded. "You know, there's an age limit for entering West Point."

"No, I didn't know that."

"You have to enter by your twenty-second birthday, so that's a consideration."

"Okay, so I have a little time."

"Not much," added Bodson. He continued, "Physically, well, you're short and wiry like me, but you'd meet the height requirement. But there's a bunch of other physical standards you have to meet."

"I'm missing a piece of my ass from mortar shells," kidded Audie. "Will that make a difference?"

Bodson laughed. "Even though you've been wounded a few times, I'm sure you'd pass muster; I don't recall a full ass being a requirement. It's mostly medical tests for eyes, ears, throat, heart rate, etc. And with a little training, you'd probably meet the other physical requirements as well."

Audie looked hopeful.

"But there's two other things, Audie. They like to see some type of record of leadership. Were you ever a Boy Scout, a group leader, captain of a sports team, or maybe did some type of community work?

Audie shook his head in the negative.

"I'm sure that would be alright," said Bodson, dismissing his own question. "You'd probably qualify because you became a noncommissioned officer; you received a battlefield commission; and of course, you were a 2nd lieutenant in command of an infantry company when you earned your

Medal of Honor. So your military record should fulfill that leadership requirement. But then there's the academic qualifications."

Bodson explained the entrance exams, parts of which were waived if a
candidate had a good track record in college or high school. Otherwise full
testing was required—and it was tough.

"You know, the academy's curriculum includes a lot of engineering and
is heavy in math, physics, and chemistry, as well as other engineering-
related subjects," explained Bodson. "Graduation bestows a bachelor of
science degree."

Audie's face grew a little long with this revelation.

"You'd probably need more schooling before you could get into the
academy," Bodson suggested. "But there's plenty of academy-oriented prep
schools across the country, and as a matter of fact, I attended one for several
months to help me get into West Point. So I'd plan on some time for that."

"But that'll make me close to twenty-two."

"Unless they waive that age requirement for you."

"I didn't know there was so much involved to getting in."

"You certainly have a quick mind, Audie, and an instinctual physical
swiftness."

Bodson tried to sound encouraging while also thinking, *That Texas mean
streak in you probably helped you survive in battle when others didn't. Beast
Barracks would have nothing on you.*

However, he got the distinct impression that Audie was disappointed in
the conversation.

He's groping for a career, reflected Bodson. *The war's over and now he's
trying to figure out what it all means . . . what to do next.*

Little did Henry Bodson know but Audie Murphy had only a fifth-grade
education, and his talk with the young man likely dashed all hopes of Audie
pursuing West Point.

After taking his leave, Henry Bodson contemplated the young man's
prospects and the skills he'd need at increasing levels of command should
he stay in the Army and broaden his formal education. What might his future hold?

*He'd be a good leader at the platoon and company level and maybe as high
as a battalion. And there's no doubt he'd be superior in training and operations in the field, just short of combat. But what about administrative duties?
There's always that burden of command. . . . Well, I guess he'd probably handle
that okay. He'd also need advance training in infantry or in a specialty. Probably okay on that as well.*

Bodson reflected on subsequent stages of advancement when command assignments become few and far between and staff assignments more often prevail.

What if he gets a staff assignment at the brigade, division, or corps level? He'd have to deal with broad operational issues, training programs, and combined or joint field operations. He'd have to deal with complex logistics issues and a lot more administrative duties.

Bodson hesitated. *I have some doubts.*

And what about senior assignments that demand high mental projections? Could he do the future-concept work? Could he make it through the advanced schooling for senior echelons—command and general staff school? Could Audie, with his education, handle that?

Again, Bodson had doubts. But he wouldn't rule out Audie Murphy.

Perhaps with more schooling and maturity, it's all possible.

At about the same time that Henry Bodson had his chance encounter with Audie Murphy, Charles Canella had one of his own in France. He was on a Paris stopover, before his deployment to Japan, when much to his surprise he ran into an armored lieutenant who had been among the soldiers who had vanished in Pilsen.

"Captain," explained the officer, "no sooner had you left than the Germans ran in and captured us all."

Again, it was that randomness of war that dictated one soldier's fate versus another's, but a randomness that West Point '41ers learned to take for granted.

★ ★ ★

Respites, for those '41ers that got them, were fleeting. Many officers immediately took on occupation duties in Germany. New regional governments had to be established, each with a myriad of directives ranging from rationing and economic development to establishing U.S. military facilities, war tribunals, and more.

The southern German region under Herb Stern's domain was once rich with wartime manufacturing, including tanks and vehicle factories, along with industry giants like Messerschmitt, which supplied much of the Nazi fighter-jet strength. Most of these companies had relied to a large degree on forced labor, primarily Polish workers, whose living conditions had been a bare step above concentration camps. With production halted, these laborers languished in "displaced persons camps." What little they had before was diminished even more so. Stern's challenge was to return as many occupants as possible to their countries of origin.

An anti-Axis coalition of more than forty countries, called the United

Nations Relief and Rehabilitation Agency (UNRRA), was providing emergency aid for this purpose, and Stern began administering a portion. A few times a week he arranged for buses to transport five hundred to six hundred displaced persons at a time to the train depot in Augsburg. They were mostly of Polish origin. Each was given a care package with enough food to sustain them on their journey—and for several weeks afterward. One day, however, Herb Stern noticed a face among the refugees; he didn't know why, but the face stuck out in his memory.

"We gave that guy a food package two weeks ago," Stern complained to one of his men. "Find out what's going on."

The man, admittedly, had hawked his food in Poland and returned for more; the camps were apparently filled with opportunists. Not that Stern necessarily blamed anyone, but there was only so much aid to go around, so his policing tasks grew by the day.

"Traffic cop" became yet another job on the growing list, as the autobahn by Augsburg often became an asphalt puzzle with accidents on the rise. To curb the incidents, Stern installed a speeding trap. Trying to think of everything, adjacent to the spot he converted a trailer into a summary court to try U.S. offenders on the spot. Soon after, the radar alert went off. Army officers nabbed their first violator. Who was more surprised, they weren't sure, the arresting officers or the speed demon—Herb Stern. Insisted Stern, "I was just testing the system!"

His officers, however, under strict orders to report all offenders, wrote up a citation. It was delivered to Stern through proper channels, at which point Stern ceremoniously tore the citation to shreds—but not before getting a good laugh at his best-laid plans for law and order in Bavaria.

For Stern, however, with occupation duty also came disquieting moments. Previously throughout the war, despite being Jewish, he had little emotion to expend on the atrocities against Jewish people occurring around him. Stern was fighting a war, doing his job, battling the Nazi enemy. He had to keep moving forward.

But during occupation duties, in the bitter cold winter of 1946–47, his emotions stood still for a moment. Stern's family had joined him oversees in Germany and, like many American military families, was living in a home usurped from members of the Nazi Party. One day Stern heard a knock on the door. On the steps stood an elderly couple in their seventies, maybe eighties. They introduced themselves.

"We are the Sommerlotts who owned this home," humbly explained the man. "All of our winter things are up in the attic. We ask if you might kindly permit us to go up there to collect some belongings to keep us warm?"

Herb Stern looked at the pair. They appeared cold and despondent. Obviously, it had taken incredible humility and despair to bring this couple back to the house from which they'd been forced. Stern knew the man had been only a low-level party member. Still, it raced though his mind what party members had done.

I have no sympathy.

Then he thought, *I can't turn them away. . . . I cannot be vindictive.*

Stern was trying to be fair in this postwar occupation, no matter his persuasion, no matter theirs, and the man before him had not been convicted of any war crimes.

The arms of the pair were soon filled with as much as they could carry from the attic. As the couple was readying to leave the house, they handed Stern three delicate porcelain pieces. "In appreciation," they said. They were exquisite pieces from Meissen, one of the oldest and most esteemed porcelain makers in Europe, collected by the very affluent. Porcelain would do little for a former Nazi Party member in postwar Germany; all the husband wanted was warm clothes for him and his wife.

With the dignity of a West Pointer—and a man willing to rise above the maelstrom—Herb Stern accepted the peacetime gifts.

16

BATAAN A YARD AT A TIME

With the war winding down, the race was on to stave off further POW deaths. While the Germans were abandoning both their POW and concentration camps, there was grave concern among the Allies that in the Philippines, the Japanese might begin mass executions rather than leave prisoners to liberation.

A high command "kill-all" order issued from Tokyo read, "Whether they are destroyed individually or in groups, and whether it is accomplished by means of mass bombing, poisonous smoke, poisons, drowning, or decapitation, dispose of them as the situation dictates. It is the aim not to allow the escape of a single one, to annihilate them all, and not to leave any traces."[1]

In December this order had been carried out in a heinous manner on the Philippine island of Palawan, where Japanese prison guards mistook two U.S. fighter jets and a seagoing convoy as a potential POW rescue effort. The Japanese ordered their American prisoners into air-raid shelters, but the structures proved fiery deathtraps as the Japanese doused them with gasoline and torched them. They laughed and cheered at the screams of despair wailing within. Those prisoners that managed to escape, engulfed in flames, were bayoneted, clubbed to death, or gunned down.

The 6th Army Rangers vowed such incidents would not be repeated, or at least only over their dead bodies. A newly formed unit of commandos, they were modeled on Colonel William Darby's Rangers, a boldly successful Army colonel—West Point graduate of '33—whose rigorously trained men were, in Darby's words, "to get to the enemy first and leave last."[2]

Among the Rangers was Woody Garrett, the gregarious and gangly former West Point champion swimmer. Garrett had a track record for boldness—some said insanity. None doubted his courage or that of any Ranger. In the previous fall of 1944 Garrett was among Rangers that conducted an assault landing in the Philippines on A-Day–3, referring to "Attack Day."

The Rangers seized four small islands, obliterating search radar to clear the way for General MacArthur's main invasion fleet of more than two hundred thousand Allied troops and seven hundred ships, the Pacific's equivalent of the Normandy invasion. During the operation, Garrett's unit found a Japanese footlocker with a neatly folded American flag inside; it was the first flag of democracy to fly over the Philippines since the country had been taken, and it welcomed back MacArthur, who had been forced out three years prior.

MacArthur had sworn, "I came out of Bataan and I shall return," and the Rangers joined him to claim what belonged to America—its soldiers. The Rangers were planning to storm a prison camp north of Manila, near Cabanatuan, where more than five hundred survivors of the Bataan Death March remained, dying of neglect and brutality. For intelligence in planning the rescue operation, the Rangers relied on aerial surveillance and Alamo Scouts. The latter was yet another pioneering new unit, trained in the Pacific Theater and focused on reconnaissance and strategic and tactical intelligence, usually behind enemy lines. Scouts had to be in exceptional physical condition, have good eyesight, be superior swimmers and marksmen, and—given the extremely dangerous nature of their missions—have extraordinary courage. Garrett's fellow swim-team member from West Point '41, Gibson "Gib" Niles, was one such man, and he joined the mission that infiltrated enemy territory to determine the layout and reinforcing elements of the Cabanatuan camp.

The rescue mission was slated for January 29. Under cover of night, the Rangers soon trekked thirty miles to reach the outskirts of Cabanatuan, crawling the last mile on their bellies to remain undetected in the open field leading up to the camp. Together with the Scouts, they got into position, only seven hundred yards away from the camp.

Two Filipino guerilla groups had been dispatched in opposite directions to hold the main road that passed by the front of the camp, while the Rangers were split into two factions, one for the front gate and the other for the rear. As diversionary cover, an American night flyer, a P-61 Black Widow, flew over the camp as a decoy, cutting out its engine to resemble a plane in distress, which distracted the guards, as intended.

The teams were ready for the raid, which was built around the elements of surprise and confusion and expected to be a fait accompli in less than thirty minutes.

A single shot designated the attack launch and hell broke loose. Hand grenades were lobbed and firing began—carbines, rifles, and automatic weapons raining on the pillboxes of the camp, the guard towers, concrete shelters, and more. Every guard station was neutralized within thirty seconds of the first shot as the Rangers stormed the compound. They appeared like strange bandito apparitions to the stunned prisoners, what with their painted faces, belts of ammunition strapped across their chests, and hand grenades dangling from their belts like bells.

Within twelve minutes, resistance dwindled to a few scattered shots, and Woody Garrett and others began carrying the emaciated prisoners—many naked and too weak to walk—out of the camp, piggyback style or on makeshift stretchers made from sticking rifles through shirt sleeves. Over 500 prisoners, some who appeared on the verge of death, were freed, while more than 200 Japanese were killed. The mission was over within a half an hour. The cost to the Allies: 2 Rangers and more than 20 Filipino guerillas, all incredibly brave.

Meanwhile, hours earlier in a tandem operation, George Johnson waded ashore from a convoy ship on to the Bataan peninsula, about seventy-five miles south of Cabanatuan. He was part of the 38th Infantry Division, charged with securing the western shore of Manila Bay and sealing off the peninsula from the plains to the north. Sealing off the peninsula would deny the enemy freedom of movement on Bataan so that Manila might be recaptured. As a division study noted, he who controls Bataan controls Manila Bay.[3]

Johnson, an artillery battery commander, was anticipating heavy beachhead battling but was stunned to find no guns to greet him. Not even a shot, just a crowd of cheering Filipinos waving an American flag. The Japanese, evidently, had prepared for an American landing farther north, and as a result, in the area of Johnson's landing, had positioned defenses inland. And that's where the 38th ran into trouble.

There were no roads on the peninsula to speak of with the exception of Highway 7, a misnomer at best. The tortuous dirt road zigzagged like a corkscrew through mountainous jungle peaks that rose to five thousand feet in places, while along the roadside there were bamboo thickets, dense underbrush, and trees that were perfect perches for Japanese snipers. Yet "Zig Zag Pass," as American troops coined the road, offered the only chance for troop land movement, especially for heavy artillery guns. The Japanese, on the other hand, had nearly impenetrable defenses in the hills surrounding the pass; Americans knew the enemy was there, but given such thick vegetation, no one knew where. Certainly not George Johnson.

He and his sergeant, along with a driver, went in search of a suitable artillery setup. When the trail became impassable for their jeep, they continued on foot with no hint of enemy forces.

Then came a loud whir.

An artillery shell exploded yards in front of the men, sending a shower of dirt in their direction.

"We gotta find some protection," Johnson exclaimed, scanning the area, "a ditch or something."

Spotting a low swale, the three sprinted to reach it and dove to the ground, hugging it. An artillery shell fell behind them.

"For Christ's sake," muttered Johnson. "They've got us bracketed."

He closed his eyes, prepared for the end, for the artillery "split" between the forward and rear lobs. But the only sound he heard was the soft chirping of birds.

Where's the next shell, he wondered. *What are they waiting for?*

The men remained low, biding their time, but no shell came. Finally, they rose and Johnson exhaled deeply. "Boy, this is an awful way to get started," he cracked.

"And we only just got here," replied his sergeant. "So much for thinking no Japs in sight."

"They're not in sight," replied Johnson. "They're part of the mountain."

In truth, the Japanese melted into the landscape, creating an altogether different type of warfare from other Allied fronts, whether the river valleys of Germany, the beaches of the Italian Riviera, or the hedgerows of France; even among the hedges, there were clues as to where the enemy lurked, not so staring at mountains of jungles. It was anyone's guess—guerilla warfare.

Johnson's unit took to stringing telephone wire around a perimeter to where they slept at night. To the wire they attached tin cans, creating a chain of makeshift wind chimes to detect if enemy troops infiltrated the grounds.

On a night soon after they arrived, the chimes began clanging and the troops bolted to their feet. They grabbed their guns and swiftly emitted a firestorm into the blackness, in the direction of the clattering cans. All went quiet, the enemy apparently dead or gone.

When the sun rose, with trepidation, Johnson and his troops inspected the violated area to determine the strength of the forces subdued. The enemy, it turned out, was a water buffalo.

The real enemy, in reality, was well entrenched in hilltop defense stations that interlocked with firing stations on adjacent ridges. Added to that, were intricate foxhole systems and command posts in caves. It was as though each hill was a fortress unto itself and each, in turn, required conquering by the Americans. But to take each hill meant navigating Highway 7 with its hairpin turns, traffic jams, and the risk of open exposure, which contributed to heavy U.S. casualties.

Still, it was a fairly narrow defense zone that the Japanese guarded. American troops, aided by Filipino guides, were able to outflank and surprise the enemy in places. The 38th took Bataan a yard at a time, a mile at a time. Within two weeks the Allies were victorious on the peninsula, though to George Johnson, the aftermath looked like the devil's handiwork, as though Bataan had been scorched. Areas of lush vegetation were leveled and charred, and flamethrowers had roasted everything—including those who had remained in caves. The stench of rotting corpses hung like a final curtain over Bataan.

But the path was cleared for MacArthur to take Manila. The 38th Division, including George Johnson, began "mopping up."

Johnson took to a two-seater plane for reconnaissance to spot any receding Japanese forces. As his pilot, Dave, swooped the plane down, Johnson impulsively shouted over the roar of the engine, "Well, let's have a little fun here!"

He took out his pistol, lowered his window, and fired at the fleeing figures of the enemy.

Take that for Sandy and Ira, thought Johnson of his classmates, killed over three years earlier in the Philippines. He finished off the clip.

Sandy Nininger—the first Medal of Honor winner in World War II—and Ira Cheaney, awarded the nation's second-highest decoration, the Distinguished Service Cross, had been avenged in the Philippines as the United States looked toward victory.

★ ★ ★

At the Pentagon, Ed Rowny, at the directive of General George Marshall, was put to work on plans for the final invasion of Japan. His part was to develop an artificial harbor, code-named "Mulberry," the same code name as that for the harbor constructed at Omaha Beach in Normandy a year earlier. In that case, a number of ships had been sunk to create a breakwater to protect the harbor, but heavy storms had torn apart large portions. Rowny wanted to ward off a similar debacle and was faced with typhoon season. Like in Normandy, he crafted a plan that would use sunken ships, but in this case they would be joined together with steel beams.

As he was planning this, he received a message: "The steel for your artificial harbor at Sagami-Wan (Tokyo Bay) is disapproved. Manhattan District Engineer."

Rowny was astounded, swearing to a fellow officer, "We can't let some damn engineer in New York interfere with our fighting a war!"

But his superiors instructed that he follow orders. He went home to Rita and, for the first time in his career, bitterly lamented his disappointment with the U.S. military.

A classmate of Rowny's was grappling with the Manhattan engineers as well, but from a far different perspective.

More than a thousand miles away, on a high desert mesa in New Mexico, sat a ramshackle town with prefab buildings, rows of barracks, unsightly apartments, and hurriedly built laboratories. Residents had begun settling in the town in mid-1943, which in truth was the ultrasecret site of Los Alamos Laboratory. Peer de Silva, who'd hoisted up the swastika at West Point four years earlier, had been serving as the Los Alamos military intelligence officer. He was also commander of the Special Engineer Detachment, or SED. Obtaining labor for Los Alamos required subterfuge, and the SED unit was the military's roundabout way of drafting young scientists and specialized technical personnel into "engineering" positions without disclosing the true purpose of their recruitment—to develop the first atomic bomb, code-named the "Manhattan Engineer District" or, simply put, the "Manhattan Project." General Leslie Groves, a West Point 1918 engineer graduate, personally handpicked de Silva to head security at Los Alamos after the West Pointer expressed concerns about attempts by the Soviet Union to secure, by espionage, highly secret information.[4]

In many ways, de Silva had been running a boot camp at Los Alamos, perhaps inspired by Beast Barracks, though his tactics met with mixed results among young, talented scientists unaccustomed to dawn inspections and drill sergeants. Some thought those fledgling soldiers resembled budding professors in uniform more than combat troops, yet by 1945 there were more than 1,800 of them, and de Silva took every precaution to secure their undertakings at Los Alamos. Mail was censored, employees had to report chance encounters with friends beyond the complex, and travel was highly restricted. Some scientists' wives, especially those who resided on-site, lived in habitual fear, unenlightened as to their husbands' true work. So restricted was the flow of information that if a child was born at Los Alamos, his or her birthplace was listed as a post office box—the secrets of the father passed on to the child.[5]

In fact, de Silva's paranoia was not unwarranted. There had long been whispers about infiltration of the top-secret facility by the Russians, though none could prove the point. De Silva kept tightening the reins, pecking away at suspicious behavior, pursuing safeguards to protect America's vital secret.

Then as the summer of 1945 rolled in on the heels of V-E Day, de Silva was charged with his most important task to date—behind the curtain of the Manhattan Project, behind the darkest veil of secrecy, he was to herd Los Alamos scientists and their handiwork to Tinian, a small island east of the Philippines and south of Japan, which the U.S. had captured in July. The handiwork the scientists were escorting was the "Little Boy" and "Fat Man" bombs, part of a trio of atomic designs that included the "Thin Man." Some said the latter was a comparison to the physique of FDR while Fat Man was Churchill, his robust counterpart. If these playful names were intercepted in communications, it was hoped they would be deciphered as conversations regarding world leaders rather than the most dangerous weapons known to man. Others countered that the names had more to do with bomb shapes than leader shapes.

What ultimately became clear, however, was that the Little Boy and Fat Man atomic bombs were to be aimed at Japan. De Silva signed for 6.1 kg of plutonium at Los Alamos on July 25, 1945.[6] The next day, President Truman issued the Potsdam Declaration, an ultimatum for the Japanese to surrender or face utter destruction. The threat went unheeded.

These maneuverings were playing out as the impenetrable walls around Los Alamos had been breached. David Greenglass, a Los Alamos machinist recruited for the Manhattan Project, was sharing sketches of atomic bomb components with his sister and her husband, Ethel and Julius Rosenberg. The actions of Greenglass reverberated all the way to the Kremlin. He was not alone in subversive actions. Theodore Hall, a New York–born Harvard graduate, and Klaus Fuchs, who was born in Germany but later became a British citizen, were also working at Los Alamos and sharing secrets with the Soviets.

Hall's contribution to the Manhattan Project, in his words written on a project personnel form dated June 14, 1945, pertained to "nuclear physics: fission." Writing that same month as to "work performed" on the Manhattan Project, Fuchs was more detailed regarding his part in the project— and he was also said to have divulged far more to the Soviets. Wrote Fuchs on his personnel form:

> Research as a member of the "Implosion group" of the theoretical division at Los Alamos: I developed the theory of the jets observed in non-lens implosions, the elimination of which is necessary in order to make the type of implosion workable. I directed the work on the theory of the hydrodynamical processes in the initiator for the implosion bomb, and worked on other implosion procedures.[7]

There was not enough time, however, for the echoes of these spy revelations to reach the Japanese Empire. Little Boy was detonated over Hiroshima on August 6, 1945, and Peer de Silva, age twenty-eight, was among the first Allied officers on the ground to witness the aftermath. Fat Man fell over Nagasaki three days later, and its path destroyed a manufacturing plant that had churned out torpedoes used by the Japanese to attack Pearl Harbor. The war came full circle. Dust to dust.

Hearing the atomic news, Ed Rowny immediately understood why the Manhattan "engineer" had denied him his steel. There was no need for a harbor; there was no need for an invasion. The Japanese were bombed into submission, and by estimates of the War Department, a half-million lives were saved when compared to estimates of American lives that would have been lost in an invasion.

A few weeks later, on September 2, 1945, the Supreme Allied Commander for the Allied Powers, General Douglas MacArthur, climbed aboard the battleship *Missouri* in Tokyo Bay. A Japanese surrender party followed, led by a foreign minister auspiciously wearing white gloves and a top hat. Walking on an artificial leg with the help of a cane, he conveyed a humbling image as he stood at attention before the world's dominant powers as battle had cast them.

Said General MacArthur, "We are gathered here, representatives of the major warring powers, to conclude a solemn agreement whereby peace may be restored. The issues involving divergent ideals and ideologies have been determined—on the battlefields of the world."[8]

At 9:05 a.m. the Japanese minister, and military leaders from his country, put the first signatures to the documents of surrender. General MacArthur and American naval commanders countersigned, followed by commanders among the Allies including China, Britain, Soviet Russia, Australia, Canada, France, the Netherlands, and New Zealand. MacArthur uttered closing words, "Let us pray that peace be now restored to the world and that God will preserve it always."[9]

As those words were spoken, a West Point '41 command pilot, Richard Kline, led a B-29 formation thundering overhead in victory.

U.S. troops began returning home in droves in the months following, though Spec Powell had arrived months earlier. After North Africa, he'd served in Anzio and then was rotated back to the states for an assignment to West Point as a tac officer. Who else happened to be at the academy but Cleo, the Army nurse he'd met in Africa and seen again in Italy. She was now working at the West Point station hospital. Powell escorted her to a commandant's reception, but upon seeing her, the commandant ordered Cleo back to her quarters. "Put on your bars," he told her. She dutifully obliged and returned wearing five overseas service bars—more than any other officer in the room. She and Spec Powell were later married in the West Point chapel.

In the meantime, Jack Norton prepared for his last jump-off of World War II: Operation Homecoming. The victory parade in New York City would be an 82nd Airborne All-American Division celebration, and Jack Norton its conductor. General Patton had observed the division's honor guard perform in Berlin and insisted it was the best ever. Norton was charged with making sure the All-Americans lived up to that reputation by putting on one of the greatest spectacles the free world had ever seen. But only about one-third of the original 82nd Airborne Division remained—the rest had not returned home.

Norton had an astounding training challenge before him. During the war, when German units were decimated, the Germans typically trained replacement units as cohesive groups before deploying them into combat. The U.S., on the other hand, was less concerned about training replacements as a whole, let alone worrying about drill order and marching formations. They needed soldiers to fight—and fast. Hence, the U.S. policy tended toward replacing individuals rather than entire units, and replacement depots popped up, "repl-depls," as they were called. In creating his postwar victory parade Norton, therefore, was taking on a division in which about two-thirds of the troops had never marched together. Some probably had never even seen a drill field. At Fort Bragg, Jack Norton began training them and drilling them, one arm length between each man, bayonets fixed, fluid lines from every viewing direction.

Norton had little time. *The odds are against us*, he thought. But to the troops at Fort Bragg, he said only, "It's the chance of a lifetime to do something right!"

Before long the replacement troops tore off their 13th Airborne Division patches. Each sewed on a new All-American patch, and on January 12, 1946, stood in place of one from the 82nd Division who didn't make it home. From the replica of the Arc de Triomphe, at Washington Square Park in New York City, the division began marching up Fifth Avenue, past crowds lining the streets that were as thick as the waters were deep off Normandy. Spectators hung over the ledges of rooftops. They waved; they cheered. They threw kisses and confetti.

An aerial carpet, like a year earlier in Holland, blanketed New York City's skies with transport planes and gliders. On the ground the All-Americans proved their mettle, as bold and undaunted as when they'd gone into Sicily, and Italy, and into D-Day and Operation Market Garden.

The 82nd Airborne was picture-perfect and Norton was triumphant. *They got it right!*

Said the gravelly voiced announcer, Dwight Weist, over the televised newsreel:

This is the jump off, this is Operation Homecoming, the last official mission of the All-American 82nd Airborne Division, their objective, the 4½-mile parade route through New York City. Reinforced with veterans from three other airborne infantry units, the 13,000 crack-fighter and paratroops of the 82nd swing to the proud cadence of the foot solider. Their first salute they throw to their comrades who must stand on the curb, whose red blood and purple hearts pulse to a parade they cannot march in. . . . These are 13,000, but they stand for 10 million and they march for many who will never march again. . . . Four million people have lined the sidewalks to see GI Joe on parade, to see victory marching down the street to become history.[10]

Sherman tanks and armor followed the marching men as each unit passed the reviewing stands, where stood Jack Norton's mentor from those early days—days behind the gray cloistered walls of the academy. It was General James "Jumpin' Jim" Gavin, accepting the final salute of the All-Americans. Operation Homecoming was Jack Norton's last assignment in World War II.

The celebrating, however, didn't end there. Norton and his classmates planned a postwar reunion for '41ers in the D.C. area. That's when Ed Rowny realized that Jack Norton was among the only officers from the group still unmarried, so he arranged a blind date. He gave Norton the address of where to collect the young lady and when the door to that residence opened, Norton found himself staring at Cheyney MacNabb, number 32 on Rowny's hops card some six years earlier.

Norton took one look at Cheyney and saw his future. Before the evening was out, he asked her, "Cheyney, give me ten good reasons why we shouldn't get married."

Cheyney struggled to come up with nine, then faltered. Jack Norton took off his West Point ring and slipped it on her finger. Within days he asked Colonel Alexander MacNabb for his daughter's hand in marriage. Cheyney MacNabb, who years earlier had seen her dreams with a West Pointer, Herb Frawley, burn up in the smoke of war, found new promise with the All-American.

★ ★ ★

West Point '41er Walter Woolwine was in France on far more somber duty. He was scanning the wintry, windswept scene before him, looking out over the gently sloping green and amber incline that led down to a beach—Omaha Beach to be exact. He gazed toward the sea, to those churning waters that had claimed so many lives. He imagined the landing ship tanks—LSTs—lining up, the thousands of soldiers fording the rough waters. Bullets ricocheting, piercing heads and hearts. Seas that turned crimson. Limbs strewn along the sand. Thinking of the invasion's cost, his head bent in reflection. It was among the most somber moments he would ever know. So many lost, his classmates among them.

There was William Gardner, among the leading infantry regiments to first hit Omaha Beach. KIA. Henry Blanchard landed three days later and was soon ambushed and killed—unaware that his English wife of two months was pregnant with a baby boy. Paul Duke, Company D, joined the Long Gray Line in Normandy, and Thomas Reagan, Company I, lost his life there as well.

Where to begin?

He hadn't expected to be back in Europe so soon, just weeks after returning home for a well-deserved leave. But any grand plans he'd had of staying warm by the fireplace with Betty were promptly interrupted with orders from Major General Robert Littlejohn. Early into his leave, Woolwine was ordered to report to the general's office one morning.

"I'm confining you to the quartermasters," Littlejohn told him.

"What does that mean?" asked Woolwine.

"It means you're staying here unless I send you somewhere." Added the general, "Did you know that Eisenhower is conducting a survey of the graves on Omaha Beach? He wants to see if the records are consistent with the burial plots."

Littlejohn looked quizzically at his lieutenant colonel. "I'll give you three more lieutenant colonels and three sergeants," the general offered. "Go to the temporary burial sites and see if they reflect with the records consistently."

And so Woolwine arrived to Omaha Beach in the blustery winter of early 1946. It was late at night. The winds whipped around him. The howling was as haunting as wolves.

Woolwine had one of his men ring up the officer in charge of the graveyard, a German—now a POW—who was supposed to be expecting them. Asked Woolwine's officer of the overseer, "Where do we stay?"

"The chaplain is in charge," answered the German, directing the Americans to the cleric's family quarters.

Woolwine knocked on the chaplain's door. It creaked open a bit, and the man inside questioned, "What do you want?"

Woolwine explained his presence and asked to enter out of the frigid night air.

"You can't come in the room," protested the chaplain.

"Why not?"

"A lady's here."

"Your wife's here?"

"No . . . ah . . . not my wife."

Woolwine blanched. The grounds were supposed to be a place of sanctity, a place to honor soldiers that lay in the cold, desolate ground, waiting for proper remembrance, not a place for a chaplain who couldn't keep his pants on.

Barked Woolwine, "You better pack your bags and be gone tomorrow!" He spun around and went back into the roaring winds.

When daylight came he got down to the dirty work, scouring the sea of crosses in the makeshift cemeteries scattered all along Omaha and Utah Beaches. There were yet more gravesites inland.

A beach is not the place to be in subzero temperatures, freezing my ass off, thought Woolwine. *But then, at least it's not the Bulge.*

Not surprisingly, it didn't take long for him to find a name on a cross that was mismatched with the records. Then he found another, and another.

During the war, Woolwine knew, casualty notices had flowed into the Army's Adjutant General's office by radio or cable and later by machine-punched cards. Added to that was information from the Red Cross along with other sources on captured and interned personnel. But when Woolwine began seeing cross numbers mismatched with Army records, he knew one thing for sure: no one knew better who lay beneath the crosses than the men who had buried their fallen comrades and marked the graves. The cross numbers, unequivocally, took precedence over machine-punched cards.

The proportion of those mismarked was not astounding—maybe one in a hundred—but given the thousands upon thousands buried in the area, the jumbled mess grew exponentially. And so did the smell of death. Woolwine tried to tune it out, to numb his senses, but at times the pungency was so overwhelming, he wished he'd thought to bring gas masks. It was then that he was thankful for the winds.

Woolwine and his team began sorting the graves, trying to restore order to the chaos of death. He was confident his team would succeed down to the last man, the last grave. Logisticians were good at connecting dots and putting them in proper order, which is exactly why the serious duty of graves' registration fell under quartermaster domain. But as the officers toiled over the grim job, a question reared up among them: "Shouldn't there be a permanent cemetery for those who lost their lives in Europe?"

Walter Woolwine's answer: "We have a lot of dead, but we have a lot of power to move them."

His commanders agreed wholeheartedly, and so the second phase of Woolwine's task began. The team was to memorialize the losses, recognize with dignity soldiers' sacrifices.

Walter Woolwine helped select the perfect spot: a long, elevated stretch of land high atop the cliffs of Omaha Beach overlooking the sea—a sea that had no beginning and no end. It was about more than the view. The location was symbolic. It was the site of the first American cemetery on European soil in World War II, the temporary American Saint Laurent Cemetery established by the First Army, two days after D-Day on June 8, 1944.

Woolwine stared out at the endless ocean from the cliff-top spot.

We'll make a fitting tribute. This will be home now.

Woolwine and his team spent a solid month or so poring over ideas, developing a vision to properly honor America's World War II heroes. They batted about concepts for buildings, ideas for spiritual and reflective elements, narratives to teach future generations about the brave odyssey called D-Day. They considered where nearly ten thousand crosses and Stars of David would lie and pondered fitting tributes to those still missing. Back and forth they went with countless architects and engineers, developing plans, scrapping them, revising, fine-tuning, till at long last, after countless alterations, the officers were satisfied. They wanted the Normandy American Cemetery to stand as one of the most striking memorials the world over, in tribute to those who fought for freedom but did not return home. Walter Woolwine also needed to inter the bodies of soldiers scattered among makeshift cemeteries in the region. His duties included bringing those soldiers to their new resting place.

It would take years to complete, but the vision of Normandy American Cemetery and Memorial had been formed. The country of France granted America more than 172 acres, in perpetuity, for its creation. Most striking was to be a soaring bronze figure, called "The Spirit of American Youth Rising from the Waves." Inscribed in bronze around the feet of that spirit would be "MINE EYES HAVE SEEN THE GLORY OF THE COMING OF THE LORD."[11]

The Spirit of American Youth would look out over a central mall with a tranquil reflecting pool and down to a domed chapel where inside a mosaic would illustrate America blessing her sons and France gratefully bestowing laurel wreaths upon them in thanks. Flanking the central mall, its paths in the shape of a Latin cross, was to be a field of thousands of marble headstones marking the dead, all perfectly aligned. Behind the bronze spirit would be a semicircular colonnade and "The Garden of The Missing." A tablet within would bear the name of those American soldiers who "sleep in an unknown grave." The avenue leading to the entrance of the Normandy American Cemetery would be lined with hedgerows—so that hedgerow heaven could prevail over hedgerow hell.

His planning job done, Walter Woolwine at long last returned home to Betty, resting easier knowing that the remains of his fellow soldiers would find an eternal home. When all was said and done, the Normandy American Cemetery held 9,387 graves, including three Medal of Honor recipients, numerous fathers beside sons, thirty-eight pairs of brothers, and four women. The Garden of the Missing listed 1,557 who gave their lives in the region. The bodies of thousands more killed in the war were moved from temporary cemeteries and repatriated to the United States at the request of kin.

17

SHIFTING GEARS

After the war, West Point '41 classmates began preparing for peace, a promise that had seemed fleeting back when they graduated but now took on new meaning. While World War II had fulfilled their service requirements, almost all graduates who survived the war continued on in their service, seeking to become career officers. Most were still under the age of thirty, yet many were put on fast tracks at the Pentagon.

The seeds of their innovation, sown at the academy, could now take root in an era of military entrepreneurship. Some, like Ed Rowny, strategized with the visionaries of the day, participating in "dream sessions" that brainstormed on America's future. These sessions were the idea of General Lauris Norstad—the "brainy, blue-eyed wonder" as *Time* magazine later called him.[1] Norstad was in charge of the Operations Plans Division (OPD) of the War Department General Staff, of which Rowny was part. It was a lean division—about eighty-five officers—formed at the outset of World War II when General Marshall decided that Army staff, numbering in the thousands, was too large and bureaucratic to plan and run the war. Marshall superimposed the OPD over the existing Army war staff, and it had since overseen the conduct of World War II.

Norstad, a brilliant Army and Air Force aviator and broad-gauge thinker, was appointed to head OPD postwar. He believed science would play a major role in the future of the military and invited some of the greatest innovators of the day—global strategists, scientists, and members of top think tanks—to participate in his dream sessions.

Officers like Rowny would gather every Wednesday afternoon in a conference room with little more than a blackboard before them, to speculate on the future. As sparks flew, the group usually ignored the scheduled finishing time of five and debated until close to midnight. No one wanted to leave for fear of missing out on a groundbreaking concept. Discussions of Stalin's expansionist goals segued into how to put ballistic missiles into space as part of an intercontinental ballistic missile force. One solution was putting ablative layers on a missile nose cone, to protect what was inside, with layers burning off in succession as the cone passed through atmospheres. This led to the question, "Well, if we can stick a missile inside, why not a man?" Thus was born the idea, in 1946, of sending a man to the moon within twenty-five years.

A naval officer invited to attend the dream sessions, Captain William Raborn, posed the idea of firing ballistic missiles from submarines. One member of the group labeled this idea "dumb," insisting water would rush into the tube when the missile was fired. Raborn introduced the concept of employing a French innovation where a volume of gas would be inserted behind the projectile, allowing the hatch to close before water rushed in. Raborn's idea was the precursor to the Polaris, the world's first submarine-launched nuclear missile, and he later became the first director of the Navy's Fleet Ballistic Missile Program.

Other ideas in dream sessions included peaceful uses for atomic energy, like powering cities during blackouts. Not every idea proved successful, but these dream sessions invigorated Ed Rowny into innovative speculation about the future.

Many from the '41 class, however, remained on in Europe, involved in far less provocative issues. Stern was still there waiting for word on a new assignment.

There was a little mix-up as General Alexander Bolling explained to him, "I have two sets of orders for you, Stern. I have orders from the theater for you to join a quartermaster group."

"But I'm not a quartermaster," protested Stern, who ranked that specialty down with cavalry.

"Well," Bolling continued, "it seems there was some confusion, and Washington issued another set of orders, obviously unaware of the quartermaster appointment."

"To where?" asked Stern.

"I have a second set of orders for you to become a student at the French War College."

Stern's eyes widened at the prospect of Paris compared to tracking buttons and buckets.

"Here's what I suggest you do," said Bolling. "Pack up all you own, get in a car, and get to Paris as fast as you can before the quartermaster can grab you."

Herb Stern was so motivated to hightail it out of Germany, he would have galloped on horseback if told to do so. He stuffed his footlocker and in no time arrived at L'Ecole Supérieure de Guerre, better known to American officers simply as the French War College.

There, like such officers before him as George Patton, he studied French military strategies, including concepts for deploying major units and the strategic use of railroads and other national assets for troop movement. He visited posts to observe forces firsthand and analyzed the relationship of the French with its Allies, usually couched in terms of World War II. The experience provided a clarifying exchange of ideas among Allies, all aimed at mutual understanding, so much so that it was replicated to varying degrees at the U.S. Army War College as well as the British and Canadian defense colleges. For his part, Stern gave lectures in French on the who, what, and where of various aspects of U.S. operations.

Though emboldened by his new knowledge, Stern was forced to pause before putting it to good use. After graduating from the war college in late 1946, he was sent back to Germany to engage in occupation duties with the 60th Field Artillery Battalion of the 9th Infantry Division.

Already, Stern had served as de facto governor to many German towns. The new assignment added policing to his repertoire. He became part of the newly created U.S. constabulary, tasked with ensuring internal security in the American zone of postwar Germany. The country had been divided into four zones of occupation: the U.S. occupied most of southern Germany; the French occupied the west adjacent to their own border and parts of Switzerland; the British were in the northwest bordering Holland; the Soviets occupied the northeast zone adjacent to Poland. Berlin, meanwhile, was jointly occupied by the four Allied powers.

In the constabulary, Stern took on the role of provost marshal for the environs of southern Bavaria, excluding the cities of Munich and Augsburg.

He shook his head in astonishment at his new role. *I'm twenty-eight years old and I'm like the police chief of southern Bavaria. What the hell do I know about policing?*

Herb Stern was about to find out.

As so was Henry Bodson.

Bodson also had remained in Germany, at first charged with maintaining order in a prison camp holding about twenty-five thousand Nazis and political prisoners. Then, like Stern, he assumed provost marshal duties. His policing took a turbulent turn one morning when he was awakened at three to news that an American soldier had been murdered in his jurisdiction in the Langen area. Rounding up a trooper platoon to help, he quickly located the scene of the incident. It had occurred outside the home of a German woman, within a row of wooden shacks. She had apparently been fraternizing with an American soldier when a fellow soldier, perhaps vying for the same woman's attention, knocked on the door. The soldier within opened the door and shot his rival point blank, killing him. The shooter fled.

Feeling like Sherlock Holmes, Bodson ordered his men to comb the grounds for spent cartridges and then tracked those found to a U.S. Army unit. The culprit was found with the murder weapon hidden beneath his pillow.

Months later Bodson attended the man's military trial. He was sentenced to hanging. While that no doubt satisfied some, Bodson reflected more on the deceased man.

To have survived a war, only to be taken by a bullet from one of your own.

Friendly fire, which Bodson had witnessed before, took on tragic new meaning.

★ ★ ★

As Bodson grappled with the notion of one American soldier turning on another, others from his class were contending with military forces as a whole, helping to reorganize the U.S. Armed Forces for peacetime. That included spinning off the Army Air Corps into a new military wing, the U.S. Air Force. Similar to the early stages of war, when '41ers were dispersed throughout service specialties, this bifurcation spread their ranks yet again. World War II bomber commanders, including George Brown, the first '41er to reach the rank of colonel, started leading an era of breakthroughs at altitude. Fresh from their pilot seats, officers began testing America's first fighter jets. Fred Ascani, the pilot who flew missions to rescue evadees from Yugoslavia during the war, became "Chief, Bomber Test" at Wright-Patterson Air Force Base (formerly Wright Field), the R & D center for the Air Force. He set the pace, checking out some hundred different aircraft including gliders, helicopters, fighters, and bombers like the high-speed experimental Douglas XB-42 Mixmaster, from which he and a classmate, Alfred Hayduk, had to bail out. Hayduk kidded that he was "helping classmates to reduce Air Force aircraft inventory." It wouldn't be long before Ascani would move on to become chief of experimental flight at Edwards Air Force Base and test pilot the pioneering Bell X-1 transonic research aircraft, working with likes of Chuck Yeager, who'd broken the sound barrier in the X-1.[2]

Classmate Charles Seamans was at Wright as "Wind Tunnel Chief" in the aircraft lab. Another '41er, Gordon Gould, was dabbling in new technologies of air communications. Some were incorporating atomic weapons into the Air Force arsenal. Still others from the class were working on rocket propulsion, creating novel bomb-loading techniques, and establishing the new Air Force branch at the Pentagon. While the so-called dream sessions had been about imagining sending a man to the moon, "new" Air Force officers were sowing the seeds to make it happen.

But not all were pleased with the Armed Forces reorganization, which included centralized control rather than a separatist approach to the services, along with a newly formed Department of Defense.

Lamented Jack Murray, "So we take two, make five, and call it one. That's unification."

He was referring to the creation of the Department of Defense, the Army with its Air Corps being spun out into Army and Air Force, and the Navy with the Marines—the latter often trying to charge off on its own.

Herb Stern knew full well how the Marines wanted to be separatists. He was part of a steering group formed in late 1947 and charged, under General Jacob Devers, with trying to standardize aspects of the Armed Forces to save costs. First things first, the group tried to tackle rudimentary tasks like standardizing clothing and equipage, ostensibly not a herculean task.

"Why can't we all wear the same boots, the same fatigues?" suggested Stern.

The steering group made presentations on ideas to the heads of the services. The Army, Air Force, and Navy all agreed on proposals like fatigue standardization. Marine Corps Quartermaster General William P. T. Hill, on the other hand, insisted there were "distinctive characteristics" to Marine attire that absolutely could not be altered.

When questioned, his reasons included, "We use a double-weave cloth, while you use single." He was referring to the appearance of a dual stripe in the fatigue.

Upon hearing that argument one Friday afternoon, a frustrated secretary of the Navy said to Stern, "I don't think the Marines realize they are part of the Department of the Navy. They will know that Monday morning."

Despite some vexing issues with new organizational structures, more satisfying was that peacetime afforded many '41 officers the opportunity to pursue higher education. Columbia, Princeton, and Yale swelled with their ranks. Class members earned master's degrees in engineering, international relations, and finance. They embarked on Soviet studies in curricula aimed at serving higher military purposes. It was preparation for one day when they might be seated at negotiating tables or pursuing high-level diplomatic relations. In their studies officers were encouraged to methodically "gaze into the future." It was just the kind of conceptual work that had caused Henry Bodson to doubt Audie Murphy's prospects for upward military mobility had the Medal of Honor winner opted to pursue a career in the Army.

★ ★ ★

Paul Skowronek was gazing at life from an altogether different perspective and region of the world—one of increasing strategic importance to U.S. control and command. Skowronek was getting to know Central America as well as the stitches in his britches. He was given a free hand in the Caribbean Defense Command's intriguing new Combat Intelligence Section under General Crittenberger.

Crittenberger noticed Skowronek's proclivity toward the subversive during the latter stages of World War II, when the young officer thrived in a photo intelligence course, flying missions over the Suez Canal and Sinai Peninsula. Now, from a base in Panama, Major Skowronek scoped out a different part of the world. Of particular concern to him was anything that presented a danger to the Panama Canal, which remained a strategic shipping route connecting the Caribbean Sea and Pacific Ocean and was still under U.S. control.

America's presence in the Canal Zone was Quarry Heights, a mountaintop setting for the key U.S. military installation in the region. Skowronek's office there exemplified his unorthodox work. It was situated in a bombproof tunnel about forty feet wide by nine feet high, bored deep into the mountain. Flanking the corridor within were offices that collectively served as an intelligence, communications, and command post for U.S. military activities. They housed four to five officers at a given time, usually made up of a couple of Air Force officers, a communications specialist, and Paul Skowronek. For Skowronek, the setting gave new meaning to "going under" in intelligence. The tunnel had direct lines to the Pentagon and was, in effect, the United States nerve center for that part of the world. In an emergency—were the canal at risk—U.S. officers from Quarry Heights would also be crammed into the tunnel for refuge.

But it was the daily activity within that most compelled Skowronek, especially the dispatches sent from the Pentagon to the communications specialist. These messages were the communiqués of a new "Special Intelligence" network that received daily updates, usually regarding Soviet activity, based on radio and telephone intercepts. So secretive was this network that it was deemed beyond top secret; only the most senior overseas commanders, such as General Crittenberger and those at Supreme Headquarters Allied Powers, were privy to its briefings. The network, in fact, reached beyond the realm of the CIA or military attachés, though information it obtained could help verify intelligence from those sources. (This Special Intelligence unit was a precursor to the National Security Agency, though the agency and acronym NSA had not yet emerged.) Skowronek just knew he was part of something monumental.

The major soon began venturing far beyond the walls of his office cavern, touring countries in the region to get a read on the politics and people.

There's so much that's new, and no one's looking over my shoulder to see if I'm upsetting the apple cart.

Skowronek was in his element.

In Panama, driving a jeep, he traveled the Pan American Highway all the way to the border of Costa Rica, along the way drawing sketches and snapping photos of every bridge he crossed—bridges that could be critical transportation arteries in the event of war. He followed the road till it disappeared and became an overgrown trail leading into the mountains, the anemic result of overambitious plans for a California–South America highway that had not yet fully panned out.

Beyond that, Skowronek took his chances traveling aboard archaic tri-motor planes run by the regional carrier TACA. Ford halted production of the tin planes two decades earlier, but they remained the air-transport workhorses for Central America and ferried Skowronek to Costa Rica, Nicaragua, Honduras, El Salvador, and beyond. He even crossed the equator via submarine to venture to Columbia, Peru, and Ecuador.

Off the coast of Ecuador, he visited Baltra Island in the Galapagos, which had been an important western air defense position in World War II for the Panama Canal as well as a transoceanic refueling station. Skowronek's intelligence gathering, however, was overshadowed late one night by the iguana that sashayed into his room as he lay sleeping. The reptile was huge—so huge in fact that Skowronek was sure it was a dragon and that he'd have to fight off with his bare hands. Instead, it proved to be the tomfoolery of the Air Force colonel who oversaw the island installation.

After his nerves calmed, Skowronek excused the prank. *The colonel must be bored to death*, he thought, *here amid giant tortoises, nary an enemy in sight except snakes.*

Such was the nature of peacetime for some officers—long stretches of monotony interrupted with pranks.

More often than not on these excursions, Skowronek didn't know what he was looking for, but he knew he'd smell something when it mattered. He'd undergone defense intelligence training to hone his intuitions.

Being in the business of looking also meant hobnobbing. At times, he chummed around with the grandsons of Ecuador's President Eloy Alfaro, who decades earlier had been ousted and barbarically murdered during a coup. Skowronek knew three of Alfaro's grandsons from West Point; they were like many sons of national leaders who sought top military training for their offspring. Unable to return to the homeland of their grandfather, the Alfaros lived in Panama. Of special interest to Skowronek was how their father, Colón Alfaro, would react as news grew of a revolutionary coup in Ecuador. The senior Alfaro also had attended West Point—he was a classmate of Crittenberger's—and had served as Ecuador's ambassador to the United States.

Will he return to Ecuador to become president? Skowronek wondered.

Colón Alfaro was headed there, intending to do just that when the revolution failed, and he was forced to return to Panama.

Skowronek kept his eye on such endless power plays in the region, many of which included coups and sham elections. Yet he always managed time for the occasional cavalry dalliance.

Late one Saturday night at a party, he ran into the commander of Panama's national police, strongman Colonel José "Chichi" Remón; Panama had no army, so the national police was its de facto military. Remón stopped by Skowronek's table, remembering the fair-haired equestrian from training with him at Fort Riley. Despite the late hour—after 3 a.m.—Remón announced to his old acquaintance, "I'm going to wake up my squadron. We'll go down to our riding stables right now, and you will pick out two of the best horses we have. They will be waiting for you and your wife at Quarry Heights at 7 a.m. . . . today and every Sunday!"

Skowronek turned to Virginia and said, "Well, there's no sense in going to sleep."

A couple of hours later the couple was pulling on their britches. No matter where in the world Paul Skowronek went, his britches were first into his footlocker.

Remón went on to become president of Panama—but was assassinated three years into his term.

By then Skowronek, given his intelligence work begun in a Panamanian tunnel, had developed a healthy skepticism toward the Soviets and their postwar aims. He doubted the U.S. and the USSR could truly collaborate.

Sure, the Potsdam Agreement was in our mutual interests. Give the Germans a taste of misery . . . reduce their industrial power . . . liquidate Nazi influence. But what now? Considering traditional rivalries with the Soviets, I don't see us sharing goals; I don't see it happening.

★ ★ ★

The Allied Control Council in Berlin had carried out occupation measures agreed to in spirit in mid-1945 at Potsdam, Germany, including measures for demilitarization, reparation, and governing the country postwar in each of the four German occupation zones. The issue of access to Berlin, however, was never satisfactorily resolved. Whereas the western Allies expected unrestricted ingress and egress, in reality Berlin was landlocked by Soviet control on all sides within the broader Soviet Zone of Germany. The Soviets had no interest in relinquishing the right to regulate traffic through that zone.

The matter came to a head when the Soviets blockaded all rail, road, and canal traffic into Berlin in March 1948, cutting off food supply routes and willing to risk starving 2.5 million Germans. To Americans in uniform it was intolerable. General Lucius Clay, West Point engineer, USMA 1918, and now U.S. commander in chief in Europe, conceived of the Berlin Airlift, an unprecedented operation to fly in supplies to the beleaguered city. Berliners needed at least four thousand tons of daily food and fuel to survive.

Chuck Schilling, a '41 engineer, commanded the rebuilding of the Rhein-Main airbase in Frankfurt to serve as the principal feeder airport for the airlift. Air Force commander and classmate Perk Perkin honed in on planning the air traffic system. Then Perkin set tonnage records, commanding a squadron of C-54 transport planes hauling coal and flour into Berlin during the early days of the airlift. As the months went by, deliveries grew to thirteen thousand tons a day.

The Cold War had begun in earnest.

At about this time Walter Woolwine was deployed to Germany, having earlier completed an MBA at Harvard. He focused on creating a new European route for fuel transport. There was concern that if the emboldened Russians crossed the northern border of their zone into western Germany, they could block fuel that flowed from the port of Bremerhaven, at the mouth of the Weser River in the North Sea, to points south. Especially penetrable along the border was the Fulda Gap, a broad, easily navigable corridor of land stretching from the Soviet Zone into western Germany.

Woolwine, however, was less alarmed than some. Ever the eagle-eyed tactician, he took notice of an idiosyncrasy in Soviet behavior:

The Soviets could shoot down a couple of our airplanes, and the airlift would collapse. But they're not doing anything. If they're not stopping our planes, then why are we worried about them going farther and crossing the border?

Woolwine began telling any superior that would listen, "We've got it made. Everyone's focused on the Fulda Gap, but now we can forget about the Russians coming west." The entire strategic picture, in his view, had shifted.

Then in May 1949, only a few months into his fuel undertaking, the Soviets lifted their blockade. At that point, given the withdrawal of the Soviets from Allied quad-power collaboration, the map of Germany was redrawn. From the U.S.-British-French tri-zone the Federal Republic of Germany was born. In the following October the Soviets established— some might say retaliated with—the German Democratic Republic (GDR). Berlin remained split between the two republics, though the GDR hardly had anything republican about it. The history set in motion when Herb Stern had heard those two simple words, "Stand down"—when Berlin was within U.S. grasp in World War II—now played out into a divided Germany. Lieutenant Colonel Walter Woolwine would help decide the fate of the western side.

The remaining Allies—France, England, and the United States—had been governing their respective zones while also implementing the Marshall Plan, the aid plan to reconstruct Europe, named for the U.S. secretary of state who envisioned it, George C. Marshall. Now came a transition as the three militaries prepared to end their occupation. Woolwine was overseeing U.S. military requirements in Germany as part of the triparties command that included political, economic, and administrative duties. He was chief of the Defense Requirement Branch within the economic branch, overseeing U.S. military procurements.

Woolwine was given little direction. "It's up to you how to accomplish objectives," he was told.

He quickly realized the job required that he not only keep a close eye on U.S. operations but also watch out for the shenanigans of the British and French militaries. One of his objectives was to keep them from taking materials and equipment out of Germany that were paid for with U.S. funds under the Marshall Plan. The Russians had already stripped their German zone of vital goods and sent them back to Russia. The French had done some of the same, much as they had in World War I. The British seemed keen on using the Marshall Plan to export items in short supply back to Britain. While Woolwine could do nothing about Russian follies, he could control U.S. directives and put a halt to those of the French and British, which is one of the first things he did.

Under the Marshall Plan, American companies provided critical supplies to help rebuild a bombed-out Germany, which needed every piece of lumber, paint, machinery, and agricultural equipment it could get. German recipients were supposed to pay for these items in deutsche marks or with credit, which was intended to support the currency and keep funds within the country's borders. Woolwine, however, discovered at one point that the French military planned on extracting deutsche marks from the German economy to purchase thirty American Cadillacs. He stopped the deal dead in its tracks. The same went for some British maneuverings. The "free" money was no longer going to provide a free ride for the French or British to take from the German economy what was supposed to be aimed at rebuilding.

They are the conquerors, and they want the spoils, thought Woolwine. *But what they're doing is draining the German economy when we need to do the opposite and get it back on track.*

Woolwine kept an eagle eye on triparty procurements. He also chaired the U.S.-U.K.-French tripartite committee charged with developing articles to govern the procurements of Allied Forces stationed in West Germany when occupation ended. More than anything, however, he began initiatives to restart the economic engines that drove Germany. Walter Woolwine, only in his early thirties, became an integral part of the German economy for the ensuing three years, inserting himself into every aspect of it from agriculture and lumber to coal, the auto industry, and more. The white-haired senior executives of German industry were learning the efficiency of West Point—à la Walter Woolwine.

Germany was on the path to recovery when he left in 1953. Allied occupation officially ended two years later.

18

In these postwar years, a number of 1941 class members disappeared off the radar screen. Peer de Silva, who had been head of security at Los Alamos during the Manhattan Project, began fading into the Moscow scenery under the shadows of the CIA. While the intelligence organization was in its early stages and had no infrastructure in Moscow, there was an American Embassy. De Silva became a "diplomatic courier," carrying classified mail between Helsinki and Moscow. There were very few Americans in Moscow, and Soviet surveillance of them was often quite blatant, but at other times de Silva encountered cunning scrutiny. As his trips grew more frequent, he acquired a knack for discerning the subversive, all the while keeping his eyes out for ways to complete his own maneuverings, such as possible dead drops for small items like film. On a broader level he tried to gauge the condition of the Soviet economy, rationing, and the mood of the public in general—any information the United States could get its hands on.[1]

De Silva was among many '41ers beginning to "go under." His classmate, paratrooper Jock Adams, conducted mysterious night jumps into the hillbilly areas of Alabama. His uniform: blue jeans. The goal: blend in with the locals as though behind enemy lines, then forge through a hundred miles of unfamiliar territory to make it back to post. He was part of the experimental Special Forces.

Other '41ers had their sights upward on aerospace and other highly classified programs. It remained an urgent U.S. priority to create missiles with longer range. Redstone, White Sands, and Sandia, sites synonymous with secret missiles and atomic programs, hosted scores of '41 officers like John Harris, who helped lead programs in their infancy. Included among their ranks were German rocket scientists, such as the brilliant Dr. Wernher von Braun, who had been recruited at war's end from the enemy. The U.S. was leaving no stone unturned to achieve weapons superiority in the face of the emerging USSR military threat building in Central and Eastern Europe, as well as the Caribbean. Many German scientists were spirited away by the Allies to keep them from falling into Soviet hands, while others disappeared into the Soviet military machine.

A '41er, Jerry La Rocca, had been part of von Braun's welcoming committee to the U.S. and was interfacing with recruited Germans as the Air Force's first experimental guided missile squadron commander. Then La Rocca took to a high-flying mission of a far different kind. He was commanding a fleet of B-17 bombers, both manned and unmanned, as part of Operation Sandstone, a series of atomic bombing tests designed to study the next generation of nuclear weapons. The tests were to be conducted in a remote area of the Marshall Islands in early 1948. Previously, experiments had been done over Bikini Atoll in the islands, but the prevailing winds there were not favorable for carrying radioactive waste away from land. Eniwetok Atoll was chosen as ideal—the new Los Alamos proving grounds in the Pacific.

In essence, U.S. forces created an open-air laboratory on Eniwetok, which included erecting a tower on the coral atoll on which to detonate a nuclear device, building communications systems and timing stations, and establishing the methods through which light and neutron generation and gamma radiation could be captured.

Early on the morning of April 14, La Rocca took off from an airbase on nearby Kwajalein Atoll. La Rocca was commanding sixteen B-17s that made up the advanced echelon of the atomic tests. Half of the B-17s were mother ships with crews. The other half was comprised of radiation-gathering drones, operated by remote control from the mother ships. The mother ships would fly in a staggered pattern around the nuclear mushroom cloud that would be created upon the atomic detonation—it was too dangerous for crewed planes to go through it. The drones, with radiation-collecting filters, would penetrate the radioactive cloud's mass and, for the most part, remain in visual sight of their mother ships.

La Rocca had done dry runs back in the states. He was prepared for his part of the air, land, and sea mission. His B-17 took off. Among the fleet, his plane would travel closest to the blast and lowest in altitude. He and his crew got ready to don hoods and goggles to protect their eyes from the blinding blast.

Two hundred feet over Eniwetok, the nuclear bomb—code-named X-Ray —was blasted on its tower.

An enormous, involuntary jolt went through La Rocca. His plane violently shook. He struggled to keep control of it, his arms shuddering, his legs trembling.

The plane's going to be torn apart . . .

The accompanying noise was deafening. *The rivets . . . I hear them popping. . . .*

La Rocca was feeling the impact of a nuclear blast yielding thirty-seven kilotons of energy—equivalent to about thirty-seven thousand tons of high explosives.

As the mushroom cloud began rising, the shock waves to La Rocca's plane subsided almost as rapidly as they'd come on, while subsequent mother ships in his team—each flying at higher altitudes—endured the next levels of the cloud's wrath. Their coordinated drones, at the same time, flew directly through the rising cloud to collect radiation samples at varying altitudes, the highest among them reaching the cloud's peak of about twenty-eight thousand feet.

Each plane and drone safely made it through the ordeal. Control of the drones was then handed off from the mother ships to ground crews for landing. A crew member was on either end of the runway to direct each drone and keep it straight. It was the first time anything like this had ever been done with pilotless planes, and La Rocca felt triumphant as the last of them landed safely.

We didn't lose any!

Sixteen days later, a second test ensued. This time La Rocca was on Kwajalein handling ground crews and electronics. The forty-nine-kiloton yield of the next bomb, code-named Yoke, was let loose. La Rocca was a good ten to fifteen miles from the blast, yet he was nearly knocked off his feet.

The first of the drones completed its task and soon returned to the airstrip. It landed but at first began weaving along the runway erratically. Then it stalled in the middle of the airstrip, its engine not responding to the remote-control orders.

La Rocca had more than a dozen planes and drones still in the air waiting to touch down. He had pilots screaming for clearance to land, and some planes would soon run low on gas, but it was not feasible for them to land with an enormous B-17 drone blocking the only runway.

La Rocca raced toward the tail of the drone and yanked at the long safety wire that went through its fuselage, connecting the wire to the throttle.

He jerked too hard. The wire snapped.

For a second La Rocca stared at the broken wire. *No . . . I can't lose fifteen planes. All that atomic data on board . . . all the crews having to bail out of the mother ships.*

Frantically, with the drone still puttering, stalled, he opened a tail door to it. He climbed inside and scampered up to the front to shut off the throttle. He was oblivious to fire crews surrounding the plane, rushing toward it with fire hoses.

Only as he jumped down from the plane did it hit him. The radiation—a feeling as though solar flares were scorching through his body.

Emergency workers turned the fire hoses on him. The gushing pressure knocked him to the ground.

La Rocca was frightened. *I can't breathe. . . .*

He was evacuated to a hospital where doctors pondered the options. La Rocca was alive and outwardly appeared fine, but there was no doubt that he'd had serious radiation exposure. Physicians realized, however, there was little they could do. La Rocca was released the next day.

The remaining drones and mother ships, he was told, had all landed safely after he had halted the errant drone. His fate, however, was left for time to tell.

La Rocca received a commendation from the major general in charge of the operation:

> 4 June 1948
> Major La Rocca,
> It is desired to highly commend you for the outstanding and successful manner in which you have participated in project Sandstone from its first inception . . . in 1947 to its completion in May 1948.
> As officer in command of the advanced echelon of Air Task Unit 7.4.2 (Drone) you supervised the movement of 203 officers and enlisted men . . . in an exemplary manner. . . . Throughout this operation you performed executive functions in air task force 7.4.2 in a most commendable manner which reflects much credit on yourself and the services of the United States Air Force.
> R. M. [Roger Maxwell] Ramey,
> Major General, USAF, Commanding[2]

★ ★ ★

While La Rocca was battling nuclear fallout, Henry Bodson had a much simpler battle on his hands. He wanted to be rotated back to the States.

At long last that happened, and he was assigned to the artillery capital of Fort Sill. When he reported for duty, his new battalion commander looked up, noted Bodson's rank and asked, "Well, who the hell wants you here? I've already got two majors in my battalion."

He was referring to the standard limit per battalion.

That's a hell of a way to welcome a soldier back from three years of combat and occupation duty. From the reception, Bodson figured his prospects for success bleak. *I'm not staying in this outfit any longer than I have to.*

Reviewing the Army's education programs, he set his sights on postgraduate studies, aspiring to one of the new guided missile programs at Cal Tech or MIT. Both institutions were trying to improve on von Braun's German V-weapon initiatives, the V standing for Vergeltungswaffen, which roughly translated meant "vengeance weapons." There was the V-1 "buzz bomb," nicknamed for jet engines that buzzed like King Kong–sized mosquitoes. Then the more powerful V-2 came into play, Hitler's so-called "brain child" because it had a guidance system, or brain, that helped steer the missile's fins. Unlike a rocket that essentially heads where it's pointed, the V-2 had steering and stabilizing systems that included a control section with gyroscopes. That control section produced electrical signals to help relay corrections necessary to maintain a trajectory path and, in turn, impacted the steering vanes in the tail assembly.[3]

Now there was hope that the U.S. could create V-2 offspring to better arm itself, and Bodson was especially intrigued by the advanced missile technology. Just as some boys are drawn to things that go blur-fast, as an artilleryman he was drawn to projectiles that seemed to have wings. He wondered if the Pentagon read his mind when a telegram from the five-sided foxhole arrived. It read, "Would you like to pull a year tour with General Electric Company in Schenectady, New York, with the Hermes missile project?"

Bodson dashed out a reply—"Yes."

The Hermes program was headed by Dr. R. W. Porter, a scientist who had recruited, prior to war's end, some of the German scientists now working on the Army's guided-missile programs. In the process of recruiting those scientists, the Army had "liberated" nearly a hundred V-2 missiles along with missile components. In fact, in August 1945, three hundred railway cars loaded with these captured components were brought to White Sands Proving Grounds, a vast expanse of uninhabited terrain in south-central New Mexico dedicated to rocket development. The U.S. fared well, racking up more than 200 combustion chambers, 180 sets of propellant tanks, 90 tail units, 200 turbo-pumps, and more.[4]

GE had responsibilities for reassembling and launching V-2s, which when erect stood forty-six-feet tall and had a diameter of about five feet. GE also had crews involved in exploration of the outer atmosphere. Scientific payloads on missiles ranged from studies on ambient pressure, solar radiation, and composition of the atmosphere to including fruit flies as missile passengers so the affects of exposure to cosmic radiation could be studied. The GE crews also tested missile components for government agencies, private contractors, and universities. Bodson would join some of these ongoing GE efforts.

Henry and Belle Bodson packed up their belongings and four-year-old Betty Ann and headed to GE in Schenectady, north of New York City. While Bodson's welcome there was much warmer than that at Fort Sill, he was stunned to discover no missile curriculum to study. The extent of his training was someone handing him a missile picture book that was elementary at best. Bodson flipped through the pages bemused.

I could probably get this at any library. So much for top-secret indoctrination.

Instead, training for the new junior engineer was on the job. Bodson began assisting in designing the internal cabling of the Hermes A-1 missile, which had a configuration nearly identical to an anti-aircraft, surface-to-air missile that had been planned by the Germans. GE, however, was redefining the concept, seeking to use the Hermes A-1 as a test vehicle for missile propulsion, flight control, and guidance.

Delving into all this, Bodson's mind flash backed to that day at Cooper Union when he'd wondered about getting in over his head. Now, fourteen years later, looking around at aerodynamic and engineering wizards, his feelings ran parallel:

I'm way out of my league . . . only a few academy courses in engineering under my belt. Rather inadequate training compared to these technically skilled experts. It'll be fascinating work, but what have I gotten myself into?

He enlisted in a GE electronics course after hours, improvising to play catch-up. Before long, he was laying out blueprints for circuitry boards and internal cabling systems, supervising the fabrication of a launching control desk, and preparing countdown time schedules and procedures.

The day came for a static test launch to navigate a missile's course from a control center—an ambitious initiative that was a far cry from Bodson's artillery students firing and hoping for the best on the beaches of Anzio. Instead, this projectile had a mind and would be given instructions. The Hermes A-1 was tethered up at a site near Schenectady. The propulsion system began firing up in mock launch, and the crew exercised its commands for control and guidance without a hitch. The team, including Bodson, was elated.

Next came the actual launch at the White Sands Proving Grounds. Henry Bodson was among a dozen or so scientists, engineers, GE executives, and military officers at the proving grounds in May 1950, all crammed into a small concrete bunker. Surrounding the bunker were miles of desert, while the city of Las Cruces lay twenty miles to the west and El Paso forty-five miles to the south. Those prepared to witness the test launch were oblivious to the scenery. All focus was on the control desk, eyes fixated on the switches and dials meant to monitor, via radar, the internal and external guidance systems of the A-1.

The missile's liquid fuel began to burn for propulsion, and Bodson's time procedures kicked into play. Three minutes till countdown. Two. The final seconds and then, "Blast off!"

As the Hermes A-1 rocketed skyward, Bodson felt triumphant.

By God, we've fired it up.

At that moment, the artilleryman officially became a rocket man. The litany of projectiles he worked on soon read like a challenging Scrabble puzzle, with Honest John and Little John rockets, Hermes, Sergeant and Corporal missiles, and more. Increasingly, Bodson's sights were focused upward. Like La Rocca, John Harris, and many other '41ers, he was ushering in an era of unheralded military experimentation that would alter war and peace—and reach new heights in innovation.

As part of the missile initiatives, Bodson oversaw the formation of the Army's first Guided Missile Battalion, based at White Sands. The battalion included about three hundred officers whose primary mission was to assist civilian contractors, such as those with Jet Propulsion Laboratory, Douglas Aircraft, and Raytheon, in launching missiles and experimental tests. One of those endeavors involved the Corporal, a missile with breakthrough technology, including an extremely powerful thrust and trajectory.

Not all was smooth sailing.

When the battalion launched its first missile, on a northerly track, Bodson watched, stunned and speechless, as it veered off-track. It headed due west, directly over White Sands's headquarters and in the direction of Las Cruces, population twelve thousand–plus. There were audible gasps of relief as the missile landed short of its maximum trajectory—and fifteen miles short of La Cruces. Midflight failure proved a godsend but what became evident was that the "guided" component of the Corporal missile was, in fact, misguided.

From that near tragic mishap, the Army's Ordnance Corps at White Sands had an epiphany: why not combine the Hermes A-1 guidance and control capabilities with the Corporal's power and thrust? If it worked, the Army would have a strategic and powerful tactical weapon, this as the Department of Defense was expediting tactical missile initiatives amid a heightened threat of Chinese offensives in Korea.

Bodson reflected, *If we have millions of Chinese opposing us, we're going to need far-reaching, guided missiles to fight them off. Ground forces alone won't do it.*

Bodson's work intensified as the guided aspects of the Hermes were combined with the Corporal propulsion system. Bodson was unaware, however, of the DOD's ulterior motive—to eventually create the first surface-to-surface guided missile capable of delivering a nuclear warhead.

He was also unaware that initiatives of classmates, like Jerry La Rocca, had been funneling into that common objective.

By now, however, a few years after surviving Eniwetok, La Rocca had developed prostate cancer. He was barely in his thirties.

He wondered, *Was it the drone?*

La Rocca knew that he'd never know for sure; much about nuclear fission and radiation still remained an unknown. He underwent four-directional radiation therapy, or "4-D," advancement in radiation treatment that minimized damage to the normal tissue surrounding cancerous areas. The cancer was purged.

La Rocca forged ahead with endeavors in electronics and in the developing new field of astronautics.

★ ★ ★

Charlie Fletcher, remembering the men he'd seen turn away from the front in the Battle of the Bulge, was in favor of military training for every able-bodied American male. He was assigned to Fort Knox in 1946 to help command the Universal Military Training Experimental Unit (UMT), formed in response to the Army's reevaluation of its general approach and methods to training recruits. The Army recognized that the rapid ramp-up of forces for World War II had involved crude training at best. In fact, the country had been ill prepared for World War I as well. Most startling, however, was that since World War II, the Army had whittled down to about six hundred thousand active troops with a small pool in reserve, compared to more than 8.2 million at the war's peak in 1945. Some experts thought there was far too much emphasis on basing national defense on atomic weapons, and UMT was viewed as an answer to the nation's challenge should rapid mobilization be needed.

It's about time, thought Fletcher. *If we'd had this in place five years ago, we could have more quickly mobilized and probably ended the war a lot faster.*

FDR had been a proponent of the UMT concept and President Truman picked up the torch, initiating directives in late 1946. Said Truman to the President's Advisory Commission tasked with exploring the concept:

I have been somewhat of a student of history, and I have discovered that great republics of the past always passed out when their peoples became prosperous and fat and lazy, and were not willing to assume their responsibilities. In other words, when the Romans and the Greeks and some of the ancient Mesopotamian countries turned to mercenary defense forces, they ended. That is, when the people of a nation would not do the necessary service to continue their government, it ended eventually one way or another.[5]

Secretary of State Marshall, Secretary of War Henry Stimson, and General Eisenhower all supported the UMT concept as well.

Under Truman's new experimental mandate, service would become compulsory for men of draft age. Importantly, UMT would also go beyond basic training. Branch training would follow basic, as would directives on health, discipline, and general education. After six months in total, trainees would be slotted for the Army Reserve or National Guard, pending any national emergency that might activate them. A key philosophical change in the training modus operandi was also the attitude for implementation.

Explained one commander to Fletcher, "The idea is to make the training effective but without degrading the position of the soldier."

"In other words," replied Fletcher, "get rid of the picture of a general staring at soldiers and treating them like dirt?"

"Exactly."

Fletcher's classmates working at the Pentagon—Jack Norton, Ed Rowny, Spec Powell, and Ace Moody—were enthusiastic and keen on well-trained soldiers. Over lunches and beers at their favorite watering spots around Georgetown, sparks flew among them as they discussed the benefits of UMT. Rowny thought adding moral and spiritual training to basic would have an impact. Norton wanted the U.S. to drop conscription altogether and adopt a universal service concept. Powell suggested that branch service not be limited to military service. Training, he opined, could be applicable to "lots of fields," and his friends agreed that the Civilian Conservation Corps, programs for the elderly and handicapped, contingencies to foster education and self-sufficiency in developing countries—they could all benefit from UMT training. The civilian applications, the '41ers figured, were nearly endless. But foremost, the classmates wanted to see better-trained troops and were unanimous in support of UMT.

Rowny relayed a story about his efforts to properly train men during World War II. Soon after arriving in Italy with his engineer battalion, he received a letter from then-senator Truman, who had been receiving complaints from constituents that Rowny was training troops too hard, including subjecting them to combat training. In truth, the men in question were in Rowny's engineer (C) battalion. That C stood for "combat," though others erroneously thought it meant "colored" because it was a black unit. Complaints about the punishing training regimes were echoed in the *Pittsburgh Courier*. Truman was considering an inspector general investigation into "white supremacy permeating the outfit" and an inquiry into the overgrueling training. Before making a recommendation, however, he wanted Rowny's view.

"I told Truman that segregation was not *my* policy but rather an Army regulation," Rowny told his classmates. "I wrote that, in my opinion, the Army would be better served if black and white soldiers served together, which was inevitable, and the sooner the better." He added, "I also said by all means, go ahead, I welcome an investigation. I admitted that, yes, I trained my troops hard—because I learned from fighting in Italy that the rate of survival in combat is *directly* proportional to the amount of sweat in training. I got a letter back from Truman saying that he decided not to pursue an investigation."

"And now," said Moody, "he's the biggest supporter of universal training."

In truth, public support for UMT was at first positive. Some believed it would make for healthier, stronger men both physically and morally, in addition to fostering a better-prepared nation. But others came out swinging at UMT, labeling it fiscally irresponsible given the enormous cost of widespread training. Others considered it a wasted exercise since no amount of training could defend against atomic weapons—weapons that would presumably make infantry obsolete. At the more grassroots level, many Americans simply wanted their men home after years of war and with threats to national security having subsided.

At Fort Knox, Charlie Fletcher had no such sense of false security as he began to help implement UMT. Like Rowny, he trained his men hard, in Fletcher's case under the auspices of General John Devine and Colonel Edwin Burba. The latter, an outstanding commander, had specifically requested Fletcher after noticing his training ethics at Fort Knox's advanced armored school a few years earlier. It was that earlier training that had taught Fletcher, the artilleryman, more than a thing or two about tanks. Now, as he trained UMT recruits, he thought back to those tank columns in the Ardennes, back to that wooded field and clothesline flapping in the breeze, back to the anti-aircraft gun he hijacked.

The outcomes could have been far different, not just for me, but also for a lot of others if not for training.

This time around, however, Fletcher and his superiors were fighting a losing war. As the UMT's experimental phase revved up, the lobbying against it ramped up. After it received initial support the doomsayers kicked in, calling it an enormous propaganda machine. Congress ultimately denied UMT's passage. Charlie Fletcher, while disappointed, was not surprised.

Always putting training on the back burner.

At home he told his wife, Johnnie, "Soon we'll be more unprepared for the next war than the last. Mark my words."

★ ★ ★

Barely a year after the UMT concept was canned, Lieutenant Colonel Ed Rowny sat in MacArthur's Pacific headquarters in the Dai Ichi building in downtown Tokyo. He was on weekend duty on June 25, 1950, when an urgent transmission came in from Korea: the North had invaded the South. The "Land of the Morning Calm," an ancient dynastic name for Korea, was anything but.

Rowny rushed to MacArthur's apartment to strategize with him and General Edward "Ned" Almond on mobilizing regional forces to protect U.S. interests and security on the Korean peninsula. It quickly became apparent that America's occupation forces in Japan were grossly unprepared for war. Their role had been more suited to a police state than battle. Troops were severely undertrained and ill equipped. Adding to those inadequacies, the majority of America's combat-ready troops from World War II had by now been separated from the service. History was repeating itself.

Of course, the U.S. did not call Korea a "war," but General MacArthur certainly did, loathing the term "police action." As the war intensified by the hour, Rowny was surprised to learn that on top of his regular duties, which focused on planning operations, MacArthur was assigning him additional responsibilities. He would be MacArthur's official spokesman, as the prior officer in that position had cracked under pressure, apparently turning to drink instead of to reporters. MacArthur, on the other hand, knew the publicity hot seat well; he'd been the Army's first press officer in 1915 and was confident that Ed Rowny could take the heat.

"Tell the press everything they need to know," MacArthur instructed, "and nothing they need not know."

What definitely became apparent to those on the ground, however, was that despite help from U.S. forces, the South Koreans were also poorly trained and ill equipped. They could not possibly beat back the ninety thousand North Koreans and 150 Soviet tanks that crossed the 38th parallel separating the two countries. North Korean forces overran U.S. and South Korean positions—including the capital of Seoul.

In the ongoing mayhem, two '41ers were captured: William "Tom" McDaniel and Paul Liles.

McDaniel had just led a counterattack, in late July 1950, when he was captured by the enemy in Taejon, which is situated roughly midway into South Korean territory. He was among several hundred American POWs then forced to march from Seoul to the North Korean capital of Pyongyang, a distance of about 120 miles. Prisoners already suffered from wounds, disease, and hunger, yet they were forced to walk some 25 miles a day. Guards shot those who could not keep up. The forced march was eerily reminiscent of the Bataan Death March, though a fraction of the troop size. It was, however, far more prolonged and went farther in distance. Bataan was some sixty miles over about five days; on this toxic traipse, surviving soldiers would see summer turn into fall—and hundreds of miles go by.

McDaniel, however, was ever-compassionate as the march began. As a young man, he had given away his only coat to a schoolmate who didn't have one. Now, as the most senior officer among the prisoners, he risked his life to intercede with the captors, trying to get food, medications, and better treatment for the prisoners. Like Tuck Brown and James Forsyth in boxcars, he also took command, organizing prisoners to help the weak and wounded so none would be left behind. Inspiring the men, he restored their will to live. McDaniel refused to be broken.

As that was occurring, the North Koreans were backing U.S. and South Korean forces into a corner down the peninsula, to "the Pusan perimeter," so called for southeastern port city of Pusan. Additional U.S. forces were dispatched from Japan and valiantly defended the perimeter with rearguard actions, but they lacked any real strength for offensive actions.

MacArthur and Almond set their sights on an amphibious invasion to land two U.S. divisions—about thirty thousand men—into South Korea. Rowny was one of three officers charged with developing that plan. The others were Colonel Lynn Smith, considered one of the best planners in the Army, and Colonel James Landrum, who'd been awarded the Distinguished Service Cross in World War II. The three recommended beachhead objectives, landing in the south on the west coast across from Pusan.

MacArthur had other ideas. He wanted to go for the throat: "Always go for the objective, and the objective is Seoul."

Seoul was considerably farther north than Pusan, and not far from the heavily fortified Demilitarized Zone (DMZ) of the 38th parallel. The closest port to Seoul was Inchon, twenty miles from the capital.

Drawing on his experience in the Philippine Islands, MacArthur suggested, "Why not terrain hop and land at Inchon?"

"First, it's very close to Seoul and the enemy would certainly defend the capital in great strength," explained Rowny. "Second, it's the most difficult of all places for a landing because the tides are so huge. Inchon has a thirty-two-foot tide, the second-greatest tidal range in the world. It would be difficult for a landing force to fight without reinforcements until those could arrive on the next tide."

"The tides are simply another obstacle to be overcome," countered MacArthur. "Never take counsel of your fears."

The three planning officers didn't; they zealously attacked the drawing board, combining their talents to draw up the plan to invade Inchon. But the Joint Chiefs were unwavering in their opinion that it was the worst place possible for an amphibious invasion due to the high tides and thirty-foot walls surrounding the port.

Undeterred, MacArthur invited the Joint Chiefs to his Tokyo headquarters and proceeded with a grand presentation outlining the merits of an Inchon invasion. After six hours of his theatrics, the decision was unanimous. Inchon it was.

Already smelling victory, MacArthur told Rowny he was convinced Inchon would go down as one of the greatest battles in history.

Rowny was convinced of something else; after witnessing MacArthur's amazing powers of persuasion and charisma, he told Rita, "I am certain he can walk on water."

Timing was a major issue in the planning. Mid-September had a combination of favorable tides, good weather, and the least historical probability of a typhoon. But it would barely allow enough time for assembling necessary troops and equipment. Still, the alternative was far worse—waiting for the next favorable tides a month later when subzero temperatures would be approaching. September 15 would be the day.

Then came the debate over invading with small boats or LSTs. The former would give the advantage of a dispersed landing force less vulnerable to enemy fire, but those small units would lack strength to attack fortified positions. LSTs, on the other hand, could land entire companies together along with supporting weapons and ammunition. However, once an LST hit the beach and troops and equipment were unloaded, they would be vulnerable to enemy attacks until the tide changed twelve hours later.

After weighing the risks, the decision was for LSTs—strength in numbers.

And so on went the debating among the trio of planning officers, the weighing of risks and rewards, down to every last minute detail and plan of contingency. Especially important to the plan was building a bridge over the Han River into Seoul. MacArthur wanted to triumphantly return there with South Korean President Syngman Rhee on September 29, a symbolic date three months following Seoul's capture. The Han, however, was not only 350-meters wide, but also one of the world's fastest flowing rivers. Ed Rowny had to amass three different types of bridges to span it—about eight tons in total—since there was insufficient bridging of any one type in the entire Pacific region. Presenting a further challenge was that the vast maze of bridges would need to be heavily anchored to prevent sections from being carried away by the swift currents.

As Ed Rowny was contemplating this, General MacArthur looked over his shoulder and announced, "Rowny, you appear to know how to build a bridge, and I want you to be the X Corps engineer."

A corps engineer was supposed to be a brigadier general; Rowny was only a lieutenant colonel. But MacArthur solved that problem as he did most others—swiftly and abruptly. He immediately made Rowny a "brevet" brigadier general, giving him a temporary promotion, though without the commensurate pay raise. Rowny didn't mind the latter, especially since the only brevet brigadier general he'd ever heard of was his hero, Polish-born General Thaddeus Kosciuszko, who was George Washington's engineer during the Revolutionary War and later the designer and builder of West Point.

D-Day soon approached, but two days out a brutal storm swept away tons of bridging material. Devastated, Rowny scrambled for replacement material to be flown in after the invasion; it was the best he could do given that the offensive was imminent.

The invasion began with the dawn high tide on September 15. Marines stormed ashore from LSTs. They swiftly set up and climbed lofty aluminum ladders and charged over the seemingly impenetrable walls of Inchon. Other troops landed on beaches to the north and south of the wall.

This first wave quickly repelled North Korean defenders, suffering only light casualties. By the time the water receded, the Marines were well established ashore. The second wave rode in twelve hours later with the dusk high tide. LSTs unloaded vehicles, tanks, and light artillery pieces and then left with the turn of the tide.

The invasion, which went off nearly without a hitch, was a complete surprise to the North. Rowny felt triumphant with its resounding success. For the next two weeks, the Marines and Army soldiers relentlessly drove the North Koreans north and recaptured the capital, Seoul.

Rowny, in the meantime, began building the pontoon bridge across the Han, at the river's narrowest point where a fixed bridge had been destroyed. Army doctrine called for never beginning such a task until the far shore was cleared of enemy weapons. The North Koreans still had artillery and mortars in place that could shell the bridge site, but the pressure from MacArthur to meet the September 29 anniversary date of recapturing Seoul loomed close.

Shortly after engineers began installing anchors to hold pontoons in place, the enemy began shelling from across the Han. A number of U.S. engineers were killed, while a supervising colonel suffered a nervous breakdown, feeling responsible for those deaths.

Still, work on the bridge continued round the clock, aided by powerful five-foot diameter searchlights that a colonel under Rowny's command, Leigh Fairbanks, had developed after World War II, allowing for fighting and working at night.

As this was playing out, however, a tug-of-war was occurring in Washington with the State Department on one side arguing that Rhee was an autocratic dictator and should not be returned to power. On the other side was General MacArthur arguing that Rhee was the duly elected president. MacArthur prevailed.

Rowny was unaware of that drama; he had enough of his own. On September 28, a heavy storm broke loose several pontoons, and they began drifting downstream. Amtracs were dispatched to retrieve them. By dawn the following morning damaged portions of the bridge were being repaired, and Rowny figured that he needed five more hours to complete the task. Then he heard that MacArthur and Rhee planned to cross the bridge in a mere two hours.

Through what Rowny considered almost superhuman effort, Rowny's teams finished the bridge in time. General MacArthur and President Rhee landed at nearby Kimpo Airfield, formed a forty-four-vehicle motorcade, and victoriously crossed the Han. They entered the blackened city of Seoul, which was still ablaze. There, in a damaged auditorium, they held a stirring ceremony commemorating Seoul's liberation, this as a stray shell hit the auditorium ceiling in the midst of MacArthur reciting the Lord's Prayer. MacArthur continued on, finishing the prayer. Perhaps it helped, as there were no further shelling incidents. Many in the audience, grateful for Seoul's recapture, wept openly during the ceremony.

Ed Rowny too was grateful, but after his harrowing bridge ordeal, other thoughts ran parallel:

I wish MacArthur could walk on water.

Though Seoul would fall and be recaptured three more times, the Inchon Invasion went down in history as a decisive victory, a bold, cleverly contrived invasion. Unlike what occurred with Berlin in the waning days of World War II, the United States would not stand down. South Korea would not fall to Communism.

Still, the war would drag on for nearly three more years, entangling '41ers like Ace Bailey, Charles Canella, and James Forsyth in its web. It was a tug-of-war in which China and the Soviet Union aided the Communist North and the U.S. supported the South. Some '41ers flew fighter wings and kept the enemy awake with napalm. They conducted "heavy drops," the sky now raining 105mm howitzers on fully assembled platforms. Ed Rowny went so far as to drop an entire bridge—albeit in sections—to span a seemingly impenetrable chasm a hundred foot wide in places. A gutsy Air Force pilot made it happen, maneuvering his rocking plane as it dropped its heavy bridge load, which was assembled to help evacuate wounded marines who had been pinned down on one side of the chasm.

Classmates Joe Gurfein and Buster Boatwright held command positions in Korea as well, the former with infantry, the latter with supporting artillery—both tackling Heartbreak Ridge. Together with Bloody Ridge, it made up the mountainous terrain that dissected the 38th parallel, at an angle running from southwest to northeast. The mountains essentially defined the parallel, and he who controlled Heartbreak and Bloody Ridges controlled it.

Needless to say, battling for domination of the ridges was fierce, and the one who stood as victor alternated back and forth. In one especially bloody engagement on Heartbreak Ridge, Gurfein reorganized his decimated battalion, got it back in position, and arranged for food and water to be brought up and the dead evacuated. Then he insisted on walking every foot of the front line in daylight under hostile fire as an example to his men. George Johnson treaded the desolate landscape as well.

Amid all the back and forth, the lights dimmed a bit for American troops on April 11, 1951. A radio operator alerted Rowny and others on MacArthur's staff to listen in on an important announcement. They heard the news that MacArthur was relieved of his duties by President Truman.

An increasingly public rift between the president and the general had been caused by monumental differences in strategies. General MacArthur believed Communism could be conquered only by attacking China and that there was "no substitute for victory." In fact, he had repeatedly sought permission to make air attacks north of the Yalu River, which runs along the North Korea–China border, and had considered laying along that border a defensive band of radiation in the form of detonated nuclear weapons. President Truman, conversely, was prepared to settle for a deadlock in Korea, allowing it to remain divided along the 38th parallel. His secretaries of state and defense, as well as the Joint Chiefs, backed his view. Truman's higher priority was countering the threat of the Soviet Union in Europe, and he considered a broader Asian war as jeopardizing European stability.

MacArthur's staff, Rowny included, was shocked and deeply saddened by the president's decision regarding General MacArthur. He had commanded in World War I, led Allied Forces to victory in World War II, been awarded the Medal of Honor, and was revered by his troops in Korea. Rowny also knew that General MacArthur could never have bombed China or invaded it without Truman's specific approval.

Nonetheless, in Rowny's view, the general was over-vocal in his opinions on war strategy, and the termination of his command was justified. He exhibited poor judgment in his correspondence with members of Congress about winning in Korea at all costs and had violated one of his own basic principles. As superintendent of the United States Military Academy after World War I, MacArthur taught what he considered the honorable way for a subordinate to act when he disagreed with his superior. He should first confidentially and respectfully try to convince his superior to change his mind. If that failed, keeping the matter confidential, he should submit his resignation. Only after his resignation was in effect should he present his arguments publicly.

Rowny was disappointed that MacArthur would violate his own honorable teachings. Yet, thought Rowny of the general's dismissal, *For an officer of his stature, it shouldn't have been like that.*

As the Korean War ultimately wound down, Woody Garrett again stormed a POW camp but one prisoner, his classmate Paul Liles, was not among the rescued—his whereabouts unknown. There were whispers that Liles had given up information to the North. In truth, he was confined to a fifty-five-gallon drum buried in the ground for a month. He was provided minimal sustenance and forced to live in his own filth. All the while, guards hellishly beat the drum 24-7.

Liles eventually succumbed to this twisted torture and, with a pistol pointed at his head, denounced the U.S. But he lived.

Another four classmates gave their lives in Korea, including Tom Mc-Daniel. After surviving the death march to Pyongyang and beyond, he was sent out with a detail under the pretense of finding food, never to be seen again. For three years afterward, he bore the label MIA, and his wife, Helen, grim uncertainty. But along the way, she learned the truth: his

North Korean guards unloaded him and other American POWs from rail cars into the tunnel of their death, in Sunchon, a city north of Pyongyang. The prisoners were massacred in nearby ravines. It occurred in late October 1950, three months after McDaniel's capture. The '41er had striven for a sense of dignity among the POWs in his group and for each man lost had held services, given prayer, and made sure each was buried with slip of paper bearing the man's name tucked inside a bottle.[6] There had been no one to do the same for Tom McDaniel.

Against this cruel backdrop, there were still moments of poignancy in Korea. On one Christmas Eve, when American supply ships were being evacuated from the port of Hungnam on the east coast, Ed Rowny helped convince General Almond to carry aboard some extraordinary cargo—one hundred thousand fleeing North Korean civilians. They had been lining up for days in subzero temperatures in the hope of being rescued from certain death at the hands of the advancing North Koreans. The refugees were squeezed onto the departing U.S. ships—atop fuel tanks and vehicles and tucked into every inch in between. As the North Korean death squads were closing in, the refugees were transported to safer territory in Pusan, making for some very special Christmas cargo indeed.

THE CHILL OF THE COLD WAR

The dust had barely settled from the Inchon Invasion when another region of Communist insurgency revved up, and Herb Stern was ordered there.

"Where the hell is Saigon?" he asked.

It was the fall of 1950, and Stern was assigned to the U.S. Military Assistance Advisory Group (MAAG) dispatched to French Indochina to help curb the growing threat of Communism in the region. More specifically, the group's role was to advise French forces on training and logistics; support them in their efforts to organize armies in Vietnam, Laos, and Cambodia; and provide those armies with combat equipment.

MAAG was also to furnish supplies and equipment to the French, who were embroiled in a dubious war against Communist nationals, the Viet Minh. In short, France had colonized the Indochina region in the late 1800s, while the Japanese wrested portions of it away in World War II. Following Japanese surrender, while the French reclaimed much territory lost, a nationalist party in the north of Vietnam, the Viet Minh—led by Communist Ho Chi Minh—declared itself a republic. The French had been trying to reestablish control of that northern area of Vietnam since.

Upon hearing of Stern heading to this hot, tumultuous area of the world, Joe Reed offered a parting warning to his friend: "If I get orders to go there because of you, I'll kill you."

Stern's own skepticism over his tour emerged the minute he stepped on Vietnamese soil. He was immediately escorted to a Thanksgiving Day party at the U.S. diplomatic mission, where he spotted the illustrious de facto ambassador, Donald Heath. Heath was clad in a purple sharkskin suit, playing the piano.

Stern tried to contain his mirth as he watched the diplomat from Kansas perform, his fingers merrily dancing across the keys.

It's a far cry from the Pentagon, Stern mused. He wasn't sure if he'd landed in Saigon—or Oz.

Stern knew Heath was a career foreign service officer, having first started out as a White House correspondent. Most recently, Heath had been U.S. ambassador to Bulgaria till he was accused by that country of espionage and declared persona non grata. The U.S. responded by suspending diplomatic relations with Bulgaria.[1] Stern lacked an inside track on the truth behind the two countries' war of words.

Stern settled into his office in Saigon, crammed into a former casino in the city's Chinatown, called Cholon for "big market." The atmosphere was frenetic, colorful, and insanely crowded. Streets were lined with small storefronts stacked like dominoes, hawking goods the likes of which Stern had never seen. Crooked awnings were plastered with Chinese and French lettering, neon signs flashed at every turn, and electrical wires crisscrossed the streets overhead like massive mounds of twisted spaghetti. Added to that was the omnipresent smell of incense mixed with occasional wafts of opium seeping out from behind the shuttered windows of opium dens.

Stern's memories of his duty governing Bavaria were bizarre. He had a feeling Indochina would shape up to be even more outlandish.

He began handling supply logistics for combat materials including guns, trucks, and artillery slated for the Vietnamese, Laos, and Cambodian armies. All these materials, he discovered, had to be filtered through the French, and not all was on the up-and-up. Looking over one of their requests, he complained to his colleague, Dick Silver, an Air Force logistician.

"The French requisitioned enough barbed wire to encircle Indochina three times," griped Stern. "Apparently, they don't want to get out and fight; they want to fence themselves in."

He also didn't think the French very clever in ordering M1 rifles for local armies. "The rifles are bigger than they are!" exclaimed Stern to colleagues. He suggested shorter-barrel carbines, but his recommendation fell on deaf ears, and M1s it was.

Shortly afterward, Stern was on the phone with his French logistical counterpart, Lieutenant Colonel Claude Robbaz, an officer with whom he'd become friends while attending the French War College.

Asked Stern, "Claude, that shipload of rifles we supplied you . . . when will you be distributing them to your army units? I need to schedule an end-use inspection."

"You're not hearing this from me," answered Claude, "but those rifles are on a ship headed to Algeria."

"Damn! *Ces merdes!*"

Stern knew "those shits," as he called his French counterparts, feared a nationalist uprising in Algeria, as in Vietnam. Apparently, the French also thought the U.S. should contribute to its efforts to contain a looming war there.

Stern thanked Robbaz for the heads-up and immediately reported the arms diversion to MAAG chief, General Francis Brink. If a ship could pivot on a dime, Brink could make it happen. The arsenal of U.S.-supplied M1 rifles, originally intended for the Cambodian army, was soon returned to Vietnam.

Another time, the French sought dozens of new U.S. M-48 tanks to deploy to the Hanoi delta. The tanks weighed nearly fifty tons.

"Where the hell are they going to use them?" asked Stern of a colleague in MAAG.

"Maybe put them on rice barges," replied the colleague, "and sail 'em up and down canals?"

Stern again turned to Robbaz, requesting a bridge survey of the delta. It showed a maximum bridge tonnage of seven. Such French antics were unending.

Though Stern modified supply requests from the French prior to relaying procurement orders to Washington, he was by no means trying to cut reasonable requests off at the pass. Sometimes, he recommended add-ons to their arms programs; the intent was not to be stingy but rather strategic in terms of U.S. interests, which were aimed at preventing a takeover of Indochina by Communists and to allow for regional armies to defend themselves against the same.

All of Stern's recommendations had to be approved by General Brink, then signed off on by Donald Heath, under whose domain fell the work of MAAG in Vietnam. Some French requests were nearly as odd as Heath's penchant for sharkskin suits.

One day, Heath called Stern to the embassy to review details of a proposed program, which included Stern's recommendations on French requests.

Reading over the list, Heath paused."Why did you delete the cots and mattresses?"

Stern felt like saying, *The question should be, "Why did the French ask for them?"*

Instead, he replied, "Ambassador, the request should be denied. I've never heard of a Communist being killed by a mattress."

"Get out!" retorted Heath.

Stern backed out of Heath's office, trying to contain his amusement. It wasn't the first time he was thrown out of a chief's office. *And it won't be the last*, he figured.

It was on days like that when, in need of a good scotch in a city sorely lacking, that he settled for heading out with his cohorts for cognac nightcaps—French cognac and champagne flowed in Saigon, less so good whiskey. The only place to get libations after ten at night was in the French brothels. So he, Dick Silver, and Joseph "Preacher" Wells, a West Pointer from '38 who was chief of the MAAG Air Force section, frequented houses of ill repute even if no ill-reputing was involved. Sure, they bought the pretty girls drinks. They listened to their dreams of saving up money to "open up a shop back home" or return to France to marry and have children. Such talk would inevitably be interrupted.

"*Mon dieu* . . . I have a client," one of the girls would say. "I'll be back in thirty or forty minutes."

The officers good-naturedly excused the break in conversation. Far be it for them to dampen the local economy. Rather than ogling ladies of the night, the three men were usually content to dish about the futility of U.S. efforts in Indochina. Conversations revolved around questions like, "Why the hell are we here?" "What idiot thought up this plan?" and "How soon can we get out of here?" Not fast enough was usually the consensus. In fact, no amount of alcohol could numb the pain, in their view, of misguided efforts by the U.S. to insert itself into hopelessly jumbled Southeast Asia predicaments.

One day Stern, Silver, and Preacher decided to go out on a limb. They sent a telegram to the Department of Defense: "Let's get out of here; it's a meat grinder."

Within two hours the officers received a reply: "Mind your own business."

Lightning doesn't travel that fast, thought Stern. *What's up with this?*

Stern plowed on in Saigon, though his counsel seemed to have little impact. It was as if all his reasoned, well-crafted advice was swept into the back alleys of the opium dens, where it dissipated in a cloud of smoke. The policy of the U.S., it seemed, was to allow the French to do what the French wanted to do.

In the face of such misgivings, Stern had to cope with the added responsibility of overseeing military shipments arriving into the port of Nha Be, downstream from Saigon; it was a safer bet for ammunition-laden ships to unload there than in the heart of the capital. Nonetheless, shipments into almost any Vietnamese port were dicey, given the guerilla tactics of the Viet Minh. Their ploys included intricate patterns of road sabotage, homemade booby traps like bamboo tubes filled with gunpowder, and clever jungle ambushes. Often the Viet Minh hid out in vast tunnel systems and in general were hard for the French to ferret out. In the words of Mao, Viet Minh political agents "moved like fish in the sea." They also resorted to bombing bars and cafes frequented by the French.[2]

For protection, Stern employed French soldiers to travel with him and board incoming ships for inspection. He quickly acquired a new talent: speed-reading manifests as Viet Minh gunfire blazed from the far shore in his direction. Granted, it was small arms, not panzers, but it led Herb Stern to wonder where the heck the "front" was. Perhaps everywhere.

Occasionally, Stern was offered exotic diversions from the meat grinder, but it did little to assuage his ambiguity about his tour. When a Cambodian prince invited him on an elephant expedition to hunt tigers, Stern politely declined, "Thank you, Your Highness. But I don't hunt the things that hunt me."

At long last, after an eternally long twelve months in the sweltering Asian heat, his tour was drawing to a close. General Brink called him into his office.

"If you're willing to stay on for another year," offered Brink, "I'll let you bring your family over and you'll get a promotion."

Stern's mind raced back to the battlefield promotion he'd earned in World War II, the orders of which had been misplaced in the thick of things.

Nothing is a certainty, and no re-upping guarantees a promotion.

His mind flashed to Bette Allyn, his six-year-old daughter whom he had not seen in over a year.

Vietnam is no place for a little girl.

With what civility he could muster, he told Brink, "General, you could give me all the stars off of your shirt, and it would not be enough to make me stay in Vietnam another day."

General Brink smirked, nodded, and replied, "I don't blame you."

An elated Herb Stern was soon on a plane leaving Vietnam. His feelings of exhilaration were replaced by surprise over his fellow passengers. The plane was loaded with pretty ladies of the night. It seemed the French had begun turning over a degree of autonomy to the Vietnamese government and the latter, in its infinite wisdom, immediately took control of two important sectors of the economy: the post office and, yes, the brothels. As a result, French hookers were being expelled from Saigon to make way for local talent.

Once stateside, scuttlebutt over the trip home flew around Stern's fellow officers: "Herb and his girls left Vietnam."

Herb was grateful that his understanding wife, Rose, had a tolerance for his antics that reached higher than Mount McKinley.

★ ★ ★

It was nearly a year later, and Stern was working in the Pentagon, when he caught up one day with General Brink, who had just returned from Asia. Brink casually updated Stern on goings-on at the mission in Vietnam. Then Stern left to grab lunch with Joe Reed, whom he had not seen in some time.

He returned an hour or so later to hushed tones at the Pentagon. "Someone on the third floor just committed suicide," he was told.

"Who?" asked Stern.

"General Brink."

He died from three self-inflicted shots to the chest. Another shot missed its mark but pierced through the wall of an adjoining office and barely missed killing the officer within—Stern's classmate, Joe Knowlton. It was June 24, 1952. Immediately, there was speculation about murder and cover-ups, but Stern knew better. Brink had been having health problems, serious dental problems as far as Stern knew, but he wondered if those problems had segued into broader mental health issues.

Stern had been one of the last officers to speak to Brink, prompting a colleague to sarcastically ask, "Did you antagonize him and send him to his death?"

Stern was not amused. To him, Brink was a very likable figure and Stern was disturbed by his death.

The next day, Donald Heath's role at the Saigon embassy was made official: he became the first U.S. ambassador to South Vietnam, further cementing America's ties to the country—and further revving up the meat grinder.

By this point in the early 1950s, the heels of many from the West Point '41 class were clicking along the halls of the Pentagon, also known as "puzzle palace" due to the lack of clarity that sometimes came from command within. Stern's classmate and friend, Roy Atteberry, was among those in the palace. He was serving in the operations section of the Army's War Plans Division when Stern was assigned to logistics. The two were surprised one day to be called into the office of General Joseph Lawton Collins, chief of staff of the Army.

"What are you doing here?" asked Stern of his classmate.

"I don't know," replied Atteberry.

It turned out that General Collins, a 1917 West Point graduate, wanted ideas from them regarding the Army's new atomic firing units, which were essentially atomic cannons with artillery-sized shells. The units would be located in western Germany and aimed at the Soviet Union to act as a defense shield.

"We're deploying these firing units to Europe," explained Collins. "They will require considerable support, but we have no plan on *how* to support them—ammunition, ordnance, security, and such. That's your job. I want you two to develop a plan and come back to me with it."

Two prior groups assigned the duty had been dismissed for their dismally inadequate recommendations. Atteberry griped to Stern that the assignment was "an opportunity to have our heads chopped off."

The pair often met in the evenings, in the confines of their homes, so they could openly brainstorm on strategies for the highly classified program. One thing was immediately clear: they could not take the units and stick them in a field. The weapons needed to be positioned like strategic—not static—chess pieces, one moving like a knight, another a bishop, another a rook, and so on—nimble pawns in the game of Cold War.

With this in mind they set about war gaming the atomic units, using maps and charts to simulate how and where hostilities might occur and in each instance plan for tactics on deployment. Their defense plan incorporated the optimal number of units, the range, strategic positions, securing ammunition depots, methods for resupplying units, and so forth. There were as many moving parts to the plan as an intricate grandfather clock with wheels, springs, and chains working in concert to make its pendulum tick. But in this case the focus was countering the ticktock of the Soviet threat, which was increasingly a perceived time bomb. Stern and Atteberry agreed that the new atomic firing weapons, positioned correctly, were an American "ace in the hole" compared to an armor-armed Soviet Union.

After nearly a month of strategizing, they presented their findings to General Collins one afternoon, midweek. They reenacted their war gaming and made closing recommendations.

"This is what I've been looking for!" the general exclaimed. He abruptly stood and announced, "I'll meet you at the airport on Friday."

"General," asked Stern, confused. "What airport and why?"

"National Airport," answered Collins. "We're going to Europe."

Neither Stern nor Atteberry had a passport; combat in World War II had hardly required one. But in this case, given no military unit to which they were attached, passports were a necessity. Less than forty-eight hours later, passports in pockets, they were on a plane headed to Paris to present their findings to U.S. commanders at Supreme Headquarters Allied Powers Europe, or SHAPE.

While word went out for those commanders to convene, the two West Pointers were briefly ordered to Frankfurt to first present their findings to U.S. division and corps commanders. Once in Frankfurt, however, the two were unable to book return flights that would get them back to Paris in time for their SHAPE meeting. They got word that General Thomas Handy's private train was heading from Frankfurt to Paris, and as Supreme Allied Commander in Europe, the general would be attending the SHAPE presentation. Stern and Atteberry rushed to the train depot to hitch a ride.

Handy was in no mood for underlings as company—or so he thought. When Stern respectfully asked if he and Atteberry might join the general's car, expressing their urgent need to get to Paris, Handy barked, "Find some other way!"

"Well general," replied Stern politely, "then there is no need for you to go to Paris."

"Why?" the general questioned.

"Because, we're your briefing officers."

Handy promptly let all aboard.

After a successful presentation, a pleased General Collins ordered the '41 pair to enjoy themselves.

"Stay on in Paris till you run out of money."

Herb Stern and Roy Atteberry had little cash with them, but orders were orders. They asked the clerk at their hotel how many francs would be required to check out. They set that much aside in the hotel's vault for safekeeping and headed out to Pigalle, the Paris nightlife district that teemed with bars, theaters, and cabarets, including the renowned Moulin Rouge.

After a night on the town, the two awoke to a collective wealth of 75¢. Stern was designated the banker for that small fortune, and the two headed to Orly to catch a military transport plane back home. At the airport Atteberry was disgruntled to discover that a boxed lunch for the ride cost $1.25.

"I guess we're not eating till we get back to D.C."

"Maybe we can get some coffee in the Azores," suggested Stern, referring to the scheduled refueling stop.

Hungry and tired, they arrived in the Azores long past midnight. Heading down a corridor toward the all-night cafeteria, they passed slot machines that served as diversions for soldiers with time on their hands between flights. For Stern, the temptation was too much. He dropped a quarter in a slot and pulled the handle.

Atteberry glanced back at his colleague. "Did you just waste money playing the slot machine?" he asked incredulously. "Now we won't have anything to eat!"

Just then the clink of coins began—and kept going. Stern hit the jackpot, and a fountain of silver poured down, nearly $50 worth of francs.

"Yes!" shouted Stern, as he began lining his pockets. "Now let's go eat!"

Corrected Atteberry: "No. There's a liquor store open. *First* we buy duty-free; then we have breakfast."

The two resembled waddling ducks when they reboarded their flight, each with four bottles of fifths in the pockets of their winter coats. The trip to Paris had proved a resounding success.

★ ★ ★

Stern and Atteberry's West Point '41 classmate Charlie Fletcher was in Europe at the time too. Fletcher was charged with unifying the command of U.S. forces in Europe as troops swelled in anticipation of Soviet aggression. Theoretically, U.S. forces in Europe consisted of Army command with a sprinkling of Air Force and Navy. But they were splintered: the Army was spread about in Germany, Belgium, and Holland; the Air Force was based in England; and the Navy covered the Mediterranean out of Naples. Each command also had their own geographic areas of responsibility when it came to noncombatant evacuation—that is, evacuating U.S. military and embassy families should the need arise—rather than drawing on one plan that worked cohesively across services and borders during crises. Furthermore, it was under the Army's domain to plan, execute, and control troop movement on the Continent in the event of war, which did not sit well with the Air Force. America's "unified" forces, in short, still weren't very unified. Generals Eisenhower and Ridgway wanted this changed.

Fletcher couldn't begin to figure out how he'd ended up as the point man in that effort. Granted he was in Special Plans, Operations, and Planning with European Command, but he was only a young major.

Yet, thought Fletcher, *someone has to come up with the ideas; someone has to figure out the details of how it would work . . . a unified European command. It might as well be me.*

Turning the options over in his mind and analyzing the anatomy of command from every angle, it soon became obvious:

The Army's not talking to the Air Force, and the Navy's off sailing on its own. We need an organization tailored like the Joint Chiefs—an organization, a European command, that is one-third Army, one-third Air Force, and one-third Navy, jointly reporting to one commander.[3]

His concept was readily accepted. He drafted the details of how it would work, and subsequently a truly joint European Command for U.S. Armed Forces was established—a command and strike central. Initially, the headquarters was based in Frankfurt, then later Stuttgart. Little did Fletcher know but one day, America's worldwide war efforts would operate along similar principles from a joint strike command out of Tampa, Florida.

Fletcher was not the one to finalize the European plans in 1952, but he was more than satisfied with the promotion to lieutenant colonel that resulted from his efforts. It was clear that Charlie Fletcher had come a long way from that one-room schoolhouse in Michigan. But then, West Point had a way of doing did that—catapulting men with promise into roles that helped shaped a nation. The West Point class of 1941 was continuing to define America's future.

Others from '41 began to feel the chilly nip of Cold War assignments. Howard Felchlin was an attaché in Moscow when his clandestine activities rankled the Kremlin. He was caught with a camera on a train, declared persona non grata and given twenty-four hours to leave the country—with his wife and five children no less, without the $3,500 in clothing they'd just purchased to survive the harsh Russian winters.

Peer de Silva was more accustomed to Soviet surprises given his work in the CIA. He was continually dealing with defectors, double agents, and even triple agents—doubles recruited and sent back to spy on the hostile service. Not much could surprise de Silva. Still, America's ambassador to Moscow, George Kennan, sat nervously across from him in a quiet hotel corner one day and made a peculiar, macabre request. He wanted de Silva to obtain for him the "L-Pill," L standing for lethal. De Silva knew exactly what Kennan referred to. They were small glass vials protected by a thin layer of mesh. One bite through the mesh unleashed cyanide, bringing on death within seconds. The CIA used to offer L-Pills to agents it parachuted into the Soviet Union, so if caught, they could kill themselves rather than disclose vital secrets under the threat of torture. De Silva facilitated Kennan's request, though the Kremlin declared the ambassador persona non grata—just like Howard Felchlin—before he needed to put a pill to use; on an official visit to Germany Kennan had given a speech in which he strongly criticized the Soviet Union, hence his supposed crime.[4]

Clearly, the Cold War was growing chillier. Whatever corner of the globe, whether capitalist or Communist, '41ers were impacting the geopolitical balance of power, just as they had when they were dispersed across every military specialty and geographic region in World War II.

Except now, they were ascending in rank up the chain of command. Jim Forsyth was advising King Hussein's military in Jordan. Windsor Anderson had NATO-related duties in Morocco, working with King Mohammed V's government. George Johnson was a military attaché at the U.S. Embassy in Cairo—an "official spy" as he viewed the position—gauging the extent of Egypt's military activities to report back to the Pentagon. Johnson was especially looking for hints of an Arab war erupting with Israel, but he also kept an eye out for new weapons and their sources. Classmate Bob Edger, meanwhile, was sourcing new nuclear weapons as commander of a secret ordnance plant in Amarillo, Texas, which had pretty coffee shop attendants at the facility's entrance as a diversionary tactic to throw the inquisitive off-track. Another '41 classmate, Jake Towers, was in Iran, while Stan Ramey and Horace Brown were rotating in and out of places like Seoul, Tokyo, and Turkey.

Class of '41er Howard "Howdy" Clark stayed stateside. In the Office of the Chief of Psychological Warfare in the Pentagon, he proposed offering a large sum to anyone who brought in the most highly advanced Russian fighter jet. Shortly thereafter, the U.S. became the proud owner of the free world's first MiG-15, complements of a North Korean pilot who reaped the hefty reward.

20

GAZING INTO THE FUTURE

As the icy standoff with the Soviets continued, none had a chillier task than Henry Bodson. Having progressed from one missile program to the next, he headed to Alaska to create battle stations of western defense in the arctic tundra. Already, about a hundred missile stations had been established near key U.S. cities, military installations, and key industrial complexes. But if Russia decided to antagonize the U.S., its closest target was Alaska, just fifty miles across the Bering Strait. The Air Force was building observation sites along the Alaska coastline, and the U.S. intended to rely on the Nike missile system as well as Air Force and Navy air defense systems for protection.

Henry Bodson's challenge was how to create Nike systems to withstand subzero temperatures and frozen tundra. He was not sure how he'd ended up with the endeavor in the first place.

Well, this is a little disturbing. . . . What do I know about air defense? All my field experience has been surface to surface.

Apparently, the powers that be figured that in the hinterlands, where there was no formula, an enterprising Bodson could figure it out.

Belle was used to dutifully trekking with her husband from post to post, but this venture was far different. She adored green grass and blooming trees. Fort Richardson, near Anchorage, had two seasons—winter and getting ready for winter. Still, like most '41 wives on hardship duty, she adapted and improvised. So it was not like visiting the dairy farm of her youth, but during the twenty-three hours of summer daylight, the Matanuska Valley grew cabbages so huge—sometimes up to thirty pounds in size—it inspired her cooking, as did Alaska king crab. In the kitchen, Belle would embark on new endeavors to make up for what she lacked in her frozen surroundings.

Henry Bodson, in the meantime, attacked the tundra with fervor. One option for housing missiles, he quickly determined, was out of the question.

He couldn't go underground. His classmate Charlie Fletcher had barely succeeded in heating the ground to insert railroad ties to support artillery back in his training days in Michigan. This was Alaska. Even Jules Vernes couldn't get far into the earth in this territory. What were the options?

Other Nike missile sites on the continent typically had subterranean facilities, which made sense for a number of reasons, including avoiding the purchase of pricey real estate near big cities. In an attack, the missiles would be raised to the surface, though such facilities were not without their elevator problems. Henry Bodson, on the other hand, had plenty of territory to work with. So he conceived an optimal surface configuration made up of two structures. The first was T-shaped, its main wing housing living quarters for troops, while the stem sheltered battery fire-control trailers. Radar systems were mounted at roof level under protective covers. Several hundred yards away a second facility housed the missiles, with launchers mounted on carriages resting on rails that would allow for them to be rolled out for use. In essence, it was similar to what the Kennedy Space Center would later use on a much grander scale for space launches. But in the case of Alaska, the '41 rocket man had created a western defense to help stave off the Soviet threat.

★ ★ ★

Like Bodson, other '41ers continued to aim skyward. Air Force classmate Jerry La Rocca, after earning multiple masters degrees, in astronautics, aeronautics, hydrodynamics, and more, earned the nation's first-ever PhD in rocket science. He headed to Cape Canaveral where launchpads had recently been established. The proving-grounds location was on a barrier island along Florida's east coast, in an isolated area of Brevard County, and its range was the Atlantic Ocean. Cape Canaveral was growing by leaps and bounds in the early '50s, its location providing room to experiment with powerful missiles with less risk to populated areas than was the case at White Sands. It also benefited from proximity to the equator, given that the rotational speed of the earth is greatest at the equator, translating into less rocket-engine thrust required for ballistic missile testing—and eventually space launches.[1] La Rocca directed the Cape Canaveral range development and became director of missile tests. General Donald Yates was commander of the missile test center, operating out of offices at nearby Patrick Air Force Base.

Yates had been the chief meteorologist on Eisenhower's team during World War II and helped select June 6 for the D-Day crossings—likely the only day that month, it turns out, that forces could have successfully crossed the channel given the desired confluence of moon, tides, clouds, winds, and seas. Coincidentally, General Yates was also the older brother of the number 2 man of La Rocca's '41 class, Elmer Yates. Brilliance apparently ran in the family. Now General Donald Yates was putting his confidence in La Rocca as director of the missile range, aptly described as "the biggest and most expensive shooting gallery in the free world."[2]

One of La Rocca's many challenges was the very real potential for a missile going errant. If a missile exploded in place, it was one thing. If it went errant postlaunch, a decision would have to be made on whether to cut off its propulsion system midflight—like abruptly cutting off a jet engine—to let the missile fall to the earth intact. The timing was critical since the missile would continue on its trajectory at the time of shutoff. There was also a risk that its parabolic path—influenced by gravitational pull—could cause it to land on one of the Caribbean islands or, if heading north in an errant direction, hit Washington, D.C. In fact, von Braun had launched a missile from White Sands in 1947 that erroneously landed in a Mexican graveyard and desecrated it, much to the chagrin of dignitaries in that country; the U.S. had scrambled to hush up that situation with apologies from the White House.

La Rocca felt much more secure with the Atlantic as his graveyard, though already he was spearheading concepts and locations for tracking stations that would, over the next decade, be installed as part of a worldwide tracking range, established in places such as Bermuda, the Antilles, the Seychelles, Ascension Island, Zanzibar, Australia, and elsewhere. Until they were in place, however, missile navigation would remain an inexact science since, as La Rocca said, there was "no tape measure long enough to reach Ascension Island," let alone accounting for the curvature of the earth.

In the end, he never had to cope with an errant missile. But his tenure included coping with a seriously errant base employee.

La Rocca's phone rang one morning at six o'clock. *Who the hell is calling me at this hour?*

"Hello, Jerry," said the voice. "It's George Brown." Brown, a rapidly rising Air Force commander, and '41 classmate, was phoning from Washington.

"What the hell is going on down there?" he asked.

"What are you talking about?" replied La Rocca.

"You've got to look at the newspaper. It says that Colonel Jerry La Rocca, commander of Cape Canaveral, has plans to put an atomic warhead on a guided missile and shoot it into the eye of a hurricane, and it's going to save lots of lives."

La Rocca was stunned. "I'll look into it and straighten it out," he assured Brown.

La Rocca, in turn, woke up General Yates. The two quickly discovered that the wacky hurricane idea was the brainchild of the base's high-ranking civil service technical director, who thought his idea would duly impress U.S. senators in southern states.[3] The director was called on the carpet.

When he reported to Yates's office, the general, with La Rocca beside him, told the director he was fired.

"You can't fire me!" protested the director.

Yates, who'd been a gymnast at West Point, class of '31, vaulted over his desk, aiming for the director. The man hightailed it out of Yates's office before the commander could tackle him.

General Yates then immediately assigned La Rocca to assume the director's responsibilities, in addition to his existing military assignments. La Rocca had his hands full but was up to the high task.

Others in his class, at the same time, were headed down—underground, that is—conducting subterranean nuclear tests. The '41ers were tackling the Soviet menace from every angle.

★ ★ ★

Though anti-Communist efforts oftentimes seemed in vain, in Korea an armistice was struck in July 1953 and a POW exchange ensued. Those freed included Paul Liles. At first, he was shunned by some classmates for relinquishing more than his name, rank, and serial number to the enemy. Until Ed Rowny, Jack Norton, and Woody Garrett found out about his torture, about the fifty-five-gallon drum.

Rowny posed the question: "What would I do to get out of it?"

His answer: "There but for the grace of God go I."

The three went on a class campaign to free the bonds that still tied Paul Liles. The consensus: rather than shun Liles, we need to sympathize with him. It was not a moral infraction the '41ers had been faced with but a moral dilemma; they had wrongly jumped to conclusions and knew to stand down.

During the period following, the remains of Tom McDaniel—killed in Sunchon—were repatriated in a United Nations' mutual exchange with North Korea, his remains identified, in part, by a broken wrist from his childhood.[4] McDaniel was later awarded the Distinguished Service Cross, the highest award given to a soldier in the U.S. Army for actions as a POW.

In the meantime, while a settlement had been reached on one Communist front, other fronts remained tense. De Silva saw his prior suspicions of spies at Los Alamos validated when it was discovered that David Greenglass, the former lab employee there, had bled atomic secrets to his sister and her husband, who in turn passed them on to the Soviets. Greenglass struck a deal, giving up information on his sister and brother-in-law, to save his wife from being implicated in the spy ring. He was sentenced to fifteen years in prison. The Rosenbergs were executed. A fiery assistant U.S. attorney in Manhattan, Roy M. Cohn, played a key role in their prosecution.

Senator Joseph McCarthy jumped in on frenzied anti-Soviet initiatives, beginning a Communist witch-hunt aimed at Hollywood, the State Department, and the Army. Honing in on the latter, he lambasted the honorable discharge of an Army dentist who had fulfilled a two-year tour—at a time when doctors and dentists were being drafted into the service—but had pleaded the fifth regarding membership in "subversive organizations."

Yet during his tour, the dentist, Major Irving Peress from New York, apparently filled every troop tooth competently, had no serious service infractions, and did not try to subvert anyone. But there was McCarthy, in front of the courtroom flashbulbs, badgering the dentist's post commander, Brigadier General Ralph Zwicker, a highly decorated World War II veteran, laying blame on him for Communism infiltrating Army ranks through men like Peress. The senator swore that General Zwicker was a Communist lover "unfit to wear the uniform."

Newspapers trumpeted the comments. The Army general staff was enraged. When it came to witch-hunts, it drew a line around its own, and the chief of staff of the Army, General Ridgway insisted that things had gone "far enough."

West Point '41er Jack Murray, who by now had a Harvard law degree and was a judge advocate, was tasked with defending Army ranks against the inquisition. Anything that McCarthy did or didn't do, if it impacted the Army, Murray was to be the point man.

The Army had, in fact, been conducting investigations into its ranks to identify those with questionable loyalty, while at the same time respecting a soldier's constitutional rights. It was obvious to Murray that McCarthy, conversely, was after headlines more than the truth. With anti-Communist fever rising to a pitch, the senator made good copy. Murray was also convinced that McCarthy had someone on the inside:

Somebody in the Pentagon, thought Murray, *is tipping him off.*

Whenever a case was initiated against a member of the Army, McCarthy and Roy Cohn, McCarthy's flamboyant chief counsel, seemed to grab hold of that person's name within days and call him before the Senate subcommittee. Murray was unimpressed, remembering how McCarthy had also called General George Marshall a dupe for Communism. No one seemed beyond the senator's fury.

Joseph N. Welch, a feisty libel lawyer from Boston, became special counsel to the Army for the McCarthy Senate hearings. Lieutenant Colonel Jack Murray was the military representative by Welch's side to help him understand the inner workings of the Army. Murray had upward of sixty people working for him, including Judge Advocate General's officers, or JAG, who toiled through the night "flyspecking" transcripts and making notations so Welch could be fully prepared when hitting the Hill on hearing days.

On the morning of the first hearing, Jack Murray told Welch, "I'll be right here at the Pentagon, keeping track of things. We'll be watching it on TV, and I'll be able to shoot anything over to you as it occurs. . . . You can call me if I miss something."

"No, Jack," replied Welch. "You're coming with me. I want you with me at the hearings."

"Why?"

"Because you're lucky."

Murray's mother didn't think so. After watching her son on TV that first day, she called him, beside herself and nearly in tears. Her son, she thought, was fighting the only man in the country who was fighting Communists.

"Mom, it just ain't that simple," replied her son. He urged her to visit him and his wife. "Why don't you come down and stay with us for a while and maybe you'll get a feel for this?"

Murray's mother agreed, but one night when Joe Welch and Secretary of the Army Robert T. Stevens visited Murray's home for drinks, she wouldn't come out of the bedroom. She wanted to live with her prejudices, her son realized, like many in America. Especially Joe McCarthy.

Jack Murray quickly tired of the senator's games, including his habit of calling up officers stationed abroad, insisting that each testify. Usually this occurred when McCarthy, in one of his favorite ploys, asked a question of Stevens that he knew the secretary could not answer. McCarthy would then demand the appearance of someone who did know. Murray's team would recall officers from halfway around the world for that purpose and notify McCarthy upon their arrival. The senator would inevitably let the officers twiddle their thumbs for weeks on end and never call them to testify. A colonel from India waited three months. Rather than a means to the end, McCarthy's antics seemed to be nothing more than egotistic ploys to force the hand of military might.

Cameras followed those antics, recording McCarthy's every move. The seating area for senators at the hearings had before it a veritable snake pit of lights, cameras, and microphones. Newspaper and magazine photographers crawled among the obstacles, passing photos on to motorcycle messengers who raced to their outlets. Senator John F. Kennedy was known to take a peek at proceedings while his new wife, Jackie, and Ethel, Robert Kennedy's wife, were frequently in the VIP section; Robert Kennedy was a constant as one of the assistant counsels to McCarthy's investigative committee. It was a media circus with Senator McCarthy even viewing nuns as photo ops, making sure that when a few visited the hearings, they got seated directly behind him to ensure that the cameras captured the angelic scene.

Jack Murray had his day before the flashbulbs as well. As he testified on the stand, McCarthy berated him, professing disbelief at every attempt by Murray to explain anything.

Next thing, thought Murray, *he's going to ask me if I'm a Communist.*

McCarthy restrained himself from doing so.

Soon after, Murray unearthed information that showed McCarthy's chief counsel, Roy Cohn, had a rather undistinguished military career. Cohn got his military service stopped before it was to start. When Cohn turned eighteen in 1945, he was subject to the World War II draft. Coincidentally, he immediately garnered an appointment to West Point through a New York congressman, which excused him from the draft. Cohn failed the strenuous West Point physical exam and was not admitted. The same congressman appointed Cohn to the academy the following year, buying Cohn time to again avoid military service; there was an uncannily resemblance to the antics of Rowny's Baltimore representative in his pay-to-play scheme, albeit this scheme had different goals. The draft ended in 1946, solidifying Roy Cohn's free pass on military service.

Murray also discovered that Cohn had since arranged an appointment to the New York National Guard, a commission he still held in 1954. And he was about to be called up for two weeks of active duty—right in the middle of the McCarthy hearings. Murray, without consulting any of his superiors, ordered his adjutant general to cancel Cohn's National Guard orders "in the name of the secretary of the Army." Secretary Stevens swiftly ratified that same order before the weekend was out.

Murray wasn't surprised. *He doesn't want to see a man in Army uniform sitting at McCarthy's table during the hearing any more than I.*

On Monday morning, when Roy Cohn took his usual place at the hearings, Jack Murray couldn't resist saying to him that he'd heard a rumor that he was supposed to go on active duty.

Cohn responded by uttering expletives—but Jack Murray got the last laugh.

The hearings droned on. Months of unceasing hearings finally ended when McCarthy castigated a young man who worked in Welch's office, accusing him too of being a Communist, something that Welch viewed as a possible career-ender for the young man. It pushed Welch over the brink and prompted an exchange that would resonate in history as a pivotal event in the demise of McCarthy's career.

"Until this moment, Senator," said Welch, "I think I never really gauged your cruelty or your recklessness. . . . Little did I dream you could be so reckless and cruel as to do an injury to that lad. . . . I like to think I am a gentleman, but your forgiveness will have to come from someone other than me."

After Senator McCarthy's usual grandstanding in response, Welch asked, "Have you no sense of decency, sir, at long last? . . . If there is a God in heaven, it will do neither you nor your cause any good."

With that comment, the gallery broke out into applause. The nail was hammered into McCarthy's coffin. His relentless intimidation had pushed public sentiment too far.

Joe Welch left the hearing rooms in the Senate building on that day June 9, 1954. He grabbed Jack Murray's arm to accompany him as he exited. Welch's head was bowed as the two tried to get by jostling reporters, but Murray saw tears in Welch's eyes. The pair turned down corridors till the last of the photographers faded out of sight, then Welch turned to Jack Murray.

"Well, how did it go?" asked Welch. "I've been waiting for him to take the bait. I had those lines written, and I rehearsed them. I wanted to make sure they stung."

"Joe, you won big, and you know it," replied Murray. "I don't cry easily, but you had me on the brink of tears. You convinced the world that that was an honest response. . . ."

Welch interrupted. "Of course it was an honest response. I felt sure that McCarthy couldn't resist something like that, but I never knew when he would strike. I was ready for him."

The Army, in this war—one of words—had at long last been prepared beyond measure. The hearings soon ended; the drama was over.

Jack Murray later summed up the confrontation: "Joe Welch had done more in five minutes to deflate the McCarthy balloon and send him back to the obscurity from which he came than all of the editorial hand wringing and executive branch dithering had been able to accomplish in the four long years of his reign of terror. . . . McCarthyism was dead and Joe Welch was the executioner."[5]

The Senate later censured McCarthy. Jack Murray was charged with picking up the pieces, from the Army's perspective, of the tangled mess left behind.

★ ★ ★

As that hearings spectacle was unfolding, the U.S. effort to contain Communism abroad continued unabated. Though Korea was cooling off, threats from Eastern Europe were building steam. Budapest, in particular, was a hot spot, as Hungarian literati and students increasingly challenged the fundamentals of Communist leadership. De Silva was CIA station chief in nearby Vienna, the "spy capital of the world." He scrambled for information as events progressed at breakneck speed. Skowronek did the same for Army intelligence at the Pentagon, where he was chief of the Soviet section. So small was that section, however, that Skowronek was stretched to the limit and wasn't allowed to leave. He moved a cot into his office.

On October 23, 1956, students and workers took to the streets of Budapest en masse in protest against Soviet oppression. They demanded freedom of expression, general elections, the withdrawal of Russian troops, and economic reform, among other fundamental demands. The uprising was short-lived—too short for the United States to develop viable options for assisting a new Hungarian government. De Silva sensed this U.S. ineffectuality from the start of independence rumblings. The only border that Hungary shared with a non-Communist bloc country was with Austria, and under its 1955 treaty with the Allies to remove occupation forces and grant it independence postwar, Austria was required to maintain neutrality. No U.S. help could flow through Austria to Hungary.[6]

In early November, the Soviet military took to the streets with tanks and machine guns to crush the revolt, killing thousands, while thousands more flocked into Austria as refugees. The Cold War was darkening. The U.S. sponsored a United Nations' Security Council resolution calling for Soviet intervention in Hungary to cease. It was vetoed—by the Soviets.

As Eastern Europe sizzled, farther south Jack Norton was appointed chief of the U.S. Military Assistance Advisory Group in Yugoslavia. In reality, he was charged with preventing the Russians from "making a quick grab" and annexing the country. The Russians had erred strategically at the end of World War II by not leaving troops behind in Yugoslavia as they had elsewhere in Eastern Europe. The country's president, Marshal Tito, though a Communist, had since strained at the leash of Soviet oppression. He broke with the Kremlin in 1948 over "Cominform," the Information Bureau of the Communist and Workers' Party, a Soviet-led organization promoting solidarity among Communist parties from various countries. Tito was expelled from the group.

President Tito had since increasingly ruled with free reign. He also had a well-trained army stocked with Russian equipment. But holding the Soviets back from a military offensive against Yugoslavia were concerns that the U.S. would intervene.[7] The Soviets also had no direct common border with the country, so they tried more subversive efforts to topple Tito, which failed.

With the Soviets having invaded Hungary, however, Tito was getting nervous and warmed to the Kremlin. To keep the two powers apart, the U.S. sought to gain President Tito's good graces by offering him military equipment and advisers.

Hence, Norton arrived to the Yugoslav capital of Belgrade, taking up residence with his family in a complex for U.S. military families. Near its entranceway, a small detail of Yugoslav army troops was stationed for security. That provided little comfort for Norton's family when rioters soon began marching in front of the building, holding signs that read "Kill the Americans!"

Jack Norton grabbed his hunting rifles and loaded his shotgun. He barricaded the apartment entrance and the door to his dining room.

If they get through that, we'll all get in the last room. I'll barricade the bedroom door and will have my shotgun ready to go.

Family life in Yugoslavia, which included the Norton's six-week-old, was harrowing, to say the least. But Cheyney was an Army brat and a tough one at that. Despite the drama beyond the walls of her confines, she got Jack off to work in crisp, pressed uniforms. She tended to the kids and school activities. She entertained visitors, oversaw the maids, and managed to fit in tennis and golf with fellow Army wives.

All the while, Tito was tracking her husband's every move. Even the Nortons' maids were grilled weekly. But Jack Norton was bearing gifts during his tenure to the tune of $780 million worth of tanks, artillery, infantry weapons, and more, as well as helping to train Tito's military. He also learned to speak the local language and regularly lunched with Tito. His efforts went a long way toward gaining the president's goodwill. More important, he befriended the leader and, in turn, Tito trusted him. Norton convinced the president to resist Soviet attempts to ensnare Yugoslavia in the eastern bloc—not an insignificant achievement as the hammer and sickle sliced away at the region with the Soviets exerting increasing influence over Czechoslovakia, Romania, and Bulgaria in addition to their displays of strength in Hungary.

If not for Norton, Yugoslavia might have been swept into the Soviet Union.

★ ★ ★

Nonetheless, a Siberian-like chill continued to linger over NATO members, so Joe Reed was dispatched to NATO headquarters in Paris. He was there from 1955 till 1957, tasked with standardizing the vast arsenals of ammunition among member countries. The dizzying variance among more than a dozen countries was wreaking havoc in terms of logistics and resupplying forces in the field. How could a unified force stock ammunition for every weapon for every country? The answer was that it couldn't.

There were economic, logistical, and tactical advantages to NATO peacekeeping forces coordinating on matters of ordnance, and Joe Reed was to solve the puzzle, formulating the optimal combination of ammunition for a collective use of force. The mind-boggling mandate included standardizing small arms, artillery, propellants, and trajectories, with that effort escalating up to standardizing the shells used on large gunships.

It's a logistical nightmare, fretted Reed. *A soldier can carry only so much ammo into battle. He needs to be constantly resupplied. We need one type for every gun—but whose?*

The problem was that each nation wanted the chosen models to be *theirs,* since there were not only significant economic issues at stake but also balance of power and vulnerability issues. Joe Reed had little faith in his ability to convince France that Germany's ammunition was superior or persuade Denmark that Norway's was better or, God forbid, tell the United Kingdom that U.S. rounds excelled. At that rate he might as well throw another Boston tea party, given the popularity contest he'd lose.

They all want it to be theirs. I know that; they know that.

Joe Reed, however, wasn't bent on convincing the naysayers. He was bent on decisions. He analyzed the fixed characteristics that were to NATO's benefit and to the benefit of the equipment employed. It was like a beauty contest—Marilyn Monroe vs. Brigitte Bardot vs. Sophia Loren. Which ammo had the right curve? The right thrust? Which could knock 'em dead?

I need the round to come out of the chamber twirling, reflected Reed, *with a high rotation to keep it from tumbling. I need to keep the cartridge nose straight on target. That's what I'm looking for.*

He took into consideration the caliber of the ammunition employed by various weapons. He examined propellants and scrutinized primer analyses, factoring in smoke and flash trajectories. He probed the types of gunpowder used, significant because it established the degradation of a barrel—the erosion caused by corrosive vapors. Then there was climatic storage. To prevent deterioration, some ammo needed to be stored at a controlled temperature with a maximum humidity level.

Between all the guns, shells, powders, chemicals, and ancillary issues that Reed was melding into a unified formula, it felt as though he had taken on the role of mad scientist. And through it all, the tug-of-war continued between this nation and that, pulling, pushing. But Reed was not one to shy away from confrontation. Twenty years earlier, he had rallied an entire West Point company to buck authority rather than ostracize a black cadet. Now, given this directive, he didn't care if the powers that be were white, black, yellow or green and whether a Frog, Brit, Kraut, or other. He roamed from one nation's NATO military ordnance specialist to the next, negotiating and all but tap-dancing. Joe Reed planned and improvised. He connived. He coerced.

The United Kingdom was the toughest opponent since it was the largest manufacturer of military weapons next to the U.S., but the two powers did not see eye to eye on weapons of choice.

Reed thought back to World War II when the Brits were flanking his left along the Siegfried Line.

Even then, they had a different view of what artillery could and should do. Nothing much, he realized, had changed.

Adding to the quagmire were vast sums of money at stake. With so many eyes following the money, Reed knew he could end up with a far different type of firefight—a blazing inferno centered on money. But Reed didn't plan to get scorched. If there was one thing he knew, it was the workings of guns.

As he liked to tell anyone that would listen, "I'm one of the two best artilleryman in the Army," to which he would add, "I can't think of the name of the other son of a bitch."

He was, naturally, referring to his best friend, Herb Stern, who at the time was stationed in Naples at the NATO headquarters of the commander in chief of Allied Forces Southern Europe, or CINCSOUTH. Part of his job was to write a defense plan for NATO's eastern border, which would be folded into the organization's overall defensive concepts.

Turkey's border with Russia figured prominently in the equation. Consequently, a month after arriving to Naples, Stern traveled with fellow NATO officers to the eastern reaches of Turkey, to the city of Erzurum near the border of Soviet Georgia.

There, the team surveyed the terrain as part of their defensive strategy. It was so rough and mountainous, however, that trying to push just twenty miles east in Turkish command vehicles took the better part of a day. On one trip Stern was subjected to nine flat tires. Fortunately, Turkish ordnance units along the border carried ample spares and, fortunately, Herb Stern was accustomed to inglorious assignments.

He took refuge from one such jumbled trip by accepting an invitation to the Turkish army officers' club in Erzurum. There, as waiters passed around hors d'oeuvres, Stern eyed a tray. *That's the most god-awful mess I've ever seen.*

"What is it?" he asked his Turkish host.

"That's sheep's brain marinated in olive oil," the host replied.

"Oh my goodness. You eat that?"

"We Turks," answered the man, "think it's good for making babies."

Exclaimed Stern, "Pass me the sheep's brain!"

It had been nearly twelve years since his daughter Bette Allyn was born, and doctors had long since told Rose there was no chance for another child, given a thyroid problem that had already prompted four operations. But Herb Stern held out hope after a renowned Johns Hopkins specialist said he could cure Rose. In the last of her surgeries, he removed a sizable chunk of her thyroid.

Whether the specialist was a miracle worker or it was the sheep's brain, Herb Stern couldn't say for sure, but nine months later Robert Stern was born to the couple. The twisted roads of inglorious assignments perhaps led to glory after all.

During the period of his assignment in Naples, Stern made monthly sojourns to NATO headquarters as part of his operational planning. While in Paris, he always capitalized on the opportunity to dine with Joe Reed and his wife, June.

One day when Reed was in Italy, he decided to reciprocate by showing up in Naples unannounced. In addition to *not* giving Stern a head's up that he was coming, Reed didn't even know where his '41 cohort lived. He knew only that there was a section of the city favored by American officers. He took his chances wandering the streets there, shouting, "Herb Stern. Where are you? Herb Stern. Herb Stern . . ." He was like a blaring foghorn, booming through a hazy mist, warning of impending doom.

Rose heard the hollering and the familiar roar to the voice. She stepped away from baby Robert, out on to the balcony of the family's rental villa. She peered over the railing to see Joe Reed standing there wearing a broad grin. Rose shook her head. Trouble had arrived. Doom indeed. She stepped inside and told Herb to break out the scotch.

Joe Reed soon returned to Paris and made his NATO ammunition decisions, including which rifle rounds would be used—the 7.62 x 51mm cartridge, or simply put, 7.62 NATO. Its performance met Reed's criteria, including working well under a wide variety of conditions from desert to altitude, hot to cold, and the rounds sustained their firepower during periods of storage. The U.S. would produce the rounds—as would other nations if they could meet the product standards. His edicts were accepted by all NATO nations for use with weapons such as the M14, which became a standard combat rifle as well as sniper rifle, and the M60 machine gun. A war within NATO had been averted. The '41ers continued to put their fingerprints on the future of America's military might, and its Allies. The round chosen by Reed remained NATO's standard round—used by infantry, weapons mounted on vehicles, aircraft, ships, and more—well into the '90s and, with some enhancements, into the next century, in addition to the 5.56 NATO round that came into use with more compact weapons developed over time.

★ ★ ★

Across the ocean from Reed, there remained fears of a broadening Soviet crisis. As a result, the United States was working furiously to create an intercontinental ballistic missile that could reach anywhere on earth. None felt that urgency more than '41er John Harris, who was working on what some called "Buck Rogers" projects.

Friends chided him, "What did you do wrong to get into a program that isn't even real?"

But everyone realized just how real things were when the Soviets launched the world's first satellite into orbit, *Sputnik*, in late 1957. The space race was on. President Eisenhower was furious but put on a show of calm for the American public.

The U.S. soon countered with a promising launch, *Vanguard*, but after reaching an altitude of only four feet, the launch exploded and sputtered miserably to the ground. The press labeled the failed endeavor as "kaputnick" and "stay-putnick."

Harris never doubted success. In early 1958, his Atlas program launched the longest surface-to-surface missile ever achieved. In December of that year the program rocketed the world's first communications satellite into space. Across the radio airwaves came the announcer's dramatic voice, sounding like a broadcast from *War of the Worlds*: "Only a handful knows the actual course plotted for the Atlas. It's a secret held by thirty-five men in the entire country. . . . The amazing communications system carried aloft, the Atlas, can record messages from earth, record them and rebroadcast them on a command signal from the ground."[8]

It was from this "new beyond" that people heard the gravelly voice of President Eisenhower delivering a Christmas message: "This is the President of the United States speaking. Through the marvels of scientific advance, my voice is coming to you via a satellite circling in outer space. My message is a simple one: Through this unique means I convey to you and all mankind, America's wish for peace on Earth and goodwill toward men everywhere."[9]

In truth, Eisenhower was on a mission. He never again wanted to be outdone by the Soviets. When he had been chief of staff of the Army, from 1951 to 1952, he had a small Army team to "gaze unfettered into the future." It was a concept he established after the war, in 1947, stipulating that a group "be divorced of all practical and mundane things of today." The team's sole function was to imagine warfare in the future and think up suggestions accordingly. It was the only service unit in history, up till that point, that was solely an "idea-thinking organization."[10]

The concept was eventually picked up by the Joint Chiefs of Staff, which formed the Joint Advanced Study Group to determine what paths the U.S. needed to forge to continue as the world's superpower. The small group developed long-term technological and strategic forecasts, peering out twenty years forward to prepare blueprints for the nation's future, including the greatest innovations on the horizon. Eisenhower, as president, now wanted to borrow that Joint Chiefs' group. It included Herb Stern.

Stern had already been immersed in heady matters for two years as part of the group from 1958 to 1960. Together with other team members, including a gutsy fighter pilot named Robert Kirtley, he scoured the country, touring top-secret arsenals as well as exploration and research centers to speak with premier scientists and visionaries of the day. He visited major missile and aircraft manufacturers. He traveled to top-secret facilities, like Los Alamos, which continued pushing boundaries by detonating the world's first thermonuclear hydrogen bomb. At Redstone Arsenal in Alabama, he convened with von Braun, the German rocket scientist. A version of von Braun's ballistic missile, in fact, helped launch the first U.S. satellite to orbit the earth. That satellite, in turn, was designed under the direction of Dr. William Pickering at Jet Propulsion Laboratory at the California Institute of Technology—another stop for Stern and Kirtley on their road tour. The scientific payload aboard the satellite aided in discovering the earth's band of radiation.

To Herb Stern, all the brilliant mavens seemed interconnected, like spokes turning the wheels of advancement. He remembered well those intellectually grueling days at West Point when mechanics, sound, heat, electricity, magnetism, and light were incorporated into classes. Now, he was witnessing firsthand how modern scientists manipulated these same forces to create the newest earth-shattering technological and military applications. At times Stern could only guess what payoffs might result, like one day when he and Kirtley visited Stanford University's research labs. There, they watched a small, spectacled scientist in a white robe hunched over small tubes from which emanated a faint glow.

"What's he doing?" whispered Stern, questioning his host.

"He's trying to convert light into energy," replied the man.

This guy's barking up the wrong tree, Stern thought. *But if something ever comes of this, it's going to be the cheapest energy ever developed.*

Little did Stern know but he was witnessing the development of solar energy, though he brushed it off as mundane lab work. The nearby streets of San Francisco held more allure to him, so he and Kirtley headed out in search of a tasty meal in the city's frenetic Chinatown. The pair walked its streets, strolling through crowded markets, passing men engrossed in sidewalk games and glancing in store windows reminiscent of Stern's Saigon days.

As they played pedestrian dodgeball, Kirtley spoke under his breath. "We're being followed."

"How do you know?" asked Stern.

Kirtley removed the omnipresent cigar hanging from his lips. "I've been noticing two men in our tracks. Where we go, they seem to go. We need to shake 'em."

"How?"

"Let's go into a restaurant," Kirtley replied.

The two ducked into an establishment, choosing seats with a door view, like mobsters wanting their backs to the wall. They explained to the waiter that they would wait to order.

Minutes later the restaurant door swung open and two suits stepped inside.

"There they are," whispered Kirtley.

The men took a table.

"Maybe FBI," speculated Stern quietly. "Hoover's inquisition. Everyone wants to know what the study group's up to."

"Either that or they want to see if we're selling secrets to the Chinese or Russians," added Kirtley. "Let's wait for them to order."

Stern and Kirtley watched as the agents placed orders and their drinks arrived. It was then that Kirtley, used to evasive action in the skies, outmaneuvered the men in black. He gave a quick nod to Stern.

"Let's leave."

He knew the men on their tail could not do the same without risking a furious Chinese proprietor chasing them with a bill—not an optimum situation for clandestine work. Kirtley and Stern purposefully walked by the agents, with Kirtley saying wryly, "Have a good dinner," to which Stern added, "Have a nice evening."

The two undercover men smiled sheepishly.

Stern and Kirtley exited, melting into the sea of Chinatown with a good laugh over the intrigue.

In truth, there were many in the upper echelons of national security that wanted in on the Joint Advanced Study Group's doings. Donald Quarles, deputy secretary of defense, was among them. Quarles had long been involved in lofty R & D issues; earlier in his career he worked in transmission development at Bell Telephone Laboratories, then later served as chairman of a Department of Defense committee on electronics, and subsequently headed special directives in air navigation and aeronautics, among other ventures.

Quarles approached Stern about a group he was helping launch at Bendix Aviation to be modeled after the Joint Advanced Study Group. Would Stern become the Army representative? The money involved would be a fortune compared to Stern's military pay grade.

Stern talked it over with his father. "Are you kidding me!" exclaimed his father. "Take it. For that kind of pay, you'd be crazy to stay in the Army."

"Dad," the younger man protested, "they just want me for what's locked inside my head from the advanced study project. They could care less about me; it's what I know that they want."

Stern thought back to three words by which he had tried to live his life: Duty, Honor, Country. He declined the job and continued his work for the Joint Chiefs of Staff.

And so it came about that President Eisenhower borrowed that Joint Advanced Study Group from the Joint Chiefs. Under the president's domain the group was given ultrasecret directives to delve into the most classified of national security matters, into a subject never before explored by a U.S. president.

"No one is to know what you are doing," President Eisenhower said. "I want to know what happens if this country is struck by a surprise attack."

An attack on the U.S. mainland had never been an issue in World War I, and though the Japanese attacked the Pacific in World War II, the mainland still remained out of reach of conventional weapons. By 1959 that was no longer the case. Technology was altering the playing fields of war—and with it, the response.

The new Joint Advanced Study Group was limited to one member from each of the services: Herb Stern represented the Army; Mike Moore stood for the Air Force; representing the Marines was Lew Walt (future four-star general and assistant commandant of the Marine Corps); Will Wehmeyer acted for the Navy. The group reported directly to the chairman of the Joint Staff, General Nathan Twining, and was also under the protective wing of the Joint Staff director, General Earle Wheeler. But ultimately the group was accountable to the president, who was singularly responsible for granting special security clearances to the officers involved. Any government agency, regardless of its secrecy, was made available to the four officers under orders signed personally by Eisenhower.

Aside from the president and Generals Twining and Wheeler, however, not even top brass within the officers' services were privy to their work. That made Herb Stern sometimes feel invisible. Walking the halls of the Pentagon, trying to gather critical information from senior echelons of the Army staff, he was routinely asked, "What do you need it for?"

Stern's pat reply: "I can't tell you."

One Army general, James Woolnough, USMA 1932, was particularly ruffled at Stern's mysterious questions. The general's long face grew longer still as the junior officer continued his inquiries.

He's got horse blinders on and wants nothing to do with anything that doesn't directly concern him.

Stern grew so frustrated he wanted to pull his hair out, except it was getting too thin to do that.

He approached an old friend, General Barksdale Hamlett, the Army's assistant deputy chief of staff for military operations. Hamlett was a well-respected, fast-rising commander whose career had included supervising logistics for the Inchon Invasion and commanding the American sector during the 1958 Berlin Soviet standoff. He had also been at the French War College with Stern, where the two had become good friends.

Stern poked his head into the general's office one day and asked, "Can I talk to you in private?"

"Come on in and close the door," the general replied.

Stern did so, saying, "This is Herb to Ham, and I need your help."

The spectacled general put Stern at ease. "This is Ham to Herb."

Stern proceeded to explain his predicament. "I'm on this project for the president, but I can't tell you what it's about except that I represent the Army. The problem is, I need to get information from the general staff, but General Woolnough . . . well, I'm not getting any cooperation from him. Frankly, he's a helluva dumb general and he's not interested in helping."

Stern detected Ham restraining a smile. *Well*, thought Stern, *he's not coming to Woolnough's defense.*

"Tell you what. Forget about him," said Ham conspiratorially. "You look around my staff, and you figure out who else you need to talk to. And I'll tell them they've *got* to talk to you. Simple as that; matter solved."

It was clear sailing from then on for Stern. All his queries on Army capabilities, organization, specialized equipment, and so forth—the who, what, where, and how of achieving national security objectives—could be answered. Those answers were critical to the group's objective, which was to address the vulnerabilities of the nation to a "first-strike" attack, along with gaps in the nation's response plans. The group's plans were also to include organizational and infrastructural improvements needed for national survival and recovery.

Herb Stern wrote to the director of the Joint Staff, describing the group's role as "providing provocative future concepts for national security," and outlined the group's broad-brush approach, which included the following major points:

1 A realistic post-attack damage analysis.
2 The role of the military services in civil defense and recovery.
3 The proper jobs of the Services in the continuation of hostilities.
4 The critically poor situation with regard to the civil defense posture of the country.[11]

The Joint Advanced Study Group was to take its military strategy out to 1975.

For a year, Stern and his three colleagues within the Joint Advanced Study Group pursued their secret quest, freewheeling among the top echelons of national security, remaining an enigma to all but the president and the Joint Chiefs' chairman and its director. When at long last the group's research was completed, its members presented their findings and recommendations to President Eisenhower in the White House. The president was joined by his secretary and defense liaison, General Andrew Goodpaster; Joint Chiefs' chairman Twining; and Lieutenant Colonel John Eisenhower, the president's son and assistant staff secretary in the White House.

After the team outlined its findings and implications, Twining turned to Eisenhower and said, "Mr. President, you know that knowledge of this project is very, very limited. What do you want me to do with this?"

"I will let these young men present their findings to the Joint Chiefs and the service secretaries," answered President Eisenhower. "Tell the Joint Chiefs they can listen, but they can't comment."

Stern was sure he saw Twining flinch. His own eyes widened. *The Joint Chiefs can't comment on our findings? Whoa.*

President Eisenhower turned back to the "young men," as he referred to them, though they were by no means novices; each had about twenty or so years of service. "Thank you for an outstanding job," the president told them, "and for answering my concerns."

The following week, on the night prior to their presentation, Herb Stern received a call from an executive to General Lyman Lemnitzer, chief of staff of the Army.

"General Lemnitzer would like to know what you're going to say tomorrow so he doesn't get blindsided," explained the executive.

"You know I'm not able to discuss the matter," replied Stern.

"You realize that this could affect your future assignments in the Army?"

"If you're threatening me," answered Stern, "then you can meet me in the Joint Chiefs' director's office at 8 a.m. tomorrow before the meeting."

Lemnitzer's executive backed off.

The next day, May 13, 1960, the Joint Advanced Study Group met in "the tank," the Joint Chiefs' strategy room situated on the third floor of a special wing of the Pentagon. Joining General Twining were Generals Wheeler and Lemnitzer; General David Shoup, the commandant of the Marine Corps and a Medal of Honor recipient; General Curtis LeMay, the vice chief of the Air Force, who was apparently filling in for the Air Force chief; and Navy Admiral Arleigh Burke, among others.

The presentation began with introductory summaries, analyses, and briefings. As requested, the findings addressed the vulnerabilities of the nation to a first-strike attack, gaps in response plans, and the organizational and infrastructural improvements needed for national survival and recovery.

Colonel Stern took over to present the second half of the findings. "How do we protect America's survival?" he hypothetically asked.

He addressed where the United States came up short and summed up the sweeping implications of the group's findings. He described an overall military posture that also incorporated space aspects as an objective for 1975, keeping the strategy flexible to allow for technological breakthroughs while not getting caught up in "new-fangled gadgets without valid military applicability."[12]

The room was quiet as the Joint Chiefs listened. No one said a word, but subtle motions betrayed their thoughts: the furrowed lines in a forehead indicating concern; a hand rising to a chin with an unspoken, "Why didn't we think of that before"; the far-away look in a set of eyes wondering, "Can that be done?" Then came the slight nods of heads from many, as though realizing it all made perfect sense.

LeMay, however, looked skeptical from the get-go, which was not surprising given his reputation for butting heads and believing that all roads of defense converged singly toward the Air Force. Herb Stern knew that reputation all too well. LeMay once told an Armed Forces Staff College gathering, "We don't need ground troops when we have air power."

That had prompted '41er Woody Garrett to rise from the audience to respectfully disagree.

LeMay barked for the younger man to "shut up and sit down."

"Sir, I will not shut up, and I will not sit down," Garrett countered. "I'm going to tell you the facts. Strategic bombing surveys show that when bombings increased against the Nazis and Japanese, it rallied them, raised morale, and made them fight harder. You cannot bomb people into submission; you can't stop onslaughts with air alone. You have to have troops on the ground."

The crowd erupted into applause at the time, infuriating LeMay.

LeMay now brought that same air of superiority into the tank as he begrudgingly listened to another '41er, Herb Stern, tell him things he didn't want to hear. The Joint Advanced Study Group's war gaming had determined that any major strike against the U.S. would include trying to disable its key retaliatory forces—and that meant the Air Force. Should that occur, there would be minimized air forces left to undertake recovery and restoration efforts. On the other hand, the Navy's critical assets—missile-laden submarines—could be expected to remain largely intact undersea, while the Army, if attacked, would do what the Army is always trained to do— move and reallocate resources. Were there to be a first-strike attack, the Army, with its established national command and control infrastructure, emerged as the primary force with overall responsibility for immediate response and national recovery.

LeMay grew increasingly piqued at the roles and missions described, his barrel chest rising till his rage boiled over. He bolted out of his chair and yelled, "I'm not going to listen to this bullshit!" He stormed out of the room like a disgruntled base runner called out—except this was no game but a meeting of the highest military leaders in the country.

Stern was stunned at the outburst. *He doesn't like the Air Force role that we laid out. The formula for success, the grand scheme . . . it doesn't give him enough power. He wants it to all be about the Air Force.*

Someone interrupted his thoughts with "please proceed."

Stern shrugged, unfazed. *Our findings are about what's best for the country, not about power plays and protecting turf.*

He finished, with those in the room taking it all in. The edicts, Stern realized, were not going to be disputed but embraced, just as President Eisenhower had known they would be. It was a fait accompli; it was clear what paths the Joint Chiefs needed to pursue for America's survival.

When the presentation was finished, the chairman simply said, "This study is going into the black box."

There were not many findings that went into the Joint Chiefs' black box—the depository that held the most highly guarded of classified secrets. So shrouded in secrecy was the box that future Joint Chiefs could retrieve documents from it to read, but none were permitted to even jot down a note from them. What the nuclear football was to the president, the black box was to the Joint Chiefs. The president's Joint Advanced Study Group findings were dropped into that black box.

Hours later General LeMay relieved his Air Force representative from the study group, holding him responsible for an Air Force role not up to his lofty expectations.

Herb Stern, meanwhile, got a call from Lemnitzer's executive. "General Lemnitzer wants to see you in his office."

Herb Stern was not terrified in the Battle of the Bulge or aboard a Saigon ship getting zinged with bullets. But Herb Stern was scared to death as he headed to Lemnitzer's office.

My career in the Army might be over. I'll be relegated to some training base in the middle of nowhere.

Arriving to the chief's office, Stern nervously asked Lemnitzer's executive, "You're going in there with me, right?"

"No. The general wants no one in there but you."

Stern entered the office and closed the door at Lemnitzer's request.

The chief of staff of the Army, standing imposingly before Stern, said, "I just got back from the White House, and I have a question for you. . . . How the hell did you swing that study?" Lemnitzer broke into a broad grin. "That's the most realistic study I've ever heard coming out of the Joint Chiefs."

Herb Stern exhaled. The rigidity in his shoulders eased.

"General, the outcome of that study was automatic. I didn't alter the findings, and I never influenced them. We just looked at a situation, as the president requested, and how to handle it."

Added Lemnitzer, "I'm very pleased with the outcome."

So am I, thought Herb Stern, *so am I.*

His career in the Army was secure. Herb Stern, however, became a hostage to his knowledge. The president had personally granted members of the Joint Advanced Study Group unlimited and top-level security access to certain agencies. Once provided those security clearances, none in the group were permitted to leave the country for two years afterward.[13]

21

LITTLE GOLD CORVETTE

The amber wheat fields surrounding the town of Fulda, in the northern German state of Hessen, gave little indication of the potent power of the land, but in 1962 those lowlands were an enormous canvas upon which armies to the east and west were drawing up battle plans. If World War III were to break out, the Fulda Gap was where it was expected to begin. That threat seemed far more imminent than when Walter Woolwine considered the same scenario a decade or so earlier.

Now, Charlie Fletcher sat poised on high alert, honed in on the gap's strategic importance. Through it, the Soviets could rapidly mobilize massive numbers of troops and tanks and then march nearly head-on to Frankfurt, the economic center of West Germany, within a couple hours' striking distance. Soviet tanks outnumbered those of the United States by about ten to one, hence the reason for Fletcher's "big guns."

Fletcher, who commanded the 210th Artillery Group, was ready to defend the Fulda Gap at all costs. His concern was not only Russian troops penetrating those lowlands and advancing on Frankfurt. If the Russians were to break through frontiers near Nuremberg, they could head southwest toward Heidelberg, and from there France was a stone's throw away.

Defending the gap required huge arsenals. Fletcher's repertoire included Honest John rockets—self-propelled and unguided—and Sergeant missiles, propelled by an independent force and guided. Both were capable of carrying nuclear warheads. There were 8-inch towed howitzers and 155mm self-propelled howitzers, the latter with a range nearing twenty miles. These too were nuclear capable. And there was more. For world powers looking to stave off a calamitous nuclear war, this western arsenal was a striking paradox.

Needless to say, thoughts of a matching, opposing arsenal chilled many gunners to the bone. Fletcher prepared his troops for what to expect. Part of training soldiers, he believed, was teaching them that the anticipation of the unknown was typically worse than the reality.

"You will feel like you're faced with overwhelming force," Fletcher told his troops, "and everything is telling you to leave and get back to a defensible position. You will feel like you're the only one fighting the enemy, like the whole world is collapsing. It isn't. Everyone else is feeling the same way. Use common sense. Do what you're trained to do and you'll get through it."

Fletcher's classmate Paul Skowronek was putting his training to use across the wall in the GDR in East Berlin. Skowronek was up against the Russians but unarmed, his duties far from routine. With Soviet studies under his belt, he had been appointed chief of the U.S. Military Liaison Mission in the Soviet Zone in early 1963. Since World War II, the U.S. and USSR had each allowed a team of fourteen men to patrol the other's side of the wall dividing East and West Germany. The Soviets had a mission in Frankfurt, while Skowronek headed the U.S. version in East Germany. The theory was that this mutual observation would prevent possible hostilities, since any miscalculation could start a new war. These were "tinderbox points," as Skowronek called them.

In essence, Skowronek was to defuse inflammatory incidents in the Soviet Zone that might cause Fletcher's high alerts to become red alerts. He was also expected to discern if Russian troops were moving into attack posture, thereby serving as an early warning system for commanders like Fletcher. Nowhere else in the world did the Russians permit such an arrangement, where tensions and dangerous misconceptions could be reduced by allowing their military establishment to be observed, if only enough to prove that they were not preparing to attack the West. And if tensions were to mount, Skowronek would serve as liaison between two heavyweights—the commander of all Soviet forces in East Germany, General Ivan Yakubovsky, who was a strapping World War II war hero, and the four-star commander of U.S. Army forces in Europe, General Paul Freeman.

In terms of the missions, each country had to provide facilities for the other side. The U.S. got the far better deal. Berlin had been badly damaged during the war, but there remained intact a lakeside country estate in Potsdam that had become the U.S. mission. Potsdam House, as it was called, was the former villa of a German prince. Crystal chandeliers and ornate mirrors adorned the main building, which had reception rooms, a large ballroom, nine bedrooms, a huge kitchen, servants' quarters, and expansive grounds.

The Soviets had long before absconded with the most valuable of the villa's former furnishings, but Skowronek and his officers didn't reside at the mission, so it hardly affected them. There was an Army headquarters five miles away in West Germany, and the officers preferred living there and commuting to Potsdam House. The mission served primarily as a communications headquarters, though nothing of a secret nature was discussed there. The villa's ancient heating, plumbing, and electric systems were constantly in need of repair by the Soviet hosts, and U.S. officers assumed that the "fixing" also involved listening devices.

The Soviet mission in Frankfurt paled in comparison to Potsdam House. Like Berlin, Frankfurt had been heavily bombed, so finding a place with living quarters, office space, and entertainment facilities, as required by liaison counterparts, had not been easy. Several civilian homes had been combined to house the Soviet mission, but it was situated a hundred miles from the nearest Soviet Army headquarters. The only reason the Russians accepted this unequal situation was because it was a time of austerity, and they were relieved not to have the burden of housing costs for U.S. officers in Potsdam, whereas the U.S had to foot the bill for Soviet officers in Frankfurt.

Costs were of little concern to Skowronek, who was given an almost unlimited budget to host lavish parties at Potsdam House as part of maintaining a rapport with the enemy. He and Virginia, who was at ease with entertaining and protocol, invited upward of a hundred guests to their elaborate dinners. Included among them was Skowronek's counterpart from the Frankfurt mission, Major General Bondarenko, and other Soviet military attachés. The British and French had missions within the Soviet Zone as well, so their officers also attended. When Skowronek first saw the elaborate dress uniforms of the latter, he decided on adjustments to his own and had his white tie and tails tailored into a military uniform complete with gold epaulettes and braiding. Virginia usually glittered in gowns and cheerfully fox-trotted her way across the dance floor. The austere Russian general, on the other hand, tended toward sternness, always donning the same light blue jacket and dark blue trousers, reflecting the somber mood of the East.

At the fetes, Skowronek tried his best to strike up conversations with the Russians, but they were cliquish; it was soon clear to Skowronek that they attended only out of duty. While Air Force General Bondarenko and his young, attractive wife were sophisticated, the ground forces were more provincial, backward in both dress and manners, and they often appeared uncomfortable. Skowronek took to holding buffets so they wouldn't be embarrassed about not knowing which fork or glass to use, or he held casual picnics on the expansive lawn, like for the Fourth of July, to put them at ease. One man in particular made them stiffen, and a nod from him meant it was either time to ease up on the liquor or to depart. It was clear to Skowronek that the man was KGB, making sure that no Soviet defected or got too chummy with Westerners.

The mutual observation—the presumed goal of the missions—in actuality meant a lot of sneaking and peeking, getting a look at each other's aircraft, estimating weapons stock, and the like. Each side was supposed to have complete freedom to travel in the other's zone. Even the Stasi, the East German secret police, were not supposed to harass Skowronek, which irked them to no end, especially given his penchant for flamboyance.

The U.S. mission had a fleet of drab, olive-colored sedans—even the chrome was painted olive—supposedly so the cars could blend into the background of wooded areas. Skowronek opted instead for his personal Thunderbird for transport. Then he discovered that the Stasi BMWs outran his old T-bird. It gave him an idea.

Why don't I order a fast little Corvette, have it shipped to West Germany, and then once I have it, I'll call Heidelberg and ask for permission to use it as my official car. What are the chances of them saying no when I tell them it outruns the East Germans?

Skowronek soon became the proud owner of a spectacular gold Stingray convertible with white leather interiors. He hit the autobahn to test the limits. The speed limit was 100 kilometers, or 62.5 mph, but Skowronek didn't care. The roads were rarely patrolled, and traffic was always light on the Soviet side since few people owned cars. Skowronek pressed on the gas and watched the speedometer needle flutter—85 mph, 100, 110. He pushed the pedal down farther.

Whoa! 135 mph—25 more than the Stasi. They're going to be mad as hell! But damn this is not a good idea if a cow strays across the road.

No strays were in sight and Skowronek savored the moment. He grinned broadly and let the wind rip through his blond hair, appearing like a spiffed-up military version of James Dean.

In the months that followed, the flamboyant mission chief was hard to miss, as though he was thumbing his nose at the Stasi, who in turn seemed intimidated by the sporty gold car. The incidents of them tailing him promptly declined.

Then one day on the autobahn he encountered a traffic jam approaching Checkpoint Alpha, the Helmstedt border crossing leading from the GDR into West Germany. The line of cars waiting to have credentials checked weaved on for nearly half a mile. It was a German holiday and the delay was an attempt by the East German police to intimidate those wanting to cross west for the day, provided they had the correct papers. The police looked under their cars, opened their trunks, peeked inside engines—any possible hiding place for an East German trying to escape the grasp of Communism.

The border guards, however, were not technically permitted to check the cars of liaison mission members like Skowronek. Rather than wait in line, he hit the shoulder and drove toward the crossing. A GDR officer hastily stepped into that lane and held up a hand for the Corvette to halt. Instead, Skowronek veered back to the main lane where he saw room to maneuver through, prompting the officer to likewise scoot over. When the officer realized that Skowronek showed no intention of slowing down, he bailed out fast. Skowronek sped forward, glancing in his rearview mirror at the incensed officer as he did so. He saw the man reaching inside his pocket, and thought, *He's going for his gun.*

Skowronek pressed on the gas, trying to make it to the safety of the Russian checkpoint, yards away, before being shot in the head. But instead of bullets shattering his windshield, he saw the Russian guard laughing at his approaching car. He glanced in his rearview mirror again and saw the GDR officer, cheeks puffed, blowing a whistle.

The East Germans tolerated Skowronek—just barely.

At times he tested the limits of Soviet patience as well. At one point he called on some of his West Point "training" to improvise on the U.S. mission's sneaking and peeking. Figuring that cross-country skiing could expand observation capabilities to remote parts of the zone, he dispatched an exploratory team to a mountain resort area to test the feasibility of espionage on ice. The team consisted of an officer, Major Paul Schweikert, and his wife.

"There's nothing expressly in the liaison agreement that says skis are forbidden," said Skowronek to Schweikert. "So why not? It'll allow us to really get behind the scenes, see what they might have hidden in the woods. It beats trying to pretend that olive sedans resemble trees. Let's give it a shot."

Schweikert reported to his boss that the experiment was short-lived. "Well, that didn't go so well," he explained. "We'd only been skiing for a couple of hours when the local commandant rounded us up. He told me that my skiing outfit was not a properly identifiable military uniform, and he kicked us off the mountain. Then we get back to the hotel and find out that our room's been cancelled."

"I'm not sure it's worth filing an official protest over this," said Skowronek. "It was a good idea, but it's probably too much pain for too little gain, so I guess we cross skiing off our list of accepted observation activities."

The jockeying was endless, but at times Skowronek pined for his old practices, like riding and jumping, so when he got wind of the skydiving world championships to be held at the Leipzig airport in East Germany, he seized on the opportunity to attend. There were, however, a few minor problems: the airport was outside the approved liaison zone and NATO did not recognize East Germany, so no NATO countries were permitted to compete.

Not to worry, thought Skowronek. *There will be plenty to whet my appetite.*

With a parachute planted conspicuously on the car seat beside him, he showed up at the site, pretending to be one of the skydivers. He slipped through with no problem and, in short order, used his Russian fluency to ingratiate himself among Soviet team members. Before long, he was roaming among the Canadian, Bulgarian, and Czech contingencies. Toward the end of the two-week competition, the Canadians invited him to join their plane for a "fun jump." But by then, the Stasi had caught wind of the gold Corvette with the funny license plate. He was barred from entry into the jumping grounds.

While he had savored the adrenalin rush of being among star skydivers, Skowronek concluded that the East fell far short of the West. Soviet skydivers had exceptional training, yet their parachutes and instruments were ill designed and poorly manufactured. But attending the event had provided side benefits. As always, Skowronek had used the opportunity to gather military, political, and economic information about Soviet activities. The threat of World War III was never far from his mind.

President John F. Kennedy, in fact, visited Berlin in June 1963. Skowronek was among U.S. officers in the dignitary receiving line representing the West, together with the chancellor of the Federal Republic of Germany, Konrad Adenauer, along with the mayor of West Berlin, Willy Brandt.

Standing at a podium overlooking the crowds gathered at Rudolph Wilde Platz, President Kennedy singled out U.S. General Lucius Clay.

"I am proud to come to this city . . . in the company of my fellow American, General Clay, who has been in this city during its great moment of crisis," said Kennedy adding, to the roar of approving crowds, "and will come again if ever needed."

President Kennedy continued on, not mincing words about the difference in freedoms between East and West.

"Today, in the world of freedom," he said, "the proudest boast is *'Ich bin ein Berliner.'*" Its translation: "I am a Berliner."

"There are many people in the world who really don't understand, or say they don't, what is the great issue between the free world and the

Communist world. Let them come to Berlin. . . . Freedom has many difficulties and democracy is not perfect, but we have never had to put a wall
up to keep our people in, to prevent them from leaving us. . . . Freedom is
indivisible, and when one man is enslaved, all are not free."[1]

Kennedy's words reverberated among countless East German citizens
on the other side of the wall, who with their shortwave radios—smuggled
in and hidden from Communist view—tuned into the Voice of America
for a window to the West. Many had high hopes that Kennedy would bring
peace to the world.

Five months later, President Kennedy was assassinated, on November
22, 1963. Shortly after, a delegation of East Germans delivered a message
to Potsdam House conveying their sorrow for America's loss. Skowronek
thought the words rang sincere.

Threats of a war, however, remained omnipresent. An event in January
1964 made that threat seem not far from reality. A coded message—marked
urgent—came into Skowronek's West Berlin liaison office from Heidelberg
headquarters. It was from the G-2, the intelligence chief. Minutes earlier,
read the dispatch, an American jet had disappeared off the radar screen
over Soviet air space. In all likelihood, it had been shot down and the three
officers on board were feared dead. The G-2 ordered a search.

Skowronek, never one to let emotion rule, didn't take time to react. He
acted—even as he mentally ticked off the punch list of requisite next steps.

*Activate the teams. Tell G-2 we're on the way. Confirm crew info. Arrange
medevac if they're still alive. Telex Washington. Contact SERB; they're gonna
try to slow this down, but this is no time for excuses. We need all-out action fast.*

Skowronek called his operations staff into his office and closed the door.

"An Air Force T-39 jet was just shot down over the Soviet Zone somewhere near Erfurt, about a hundred kilometers into the zone," Skowronek
explained. "Three officers were on board. We need to see if any survived.
Get every officer available and send out search teams. Do whatever you
need to do to bring these men back."

Skowronek read off the jet's last known coordinates.

"Any questions?" he inquired, as he glanced around at his team. "No?
Okay. Get everyone moving. Now! I'll call SERB and let them know we're
coming."

The officers filed out of the office as Skowronek dialed Colonel Pinchuk,
his go-between at SERB, the Soviet External Relations Branch. SERB was
the local entity that handled day-to-day problems with missions in the Soviet Zone, since the headquarters of the commander in chief was situated
a hundred miles away.

"Look, there's been an accident," said Skowronek to Pinchuk. "We've had a U.S. Air Force jet go down in the Soviet Zone near Erfurt. We want teams to go in and see if there are survivors, and if not, we at least want to retrieve the bodies."

Grudgingly, Pinchuk acquiesced to the search, but it was clear from his agitated voice that Skowronek would get no further assistance; it was not the Soviet's fault that the U.S. had invaded East German air space.

Skowronek's situation was aided little by reports that quickly leaked out to the wire services. Between Washington and Moscow, a war of words ensued. Secretary of State Dean Rusk condemned the incident as an "inexcusably brutal act of violence." He demanded those responsible be punished. Tass, the Russian news agency, called the U.S. explanation that the jet had strayed off course "incoherent and unconvincing."

A Soviet Embassy official in Washington retorted, "One would not expect a plane to intrude into the territory of another state one hundred kilometers just by error."

Tensions mounted almost as rapidly as the Berlin Wall went up a few years earlier; in a matter of hours it splintered German families between East and West. Skowronek contemplated the downed jet.

Of course it was an intelligence mission. I need to keep a lid on things, and I need to keep this from reaching a boiling point. But first, if any of the officers are still alive, I need to get them out before they can be interrogated.

It was nearing nightfall when his teams spotted campfires in the hills surrounding the Vogelsberg Mountains, an area through which the Fulda River runs. Russian army sentries prevented the U.S. officers from investigating further by claiming that a military exercise was in progress. But the teams had been instructed to do everything possible to find the American officers, so two teams pressed on and tried to evade the cordon of guards. They were immediately surrounded and arrested.

Amid the chaos, a third team was able to skirt away and find a hiding place on a hill for the night. As the faint glow of dawn arrived, they saw it. The jet. Rays of sunlight glinted off the tail and a torn wing. The men snapped photos of Russian soldiers collecting the strewn parts.

That same morning, Colonel Pinchuk called Skowronek. "We have detained four of your men," he pronounced. "They attempted to enter a restricted area where we were undergoing military exercises. They were told they could not proceed but chose to ignore our commands. They are now being held at our military headquarters in Erfurt."

"Listen," replied Skowronek. "Things are spiraling out of control, but you and I have always smoothed things over in the past. We need to talk in person before things get any worse. Can I meet you in Potsdam in an hour?"

There was a slight hesitation, and then "Da." Skowronek breathed a sigh of temporary relief.

As Skowronek drove to the SERB office in Potsdam, the situation between Washington and Moscow grew increasingly dire, increasing the pressure on him. He rehearsed in his mind every scenario he might have to tackle and every possible objection to U.S. explanations and objectives. It went better than expected.

Skowronek explained to the SERB chief, "We are aware that our aircraft was shot down. We understand that. But we still have a right to rescue our officers . . . or to retrieve their bodies, whichever the case may be. We would give you the same respect were it your officers. All I'm asking is that we be permitted to bring in some trucks and an ambulance to remove what is ours."

The Russian rubbed his chin as though deliberating.

Skowronek pressed on. "I hope there never comes a day when you have to ask the same of me—to retrieve your comrades—but if you ever do, I will do the same for you."

The comment seemed to sway the officer and he gave a slow, deliberate answer. "I must . . . contact the commander in chief . . . to request permission."

Skowronek nodded, relieved that he'd gotten that much. He thanked Pinchuk.

Soon he received an answer. His military convoy and an ambulance would be permitted to the crash site to retrieve the wreckage. The mission's "ambulance" was actually nothing more than a Ford station wagon outfitted with a police siren and red-cross insignias. It pulled up to the site with its lights whirling, followed by a wrecker, a flatbed, and two 2½-ton trucks.

Skowronek and his crews disembarked from their vehicles and surveyed the charred scene. They saw body parts strewn everywhere. Jaws dropped; gasps were audible. For a moment, time stood still. Each man seemed to reflect on some silent prayer, some hope that the fiery crash had ended quickly for their fallen colleagues.

"God bless their souls," Skowronek muttered.

He had not thought to bring a chaplain.

Regaining his composure, he ordered the grisly undertaking to follow. His team needed to pick up all the remains, all the pieces, one by one; leave no man, or part of a man, behind.

A young airman among his group lurched off to the side and vomited. Then he collapsed, moaning between sobs, "I can't do this."

Skowronek nodded understanding.

The remains of the officers were later flown to the U.S. Air Force base in Wiesbaden in West Germany, where the widows and children of the officers lived. The T-39 jet parts were hauled back to West Berlin for the crash to be investigated.

Two months later, in March 1964, the Soviets were conducting large maneuvers in a restricted area near the border. Charlie Fletcher was still on the western side, manned and ready. An Air Force RB-66 reconnaissance jet was dispatched over the Russian maneuver area. This time, there was no question that the jet was an intrusion, but the U.S. could not afford to forgo the reconnaissance. If the house of cards was to fall, it didn't want to be left playing the part of joker.

As in the prior incident, the aircraft disappeared from radar screens, and again Skowronek immediately dispatched search teams. He was relieved to find out that the three-member crew had ejected, though the Russians had captured them. But they were alive. Word trickled in that the lieutenant navigator was seriously injured, having borne the brunt of a tumbling jet tail. He was being treated at a Soviet military hospital. The other two were unharmed. All three, however, were branded as spies to be put on trial in the GDR.

The touch-and-go saga with the crew went on for nearly a month but again, Skowronek negotiated to obtain their release. As he was loading the injured lieutenant into his ambulance, the Soviets insisted the mission chief sign release papers. Ten doctors stood by, watching and waiting. Skowronek noticed no markings on the physicians' white coats.

That's odd. No identification. I bet they're all East Germans. And if I sign the papers that will imply that the U.S. is acknowledging the GDR. Like hell!

Skowronek, with the injured lieutenant loaded, jumped into the ambulance and ordered the driver to speed away.

Given such incidents, Skowronek knew there was a chance that the East Germans would "get him" some other way. Particularly questionable were some characters at local hotels. The drab and dreary conditions in the country made Communist officers throng to hotels, since they were about the only places for good meals. A few even had cabarets. Skowronek liked visiting the hotels because the spending habits of patrons clued him into the Soviet and GDR economies. He could also order chateaubriand for the equivalent of seventy-five cents, given the deflated local currency; Russian caviar and toast were forty-five. Tipping was not customary, but

Skowronek got in the habit of handing out the new Kennedy half-dollar in appreciation of good service; it was usually prized among recipients.

The young ladies that crossed Skowronek's path, however, sometimes appeared suspect.

Are they honey traps?

One day while staying in an East German hotel, he ordered room service. A lithe young woman in a miniskirt arrived shortly afterward and set down his hot chocolate.

There is no way this woman is room service staff. She's a stunner . . . far too pretty to be doing kitchen work. Something's out of place.

The woman poured his beverage.

Skowronek paused. *Are there knockout drops in it? Is it a setup for compromising photos?* Then he picked up his cup and drank, deciding that the East Germans would not be so obvious in trying to do him in.

The young lady seemed to hesitate as though waiting for a proposition. But Skowronek knew better. He gave the girl a good tip for the hot cocoa and sent her on her way.

Some time later, a fellow diplomat relayed to the mission chief words he'd heard uttered by General Yakubovsky. "I know they want me to get rid of him," said Yakubovsky, referring to Skowronek. "But I like him!"

Skowronek continued on with his sneaking and peeking.

22

ANTICIPATING NEW FRONTS

While the Fulda Gap was the anticipated route for a Soviet invasion of West Germany, the United States feared Communism was on the move *everywhere*. The Soviets had aggressively taken over Poland and Hungary. They were on the move in Mongolia. And in the year prior, America had felt Communism breathing down its red neck only ninety miles from Florida's shores in Cuba. But the ill-fated Bay of Pigs invasion in April 1961 by CIA-trained Cuban exiles had failed to topple Castro, Communism, or the threat of nuclear weapons within striking distance of the U.S.

Ed Rowny, like Skowronek, had intensely studied Soviet ideology. While pursuing his master's degree at Yale postwar, he had been exposed to leading experts on the Soviet Union as well as nuclear weapons. Chief among them was Gabriel Almond, who wrote the magnum opus *Appeals to Communism*, and Bernard Brodie, who wrote *The Absolute Weapon*, which foresaw how atomic weapons could be used as a deterrent to war.

Rowny now sensed the Soviets feeling particularly emboldened. The star of Premier Nikita Khrushchev was on the rise, while at the same time the Kremlin perceived a general weakness in U.S. power.

Rowny debated with his former professors at Yale whether a domino effect would spread Communism to other parts of the world like Southeast Asia. The consensus was that if Communists used surrogates like the Vietcong, they could take over South Vietnam, which would provide them a base with which to move against Thailand and Burma in one direction and Indonesia in the other. Each of those countries already had strong Communist insurgencies in place that the Soviets could exploit. Korea might also then be lost, given cooperation between the Soviets and China, albeit theirs was a shaky alignment steeped in distrust. The dominoes would tumble. Consequently, keeping the Soviet Communists from taking over Vietnam was considered vital.

An atomic bomb in retaliation against Soviet aggression, however, was not in the cards. America had altered its strategy from massive retaliation to that of graduated response. The revised strategy involved at first relying on conventional weapons while the U.S. had time to determine alternatives before risking countless civilian casualties. NATO was considering this flexible response as well. Such a response required alternative methods of warfare. Jack Norton and Ed Rowny were keen on the prospects of arming helicopters. They discussed it at length in 1959 while at the National War College together; up to that point helicopters remained used primarily for transporting troops and supplies. The pair also talked about how the next fronts might be "everywhere," in contrast to defensive lines like the Siegfried and Gothic Lines in World War II.

Rowny and Norton were not alone in wanting to alter the art of movement in war. Spec Powell had participated in the Army's "eagle flights" initiative, which involved taking senior Army officers from different specialties, like Powell as an engineer, and giving them aviation training to expand the thinking and abilities of Army Aviation. Although the former Army Air Corps had become the U.S. Air Force in 1947, the Army retained aviation assets for command and control purposes, medical evacuations, reconnaissance, and supply missions.

Powell subsequently became director of a development unit tracking the progress of equipment, being developed anywhere in the world, that might have Army Aviation applications. Items ranged from fire-resistant flight suits and various types of aircraft to crash rescue equipment. Powell's unit conducted engineering tests on items and identified their capabilities and limitations. He also learned to fly helicopters, which in his view was not out of line with his engineering background, particularly the idea of adding a vertical dimension to combat.

The helicopter is directly tied to obstacle crossing. And obstacle crossing is the principal role of the engineers in the battle area.

Powell also thought it time to view the helicopter as a weapons' platform.

Before long he was assigned to the office of the chief of research and development in the Pentagon. It was 1961, and it was a far cry from his days at the Pentagon years earlier, what with Defense Secretary Robert McNamara's reliance on his new intellectual "whiz kids," which he recruited from the Rand Corporation to modernize the Department of Defense. Not many in the Armed Forces seemed pleased with the staffing, Powell included.

We're servants of civilian masters, he thought. *Bright young men . . . but they know absolutely nothing about what they're doing in the secretary of defense's office.*

Powell took to wearing civilian clothes given the attitude of McNamara's staff, which seemed to view those in uniform as fools to be talked down to. But it was hard to mistake Powell for anything short of brilliant.

Ed Rowny's experience with the secretary was hardly more agreeable. A second Berlin crisis had been brewing, and it culminated in August 1961 with the Soviets commencing construction of the Berlin Wall separating the west side of Berlin from the east side and the rest of the German Democratic Republic (GDR). Rowny, who was on the Joint Chiefs' staff, helped plan massive airlifts into the beleaguered city. He had yet more maneuverings to grapple with when the chairman of the Joint Chiefs, General Lyman Lemnitzer, gave him more orders one Friday afternoon, part of which involved McNamara's whiz kids.

"Tie a can on them," Lemnitzer told Rowny. "Quiet them down, and plan for the build up in Germany."

Lemnitzer explained that he wanted Rowny to write an outline augmenting troop structure and improving the logistical situation in Europe given the Berlin crisis. The original deployment of U.S. troops in the region had been designed around a "trip wire" strategy, meaning that the United States had a threshold, which if crossed, would trigger massive retaliation. The trip wire was a thin line of troops. Were that breeched, the response previously would have been massive retaliation in the form of a nuclear attack. Now Army troops as well as tanks and ammunition needed beefing up for the new graduated response strategy.

After Rowny's plan was approved, he reported to the defense secretary's offices over the weekend to begin arranging a staff to implement it.

Come early Monday morning, McNamara asked him, "Well, what are your conclusions?"

Rowny explained that he didn't even have his staff in place, let alone having gone through the process of a "sound military decision" or SMD. This was West Point thinking, Army thinking . . . Navy thinking. It involved stating the problem; appraising how the enemy, based on intelligence, perceived the problem; making three to four assumptions about the situation; developing two to three options; weighing the pluses and minuses of each; and making a systematic analysis to draw a conclusion.

McNamara wanted none of it. "You've got a lot to learn, young man," scolded McNamara. "To hell with all this nonsense about pluses and minuses, yeas and nos, positives and negatives. If you don't know what the conclusions are before you start, you're not my kind of man."

McNamara's theory, Rowny learned, was that officers should know the desired outcome before filling in the blanks on how to achieve it. It was a far cry from West Point where cadets had to figure out the approach to the solution.

Unfazed, Rowny went about his plans, tackling the problems in the logical manner that he knew best—as his military training dictated—to formulate sound military decisions. His plans were then smoothly implemented, boosting NATO's troop strength and logistical support to deter Soviet aggression. Lemnitzer's plan for discreetly blowing the whiz out of the whiz kids, with a weapon called Ed Rowny, worked like a charm.

His '41 classmate Air Force Brigadier General George Brown was, at the same time, the primary action officer designated to help with the movement of troops and supplies to address the Berlin crisis. The strategy included establishing a logistical command center and opening up ammunition depots. A '41 classmate coordinated emergency plans for the defense of the encircled city.

As these events were occurring, Roswell Gilpatric, deputy secretary of defense, while addressing a U.S. audience, relayed a not-so-subtle warning to the Kremlin: "Berlin is the emergency of the moment, because the Soviets have chosen to make it so. . . . The fact is that this nation has a nuclear retaliatory force of such lethal power that an enemy move which brought it into play would be an act of self-destruction on his part."[1]

The following week, in late October 1961, the U.S. and the Soviet Union engaged in a provocative tank standoff in Berlin, their guns aimed at each other barely a hundred yards apart by the main east-west checkpoint along the wall, called "Checkpoint Charlie." Through back channels President Kennedy was able to defuse the situation, and the Soviets began removing their tanks. They moved one back. Then the U.S. did the same. One by one the tanks on each side retreated. The Soviets had chosen not to self-destruct, and by early November the crisis had passed.

McNamara and Lemnitzer congratulated Rowny on his successful part in the showdown, and he was rewarded with a plum assignment. He became deputy to the commander of the 82nd Airborne Division.

In the meantime, Spec Powell had written a memorandum to the Army staff calling for "bold new approaches to mobility." He joined with Rowny, along with classmates Jack Norton and Ace Moody, to promote these air mobility efforts, collectively referring to themselves as a cabal. The cabal knew there would be resistance to their efforts since the Army general staff, dominated by armor officers, incorrectly assumed that each new helicopter, within a fixed budget, would mean one less tank. The cabal knew it wasn't a zero-sum game.

Garnering a fair share of defense budgets, however, involved jockeying for position both within and between services. Every year each service chief submitted to the chairman of the Joint Chiefs a projection for the next fiscal year of what he intended to accomplish, along with necessary projects and a price tag for each. After weighing these submissions, the chairman recommended final figures to the president. Naturally, the chairman's wish list usually exceeded the president's targeted amount, so the president had to decide whether to submit the chairman's budget to Congress for review—or more typically, advise the chairman on how much each service chief's request would be cut.

The West Point '41 cabal forged ahead with their ideas, trying to outmaneuver the services' jockeying.

Jack Norton was at Continental Army Command (CONARC), which was responsible for all Army combat forces in the continental United States. For his part of the cabal effort, Norton presented a plan to General Hamilton Howze on greatly increasing Army air mobility; Howze was a former cavalryman who became the first director of Army Aviation in 1955 and had since pioneered concepts for Army Aviation in combat. Norton proposed to him, among other matters, significantly increasing the inventory of helicopters in the Army. Helicopters would retain traditional uses such as command and control, and medical evacuation, but added to that would be two new purposes: serving as lightly armed troop carriers and as heavily armed gunships offering fire support.

Ace Moody's cabal undertaking was to persuade Secretary of the Army Cyrus Vance that these concepts would help the Army better accomplish its mission. Spec Powell was tasked with convincing the whiz kids that the plans for air mobility efforts could be cost-effective. Ed Rowny would demonstrate through field exercises that it could all work.

Powell's "bold" memorandum on new approaches to mobility, though drafted by Powell, was ultimately sanctioned and signed off under McNamara's name—as though air mobility was all his idea. But Spec Powell didn't care how the final goals were accomplished; it wasn't about glory but getting the job done.

In reality, he thought, *If I tell anybody in the Army staff that I'm doing this, I'll have my throat cut.*

Powell knew that if Army hierarchy, which favored a large tank force, discovered the cabal was responsible for cutting their tanks to provide resources for helicopters, all four in the cabal would probably have their throats cut, not just him. But they had pulled it off.

Subsequently, the Howze Board was established, with General Howze at its helm, to test the new concepts. Powell thought it interesting that much of the driving force behind the development of Army Aviation came from former cavalrymen like Howze, who saw helicopters as tools with which to apply the tactics learned as horse cavalrymen. The concept of "air cavalry" was taking hold. The Howze Board would bring the concept to the next level.

It was mid-1962. Norton was designated the Howze Board chief of staff while Rowny became the director of tests. Rowny had at his disposal three regiments of the 82nd Airborne; between aviators, pilots, and mechanics there were about seven hundred men involved. One hundred helicopters and thirty fixed-wing aircraft were ordered to Fort Bragg, North Carolina, for the tests. There, around farm country, the whirling of rotor blades became so incessant that traumatized turkeys huddled en masse and suffocated. Rowny had to buy up thousands of them to pacify the disgruntled locals and in turn donated as many as he could to local hospitals and orphanages.

In the meantime, a new generation of "weapons" was emerging. Rowny had teams experiment with using helicopters and fixed-wing aircraft in "vertical envelopments." He experimented with helicopters in guerilla warfare. Helicopters would fly a few hundred feet off the ground trying to spot targets. From low vantage points, they could fire machine guns and rockets to strike insurgents more accurately than if fired from an airplane at high altitude. Fixed-wing tests included using lightly armed planes for close air support, with planes hugging the "nap of the earth," flying just above the treetops.

"We are striving mightily not to be accused of fighting with the tools and concepts of the last war," Rowny noted on air mobility. "Concepts lag years behind the tools; The rifle was in use fifty years before we used it in battle. We are accelerating our thinking on how the new tools now available can be used."[2]

The final Howze Board recommendations were submitted to the Army in August 1962, embracing the concept of air mobility. Out of the Howze Board recommendations came plans to create a new air assault division within about six years.

★ ★ ★

Later that same year, Rowny was helping his wife unpack at their newly rented home in Washington, D.C., early one morning when a limousine pulled up to deliver a note from Cyrus Vance. He wanted to speak with Rowny immediately in his office over breakfast.

Rita was annoyed. "You're leaving for Korea in forty-eight hours," she complained. "You're going to be gone for a year, and I've got a whole house to unpack and five children to care for. It's not the time to be running off."

"You know I can't say no to the secretary of the Army," replied her husband. Then he was out the door.

Over the meeting, Vance explained to Rowny that he was impressed with the Howze Board's tests on arming helicopters and was considering equipping some in Vietnam. "What do you think of the idea?" he asked. "How do you think they can best be used?"

Rowny had no shortage of ideas. He explained how helicopters could be used for command and control purposes to ferry commanders around the battlefield to meet with subordinates. They could deliver critically needed supplies of ammunition and food to units. The survival rates of the wounded could be increased by rapidly transporting them via helicopter to MASH facilities. He added, "In World War II, 90 percent of soldiers with head and belly wounds died. By the end of the Korean War, 90 percent of those casualties survived. Just think how many more would survive if we could airlift them by helicopter."

These were compelling notions, and Vance urged Rowny on.

"The greatest use," he told Vance, "is to arm them with rockets and machine guns. We'd be adding new elements of surprise and mobility into combat. They could escort helicopters carrying troops and do reconnaissance. And they could spot insurgents from the air. Just think of the highly discriminating firepower they could use to fight guerrillas."

Vance liked what he heard. "Any suggestions on who's most qualified to test the ideas in Vietnam?"

Rowny told him there was no shortage of qualified officers from the Howze Board and suggested one name in particular. Then he left to help relieve Rita of her misery back home.

The next morning, Vance's limousine returned to the Rowny residence. Again, a breakfast meeting was requested. Again, Rita was furious, and again, Rowny had little choice.

At the meeting Vance explained his intrusion into Rowny's move. "The Army chief of staff and I have been talking, and we've decided that *you* are the one who should go to Vietnam."

"But . . . but I'm supposed to command the 1st Cavalry in Korea," protested Rowny. "I'm leaving tomorrow. My uniforms are already in South Korea getting the division's insignia sewn on to them."

Vance dismissed his objections. "So you'll get new uniforms and a new insignia. Call the unit whatever you'd like. You can choose twenty-five

Army officers to go with you, and we'll give you twenty-five civilian scientists from think tanks working with the Army."

The idea, he explained, was that the Army would conduct helicopter testing partly under the guise of nation-building projects, seeking ways to improve the lives of the South Vietnamese civilian population while also helping its military. This way the U.S. Air Force and Navy, both opposed to the Army arming helicopters, wouldn't get bent out of shape. The Air Force in particular wanted to be the sole provider of combat air support.

Vance added one other note: "By the way, unfortunately, I'm sorry to say, your promotion will be on hold."

Rowny's dismay was palpable; he was perplexed as well. His assignment to Korea had been accompanied by the promise of promotion from brigadier to major general.

Explained Vance, "You'll be reporting to Brigadier General Stilwell, who's in charge of Army support for the Vietnamese in Saigon. If we give you your second star now, we'd have to give *him* one, and we're not prepared to do that."

Ed Rowny's future, so well orchestrated just hours earlier, had taken a major detour. He licked his wounds and returned home to let Rita know that he now had plenty of time to unpack boxes.

★ ★ ★

Rowny was not the only West Point '41er caught by surprise with assignments to Southeast Asia. Henry Bodson was diverted from White Sands to Cambodia to help advise the country's fledgling military. Bodson didn't understand why, as there wasn't a single missile in the whole country.

Herb Stern, who was commanding and training a six-thousand-strong artillery and infantry regiment in the snows of Colorado that winter heading into 1962, was informed that his troops were being sent to Vietnam. He griped to fellow officers that he would have made training more weather-appropriate had he known.

As the days went by, however, Rowny ruminated on this new assignment and found its silver lining.

Maybe going to Southeast Asia isn't so bad. Experimenting with armed helicopters in combat could be a really fascinating assignment. Maybe I'll make the idea work.

On his way to Vietnam, Rowny had a stopover in Hawaii and paid a courtesy call on Navy Admiral Harry Felt, commander in chief of U.S. Pacific Command. Felt's command included forces in Vietnam. The admiral hadn't received any orders from the Joint Chiefs regarding armed helicopter experiments, and he argued with Rowny that such undertakings would adversely affect the Air Force and, consequently, the Navy's roles and missions. He would have none of it.

Hell, I got some tap dancing to do, thought Rowny. *I've already got jerry-rigged Hueys in transit to Vietnam.*

Rowny put in a call to Vance who, in turn, found the new Chairman of the Joint Chiefs, Maxwell Taylor, unresponsive to roadblocks put up by Felt; the chairman had been brought out of retirement only weeks earlier and wasn't interested in tackling roles and missions. Vance had to get McNamara to issue orders directly to Taylor, who transmitted them to Felt.

Everything was resolved. Or so Rowny believed. But soon after in Saigon, he arrived to his new offices one morning to find his desks, file cabinets, and typewriters out on the street. Apparently yet another commander had disowned Rowny's mission, having not been provided orders. Rowny was unceremoniously evicted.

Sitting on his desk on a sidewalk in the sweltering heat of Saigon, he shook his head in bewilderment. *Maybe helicopters are not my ticket to a glorious career.*

At that moment an old friend happened to be passing by, a brigadier general who headed the U.S. Air Force component in Vietnam and who Rowny knew from the National War College. "What in Christ's name are you doing out here on the street?" Rollen "Buck" Anthis asked.

Rowny explained as best he could comprehend.

"That's shameful," said Anthis. "You know, in principle, the Air Force isn't behind the air mobility concept. But I have plenty of space in my Saigon headquarters." Added Anthis, "You're welcome to share it till you get things straightened out. There's certainly no reason for you to be out here."

Rowny couldn't agree more and was glad to be rescued from the sweltering heat. Eventually, he found his own space—in a burned-out warehouse. Thanks to an enterprising can-do officer on his staff who knew well how to cover his requisition tracks, it was converted into one of the snazziest offices in the city, complete with silk wallpaper. Rowny and his teams now were ready to move into high gear. ACTIV, or Army Concept Team in Vietnam, as Rowny had named his initiative, kicked off.

The teams began launching a few dozen civilian-related experiments. On the nation-building front, they started digging deep-water wells to improve the water supply. They tried introducing new rice-harvesting techniques to reap more per square meter of paddy. And they dug large ponds to encourage fish farming, among other initiatives.

But the testing of helicopters was the main task, and there was no shortage of ideas—some boldly out on the edge. The ACTIV scientists, mostly from Johns Hopkins, were nothing short of brilliant. One had made millions on inventions, including a carton to separate eggs so they wouldn't break. He'd also created the six-pack carrier for beer, figuring that when a man bought beer he usually wanted more than one, which was one of the reasons why the scientist had become a rich man.

Ed Rowny planned to combine the scientists' ideas on arming helicopters with his own. He had twenty-six Hueys to work with: fifteen of the UH-1A version and eleven UH-1Bs, the UH standing for "utility helicopter," from which came the nickname "Huey."

Ostensibly, these helicopters were not to be used for combat, since the U.S. was relegated to a supporting role alongside the Vietnamese military. Instead, they were to mainly serve as armed escorts for the Army's unarmed Hueys and Chinook choppers that transported troops or performed reconnaissance. ACTIV personnel, however, were permitted to instruct Vietnamese pilots in maneuvering helicopters in combat. At times that proved troubling but also opportune. The Vietnamese pilots were prone to air sickness, which gave Rowny and his colleagues a chance to skirt the rules and assume the helicopter's controls and machine guns, which was their ultimate objective.

Soon the role of ACTIV's armed escorts grew. The Air Force had been using its own planes for many escorts, but that proved dangerous. As they approached their objectives, the pilots had to veer off at a high altitude or risk crashing into the ground. Because armed helicopters could fly at much lower altitudes, they could break off considerably later, giving them a huge advantage with last minute, suppressing fire. But again this bumped Rowny up against the Air Force.

General Buck Anthis came to the rescue with a solution. He helped establish a "one-minute" rule, whereby in the final minute before troop carriers prepared to land, the fixed-wing support of the Air Force would break off and ACTIV's armed helicopters would take over. Soon, one minute was extended to three and even five minutes.

Technical advancements with helicopters were also progressing. They attached listening and radar devices on them to create a Doppler effect. When the enemy fired, the devices tracked, through pitch and wavelengths, the source of fire so U.S. officers could get fixes on enemy positions and automatically return fire.

Another idea involved rigging goggles that allowed for coordinating the pupil movement of a pilot's eyes with the aim and fire of the helicopter's machine guns. Wherever the pupils turned, so too would the gun. It was an earth-shattering idea that held promise, though it would take decades to fully develop.

Teams began improving the helicopter's structure. Blades were fine-tuned so that the thwapping noise was reduced, lessening the chances of alerting the enemy to a chopper coming in low and fast. Strong plastics replaced heavy metal parts to lighten up the structure, and fire-retardant materials were built in so that if a helicopter crashed, chances of it bursting into flames were reduced.

Scientists competed with one another trying to come up with ideas. Their innovations included sensors so discerning that they could detect the body heat of enemy soldiers under the jungle canopy. They played with elements of night vision as well. Less successful, however, was toying with the sense of hearing. When they put powerful listening devices on the front lines, the Vietcong quickly caught on and stopped talking. U.S. helicopters ended up firing on countless deer and rabbits instead of the enemy; in places, it looked more like hunting season than war.

There were, in fact, many hiccups in ACTIV efforts, such as the time when Rowny, wanting to show off the helicopter's prowess, took a reporter out to cover a large operation named Ap Bac. One helicopter was downed in the operation, and another five were subsequently shot down attempting to rescue the pilot of the first. The press labeled the operation a fiasco, stating that six helicopters were destroyed, though that was not true. The five damaged rescue helicopters were lifted out by other helicopters with slings. Only the first downed chopper, too badly damaged for repair, was lost. The wounded pilot of the first helicopter was rescued, and there were no other casualties.

After reading one account of the events, Rowny asked the reporter, "Did we witness the same operation?"

Replied the reporter, "Ed, the readers don't want to read anything about these military skirmishes. What they're interested in is Madam Nhu, the Dragon Lady."

Nhu was the beautiful and diabolical sister-in-law of South Vietnam's bachelor president, Ngô Dình Diêm. The "First Lady" sometimes got more ink than American soldiers risking their lives.

While Rowny's work didn't particularly rate with the press, it did with the chain of command. General Joseph Stilwell Jr. was reassigned at the end of 1962, allowing Rowny to finally put on his coveted second star.

A few months later, he was in a chopper taking off when a sniper's lucky shot caught the tail rotor. Immediately, the pilot engaged the auto-rotation mode so the helicopter would drift rather than plunge to the ground. But it spun faster and faster earthward. The two gunners manning the doorway machine guns were thrown out of the gyrating machine, while Rowny remained strapped in the back as it jolted to the ground. He survived, albeit with mild burns. The gunners suffered minor injuries, but the quick-thinking pilot suffered two broken legs.

"He'll be dead in the morning," the aid-station surgeon told Rowny of the latter.

He was right. Due to the leg breaks, an embolism formed, killing the pilot.

War, as Rowny knew all too well, didn't wait on mourning. He continued his helicopter experiments.

Several months later, he jumped out of one in a demonstration to Vietnamese paratroopers, but a gust of wind badly jarred his landing, causing his shoulder to dislocate. As he stood in severe pain, his arm bent nearly at a right angle, the Vietnamese paratroopers thought he was saluting them. Through gritted teeth he had to convince them otherwise, and they finally got a helicopter to come evacuate him. Along the way to the medical station, the pilot spotted enemy troops and began chasing them in earnest, wanting to show the American officer how effective armed helicopters could be. He didn't need to convince Rowny, who at that moment was more interested in a hospital bed.

The injury ended Rowny's tour in Vietnam, and he returned to the States. Shortly afterward, a package arrived at his home in D.C. It was his 1st Cavalry uniform, last believed to be with a tailor in South Korea. After Rowny failed to show up there, it was forwarded to the Army unit handling the effects of deceased persons. But Rowny was very much alive.

So was Peer de Silva. He was appointed station chief of the CIA in Saigon in 1963, one of the hottest seats in intelligence.

23

TRIALS AND TRAUMA OF THE VIETNAM ERA

Walter Woolwine had by now become the treasurer of the United States Military Academy at West Point. He was, in essence, the academy bank account, receiving a monthly disbursement from the Army that, in turn, was used to fund books, meals, and other operating details of the academy and its nearly three thousand cadets. He also safeguarded cadet monies put away toward graduation day, when each would need to dole out about a thousand dollars for uniforms; unlike reservists, whose uniforms were supplied gratis, the Army seemed to think that since West Pointers got paid, they could afford the style in which they might be killed.

About a year into Woolwine's tenure, General William Westmoreland became superintendent of the academy. Westmoreland, not one to be outdone by the Navy, wanted West Point to surpass the four thousand officers in training at Annapolis. It was "Go Army!" thinking. It was also expensive thinking, increasing capacity to accommodate a thousand more cadets. Seeking a collective strength in force, Westmoreland approached the Air Force Academy superintendent about a similar expansion there, and the two academies pushed the concept through their respective services as well as through Congress.

For Walter Woolwine, Westmoreland then became a boss with a checkbook. The general gave his treasurer one simple caveat: "Keep it under $100 million."

Woolwine, used to pinching pennies on C-rations and laundry detergent, had no qualms about staying within budget. Now he needed an expansion plan. Two sets of prior engineering plans had been nixed for not adequately fulfilling the vision of West Point. One situated buildings miles away from the academy. In Woolwine's view, a separate campus would create internal rivalries not in keeping with the corps concept. On the other hand, he had a simple revelation as he stood in a wing of the mess hall one day.

The wing seats 1,100. We simply need a structure of about similar size. And in front of the mess hall is a large piece of real estate that we use only once a year, for graduation. . . . All we need to do is move Thayer.

General Sylvanus Thayer was an early West Point superintendent who became known as the "father of the Military Academy," and his statue overlooked the plain.

Woolwine grabbed the commandant's attention, cleared the table where cadets placed their swords during meals, and proceeded to sketch his idea for an expansion in front of the mess hall. Westmoreland came over next. Woolwine explained the plans: how there would be little or no interference with the cadets' education and daily lives while an expansion was underway, how Thayer really belonged next to the superintendent's house since the former had been a sup, and how a new facade could exactly resemble the current one to please old-timers. And, new barracks could be built outside existing quarters, making them wings off of the mess hall.

Right then and there, Westmoreland approved the plan without change, including the new barracks and an expanded mess hall to fit the extra thousand or so cadets. "Send it to the district engineer."

Those plans, drawn up on a mess hall table, together with the eventual conversion of the riding hall into an academic building, would help bring the academy into the next century. Woolwine and Westmoreland, however, would not see them coming to fruition. They would be at war.

★ ★ ★

It was just weeks after the assassination of President Kennedy and the assassination of South Vietnam President Ngô Dình Diêm—both in November 1963—when Peer de Silva was slated to become the Saigon station chief. The U.S. had not yet deployed combat troops to Vietnam, aside from Green Berets training the South Vietnamese army in counterinsurgency, but there remained concerns in Washington that if Vietnam fell to Communism then so too would Southeast Asia. President Lyndon B. Johnson was trying to wrap his hands around the quagmire, but the South's struggle against the Vietcong was becoming entirely discombobulated in the wake of Diem's demise.

There was no order of succession in place for the former president, who had been a strong leader. Questions were asked, between Washington and South Vietnam, about who could fill his shoes. One of the most logical choices didn't want the job; he wanted to retire and grow orchids. Other generals coming up the line were ambitious, but it was unclear if they were capable of handling a high political position. Still other generals desiring the appointment got caught up with in-fighting, and their allegiances and trustworthiness—from a U.S. point of view—were unknown. The lack of a clear leader and an order of succession resulted in chaos.

Mike Greene and his family had been in Saigon during the Diêm coup, when there were attacks throughout the city, including the ransacking of houses around the Greene's neighborhood. Now, Peer de Silva was trying to make heads or tails of the situation, especially the Vietcong's "unceasing application of violence and terror against segments of the rural population," as he saw it. He pondered whether the CIA programs had worthwhile goals, how they might counter the Vietcong, how to break the Vietcong stranglehold. Orthodox military tactics, he realized, could not prevail against small and highly mobile Vietcong units. He helped spearhead the concept of "people action teams," intermingling local militia with the population, such as farmers, to gain their trust and break Vietcong strangleholds over them.[1]

Instead, the U.S. military opted for a military solution. De Silva was not optimistic about the prospects and thought that the three "heavenly stars" who had aligned to dominate policy—Secretary of Defense McNamara and Generals Maxwell Taylor and William Westmoreland—perhaps "came to the wrong war."[2]

Needless to say, the place for a wrong war was no place for kids. Peer Jr. "Perry," Paul, and Cathy, ages seven, three, and two, respectively, lived behind twelve-foot cement walls crowned with broken glass and guarded by round-the-clock South Vietnamese army security. Each weekday a military bus, armed with M-16–laden military police, would pull up to retrieve Perry before heading to the school for Army dependents. The MPs would secure a path for him to enter the school complex, and then Perry would pass endless yards of barbed wire before he was free to be a kid.

The children's diversions in Saigon were few: Perry acting as projectionist for movies at their walled-in home; taking a Huey to a private beach; a birthday party complete with armed guards.

The dogs fared far worse. Black dogs were a favorite among the locals—as a delicacy of the local cuisine, that is. The de Silva's black poodle disappeared. Then another.

The dogs turned out to be the least of it.

One day in the sweltering heat came a chilling revelation: a Vietcong courier was captured and on his person were detailed drawings of the American school, complete with guard schedules, details of the facility and playground, school bus information, and more—it appeared a war on American soldiers was about to be extended to their young families, had it not been thwarted.[3]

Mike Greene's wife, Eileen, took the attitude that fear begets fear; if she reacted to her own fears by being overly restrictive regarding her teenage children's activities, then they too would live in fear. Instead, while her husband was busy serving as secretary of Westmoreland's general staff, she tried to make life for their four kids as normal as possible. That included allowing Mike Jr. to motorbike around Saigon with his American friends. When some of the teenagers ignored curfew restrictions, however, the American ambassador banned the use of motorbikes by all military dependents. The kids, broken up over the edict, enlisted Colonel Greene's help in reversing it, swearing on their honor that if he helped them, never again would they break any rules. Greene accomplished the task and the young men kept their words of honor, becoming lasting fans of the colonel.

The adults too tried to maintain normalcy amid the worsening conflict. Granted, Peer de Silva took precautions, like altering his daily route to work and staggering visits to the swimming pavilion, but there were routine pleasures for both the de Silvas and Greenes. They shared in the occasional bridge game or dinner parties hosted at their respective homes.

Never far from Eileen's mind, however, were evacuation procedures. She rechecked the protocol so many times that she lost count, mentally packing her bags so she could be ready in an instant. When that time finally came in February 1965, and she was told "Now!" she didn't hesitate. Each family member was permitted one suitcase, and into those collective bags went all of the Greenes' silver, fine linens, and precious collectibles from Asia.

Explaining her priorities to the children, said Eileen, "We can always buy new shoes and underwear back home."

The family's exit from Saigon was in concert with the push by the DOD to relocate military families and the State Department to usher out U.S. civilians—all in response to orders from President Johnson to vacate Vietnam. The war was heating up.

A boiling point came in early spring. On March 30, 1965, Peer de Silva was in his office at the American embassy, casually discussing issues on the telephone with one of his section chiefs. While speaking, he absentmindedly glanced out the window and noticed an old Peugeot, apparently with engine trouble, being pushed up to a position directly below his window. A man raised the hood to look under it. It was then that de Silva saw, jammed between the seats, an object he knew all too well—a "time pencil," a detonating device. It immediately clicked in his mind. It was a bomb. He instinctively fell away from the window—just as 350 pounds of C-4 exploded.[4]

De Silva came to. He was bleeding. An ear was hanging loose, his lip drooping. His neck seemed to have a large wound. And de Silva couldn't see. He couldn't see the shrapnel that blasted through the seven-year-old boy in the portrait on the wall—slicing Peer Jr.'s eyes. De Silva couldn't see the mounds of rubble around him or the iron grates to the windows that had been blown into the streets. Someone came to his aid and led him down the embassy stairs, but he couldn't see who was on a stretcher that he passed. It was his secretary, Barbara Robbins, the first female employee of the CIA ever killed in the line of duty—and at only twenty-one, the youngest employee ever killed. She was also the first American woman to lose her life in the Vietnam War.[5]

Peer de Silva survived but was partially blinded from the blast that killed 22 people and wounded more than 180.

Nine days later, de Silva's classmate and friend Ken Kennedy was at a planning conference in Pearl Harbor. General Westmoreland gave Kennedy less than twenty-four hours to create a base development plan for two hundred thousand Army, Navy, Air Force, and Marine forces to enter Vietnam. He tapped Jack Norton as deputy commanding general of the U.S. Army, Vietnam. Despite any misaligned stars, the U.S. was officially entering the Vietnam War. Officers from West Point '41, thrust into leadership at young ages in World War II, were now called on to enter the upper echelons of their third war.

Evelyn Canella waved her husband off optimistically. "Charles, if you're going to Vietnam," she insisted, "we'll certainly win the war."

When Charles Canella got to Vietnam, he had serious doubts. Once known as "make 'em or break 'em Charlie" in training, Canella had become an old hat at taking over failed commands. But Vietnam was different. As senior adviser to the commanding general at an Army of the Republic of Vietnam (ARVN) military training center at Quang Trung, he handled fifteen thousand South Vietnamese trainees. While on one hand he liked many of those he coached, on the other hand, he was exasperated.

The training is abysmal, they don't understand tactics, and no one knows which end of a rifle to shoot. They don't want to fight, and you can't make them fight.

Canella got in the dust on a daily basis with soldiers, but he couldn't get the Vietnamese commander to show up to do the same. He wrote a lengthy memorandum to top U.S. brass describing the dismal situation. The response wasn't what he hoped for. General Westmoreland had approved the training, so Canella got his neck pulled back. He was a commander not permitted to command as he saw fit. It brought back recollections of World War II, when he'd received those shocking orders to put up roadblocks and turn back Czech refugees. Now, like then, he was the boots on the ground, the eyes on the front, but the commanders behind gray walls in the puzzle palace and the whiz-kid bean counters thought they knew better.

De Silva returned to the maelstrom briefly, but he too was disillusioned, especially regarding the outlook for the Vietnamese people. He didn't understand why the U.S. disapproved of people in Vietnam acting like Vietnamese, but then he never understood the U.S. criticizing Koreans for being Koreans and the Chinese for being Chinese. In de Silva's view American officials moralized—wanting others to act like them.[6]

Back at the puzzle palace, others forgot that old adage about never volunteering. Class of '41er George Brown called his tour as military assistant to McNamara, "a traumatic experience." Another from the class labeled the secretary "the strangest man I've ever met." McNamara whittled down everything, including winning battles, to numerical analyses, or "ICE" for Index of Combat Effectiveness. It seemed that McNamara was sure that the sheer quantity of troops, artillery, shots fired, and so forth would predict the outcome of battles; leadership qualities had little bearing. Some even thought an assignment in the armpit of Southeast Asia was preferable to any further duty working at the Pentagon with McNamara. Military commanders didn't easily suffer bureaucrats.

The top '41 graduate, Ace Moody, headed to Vietnam as assistant deputy commander of the 1st Cavalry Division (Airmobile), an assault helicopter unit that had come to fruition largely due to the efforts of the classmate cabal. He joined Jack Norton, who was returning to combat to lead the division. It was Norton who had recommended employing this new airmobile division to Vietnam, which had at first been commanded by Major General Harry Kinnard. The division had to tackle far different terrain than in World War II or Korea, but as Spec Powell put it, "You have to be smart enough to take the good out of what you have learned and extrapolate it into the new conditions that you haven't encountered yet."

At their disposal, Norton and Moody had attack helicopters, scout helicopters, lift helicopters, a new Mohawk for reconnaissance, and more. The sky began to rain birds. Sadly, Ace Moody didn't get to see the fruits of this progress. He died of a heart attack at the age of forty-nine soon after arriving in Vietnam in March 1967. Norton and Rowny swore it was due to his time previously working for McNamara.

Under Norton's command, the 1st Cavalry Division went on to earn seven Medals of Honor, the highest number earned by an Army division. What the tank was to World War II, the helicopter became to Vietnam.

Many in the class, however, had conflicted emotions about the war.

George Brown had little time to reflect. He pinned on his fourth star—that of a full general—on his way to Southeast Asia to command air operations at the war's height. Still, Brown knew—just as Woody Garrett had made plain years earlier—that despite all the tactical air power and helicopter gunships at his disposal, there was no absolute substitute for ground operations; in the case of Vietnam, airpower missed enemies who were underground.

★ ★ ★

While some West Point '41ers were heating up the skies in Vietnam, Joe Reed was on a different tack, undertaking a massive directive to bring America's Armed Forces into the twenty-first century. He was pondering the Army's massive computers that were so bulky they were lugged around in 2½-ton trucks. Reed was trying to figure out a way to arm the troops with them.

I've got to take computers down to where the rubber meets the road.

For a crack artilleryman, it wasn't totally out of his realm, since he had been working in R & D for the Joint Staff as well as the Office of the Chief of Staff, and this new directive came on orders from General Creighton Abrams, Army vice chief of staff. Given America's role in Vietnam growing ever more convoluted, Abrams thought it time to come up with new ideas. Keeping track, by hand, of thousands of personnel and their military occupation specialties (MOS) was hard enough, let alone tracking the logistics behind thousands of tons of equipment heading to Vietnam. At the same time, the Office of the Secretary of Defense (OSD) determined that the Army's existing computer systems were too costly and disorganized. Abrams turned to the insight of Reed to tread a new path.

Reed saw his appointment from a different angle, telling friends, "I floated in and Abrams grabbed me out of the sink."

Reed was appointed the commanding general charged with establishing the Computer Systems Command at Fort Belvoir, Virginia. He looked around at the role of the computer in the military:

There's a lot of different problems. The only time the Air Force is looking at a computer is when they're in the front seat as a pilot. The Navy . . . their computer is in a steel bubble floating around on the ocean. They both only use computers to administer or run equipment.

He considered the drastic difference between those services and what he needed to do for the Army: *They man the equipment; we equip the man.*

Equipping the man, given the amount of boots beating the ground, was a task of mind-boggling proportions. The Army was way behind the eight ball.

We've been floating along, trying to get along, but no one's done anything smaller than a communications center.

He pondered what needed to be done. *We have to make things smaller. That's a given. We need standard operating procedures from top to bottom, and we need our computers to have a language of their own; otherwise we'll have roadblocks stopping our messages. Theoretically, we need to make it to where the whole service comes down to one button. But we need to test every button to get there.*

Joe Reed, the humble southern boy who'd grown up in an orphanage and morphed into a fine officer at West Point, was now ushering in America's computer age. Granted, it wasn't all smooth sailing for the brigadier general. Reed realized that his staff members—about thirty culled from various other units—were fairly ignorant about what they were doing, but more important, at least they knew what they were *trying* to do. One of those objectives was computerizing tactical fire direction systems, or TACFIRE. Reed was trying to automate artillery so that in the future, if someone like he, Stern, or Fletcher—whether it be at a crossroads in the Bulge or facing down Emperor Wilhelm—need not try to calculate targets by visual observation, slide rules, and firing tables. They could input all necessary data into a computer and let it tell them how to knock the emperor off his horse. In essence, the computer would replace the fire directions center. Added to that was MOS tracking, inventory control, and more. There would be no orders like those sending Skowronek to Oran when he was supposed to be in Italy. Computers would sort it all out.

While Reed was pursing these efforts, at the same time he considered his unit a transient phenomenon. On one hand, if the unit didn't get it right, the OSD made it clear there would be no computers. "We can't continue to let a thousand flowers grow," the OSD told him.

On the other hand, if Reed's directive was on target, the sooner he put his unit out of business, the better for the Army.

The Army's computers needed to all start talking to one another, so Reed began organizing them under one point of control. That brought on another entirely distinct challenge. Every top commander needed to be on board, which meant four-star generals exchanging their computers for what the new Computer Systems Command was developing.

Said General Abrams to Reed, "You're going to take a safari all around the Army to all of the commanders, and you're going to straighten out their situations."

"But I'm only a one-star general," protested Reed.

"Don't look while they stare," replied Abrams. "If you get to stuttering, take this little letter I'm going to give you and have them call the number on it; it'll get things straightened out."

Joe Reed was off on his worldwide tour. Surprisingly, he encountered less resistance than anticipated, till he came across General James Polk, commander of the U.S. Army in Europe, or USAREUR. Polk began dumping on Reed all the reasons why the Army should not mess with his systems. Reed explained that the Army could not have in service a piece of equipment that did not fulfill its proper place in the system. But the general insisted *his* computers remain under *his* domain, despite his own staff advising to the contrary.

Reed listened politely to the general's grandstanding and then finally, after half an hour of his rhetoric, pulled out a letter. "Sir, please read this letter, and if you've still got any objections, then call the number on it."

As Polk looked over the letter, Reed heard an audible gasp as the general saw the phone number on it. It belonged to General Abrams, vice chief of staff of the Army.

Every general was then on board. The new systems began revolutionizing aspects of the soldier's daily work life, and the Computer Systems Command rapidly grew to encompass 2,700 professionals in seventeen installations worldwide. Polk wound up being an enthusiast who saw the possibilities.

★ ★ ★

Reed was deep in the thick of things when Charlie Fletcher was at the Army War College directing its first-ever military strategy course, which he had devised and written. When the time came for the '67 summer break, he and Johnnie headed to his hometown in Michigan with the kids, back to where his ancestors had built a log cabin and where the Fletchers' century-old home now stood. Little had changed since Fletcher left home for West Point at the age of sixteen. His mother and father lived on in the house; the county fair still remained a huge area draw; the red covered bridge still spanned the St. Joseph River; bald eagles continued to soar over farms dotting the landscape. Gone, however, were the days of the one-room schoolhouse.

On their first evening back in Centreville, Charlie Fletcher's father broke out a fine vintage of wine over dinner. He stood up with great fanfare, looked across the table to his son, and with a beaming smile, raised his glass. "A toast to the new general," he proudly announced. "May his stars multiply."

Charlie Fletcher sat momentarily stunned, as though his father was speaking to someone behind him.

General? What is he talking about?

Little did Fletcher know but Herb Stern, who was also at the war college at the time, had glimpsed the commandant's notification of general officer promotions and there was his classmate's name, Charles William Fletcher, with two new words before it—Brigadier General. Knowing his friend's vacation destination, Stern tracked down the phone number to his boyhood home by telling the registrar's office, "This is an emergency. Colonel Fletcher just got promoted! You *have* to give me his family's number."

The realization settled in with the younger Fletcher as the family raised glasses in celebration. From his days riding Sally, to the Battle of the Bulge, to the chill of the Cold War . . . like Joe Reed, this brigadier general had come a long way from humble beginnings.

Within months, however, he would embark on a new type of schooling—learning about the rugged terrain of the Demilitarized Zone of Korea, that buffer zone between North and South Korea, along the 38th parallel.

★ ★ ★

It was early 1968 when Charlie Fletcher became the commanding general of I Corps Artillery in Korea. In essence, he commanded "controlling and patrolling." Despite the armistice signed nearly fifteen years earlier between North and South, tensions remained high. Fletcher had two howitzers in position by his headquarters, ready to engage on a few minutes' notice. All his men had to do was load and fire. Another half-dozen units could be moved on short notice into strategic positions.

That time came on Sunday, January 21, in a fast-moving blur of events. Thirty-one commandos from North Korea's 124th Special Forces, disguised as South Koreans in overalls, had days earlier breached the DMZ, crossing in the U.S. section near the city of Yeoncheon. Undetected in their small units, the commandos regrouped and made it to the outskirts of Seoul with the goal of infiltrating the city to assassinate South Korean President Park Chung-hee. By entering South Korea through the U.S. zone, they hoped to place partial blame for their actions on the U.S., thereby creating friction between it and South Korea.[7]

Before approaching Seoul, the commandos rid their overalls to reveal Republic of Korea (ROK) uniforms like those worn by the South Korean army. This allowed them to proceed undetected past numerous military checkpoints, that is, until a South Korean officer at a final checkpoint—just eight hundred meters from the presidential Blue House—questioned what was beneath the men's bulky overcoats. In response, the commandos began firing, attempting to gun the rest of the way to reach their objective. South Korean tanks converged on the scene, their firepower far exceeding the expectations of a commando unit whose strength was stealth. Abandoning their mission, the commandos began retreating.[8]

That's when Charlie Fletcher's mission began with a red alert: "The commandos are fleeing north."

He moved his firing units into position and lay in wait. "Either they kill us or we kill them," Fletcher told his officers. "We know which way they're moving, but it's rough terrain. The 2nd and 7th Divisions are out looking, but rest assured, we're going to take them. Don't let any chance go by, because they will fight to the last man."

And so they did—nearly to the last man. As the commandos tried to navigate the cold and formidable mountains leading north, almost all were subdued. Most were killed singly, in blazing firefights with American infantry. A few were said to have committed suicide rather than suffer capture. One successfully made his way back to North Korea. Another young commando threw down his arms in surrender.[9]

While Charlie Fletcher's unit remained armed and ready, the situation went from bad to worse. Two days after the commando attack, North Korean patrol boats off the coast of Korea fired upon a U.S. Navy intelligence ship, the *Pueblo*, killing one of its crew and wounding others, including the ship's commander. While the ship was supposedly operating in international waters, the North Koreans boarded it, and the remaining crew of more than eighty was bound, blindfolded, and transported to Pyongyang. There the Americans were imprisoned and charged with spying for allegedly impinging on North Korea's twelve-mile territorial limit. Forced confessions were elicited under threat of torture. The Americans lingered in prison.

It was fifteen years since Paul Liles had been confined to a fifty-five-gallon drum in Korea, twenty-one years since Fletcher pushed universal military training for the U.S. to be able to quickly mobilize. Little had changed. The U.S. strained at the seams in terms of a military buildup in Korea. Resources were spread thin.

A week later, the North Vietnamese and Vietcong launched the Tet Offensive, an extensive series of surprise attacks against cities, towns, and hamlets throughout South Vietnam. It was the most far-reaching offensive up to that point in the Vietnam War, launched on the important lunar New Year holiday, "Tet."

As the debacle of Vietnam deepened in intensity, the *Pueblo* crew languished and the months went by.

Finally, Christmas of 1968 approached, and negotiators reached an agreement: the U.S. would admit the ship's intrusion into North Korean territory, apologize, and pledge to cease further action. In return, the *Pueblo* crew was permitted to walk across a bridge to freedom in South Korea.

24

PERMISSION TO WITHDRAW

As the '60s drew to a close, Charlie Fletcher, having returned stateside, was at the Department of Defense, tasked with industrial preparedness. His goal was to determine how the United States could take a war footing— its stockpile of weapons and mobilization strategies—and plan in the future to have a graduated response by industry rather than a full-blown mobilization.

Fletcher deliberated, *Not all wars will be a world war. We need to scale up only to the level required by the situation. We need stages of intensity from a limited mobilization, up to reworking a full mobilization like in World War II.*

Charlie Fletcher was in his element. Preparing.

His '41 classmates remained spread around the world, sharing holiday and reunion greetings as the decade progressed:

George Brown expressed fond sentiments over his location—commander of a task force running atomic weapons tests "from the Land of Enchantment" in New Mexico.

A classmate, Joseph Brown, echoing sentiments shared by many about the puzzle palace, wrote, "WANTED! To exchange small home in Arlington on the Potomac for castle on the Rhine, hut in Hawaii, French chateau, or quarters on post. Be of light heart—there is room for you at the Pentagon."

Spec Powell was ready to take him up on it: "Even the puzzle palace looks good after a year in Iran."

Still another, Robert Johnson, kept up the black-class humor by commenting that he'd "escaped" the Pentagon, been "resentenced," gone through "rehabilitation" in Germany, and then ended up in "maximum security" at the Aberdeen Proving Ground.

Wrote James Green from the class: "Am working for the Boeing Company to help put a man on the moon. May he be one of the sons of '41."

Classmate Jerry La Rocca had been helping to make that moon shot happen. He had been the scientific adviser to President Kennedy, and under the auspices of the government-sponsored Arnold Engineering Development Center, designed the world's first "supersonic diffuser." In short, La Rocca helped bring space to earth. The supersonic diffuser was a test chamber that simulated on the ground what a rocket would encounter attempting to reach space. There had been enormous challenges trying to lighten a rocket load so its velocity could pass the earth's gravitational field, but the larger the booster rocket, the heavier the load, which caused the rocket to fall back to earth. The solution was to have the heavy "first stage" rocket jettisoned during ascent to lessen the load, after which a "second stage" rocket would ignite and further propel the rocket into space.

The problem was trying to figure out how to get the second stage to ignite at that different atmosphere. The supersonic diffuser was the answer, and La Rocca called on famed aerodynamic scientist Dr. Bernhard Goethert to help build it. The supersonic diffuser simulated conditions for a space vehicle flying at high speed and reaching a hundred-plus miles in altitude, at which point its second stage would ignite to push the vehicle past the earth's gravitational pull.

While outward appearances suggested these efforts were aimed at seeking to explore where none had gone before, La Rocca's initiatives were, in truth, far more focused on defense. He was ever cognizant of a world at risk. U.S. intelligence officers had broken through codes to learn that the Russians wanted to "own" the moon so they could plant atomic weapons there, which could theoretically be aimed at any spot on earth. La Rocca had confidentially relayed this to President Kennedy when he'd been in office, which contributed to the urgent thrust to put a man on the moon.

Making that moon shot happen meant overcoming endless obstacles. Getting a man to the moon was one thing, but then came the next question asked of La Rocca: "How do we get them back to earth?"

La Rocca's answer: "If we have a space capsule returning, we don't know for sure if the astronauts will be alive or unconscious or semiconscious. So we don't know if they'll be capable of flying. We need features to aid their landing so they don't come crashing back to earth at such a high speed that it burns apart the capsule and the astronauts inside."

La Rocca, with his days bailing out of fighter jets a not-so-distant memory, pioneered the concept of employing a parachute to slow down a space capsule as it neared the earth after reentry. He was also concerned about the sleep deprivation that early astronauts encountered in space, returning to earth like "zombies" that had not slept in days. He tapped physicians for possible answers, ultimately determining that the pineal gland in the brain, which produces melatonin to induce sleep, malfunctioned when beyond the earth's electromagnetic field, the Van Allen belt. The solution, La Rocca decided, was to create an electromagnetic field for the astronauts within the space capsule. Future astronauts then slept.

In the end, the '41er reached new heights when he became deputy director for Apollo tests, quality assurance, and astronaut training at North American Aviation, which was building the Apollo command and service modules and developing entry monitor systems. La Rocca ensured that every aspect of an Apollo capsule had the quality to successfully land a man on the moon—and return safely to earth. He also oversaw the familiarization and training of astronauts such as John Glenn, Neil Armstrong, and Buzz Aldrin on Apollo operations, capsule functioning, and the lunar excursion module.

While James Green was denied his wish that a moon landing include a class son, due to the contributions of '41er Jerry La Rocca, Armstrong and Aldrin successfully took those steps for mankind. The high aspirations of '41 class officers never ceased.

In fact, numerous officers like La Rocca had by now joined the ranks of private industry. Many remembered well the higher mathematics they'd learned at West Point and did some calculations: There were seven thousand colonels on active duty in the military. Taking a thousand off the top and the same off the bottom—those too young or too old to be considered for promotion to general—left five thousand colonels. In 1967 about fifty were promoted to general.

"You don't have to be in first section math to figure that at 1%," wrote one from the class.

Rather than sweat out the generals' list, most '41ers chose to retire or enter private industry. But they saluted their forty class members who had made it, their "1 percenters," including Roy Atteberry, Buster Boatwright, George Brown, Pete Crow, Charlie Fletcher, Larry and Mike Greene, Ace Moody, Jack Norton, Spec Powell, Joe Reed, Ed Rowny, and Walter Woolwine.

By that point, the twenty-fifth reunion for the class of 1941 had come and gone. Classmates debated whether the academy's rigid standards had wavered over the decades, though most agreed with George Johnson that from the minute they graduated, the corps had "gone to hell." Few West Point classes, in their view, could compare to theirs.

Still, even if the corps didn't shine as brightly, most '41ers had enough faith in the academy to encourage sons to follow in their footsteps—or their prior example paved the way. John Murray Jr. graduated from the academy, throwing his cap in celebration twenty-three years after his father.

Joining him that year was the son of Joseph H. Ward, who'd been killed in Germany just prior to V-E Day. Soon came Roy Atteberry's son, along with the namesakes of Charles Canella and John Norton. Jim Fowler had not one, but two sons attend the academy, a testament to his admiration for West Point; graciously, he did not fault the academy for his treatment as a cadet but rather the time and place. He proved to be a pioneer paving the way for the likes of his sons. Charlie Fletcher Jr. also put on the grays, but the Fletchers encouraged their second son, James, to pursue his talent for architecture. Still, he chose the academy.

"If I was here because you wanted me to be here, I could never have made it," he wrote to his parents during plebe week.

Being headstrong was apparently a Fletcher gene. So too was Duty, Honor, Country. The generational lines of those in gray connected to the class of '41 grew. Other class sons attended the Air Force and Naval Academies.

Among the gains, however, were devastating losses, as '41ers began losing their children to Vietnam. The Tet Offensive claimed Larry Greene's only son, 1st Lieutenant Lawrence D. Greene. While leading forward elements of his command in an airborne operation, he was killed by a sniper's bullet as he went to the aid of a wounded radioman.[1] Ed Rowny thought his former roommate was never the same afterward. Yet the senior Greene went on to command in Vietnam. Duty, unquestionably, came with degrees of heartbreak. There was some comfort for him being able to sit next to his younger brother at Military Assistance Command (MACV) events in Vietnam. The two were known as "Big Greene" and "Little Greene." None doubted the tall orders both had seen in their lifetimes.

★ ★ ★

As the '60s drew to a close, General Creighton Abrams became commander, U.S. MACV Vietnam. He assumed control from Westmoreland, who'd been appointed chief of staff of the Army. President Richard Nixon, in effect, tasked General Abrams with winding the war down, pursuing a "Vietnamization" policy that involved an orderly turnover of military operations to South Vietnam. Abram's deputy was General Frederick Weyand. Alongside him was Major General Walter Woolwine, who initially served as the commanding general of the 1st Logistical Command and later as assistant deputy commander, U.S. Army, Vietnam. Of the two deputies, Abrams always seemed to dispatch Woolwine whenever there was a screwup, when everything went abysmally wrong, when level-headedness blew out the window, when hell needed to be sorted out. Walter Woolwine didn't mind chasing the devil.

The West Pointer, at six three, was as trim and lanky as ever, though his hair was now salt and pepper and the corners of his eyes crinkled in contemplation. But an omnipresent glint remained in his eyes—part brilliance, part incorrigibility—and his humor still cracked like a whip when chaos called for a degree of levity.

There were upward of a half-million U.S. troops in Vietnam, the majority of which rotated out every twelve months, as though Woolwine didn't have enough to keep track of without that revolving door. He directly oversaw fifty thousand troops, among the larger commands that those from his West Point class had tackled.

Under Woolwine's domain were the broad logistics that kept the war effort propelled forward—connecting operational requirements A to B to X, Y, and Z. For anyone who thought logistics was just "gitten' stuff," they'd have thought twice upon witnessing Woolwine operate his vast logistical puzzle.

Through his doors flowed the materials of war. The supply requirements were dizzying, as though he was running the economy of a small nation that produced little—and imported nearly everything. There were construction materials, generators, refrigerators, and petrol—tens of thousands of gallons of the latter pumped hourly though pipelines snaking inland to feed fighting machinery. Supply lines included a constant flow of Hueys, tanks, artillery, ammo, and spare parts loaded on to transport crafts that in turn needed patrol boats to guard against ambushes. Barbed wire and sandbags were critical; radios and field telephones always seemed in short supply.

Then came food rations for the small nation of men, which for starters, guzzled 1.5 million gallons of milk a month.[2] Complicating matters was when rations had to be air dropped via parachute into remote areas, such as when infantry got cut off. Add in to the logistics equation millions of pounds of monthly laundry and the mind-boggling paper trail for this vast arsenal of supplies that was still being tracked by manual input; it was but a short time since Joe Reed began the initiative, under General Abrams, to implement computerized command systems into the Army.

Walter Woolwine certainly didn't need a debacle to get a headache. By his estimates Vietnam was the most difficult logistical operation the Army had ever seen, trying to establish secure supply bases in an underdeveloped country ten thousand miles from the U.S. mainland and in the midst of combat operations. Unlike in World War II, where logistics could bring up the rear behind the front, there was also no cohesive front in Vietnam. Supplies had to go up, down, sideways, and at times at crosshairs. Meanwhile, Woolwine was trying to transport supplies while building roads to transport the same—*and* trying to leave twenty feet clear on other side to reduce the chances of ambushes *and* arming the skies with guns while doing all this on the ground. It was a far cry from World War II's "Red Ball Express," where supply convoys could steam nearly four hundred miles to the front.

Despite the challenges, Westmoreland reported to Congress about logistics in Vietnam, saying, "No commander in the field has ever had to look back over his shoulder to make sure his supply and support was following him. He knew it was there. No operation ever had to be delayed because of lack of supplies to perform the operation."[3]

Performance required innovation on Woolwine's part. Mental light bulbs were always blinking behind his eagle eyes. One of his illuminating ideas: *Let's train some Thai girls to work at computers.*

Secretarial work was, after all, still a woman's domain, and Woolwine knew it would be easy to find a willing workforce near Bangkok. He set up a computer training school and soon, by popular demand, had rotated four graduating classes through it with more on the way. Woolwine turned to this computer effort to centralize a database of troops killed or missing in action, having never forgotten the mayhem of mismarked graves along Omaha Beach; soldiers had died fighting for their country but yet couldn't be properly identified for their place in history.

After hearing about some kills in the badlands of Vietnam—with nothing done about recoveries—Woolwine started a crusade.

We've got to start a method of collecting information when people are still on the ground . . . in the area. It has to be done.

His ideas for identification mostly fell on deaf ears. He got responses from fellow commanders like, "We're busy as hell" or "Wait till the war's over." Waiting till war's end was exactly what Woolwine did *not* want to do. At that point, he figured the information of those unaccounted for was (*a*) not likely to be under U.S. control and (*b*) not likely to be shared with an exiting enemy.

Woolwine approached General Abrams. Though only slightly more inclined to listen than others, the general lent his assistant deputy an ear. The latter laid out his case. "Listen, we should be gathering ID on planes as soon as they're shot down," said Woolwine. "The same with ships bombed or torpedoed. The sooner we start tracking, the better chance of identifying the missing. When we put it off, our success rate drops exponentially."

Woolwine wasn't looking to establish a complicated system, he explained, but something basic. He wanted all divisions on the ground and all headquarters locations to collect information on where people died, when they died, with that information sent to a newly created graves registration office in Vietnam.

Abrams signed off, and Woolwine began implementing his plan, centralizing the information about America's losses. He put names to the deceased, faces to the losses, created records for loved ones. He thought it unlikely that there would ever be a proper tribute to the thousands lost in such an unpopular war—no chapel or reflecting pool like on Omaha Beach, no bronze statue remembering the "Spirit of American Youth." Still, one dog tag at a time, he worked toward the process of honoring those lost. For Walter Woolwine, it was about the honor in Duty, Honor, Country.

But the majority of the time, he and other commanders remaining on in Vietnam were running the clock out on a war. In doing so, contemplated Woolwine:

What do we need to leave behind for forces assigned to stay? I don't want it to be an asshole place like in Korea. That was like the plague after the war—shit facilities and shit weather.

Woolwine couldn't exactly create a country club, but he could build proper, permanent facilities for troops. That included decent barracks with fans, which he planned for Long Binh, near Saigon.

Forget sweltering in the heat trying to sleep. And I'll fix up a recreational area. Yes, at least let them have a movie theater.

Added to that, he threw in a golf range and a swimming pool.

For all the looking forward, Woolwine also had the gargantuan task of moving back. As the Vietnamization policy took hold, he had to reverse gears to untangle the massive spider web of logistics. He had to begin packing up so America could go home. "We need to get lean," he told his staff. "We don't want to end up with tremendous excesses as this redeployment proceeds, because that'll require keeping people around for long periods of time. And the goal is to get out."

Getting out, simply put, was not just about soldiers. Woolwine could not leave hundreds of tons of critical military equipment and materials around that might fall into enemy hands, not to mention the dollar value of those supplies. So the general set about redeploying everything physically and logistically possible. Air vehicles were easy enough—fly them out. In terms of the heaviest equipment, like tanks and artillery, U.S. interests were best served, he determined, if those items were primarily redeployed to nearby nations, like South Korea and Thailand, with strategic ties to the U.S. He went down the list of equipment and materials, factoring in the bulk, weight, and cost of transport. Like the circles on a bull's-eye board, as items got lighter and smaller, the radius to which they were dispersed grew wider, spreading to America's military bases around the world till the widest bands of supplies rippled back to America's shores.

Still, despite his best-laid plans, as troops left Vietnam, inevitably deserted posts were strewn with leftover guns, ammunition, and more. Woolwine made sure that cleanup crews followed.

We're not leaving anything behind worth leaving.

Opportunists, he knew, made hefty sums over equipment abandoned in World War II. Woolwine didn't plan to let that happen again. The Joint Operations Area Command for Vietnam, under the auspices of the Department of Defense, spent months surveying exited areas and signed off on a job well done. After it was all wrapped up, computations were made on the value of materials "saved," and Walter Woolwine saved the Armed Forces and American taxpayers $100 million. For that, he was awarded the Legion of Merit.

Woolwine, however, preferred to shower the accolades on his troops, the fifty thousand worker bees that had driven the challenging feat to fruition. Forget what Americans back home were saying about a "wrong" war—as if there was ever a right one. No matter the background of the young American who had arrived in Vietnam, whether willing or not, in Woolwine's view each had shouldered his responsibility to his government and country. Walter Woolwine parted Vietnam with the lasting impression that his men had done their duty effectively and with motivation. Maybe, just maybe, U.S. troops had come much further than Charlie Fletcher could ever have imagined decades earlier.

Woolwine, however, never imagined that there would be no U.S. forces *at all* kept on in Vietnam. While the South Vietnamese temporarily enjoyed the facilities he'd built, ultimately, his movie theater, golf range, and swimming pool became bounty for the North Vietnamese. Talk about a screwup.

★ ★ ★

As Woolwine was winding things down, Charlie Fletcher was conducting his own calculations on the U.S. exit from Vietnam. As director of ground ammunition in the Department of Defense, he was charged with predicting the reduction in ammunition that would be required as the U.S. phased out operations. Ammunition was not typically stockpiled but rather cranked up to a wartime footing and cranked down in anticipation of war ending. Fletcher ordered reductions in the output of U.S. production as combat units began returning home. At the same time, it was essential to ensure that this did not create ammunition shortfalls for troops remaining on in Southeast Asia, whether ground, air, or naval. It was left to Fletcher's determination how regiments were to be supplied, including how many days' worth of ammunition to keep in Okinawa, the main spot for channeling supplies to the front. His was a fine art of manipulation, making sure that troops did not run low while ramping down the war effort.

In general, it was a smooth transition, so when the Department of Defense later needed to know how much ammunition to leave the South Vietnamese for self-defense after the U.S. exit was complete, it again turned to Fletcher. He was dispatched to Honolulu, to a meeting sponsored by the Commander in Chief Pacific, or CINCPAC. Fletcher, representing the DOD, argued for a 120-day supply to protect the South. A young representative from the State Department thought 60 days sufficient. Fletcher stared in astonishment at the young man, who had probably never looked down the barrel of a shotgun. It seemed yet another instance where combat numbers were based on spreadsheets—just as Moody had experienced with the Index of Combat Effectiveness—rather than a logical strategy to retain command and control.

It became a moot point when Congress passed the Case-Church Amendment in June 1973, prohibiting further direct U.S. military involvement in Vietnam, including firing support. That was the day, in Fletcher's view, the Vietnam War was truly lost.

We've condemned the South to defeat. North Vietnam will get all the support they need from the Russians, and while the South still has the will to fight—they won't have the means.

★ ★ ★

During those last years of war, General Creighton Abrams left Vietnam to become Army chief of staff in 1972. Soon after he was diagnosed with lung cancer. As he lay terminally ill at Fort Myer, by Arlington National Cemetery, Ed Rowny visited him once or twice a week.

On one visit, Rowny was caught off guard by the general's question: "Why are you a Catholic?"

"Because my parents were Catholic," answered Rowny.

"Do you believe in God?" asked Abrams.

"Yes."

Questioned Abrams, "Why?"

"Because there's no risk involved," answered Rowny. "If I said I did not believe in God and there is one, I'd go straight to hell. If there is a heaven and I believe, then I stand a chance of getting in."

Abrams smiled. "Sound thinking."

The following week, Abrams converted to Catholicism. He died soon after.

After hearing the news, Rowny thought back in time . . . to the three wars he'd seen, different countries, different conflicts. The clock had ticked away at the decades, but it seemed time changed little when it came to the soul of a soldier.

Thought Rowny, *There are no atheists in foxholes*.

Henry Bodson was searching for answers as well, in his case to the mysterious illness that inflicted his wife, Belle. She was prone to tripping and dropping things, feeling weakness in her limbs, and rapidly losing weight. Soon she could barely speak or swallow. The diagnosis came down: ALS, or Lou Gehrig's disease, the degenerative disease that wastes away muscles. Within six months she was chair-bound, and then one day she passed out. She ended up at Walter Reed Hospital, needing twenty-four-hour care. Duty and Honor took on new meaning for Henry Bodson.

He was now a civilian employee on the Army staff at the Pentagon, advising on military aid to foreign countries. Every evening after long workdays, he would faithfully navigate the unrelenting traffic and nearly hour-long trip from Arlington to Walter Reed to see his wife, usually not returning home till well past eleven. Day in, day out, and the weeks turned into months. Only on Sundays was there a reprieve when his son stepped in for him. But Henry Bodson didn't mind.

Walter Reed attempted to discharge Belle, but Bodson couldn't find a single nursing home that would take an ALS patient. The hospital assigned a lieutenant to fix that, but he had no better luck then Henry. It was an era with limited knowledge of the disease, limited interest in helping. And so Belle remained at Walter Reed, and Henry continued his daily visits, soldiering on to keep Belle's spirits up as the days and months turned into eight years. Then at long last Belle succumbed to her illness and was laid to rest at Arlington National Cemetery to wait for Henry.

In fact, many '41 officers would survive their OAO, their one and only, the backbones to their lives, the ones who had made it all possible for them to achieve what they had achieved. Many felt their wives should have received combat badges for support services. They'd brandished pistols to ward off intruders in strange outposts, learned to evacuate on a dime, been separated from their husbands for years at a time. As Rita Rowny figured it, she had cumulatively spent seven years on her own, raising five kids while her husband was on overseas hardship tours. It would not be long before Ed would have to nurse her for nine years, eventually losing her to cancer. James Forsyth and Joe Reed lost their beloved wives as well, as did Walter Woolwine. And darling Cheyney, after losing one '41er, had gone on to forty-six years with Jack Norton before he lost her. On went the list, officers hardly expecting to survive three wars and then outlive their wives.

The spouses remaining, like Alice "Skip" Brown, the tenacious Johnnie Fletcher, together with Eileen Greene and Ruth Adams, were often the glue that kept everyone connected as '41ers crossed over into retirement.

By 1974 only nine '41 officers remained in uniform. One, Jack Norton, retained his affinity for choppers, supervising the building of a new assault helicopter. It was called the Black Hawk. George Brown also still wore stars. A friend of his returned to the Catholic high school that both had attended.

Sister Mary Baptista asked, "What ever happened to that nice boy, George Brown?"

"Sister," answered the friend, "he is now the chairman of America's Joint Chiefs of Staff."

Replied the Sister, "Oh . . . he was such a good boy."

The president had chosen Brown for the highest uniformed position in the nation, the hopes of a bright black class borne out.

The last of U.S. troops were soon withdrawn from Vietnam in 1975, and the South found itself unable to defend itself. That didn't surprise Charlie Fletcher. But such issues were for the next generation of West Pointers to figure out, two of which bore his family name. West Point '41 was wrapping up its duty.

In many ways, the days of military entrepreneurship were also wrapping up. Jack Murray lamented that going forward, a military man would need to be a genius to cut his way through the layers of bureaucrats in Washington. Decisions regarding combat command, he figured, would be made by politicians, a far cry from the days when '41ers assumed commands in war without prompting or asking permission. Murray complained that the way things were going, commanders would not even be able to "bomb an outhouse" without first asking. Still, Murray didn't give up hope. When asked to be a visiting professor at his alma mater, he said yes before asking if he'd be paid. He would have done it for nothing. West Point did that to men of promise.

As the class of West Point '41 culminated its four decades of service— decades that encompassed three wars, a Cold War, and eight presidents— the bonds between members remained indelible, bonds that went back to that steaming July day along the Hudson in 1937. Many from the class were still planning, improvising, and conniving, but it wasn't for appointments this time. Instead, they were ensuring that the sacrifices of classmates not be forgotten.

In 1977 they dedicated Nininger Hall at West Point. On the top floor of the building, to be funded in perpetuity by the class, was the Honor Committee Room. It was soon furnished with dozens of beautiful chairs purchased by class members—as though a show of arms reaching out to the Medal of Honor winner, Sandy Nininger.

At the commemorative service, there was talk among '41ers and family members about how some people were all too ready to complain about what was wrong with Duty, Honor, Country.

Those connected to the West Point class of 1941 knew differently. Its class members had lived and died by that creed. As General Douglas MacArthur said, "They are your rallying points to build courage when courage seems to fail, to regain faith when there seems to be little cause for faith, to create hope when hope becomes forlorn."[4]

After battling in the sands of Africa and the skies off Sicily, on to the beaches of Normandy and through hedgerow hell, up the Apennines and on to Bataan, Inchon, and the quagmire of the jungles of Vietnam . . . West Point '41ers knew about courage and hope and faith. Above all, they knew about the truth, having commanded countless men whose lives had been under their control. They knew that the truth mattered.

As the 1970s drew to a close, so too did the military service of one of the most remarkable classes to ever graduate West Point. Peer de Silva re-emerged from the shadows to publish memoirs of his CIA days, his writing skills honed, he insisted, by those countless responses to *New York Times* complaints about his swastika prank decades earlier. His heart failed a month before his memoirs were published, but at long last his classmates finally gained insight as to what he'd been doing all those years. George Brown succumbed to cancer in his second term as chairman of the Joint Chiefs. The honorary pallbearers were his classmates.

Ed Rowny was alive and energetic as ever, but in a display of moral courage retired rather than support a Carter administration arms treaty with the Soviets that he considered not in America's best interests. It was unequal; the Soviet's cache unverifiable. Rowny relinquished his thirty-eight-year military career, three stars—and prospects for a fourth—so he could testify against the treaty. It was never ratified and the next president, Ronald Reagan, tapped Rowny's expertise by making him the chief negotiator for nuclear disarmament.

Other classmates learned to finesse eighteen holes with flair. Some also did exceptionally well in second careers. Charles Canella turned to making 'em—not breaking 'em—in the stock market. Classmates like Herb Stern were among his best clients.

In retirement, rather than meeting on battlefields, class camaraderie continued at ad hoc supper clubs. The artillery crew of Fletcher, Reed, and Stern rotated among their D.C.-area homes, inevitably trading stories of war and peace, with Reed and Stern chiding Fletcher for always getting to "play with the big guns—with artillery as big as Volkswagens." Jack Norton, Mike Greene, Henry Bodson, and Ed Rowny usually joined them, and classmates passing through D.C. sometimes dropped in. Down south, Charles Canella moved into the same Florida retirement community as Larry Greene, Spec Powell, and Buster Boatwright. And so on went the unbreakable bonds of classmates.

Reunions, however, remained the big bashes. After seeing so much change—a metamorphosis of America over the decades, from the Depression to wars, to landing a man on the moon and more—the class was a hard group to shock. But they were truly stunned when Dr. Henry Goodall walked through the doors of the fortieth reunion at West Point.

Goodall was the son of '41er Henry Blanchard, who had married an English woman early in World War II, and then was killed in Normandy. Goodall was born seven and a half months after his father died. For years Goodall had been seeking his father's legacy, which eventually brought him to the academy one spring day in 1981. There, quite by accident, he stumbled upon the fortieth class reunion. But to Blanchard's classmates, it was no accident. Henry Goodall had come home. Class members embraced him as though their lost comrade was standing before them.

By Christmas, 1985, the classmates were still relying on wry humor to sum up the years in their seasonal greetings. Ace Bailey passed on a quote from the veteran Indian scout of General George Custer: "I reckon them young fellers from West Point know all the book larnin,' but they ain't had a chance at anything else, and ginerally, if one of 'em knowed half as much as he thinks he does, you couldn't tell him nothing."

Woody Garrett by then had three sons, including one who was a lieutenant colonel at Fort Bragg. His in-your-face style hadn't softened over the years. Now he challenged his classmates: "My three grandsons can whip yours!"

There was no follow-up to discover if he had any takers.

Another classmate recognized the passing of time very honestly: "It's still a great adventure to limp, hobble, drag, or if you're lucky, to charge along the trail so well marked by those who have gone before us."

Still another classmate was not pleased when his wife received a condolence call from a '41er who had heard that the classmate had reported "present" at the "Last Great Assembly." In fact, the classmate was very much alive.

As threats of a nuclear showdown with the Soviets hovered menacingly, perhaps most fitting was the simple prayer request of classmate Jim Healy: "God Bless America—and please hurry."

Rowny was doing his part in that equation, having progressed to special adviser on arms control for President Reagan, helping to negotiate the end of the Cold War. In the process he taught the president the Russian expression, *doveria no proveri*—trust but verify. Upon leaving office, Reagan presented Rowny with the Presidential Citizen's Medal for being "one of the principal architects of America's policy of peace through strength. . . . He has served mightily, courageously and nobly in the cause of peace and freedom."

The Iron Curtain came down. Germany was reunified. The statue of Emperor Wilhelm rose again, his horse kicking up its hooves where the Rhine meets the Mosel, much to Charlie Fletcher's delight; he'd never talked publicly about what he'd done to the emperor half a century earlier for fear of someone suing him.

★ ★ ★

In late May 1991, nearly 350 classmates returned to the West Point plain. It was fifty years since some strapping young men—and some scraggly young men—had walked through its cloistered gates to find their worlds turned upside down. Now they were celebrating the memories. The crowd gathered on the parade grounds for the alumni procession of graduation week. The granite figure of General Sylvanus Thayer stood watch over the plain. The cast figures of three alumni who commanded many in the crowd looked on approvingly—Generals MacArthur, Patton, and Eisenhower. And George Washington, who defended America from his Revolutionary War headquarters at West Point, sat astride his horse nearby. Several generations of more recent defenders joined the class of 1941 on its field of freedom. Thousands of spectators were in the stands.

The skies were clear for this June Week tradition. Till the sound of an oncoming plane distracted those gathered. It was a small plane, a Cessna, approaching from the direction of the Hudson River. A lone figure dropped out from it, and a parachute opened. There were gasps among the crowds. Puzzled eyes were fixed on the sky, and the chatter grew louder as the skydiver loomed larger, heading in the direction of West Point. Trailing behind the figure was a blue billowing canopy, moving with the winds of West Point toward the parade grounds.

The skydiver maneuvered the canopy past Flirtation Walk, past the Kelleher-Jobes Memorial, till it was directly above the plain. Then the person dropped to the ground, landing near the superintendent's box. Two men rushed to help the skydiver unleash his chute while a third snapped photos. The man ripped the helmet and goggles off his head and unzipped his jumpsuit, stepping out of it in coat and tie. He brushed back dangling locks of ivory white hair from his face and broke into a grin so broad it seemed wider than the Hudson River. It was Colonel Paul Skowronek— seventy-five years old—and the men helping him were his classmates, former combat pilots Burt Andrus and Wayne "Fox" Rhynard, along with quartermaster Jack Christensen. The crowds went wild with applause at this fiftieth reunion surprise.

The jump was also a surprise to the superintendent, but the '41 committee that set up the stunt decided to beg for forgiveness afterward rather than ask permission beforehand. Besides, the '41ers figured the sup would be hard-pressed to argue with their pat explanation.

"We are saluting our comrades who jumped into Normandy." The spectacle was a fitting tribute to those not on the parade grounds in 1991, but in spirit they all gripped hands.

That same day, Paul Skowronek swore to classmates that he'd jump again at the fifty-fifth reunion, which drew good laughs. Never doubt the word of a West Point '41er.

At age eighty, in 1996, Skowronek was up to his old airborne tricks. Jack Norton was on the ground serving as Pathfinder, holding a two-way radio to communicate with Skowronek in the air, prompting and directing him on wind conditions as he jumped once again. This time when Skowronek landed, military police rushed toward him, saying something about "arresting" the graduate.

"You can't," insisted Norton. "We're in the parade!"

West Point '41 was going out with the same unmistakable flair as when it entered the academy half a century earlier. Paul Skowronek repeated the skydiving stunt one more time, at age eighty-five for the sixtieth reunion in May 2001. He would have been back for more jumps had 9/11 not ushered in a new era of aerial security.

As they entered their twilight years, however, some class members, like Jack Norton and Ed Rowny, felt their work still unfinished. They grew disappointed with what they perceived as deteriorating standards at West Point. Some among higher echelons of the academy thought West Point should become more like an Ivy League college, which Norton and Rowny considered misguided. They also discovered that the retention rate of officers who stayed on in the Army beyond their five-year obligation had dropped dramatically. A full 90 percent of graduates from 1941 had continued in the service for twenty years, and over 65 percent pursued a thirty-year career (after thirty years officers who had not reached general rank were automatically designated for retirement). In contrast, only about a quarter of the classes in the 1980s stayed on for twenty years.

Rowny and Norton also learned that the high standards of honor had suffered. So many '41ers had lived and died by that honor code. Hume Peabody killed over Gibraltar. David Taggart in Tunisia. Paul O'Brien over Rangoon. Thomas Cramer and Marshall Carny over Italy. Paul Duke, William Gardner, and Thomas Reagan lost to the Normandy invasion. William Kromer in the Bulge. Edgar Boggs in Luzon. And Donald Driscoll in Korea, among so many from the '41 class that stood fast to their code of honor—because the truth mattered.

But things had changed. Whereas four out of five cadets in the '41 class said they would inform on a classmate who violated the honor code, only one in five surveyed from the 1991 class said they would do the same. Norton and Rowny, disheartened by all of this, teamed with fellow retired generals, John R. Deane and John Carley, from the classes of '42 and '45, respectively. The foursome wanted to help shore up standards to keep the corps from "going to hell." The officers met with cadets and gave speeches. They were relentless, continuing their efforts over the two decades to follow.

Congress had also changed the Regular Army commissions of academy graduates in 1992, instead making graduates Reserve officers. Herb Stern would have none of it, and with Rowny and Norton, tirelessly walked the halls of Congress—for more than seven years—till a bill was passed restoring Regular commissions.

Progress by '41ers was made on many fronts, but restoring strict adherence to the honor code that had so defined their class proved elusive. A dean complained that such a concept was "too tough on the cadets."

It was a different era, an era when corners could be cut, or so thought many from West Point '41. Duty, Honor, Country had defined their lives and actions. Perhaps no actions were more symbolic of that code than that of classmate Buster Boatwright. In his twilight years, at age eighty-eight, he lay hospitalized in a long-term coma. Charles Canella relayed the final salutation of his classmate and friend:

"He suddenly awoke from the coma, saluted sharply, and said, 'Sir! Permission to withdraw, sir!'"

And with that, another of the West Point class of 1941 joined the Long Gray Line, never forgetting his command.

And when our work is done,
Our course on earth is run,
May it be said, "Well done;
Be thou at peace."
E'er may that line of gray,
Increase from day to day,
Live, serve, and die, we pray,
West Point, for thee.

EPILOGUE

Rarely in modern history have young officers been propelled into leadership so quickly and risen so rapidly as those from West Point '41, thrust as they were from the fields of training at West Point into commands in World War II. Few could have foreseen that twenty-five-year-old officers would end up commanding battalions in war, positions that otherwise would have required some twenty-plus years of peacetime service.

Only in one other period of history did anything remotely similar happen, and that was with West Point graduating classes during the Civil War. But those classes were small, only about forty-five cadets in total, and their ranks were divided as they split to fight for either North or South—and against one another. World War I, on the other hand, did not push West Point officers into high commands with such urgency.

"They were eased into war," said Herb Stern, "not bombed into it."

West Point '41 was different, its 424 officers graduating and immediately influencing the course of training, the course of war—and later the course of peace and the future.

As Stern noted in retrospect, "How did I, a twenty-something kid from a small country town cope with this blind exposure to the military and suddenly to war? Beats the hell out of me, but 424 of us did just that. We hitched up our belts a notch or two and tackled the world, which is a lot better for our efforts."

Theirs is a story not just of leadership and courage—but one of innovation. Officers from West Point '41 commanded in an era of unheralded latitude in military entrepreneurism. The words "do something, do anything, just do it" were instilled in them from their earliest days at West Point. It wasn't enough for these officers to work harder; they had to work smarter. Those concepts followed them into battle in World War II, Korea, and Vietnam, where there were few bureaucracies to dissuade them from experimenting. Then, in unique periods of peacetime, where weapons and space races were as furious as war, they were encouraged to continue striving toward the seemingly impossible.

Their work with missiles led to communications satellites that changed the way the world connects and in turn gave rise to GPS technology to navigate the world. The Army's computer command center helped usher in the Internet age. Their work on atomic cannons created defense shields that deterred aggression, helped stave off a third world war—without a shot fired—and aided in bringing down the Iron Curtain. The combat helicopters they created, and used successfully in Vietnam and the Gulf Wars, led to the sophisticated model that helped capture the world's most wanted terrorist, Osama bin Laden. And through some '41 initiatives, infantrymen are now being replaced with robots that can distinguish terrorist from civilian through motion, smell, and more.

Class efforts at innovation went far beyond the military to profoundly impact civilian life.

"For every dollar spent in military labs," said Ed Rowny, "America gained nine dollars in civilian production in return."

Such production ranged from solar energy, like that seen in a lab in its infancy, to innovations like the pilot's head-mounted, vision-tracking helmet tested in its infancy in Vietnam to direct firing in combat. It now has surgical applications.

The breakthroughs of West Point '41 ranged from the micro—finessing the proximity fuse—to the macro, such as improving tank warfare, nuclear-powered submarines, and putting men on the moon. Class officers delved into the mundane, such as overseeing labs that created freeze-dried coffee and meals ready to eat (MREs) as well as the practical, like cold-weather gear and searchlights that turned night into day. They helped create night-vision goggles, stealth planes, and the first drones. And so on reads the roll call of breakthroughs on which West Point '41 left its mark. This book only scratches the surface. The boundaries that officers crossed impacted one century and persevered into the next; to this day NATO's ammunition still bears the mark of '41 standardization. Through it all the mantra of the class continued to be "I was just doing my job."

When this book was started, following the seventieth class reunion at West Point, there were fewer than forty surviving class members—but tucked into the brilliant minds of these officers remained such a wealth of history.

Fortunately, with *West Point '41*, we were able to record some of that history so that it may burn like an eternal flame, perhaps inspiring future generations in the principles of Duty, Honor, Country. As was written in the West Point '41 graduating yearbook beneath Sandy Nininger's photo—"'tis not what man does which exalts him, but what man would do."

ACKNOWLEDGMENTS

It was graduation week at West Point in 2011, and at the invite of our good friend General Edward Rowny we attended seventieth reunion festivities for the West Point class of '41. We were quickly awestruck by class members we met—by their close camaraderie, their remarkable stories of service, their vivacity and humor. This was a unique group of men, we knew, and together with General Rowny, we immediately set about making sure their stories would not be forgotten.

To General Rowny for helping us launch this *West Point '41* book endeavor, we are forever grateful, and we are honored to have him as a mentor and friend. Thanks to Herb Stern, for countless hours helping us fine-tune the manuscript and leaving us with treasured stories of humor in the midst of war. Charlie Fletcher gave us a commander's keen candor that was always refreshing, while usually wrapped with wry wit. Charles Canella was also no-holds-barred. And Joe Reed, what can one say about this one-of-a-kind officer who was at once brilliant and incorrigible—except thank you for sharing.

Special thanks to Henry Bodson for an education in missiles and his meticulous attention to detail, and to Paul Skowronek for allowing us to live life in the fast lane vicariously. Colonel La Rocca . . . it took us two years to find him, but he was worth the wait. And Walter Woolwine's endeavors in creating the Normandy American Cemetery touched us in ways that words cannot express. Our deep gratitude goes out to James Forsyth; we were humbled by the quiet dignity and kindness of this fine officer. We will also treasure the eternal skip and hop in George Johnson's voice. Additional thanks go to Mike Greene, Stan Ramey, and Windsor Anderson for sharing their recollections of West Point life and service. Other moments shared with '41ers were fleeting, but we were honored nonetheless for time with Ace Bailey, Robert Edger, and Jacob Towers.

Our gratitude goes to '41 wives who continued on in their "service" contributing to this book, namely Johnnie Fletcher, Dottie Harris, Evelyn Canella, and Eileen Greene, and we are thankful for assistance from the families of Peer de Silva, Jack Murray, John Norton, and Spec Powell, among others.

West Point '41 would also not have come together without our exceptional literary agent, Andrew Lownie, who believed in us and guided the honing of our literary skills. Thanks as well to our good friend and talented personal editor, Marci Baker, whose advice on numerous projects helped bring us to the authorship point we have reached today. And an enormous thanks to Boots Butler—just because. We'd also like to acknowledge the important work of Dr. Ron Dawe with Post Traumatic Stress Disorder, or PTSD.

Lastly, our appreciation goes to Brigadier General Michael Meese (ret.) for his astute assistance assuring the accuracy of certain campaign excerpts. Thank you also to Stephen Hull at University Press of New England. His remarkable historical knowledge helped *West Point '41* further shine.

APPENDIX
UNITED STATES MILITARY ACADEMY CLASS OF 1941

Graduates listed below retired upon completing their service unless otherwise noted.

Capt. Harwell Leon Adams	Army, Hon. discharge 1954
Capt. Howard Frank Adams	Army Air Corps, KIA 1943
Lt. Col. Jonathan Edwards Adams Jr.	Army
Col. George Roopen Adjemian	Army
Col. Joseph Patrick Ahern	Army
Lt. Col. Richards Abner Aldridge	Air Force
Lt. Col. Michael Frank Aliotta	Army
Lt. Col. Windsor Temple Anderson	Air Force
Capt. George Lincoln Andrews	Army, Died in accident 1945
Col. Burton Curtis Andrus Jr.	Air Force
Lt. Col. Clare Hibbs Armstrong Jr.	Army
Maj. Gen. Fred John Ascani	Air Force
Col. John Earl Atkinson	Air Force
Brig. Gen. Roy Leighton Atteberry Jr.	Army
Capt. Emory Ashel Austin Jr.	Army, KIA 1943
Lt. Col. Hamilton King Avery	Air Force
Capt. Harry Kendall Bagshaw	Army, Hon. discharge 1954
Lt. Col. Leslie Wilmer Bailey	Army
Col. Frederick John Baker	Air Force
Col. Clinton Field Ball	Air Force
2nd Lt. Cargill Massenburg Barnett	Army, Died in accident 1942
Col. John Coles Barney Jr.	Army
Col. Sam Hardy Barrow	Army
Col. Jack Leith Bentley	Air Force
Col. Leon Herman Berger	Air Force
Col. Harry Charles Besancon	Army
Lt. Col. Curtis Francis Betts	Air Force
Lt. Col. Mortimer Buell Birdseye Jr.	Army
Lt. Col. Hill Blalock	Army, Resigned 1947
Capt. Henry Nathan Blanchard Jr.	Army, KIA 1944
Maj. Gen. Linton Sinclair Boatwright	Army
Col. Henry Richard Bodson	Army
Capt. Edgar Clayton Boggs	Army, KIA 1945
Col. Robert Channing Borman	Army
Col. Henry Boswell Jr.	Army
Col. William Wallace Brier	Air Force
Maj. Leon Arthur Briggs	Air Force
Capt. Robert Hendrick Brinson Jr.	Army, Retired disabled 1944
Brig. Gen. John Adams Brooks III	Air Force
Col. Earl Vincent Brown	Army

Mr. Earle Wayne Brown II	Army, Resigned 1947
Col. Edwin Watson Brown	Air Force
Gen. George Scratchley Brown	Air Force
Col. Horace Maynard Brown Jr.	Army
Col. Joseph Tuck Brown	Army
Col. Robert Duncan Brown Jr.	Army
Col. Earl K. Buchanan	Army
Col. John William Burtchaell	Army
Col. Charles Manly Busbee Jr.	Army
Col. Edwin Boynton Buttery	Army
Col. John Wilson Callaway	Army
Lt. Col. John Holmes Camp	Army
Lt. Col. Victor Woodrow Campana	Army
Col. Raymond Potter Campbell Jr.	Army
Col. Charles Joseph Canella	Army
Col. Charles Arthur Cannon Jr.	Army
Col. Vincent Paul Carlson	Army
Maj. Charles MacArthur Carman Jr.	Army, Resigned 1948
Capt. Marshall Warren Carney	Army Air Corps, KIA 1943
Lt. Col. James Henry Carroll	Army
Lt. Col. Bruce Campbell Cator	Air Force
Maj. Theodore Bernarr Celmer	Army
Maj. Gen. Curtis Wheaton Chapman Jr.	Army
Mr. Atanacio Torres Chavez	Philippine Army
1st Lt. Ira Boswell Cheaney Jr	Army, KIA 1942
Col. John Moore Christensen Jr.	Army
Lt. Col. Wadsworth Paul Clapp	Army, KIA 1945
Col. Howard Warren Clark	Army
Capt. John Calvin Clark	Army, Resigned 1946
Col. Robert Evarts Clark	Army
Col. Thomas James Cleary Jr.	Army
Lt. Col. Herbert Campbell Clendening	Army, Resigned 1954
Col. William Eugene Clifford	Army
Col. Roy J. Clinton	Army
Col. Robert John Coakley	Army
Col. Harrington Willson Cochran Jr.	Army
Col. Wharton Clayton Cochran	Air Force
Col. Floyd Sturdevan Cofer Jr.	Air Force
Col. Norman Kitchener Coker	Army, Resigned 1946
Col. Sears Yates Coker	Army
Col. Clifford Elbert Cole	Air Force
Lt. Col. Robert James Colleran	Army Air Corp, Resigned 1947
Col. Leroy Pierce Collins Jr.	Army
Lt. Col. Tom Depher Collison	Army
Capt. Lanham Carmel Connally	Army Air Corp, KIA 1945

Col. David Cooper	Army
Lt. Col. George William Cooper	Army
Mr. Robert Lawrence Cooper	Hon. discharge upon graduation
Maj. Gen. Thomas Goldsborough Corbin	Air Force
Maj. Richard Waggener Couch	Army, Resigned 1954
Col. James Isaac Cox	Air Force
Maj. Thomas Rees Cramer	Army Air Corp, KIA 1943
Lt. Gen. Duward Lowery Crow	Air Force
Capt. Robert Lloyd Cummings	Army, KIA 1944
Lt. Col. William Kneedler Cummins	Air Force
Lt. Col. Thomas Winston Curley	Army
Col. Gwynne Sutherland Curtis Jr.	Air Force
Lt. Col. Albert Samuel Dalby	Army
Lt. Col. Carroll Freemont Danforth	Army
Col. Paul Chester Day	Army
Col. John Breed Deane	Army
Col. Eric Thomas de Jonckheere	Air Force
Lt. Col. Richard Delaney	Army
Maj. Gen. Edward Harleston deSaussure Jr.	Army
Peer de Silva (former Lt. Col.)	CIA Station Chief
Lt. Col. John Vincent D'Esposito	Army
Col. Kenneth O'Reilly Dessert	Air Force
Col. Robert Putnam Detwiler	Army
Lt. Col. Truman Eugene Deyo	Army
Capt. James Henderson Dienelt	Army Air Corps, KIA 1943
Maj. Junius Edward Dillard	Army, Resigned 1947
Maj. Peter Kirkbride Dilts	Army
Col. Robert Toombs Dixon	Army
Maj. Donald Lyons Driscoll	Army, KIA 1953
Maj. Heister Hower Drum	Army
Capt. Kenneth Oswalt Due	Army, Retired disabled 1947
Maj. Paul Demetrius Duke	Army, KIA 1944
Maj. Ernest Durr Jr.	Army, KIA 1945
Col. John Jay Easton	Air Force
2nd Lt. Dan Holton Eaton	Army, Died in accident 1941
Col. Robert Huff Edger	Army
Capt. Bruce Wilds P. Edgerton	Air Force, Resigned 1949
Col. Clarence Lewis Elder	Air Force
Col. Harry Howard Ellis	Army
Lt. Col. Harry VanHorn Ellis Jr.	Army
Lt. Col. Robert Vaughan Elsberry	Army
Maj. Gen. Andrew Julius Evans Jr.	Air Force
Col. Lyman Saunders Faulkner	Army
Col. Howard Lawrence Felchlin	Army
Col. Thomas Legate Fisher II	Air Force

Col. Francis Cornelius Fitzpatrick	Army
Col. Charles Llewellyn Flanders	Army
Brig. Gen. Charles William Fletcher	Army
Lt. Col. James Paul Forsyth	Army
Maj. Horace Grattan Foster Jr.	Army Air Corps, KIA 1943
Maj. Gen. Hugh Franklin Foster Jr.	Army
Col. James Daniel Fowler	Army
Capt. Elkin Leland Franklin	Army Air Corps, KIA 1944
2nd Lt. Herbert Welcome Frawley Jr.	Army Air Corps, KIA 1942
Lt. Col. Ralph Earl Freese	Air Force
1st Lt. William Gardner	Army, KIA 1944
Col. Robert Willoughby Garrett	Army
Col. David Gabriel Gauvreau	Army
Col. Edward Joseph Gelderman	Army
Maj. Gen. Felix John Gerace	Army
Lt. Col. Frank Austin Gerig Jr.	Army
Col. Willard Russell Gilbert	Air Force
Maj. William Graham Gillis Jr.	Army, KIA 1944
Brig. Gen. William Thomas Gleason	Army
Maj. Gen. Guy Harold Goddard	Air Force
Lt. Col. Howard Clarke Goodell	Air Force
Lt. Gen. Gordon Thomas Gould Jr.	Air Force
Col. Denis Blundell Grace	Army
Col. James Weatherby Graham	Army
Col. Paul Gray Jr.	Army
Col. James Oscar Green III	Army
Brig. Gen. Lawrence Vivans Greene	Army
Brig. Gen. Michael Joseph Lenihan Greene	Army
Lt. Gen. William Charles Gribble Jr.	Army
Col. Joseph Stanley Grygiel	Army
Col. Joseph Ingram Gurfein	Army
Col. William Harold Gurnee Jr.	Army
Lt. Col. Max Woodrow Hall	Air Force
Capt. Fred Milas Hampton	Army Air Corps, Died in air accident 1942
Col. Edwin Forrest Harding Jr.	Air Force
Capt. Matthew Gordon Harper Jr.	Army, Hon. discharge 1954
Lt. Col. Charles Knighton Harris	Army
Col. John Frederick Harris	Air Force
Col. Matthew Clarence Harrison	Army
Col. Harry Canavan Harvey	Air Force
Col. Mills Carson Hatfield	Army
Col. Auburon Paul Hauser	Army
Capt. John Nathaniel Hauser Jr.	Army, Died 1944
Col. Alfred George Hayduk	Air Force

Col. James Gerard Healy	Army
Col. Donald Haynes Heaton	Air Force
Maj. Roy George Hendrickson	Army
Col. John Miles Henschke	Air Force
Maj. Leo Charles Henzl	Army, Resigned 1956
Lt. Col. William John Hershenow Jr.	Air Force
Lt. Col. Ralph Robinet Hetherington	Army, KIA 1944
Lt. Col. Merritt Lambert Hewitt	Army
Col. George Luther Hicks III	Air Force
Col. Arnold Jacob Hoebeke	Army
Lt. Col. William Morris Hoge Jr.	Army
Maj. Justus MacMullen Home	Army Air corps, Died in air accident 1944
Lt. Col. Robert William Horn	Air Force
Maj. Frank Benton Howze	Army, KIA 1950
Maj. Gen. Burnside Elijah Huffman Jr.	Army
Mr. Charles Herbert Humber	Disability discharge at graduation
Maj. Thomas Abbott Hume	Army, KIA 1951
Col. Stanton Claude Hutson	Army, Resigned 1954
Lt. Col. Henry Durand Irwin	Army, Resigned 1947
Capt. Harry Lee Jarvis Jr.	Army Air Corps, KIA 1943
Col. Allen Jensen	Army
Col. Allan George Woodrow Johnson	Army
Col. Malcolm Corwin Johnson	Army
Col. Robert Paul Johnson	Army
Capt. Charles Edwin Jones	Army Air Corps, KIA 1943
Brig. Gen. Morton McDonald Jones Jr.	Army
Capt. Perry Thompson Jones	Army, KIA 1945
Col. James Lawrence Kaiser	Army
Col. Robert Bernard Keagy	Army
Lt. Col. Reynolds Robert Keleher	Army
Brig. Gen. Roy Skiles Kelley	Army
Col. Straughan Downing Kelsey	Air Force
Lt. Col. Paul Richard Kemp	Army, Resigned 1949
Brig. Gen. Kenneth Wade Kennedy	Army
Col. Benjamin Berry Kercheval	Army
Col. James Henry King	Army
Capt. Riley Smith King	Army, Resigned 1948
Col. Edwin Charles Kisiel	Army
Col. Richard William Kline	Air Force
Col. Wendell Pollitt Knowles	Army
Col. Joseph Lippincott Knowlton	Army
Lt. Col. Stephen Thaddeus Kosiorek	Army
Col. Robert Sealey Kramer	Army
Capt. William Annesley Kromer	Army, KIA 1944

Col. David Ernest Kunkel Jr.	Air Force
Col. Ralph Edward Kuzell	Army
Col. Gerard Anthony La Rocca	Air Force
Col. James Raine Laney Jr.	Army
Col. Robert Edward Lanigan	Army
1st Lt. Paul Rutherford Larson	Army Air Corps, KIA 1942
Lt. Col. Angelo Augustine Laudani	Army
Col. Wallace Michael Lauterbach	Army
Col. Roger Longstreet Lawson	Army
Maj. Thomas Roger Lawson	Army, Retired disabled 1946
Col. Moody Elmo Layfield Jr.	Army
Lt. Col. Lee Bradley Ledford Jr.	Army
Maj. Glenn Alfred Lee	Army, Resigned 1951
Col. John Clifford Hodges Lee Jr.	Army
Col. Lynn Cyrus Lee	Army
Lt. Col. Richard Mar Levy Jr.	Army
Lt. Col. Paul Von Santen Liles	Army
Lt. Col. John Charles Linderman	Army, Retired disabled 1947
Brig. Gen. Frank Holroyd Linnell	Army
Col. William Miles Linton	Army
Capt. Frank Ely Locke	Army Air Corps, Died in air accident 1942
Maj. Gen. John Langford Locke	Air Force
Lt. Col. Clarence John Lokker	Army Air Corps, KIA 1944
Lt. Col. Mercer Presley Longino	Army
2nd. Lt. Robert Gilman Loring	Army, Resigned 1943
Col. Samuel Bertron Magruder	Army
Col. Clinton Earle Male	Army
Maj. John Benjamin Manley Jr.	Army, Resigned 1956
Col. Harley Truman Marsh Jr.	Army
Mr. Rudolph Adolph Matheisel Jr.	Hon. discharge upon graduation
Col. Walter Edward Mather	Army
Col. Charles Fuller Matheson	Air Force
Col. Thomas Ward Maxwell	Army
Col. Charles Dorsey Maynard	Army
Col. Ben Isbel Mayo Jr.	Air Force
Lt. Col. Benjamin McCaffery Jr.	Army
Col. Jack Curtright McClure Jr.	Air Force
Maj. Ralph Allen McCool	Army, Resigned 1948
Col. Joseph Andrew McCulloch Jr.	Army
Lt. Col. William Thomas McDaniel*	Army, KIA 1950
Lt. Col. James Edward McElroy	Army
Col. Edward Joseph McGrane Jr.	Army
Col. George William McIntyre	Army
Lt. Col. John Carl McIntyre	Army

Col. Gregg LaRoix McKee	Army
Col. James Fuller McKinley Jr.	Army
Col. Donald Leroy McMillan	Army
1st Lt. Rob Reed McNagny Jr.	Army Air Corps, Died in air accident 1943
Col. John William Meador	Air Force
Col. Arthur Lloyd Meyer	Army
Lt. Col. John Field Michel	Army
Lt. Col. LeMoyne Francis Michels	Army, Resigned 1947
Col. Maurice Guthrie Miller	Army
Col. John Millikin Jr.	Army
Brig. Gen. William LeRoy Mitchell Jr.	Air Force
Col. Walter Francis Molesky	Army
Maj. Nelson Paul Monson	Army
Brig. Gen. Alfred Judson Force Moody	Army
Col. George Bissland Moore	Army
Col. Walter Leon Moore Jr.	Air Force
Col. Miroslav Frank Moucha	Army
Lt. Col. Maynard George Moyer	Army, Retired disabled 1957
Lt. Col. Walter Raleigh Mullane	Army
Maj. Charles Love Mullins	Army Air Corps, Died in air accident 1943
Maj. Charles Robert Murrah	Army, Resigned 1946
Col. John Francis Thomas Murray	Army
Col. Alexander Frank Muzyk	Army
Lt. Col. Francis Joseph Myers Jr.	Army
1st Lt. Harold Edward Nankivell	Army Air Corps, Died in air accident 1942
Lt. Col Roger Stevens Neumeister	Army, Resigned 1955
Col. Gibson Niles	Army
1st Lt. Alexander Ramsey Nininger Jr.	Army, KIA 1942
Col. Harold Wesley Norton	Air Force
Lt. Gen. John Norton	Army
Maj. Paul James O'Brien	Army Air Corps, KIA 1943
Maj. Thomas Courtenay O'Connell	Army
Col. Roderic Dhu O'Connor	Air Force
Col. Richard Magee Osgood	Air Force, Resigned 1955
Col. John Roy Oswalt Jr.	Army
Col. Robert Edward Panke	Army
Lt. Col. Samuel Wilson Parks	Air Force
Capt. Hume Peabody Jr.	Army Air Corps, KIA 1942
Reverend (Col.) Joseph Scott Peddie	Air Force
Lt. Col. Charles Leonard Peirce	Army Air Corps, KIA 1944
Col. Irving Richard Perkin	Air Force
Maj. William McVay Petre	Army, Resigned 1946

Maj. Gen. George Bibb Pickett Jr.	Army
1st Lt. Robert Patterson Pierpont	Army, KIA 1944
Col. Paul Edgar Pique	Army
Col. George Henry Pittman Jr.	Air Force
Capt. Stephen Kellogg Plume Jr.	Army, Resigned 1953
Maj. Ernest Franklin Poff	Army
Maj. Richard Bradford Polk	Army Air Corps, Resigned 1946
1st Lt. Hector John Polla	Army, KIA 1945
Lt. Col. Edgar Thornton Poole Jr.	Air Force
Brig. Gen. Edwin Lloyd Powell Jr.	Army
Col. William Doyle Pratt	Army
1st Lt. Max Price	Army Air Corps, Died in air accident 1943
Col. William Augustus Purdy	Army
Col. Paul Wyman Ramee	Army
Col. Stanley Meriwether Ramey	Army
Col. Richard John Rastetter	Army
Capt. Thomas Edwin Reagan	Army, KIA 1944
Col. John Gabriel Redmon	Army
Brig. Gen. Wilson Russell Reed	Army
Lt. Col. Robert Stanley Reilly	Army
Col. Wayne Edgar Rhynard	Air Force
Col. John Rose Richards	Air Force
Col. Herbert Richardson Jr.	Army
Lt. Col. James Richardson	Army
Lt. Col. Harry Niles Rising Jr.	Army
Maj. John Leonard Robinson	Army, Retired disabled 1951
Col. Paul Crawford Root Jr.	Army
Capt. Robert Harold Rosen	Army, KIA 1944
Col. Bert Stanford Rosenbaum	Air Force
Lt. Col. John Ellis Rossell Jr.	Army
Col. William Faye Roton	Army
Lt. Gen. Edward Leon Rowny	Army
Col. James William Roy	Army
Col. Daniel Salinas	Army
Col. Lloyd Robert Salisbury	Army
Col. Robert Walter Samz	Army
Maj. John Raymond Sands Jr.	Air Force, Died in air accident 1947
Col. Willis Bruner Sawyer	Air Force
Brig. Gen. Charles Henry Schilling	Army
Col. Raymond Ira Schnittke	Army
Col. John Edward Schremp	Army
Capt. Bernard Schultz	Army, Resigned 1947
Brig. Gen. Richard Pressly Scott	Army
Col. Charles S. Seamans III	Air Force

Brig. Gen. William Thomas Seawell	Air Force
Lt. Gen. George Philip Seneff Jr.	Army
Lt. Col. Martin Andrew Shadday	Army
Col. Thomas Wilson Sharkey	Army
Mr. Thaddeus J. Shelton	Disability discharge upon graduation
Col. Joseph Meryl Silk	Air Force
Maj. Walter Singles Jr.	Army, Resigned in 1947
Col. Paul George Skowronek	Army
Lt. Col. Edgar Mathews Sliney	Air Force
Maj. George Lawrence Slocum	Army, Resigned 1949
Col. Bradish Johnson Smith	Army
Lt. Col. Cecil Leo Smith	Army
Col. Albert Howell Snider	Air Force
Col. Benjamin Alvord Spiller	Army
Col. Frank Pleasants Stainback Jr.	Air Force
Col. George Winfield Stalnaker	Air Force
Col. Frederick Clinton Stanford	Army
Col. William Frank Starr	Army
Col. Herbert Irving Stern	Army
Col. James William Stigers	Army
Col. George Hamilton Stillson Jr.	Air Force
Col. James William Strain	Army
1st Lt. Maxwell Weston Sullivan Jr.	Army Air Corps, KIA 1943
Lt. Col. James Rayford Sykes	Army, Resigned 1955
Capt. David Burch Taggart	Army Air Corps, KIA 1943
Col. Peter Schuyler Tanous	Army
Col. Patrick Henry Tansey Jr.	Army
Brig. Gen. Robert Mack Tarbox	Army
Lt. Col. Joseph Scranton Tate Jr.	Army Air Corps, KIA 1943
Lt. Col. George Lawrence Theisen	Army
Col. Joseph Jackson Thigpen	Army, Resigned 1947
Lt. Col. Arnold Ray Thomas	Army
2nd Lt. Charles Edwin Thomas III	Army Air Corps, Died in air accident 1942
Col. Alden George Thompson	Air Force
Col. Clyde Arnold Thompson	Air Force
1st Lt. Donald Vincent Thompson	Army Air Corps, Died in air accident 1942
Lt. Col. Jesse Duncan Thompson	Air Force
Col. Harold Alexander Tidmarsh	Army
Maj. Richard Gentry Tindall Jr.	Army, KIA 1945
Col. Oscar Charles Tonetti	Army
Mr. Arnold Svere Torgerson	Grad/no commission (physically disqualified)
Maj. Jacob Heffner Towers	Army

Col. Richard VanPelt Travis	Air Force
Lt. Col. Harry White Trimble	Air Force
Col. Malcolm Graham Troup	Army
Capt. Francis Joseph Troy	Army, KIA 1945
Col. Robert Merrill Tuttle	Air Force
Col. Max Campbell Tyler	Army
Lt. Col. John Gavin Tyndall II	Army
Col. Jess Paul Unger	Army
Col. Ralph Reed Upton	Army
Col. John Webb VanHoy Jr.	Army
Col. William John Dooley Vaughan	Army
Lt. Col. Dick Stanley von Schriltz	Army
Lt. Col. Robert Graham Waitt	Army
Maj. James Philip Walker	Army Air Corps, KIA 1943
Lt. Col. Edison Kermit Walters	Air Force
Maj. Joseph Hester Ward	Army, KIA 1945
Lt. Col. Thomas Martin Ward	Army, Resigned 1946
Col. Leroy Hugh Watson Jr.	Air Force, Died 1959
Lt. Col. Joseph John Weidner	Air Force
Lt. Col. George Hollenback Welles	Army
Lt. Col. Ben Marshall West	Air Force
Maj. DuVal West III	Army, Resigned 1947
Col. Ernest Jeunet Whitaker	Army
Col. Alpheus Wray White	Air Force
Capt. Lester Strode White	Army Air Corps, Died in air accident 1943
Lt. Col. Theodore Knox White	Army, Died 1953
Col. Charles Gleeson Willes	Air Force, Died 1956
Col. Isaac Owen Winfree	Air Force
Col. Roscoe Barnett Woodruff Jr.	Air Force
Col. David Seavey Woods	Air Force
Col. William Hunter Woodward	Army
Lt. Gen. Walter James Woolwine	Army
Maj. Gen. Elmer Parker Yates	Army
Lt. Col. Edward Benedict Zarembo	Army
Lt. Col. John Henry Zott Jr.	Army

*McDaniel was a major when declared MIA and was subsequently KIA. His promotion to lieutenant colonel was posthumous.

NOTES

Chapter 1. Hell on the Hudson
1. MacArthur, "MacArthur's Address."

Chapter 2. Upon the Fields of Friendly Strife
1. Lokker, "Blue Monday," 1.
2. Ibid., 1.
3. Roosevelt, *Graduation Address*.

Chapter 4. Pass the Ammunition
1. Kuehn, "Japanese Activities," 147.

Chapter 5. Humble Honor
1. J. Bailey, "Philippine Islands," 4, 9.
2. Chen, "Invasion."
3. Esposito, *West Point Atlas*, maps 122–24.
4. Mabunga, "Memorial Day 1994."
5. Ibid.
6. Many historical accounts cite Colonel Clarke as calling in the reserve, but Philippine Scouts recounted in later years that Clarke had, in effect, withdrawn from active battle command in early January. He was soon relieved of his duties and sent to Australia, where he engaged in noncombat duties.
7. Colonel (ret.) Frederick J. Yeager to Colonel Burton C. Andrus Jr., USMA Class of 1941, *Gold '41*, 197.
8. "Alexander Ramsey Nininger, Jr."
9. "World."
10. Yeager to Andrus, in USMA Class of 1941, *Gold '41*, 197.
11. Lieutenant General Jonathan M. Wainwright soon surrendered the remaining forces on Corregidor and became the highest-ranking U.S. prisoner of war, held captive until August 1945.
12. "Radio Navigation."
13. *"Admiral Marc Andrew Mitscher."*
14. "Hydraulic Catapult."
15. "Doolittle Raid (Hornet CV-8)," 4.
16. Trueman, "Battle of Guadalcanal."

Chapter 6. Baptism into War
1. "Fort Bragg," 106.
2. Helgason, "Ships Hit by U-boats."
3. Ibid.
4. Niderost, "Baptism of Fire."
5. Craven and Cate, "Defeat and Reorganization," 156.
6. Powell, "True Story."

Chapter 7. Jump Time in Sicily

1. Birtle, "Sicily," 9.
2. Accounts of total gliders range from 139 to 144. "Operation Husky," 1.
3. Birtle, "Sicily," 8.
4. Ethier, "World War II."

Chapter 9. Gothic Fronts

1. Goodman, *Fragment of Victory*, 19–20.
2. Oland, "North Apennines," 3.
3. Ibid., 3, 190.
4. Ibid., 38, 39, 48.
5. Years later, when the United States conducted joint military maneuvers with Germany, Ed Rowny met a German officer who served in Italy in World War II. The officer told Rowny he was in the Apennines, "looking down on those poor miserable American soldiers." Rowny replied that he commanded some of those poor miserable soldiers. The officer, as it turns out, commanded the unit that came up against the 10th Mountain Division in the foxholes and lamented having been tricked at the time.

Chapter 10. The Nose of the Bulge

1. Fox, "Lessons Learned," 5–6.
2. MacDonald, "United States Army," 136, chap. 6, note 58.
3. Ryan, "Bridge," 142.
4. Gavin, "Graphic History," 1.
5. MacDonald, "United States Army," 139.
6. Ibid., 157.
7. Major General James M. Gavin to Marjorie Rosen, USMA Class of 1941, *Gold '41*, 120.
8. Stoy, "Other Side."

Chapter 11. Contact at Houffalize

1. Stoy, "Other Side."

Chapter 13. Bittersweet Freedom

1. Bradford, "The Way It Was."
2. This incident, resulting in the death of approximately fifty British officers, became the subject of the 1963 movie *The Great Escape*.
3. Diggs, "Itemizing, "October 1, 1944, 2.
4. Diggs, "Itemizing," December 1, 1944, 2.

Chapter 14. Victory Europe

1. "Army Battle Casualties," 80–81.

Chapter 16. Bataan a Yard at a Time

1. "Bataan Rescue."
2. "Americans Specialize."

3. "Avengers of Bataan," 10.

4. "50th Anniversary Article."

5. Ibid.

6. Sublette, "Nuclear Weapons," sec. 10.6.

7. Fuchs, "Manhattan Project."

8. United News. "Japanese Sign Final Surrender!"

9. Ibid.

10. Weist, "82nd Division."

11. "Normandy American Cemetery."

Chapter 17. Shifting Gears

1. "NATO."

2. "The X-1 Research Airplane."

Chapter 18. Going Up, Under, and Over There

1. De Silva, *Sub Rosa*, 17, 23, 24, 31.

2. Ramey, Commendation memo.

3. "V-2 Rocket Components."

4. "V-2 Rocket."

5. Truman, "Remarks."

6. McDaniel, *Major*, chap. 8.

Chapter 19. The Chill of the Cold War

1. "History of Relations."

2. Luelliot and O'Hara. "Tiger and the Elephant."

3. The Marines, at the time, were counted in with the Navy.

4. De Silva, *Sub Rosa*, 73.

Chapter 20. Gazing into the Future

1. Lethbridge, "Missile Ranges Takes Shape," chap. 2.

2. "Donald Norton Yates."

3. As explained in Landsea, "Tropical Cyclones," using a nuclear weapon for hurricane modification neglects the problem of released radioactive fallout on land. From a scientific perspective, "the main difficulty with using explosives to modify hurricanes is the amount of energy required. A fully developed hurricane can release heat energy at a rate of 5 to 20 x 10^{13} watts and converts less than 10 percent of the heat into the mechanical energy of the wind. The heat released is equivalent to a ten-megaton nuclear bomb exploding every twenty minutes."

4. McDaniel, *Major*, chap. 11.

5. Murray, "Army-McCarthy Confrontation," 26–27.

6. De Silva, *Sub Rosa*, 123.

7. Ritter, *War on Tito's Yugoslavia?*

8. Universal-International News. "Atlas in Orbit."

9. Ibid.

10. Osborn, "Creative Collaboration by Groups."

11. Stern, "Comments," 1, 2.

12. Ibid.

13. At the writing of this book, in late 2013, Herb Stern considered the majority of key findings and directives of President Eisenhower's Joint Advanced Study Group to be as relevant and critical to national security as they were in 1960, and he therefore would not disclose additional details.

Chapter 21. Little Gold Corvette

1. Kennedy, "One Day in Berlin."

Chapter 22. Anticipating New Fronts

1. Kennedy, "One Day in Berlin."

2. Watson, "Air-Assault Unit."

Chapter 23. Trials and Trauma of the Vietnam Era

1. De Silva, *Sub Rosa*, 220–21, 234.

2. Ibid., 220.

3. Ibid., 254.

4. Ibid., 265–67.

5. Shapira, "Barbara Robbins."

6. De Silva, *Sub Rosa*, 273–74.

7. GI Korea, "Korea."

8. Ibid.

9. Ibid.

Chapter 24. Permission to Withdraw

1. "Lawrence Douglass Greene."

2. "U.S. Army, 1st Logistical Command."

3. U.S. Army, "Talk with the CG," 5.

4. MacArthur, "MacArthur's Address."

BIBLIOGRAPHY

Personal Interviews with '41 Classmates and Families

Note: Dialogue in *West Point '41* is verbatim and was either relayed directly to the authors by classmates and their families in personal interviews or in a few cases was taken from oral histories. The only two exceptions are Lieutenant Colonel Leslie Bailey and Peer de Silva, whose published books were relied on (excerpts from the former reprinted with permission by Leslie W. Bailey Jr.). Personal interviews took place at the residences of classmates, at West Point, and via phone interviews that were ongoing over the course of more than two years.

Anderson, Windsor T. Telephone interviews with Anne Kazel-Wilcox, 2011–12.

Bailey, Leslie W., Jr. Telephone interviews with Anne Kazel-Wilcox, 2011–13.

Bailey, Leslie W. Telephone interviews with Anne Kazel-Wilcox, August–September 2011.

Bodson, Henry R. Personal, telephone, and e-mail interviews with Anne Kazel-Wilcox and PJ Wilcox, 2011–13.

Canella, Charles J. Telephone interviews with Anne Kazel-Wilcox, 2011–12.

Canella, Evelyn. Telephone interviews with Anne Kazel-Wilcox, 2011–13.

Cushman, John H., USMA 1944 (Lt. Gen, ret.). Telephone interview with Anne Kazel-Wilcox, July 29, 2011.

De Silva, Peer, Jr. Telephone and e-mail interviews with Anne Kazel-Wilcox and PJ Wilcox, 2012–13.

Edger, Robert H. Telephone interview with Anne Kazel-Wilcox, 2011.

Fletcher, Charles W., and Johnnie Fletcher. Personal, telephone, and e-mail interviews with Anne Kazel-Wilcox and PJ Wilcox, 2011–13.

Forysth, James P. Personal and telephone interviews with Anne Kazel-Wilcox and PJ Wilcox, 2011–13.

Greene, Eileen. Telephone interviews with Anne Kazel-Wilcox, 2012–13.

Greene, Michael. J. L. Personal and telephone interviews with Anne Kazel-Wilcox and PJ Wilcox, 2011–12.

Harris, Dorothy "Dottie." Telephone interviews with Anne Kazel-Wilcox, 2011–12.

Johnson, Allan G. W. Johnson Telephone interviews with Anne Kazel-Wilcox, 2011–12.

La Rocca, Gerard A. Personal, telephone, and e-mail interviews with Anne Kazel-Wilcox and PJ Wilcox, 2011–13.

Norton, John Jr. Telephone interviews with Anne Kazel-Wilcox and PJ Wilcox, 2011–13.

Patterson, John A. Telephone interviews with Anne Kazel-Wilcox, 2013.

Powell, Clelia "Cleo." Telephone interviews with Anne Kazel-Wilcox, 2012.

Ramey, Stanley M. Telephone interviews with Anne Kazel-Wilcox, 2011–12.

Reed, Wilson R. Telephone interviews with Anne Kazel-Wilcox, 2011–12.

Rowny, Edward L. Personal, telephone, and e-mail interviews with Anne Kazel-Wilcox and PJ Wilcox, 2010–13.

Skowronek, Paul G. Personal and telephone interviews with Anne Kazel-Wilcox and PJ Wilcox, 2011–13.

Stern, Herbert I. Personal, telephone, and e-mail interviews with Anne Kazel-Wilcox and PJ Wilcox, 2011–13.

Towers, Jacob H. Telephone interviews with Anne Kazel-Wilcox, 2011.

Woolwine, Walter J., Jr. Personal, telephone, and e-mail interviews with Anne Kazel-Wilcox and PJ Wilcox, 2011–13.

Other Sources

"The 1944 Christmas Package." *Prisoners of War Bulletin* 2, no. 11 (1944). American National Red Cross. Accessed August 2012. www.archive.org.

"The 505th Parachute Infantry Regiment: Unit History." 82nd Airborne. World War II. Accessed July 2012. www.ww2-airborne.us.

"50th Anniversary Article." Los Alamos National Laboratory. [Ca. 1993]. Accessed June 2012. www.lanl.gov.

"82nd Airborne: Normandy (Operation Neptune)." *Preserving Their Sacrifice*. World War II Archives, National Archives and Records Administration, College Park, MD. Accessed April 2012. www.wwiiarchives.net.

"Admiral Marc Andrew Mitscher, USNR 1887–1947." Naval History and Heritage Command. Accessed July 2013. www.history.navy.mil.

"Alexander Ramsey Nininger, Jr." *Military Times, Hall of Valor: Medal of Honor*. Accessed January 2013. http://projects.militarytimes.com.

"Americans Specialize in Killing Germans by Night." *Daily Oklahoman*, April 27, 1944. Accessed October 2012. http://darbysrangers.tripod.com.

"Army Battle Casualties and Nonbattle Deaths in World War II. Final Report, 7 December 1941–31 December 1946." Statistical and Accounting Branch, Office of the Adjutant General. June 1, 1953. Accessed August 2012. www.ibiblio.org.

Association of Graduates. *The Register of Graduates and Former Cadets of the United States Military Academy, West Point*. West Point, NY: Association of Graduates, United States Military Academy, 2010.

"Avengers of Bataan." 38th Infantry Division Headquarters. Historical Report M-7 Operation. August 8, 1945. Accessed October 18, 2013. http://corregidor.org.

Bailey, Jennifer L. "Philippine Islands: Introduction; The U.S. Army Campaigns of World War II." U.S. Army Center of Military History. Accessed July 2013. www.history.army.mil.

Bailey, Leslie W. *Through Hell and High Water: The Wartime Memories of a Junior Combat Infantry Officer*. New York: Vantage, 1994.

"Bataan Rescue: People and Events; Japanese Atrocities in the Philippines." PBS. Accessed October 2012. www.pbs.org.

Berkhouse, L. H., F. R. Gladeck, J. H. Hallowell, C. B. Jones, E. J. Martin, F. W. McMullan, and M. J. Osborn, W. E. Rogers. "Operation Sandstone 1948." Defense Nuclear Agency as Executive Agency for the Department of Defense. December 19, 1983. Accessed April 2013. www.dtic.mil.

Birtle, Andrew J. "Sicily: Introduction, the U.S. Army Campaigns of World War II." U.S. Army Center of Military History. Accessed July 2013. www.history.army.mil.

Bodson, Henry R. "Anecdotes about Audie Murphy." 1974. Private collection of Henry Bodson.

———. "Loading Plan for Amphibious Operations, Battery 'B,' 39th Field Artillery Battalion." August 1944. Private collection of Henry Bodson.

Bowditch, John, III, with assistance from Robert W. Kerner and the Historical Division, War Department Special Staff. "American Forces in Action: Anzio Beachhead, 22 Jan–25 May." Historical Division, War Department. October 1, 1947. Accessed June 2012. www.ibiblio.org.

Bradford, Brad. "The Way It Was." *Oflag 64 Association, Capture and Camp Life.* Accessed 2012. www.oflag64.us.

Carey, Norman C. "The Normandy Campaign." Part 1 of *The European Theater.* 35th Infantry Division in World War II, 1941–1945. Accessed February 2012. www.35thinfdivassoc.com.

———. "Northern France: The Vire River Campaign, Mortain." Part 2 of *The European Theater.* 35th Infantry Division in World War II, 1941–1945. Accessed April 2012. www.35thinfdivassoc.com.

Chen, C. Peter. "Invasion of the Philippine Islands, 7 Dec 1941–5 May 1942." World War II Database. Accessed July 2013. http://ww2db.com.

Cockrell, James Leroy, Jr. "A Narration of World War II Experiences by One Soldier." *Capture and Camp Life.* Oflag 64 Association. Accessed 2012. www .oflag64.us.

"Commander Howell M. Forgy. USN (ChC), (1908–1972)." Naval Historical Center, Department of the Navy. Accessed February 2012. www.history.navy.mil.

Conant, Jennet. *109 East Palace: Robert Oppenheimer and the Secret City of Los Alamos.* New York: Simon and Schuster, 2005.

Conroy, Fay. "Church Tower, Windows Pay Tribute to Paratroopers Who Jumped into First Town Liberated during World." U.S. Army. June 2, 2009. Accessed April 2012. www.army.mil.

Craven, W. F., and J. L. Cate, eds. "Defeat and Reorganization." *The Army Air Forces in World War II.* Vol. 2 of *Europe: Torch to Pointblank, August 1942 to December 1943.* HyperWar Foundation. Accessed July 2013. www.ibiblio.org.

De Silva, Peer. *Sub Rosa: The CIA and the Uses of Intelligence.* New York: Times Books, 1978.

Diggs, Frank, "Itemizing." *Oflag 64 Item,* December 1, 1944. Accessed February 2012. www.oflag64.us.

———, ed. "Itemizing." *Oflag 64 Item,* October 1, 1944. Accessed February 2012. www.oflag64.us.

"Donald Norton Yates." Bowdoin College. Accessed August 2013. http://library .bowdoin.edu.

"The Doolittle Raid (Hornet CV-8): America Strikes Back." USS Hornet Museum. Accessed July 2013. www.uss-hornet.org.

Esposito, Vincent J. *The West Point Atlas of American Wars.* Vol. 2, *1900–1953.* New York: Praeger, 1960.

Ethier, Eric. "World War II: George S. Patton's Race to Capture Messina." *American History,* April 2001. Accessed June 2013. www.historynet.com.

Forsyth, James. Letters and postcards written from Oflag 64 POW camp to family members. Private collection of James Forsyth.

"Fort Bragg with 67,000 Men, It Is Army's Biggest Camp: Negro Engineers Sing on Parade." *Life*, June 9, 1941. Accessed October 15, 2013. http://books.google .com.

Fox, Jennifer B. "Lessons Learned from Operation Market Garden." Air War College. April 8, 1944. Accessed August 2013. www.dtic.mil.

Fuchs, Klaus, E. J. "Manhattan Project." Scientific Research and Development Personnel, Los Alamos National Laboratory. June 27, 1945. Accessed June 2012. www.lanl.gov.

"Gardelegen Massacre, 13 April 1945: Prisoners Burned to Death inside a Barn." Scrapbookpages.com. Accessed December 2012. www.scrapbookpages.com.

Gavin, James M. "A Graphic History of the 82nd Airborne Division, Operation 'Market,' Holland 1944." Combined Arms Research Library. 1944. Accessed October 2013. http://cgsc.cdmhost.com.

GI Korea. [pseud.]. "Korea from North to South." *DMZ Flashpoints: The Blue House Raid*. ROK Drop. December 30, 2008. Accessed August 2012. www.rokdrop.com.

Goodman, Paul. *A Fragment of Victory in Italy, the 92nd Infantry Division in World War II*. Nashville: Battery, 1993.

Greene, Michael J. L. "Contact at Houffalize." *Armored Cavalry Journal*, May–June 1949. Private collection of Michael J. L. Greene.

Hall, Theodore, A. "Manhattan Project." Scientific Research and Development Personnel, Los Alamos National Laboratory. June 14, 1945. Accessed June 2012. www.lanl.gov.

"Hall of Valor." *MilitaryTimes.com*. Accessed 2013. October 2013. http://projects .militarytimes.com.

"'Have You No Sense of Decency': The Army-McCarthy Hearings." *History Matters: The U.S. Survey Course on the Web*. American Social History Productions. Accessed February 2013. http://historymatters.gmu.edu.

Helgason, Gudmundur, ed. "Ships Hit by U-boats, West Irmo, American Steam Merchant." Accessed July 2013. http://uboat.net.

"Hell in the Hedgerows." *The Story of the 225th AAA Searchlight Battalion from Omaha Beach to V-E Day*. Skylighters. August 20, 2001. Accessed April 2012. www.skylighters.org.

"History of Relations between the U.S. and Bulgaria." Embassy of the United States, U.S. Department of State. Accessed July 2013. http://bulgaria.usembassy .gov.

"Hydraulic Catapult, USS Hornet Aircraft Carrier Museum." WW2HQ. Accessed July 2013. www.worldwar2headquarters.com.

"Indochina." *Encyclopœdia Britannica Online*. Accessed August 27, 2013. www .britannica.com.

Joel. "Operation Ladbrooke Gets Broke." *Today's History Lesson*. July 9. Accessed August 2013. http://todayshistorylesson.wordpress.com.

"Kasserine Pass Battles: Readings." Vol. 1. Parts 1 and 2. U.S. Army Center of Military History. Accessed July 2013. www.history.army.mil.

Kennedy, John F. "One Day in Berlin." Remarks at the Rudolph Wilde Platz, Berlin. John F. Kennedy Presidential Library and Museum. June 26, 1963. Accessed August 2013. www.jfklibrary.org.

Kerkhoff, Roel. "Remember September '44." Accessed July 2012. http://rememberseptember44.com.

King, Michael J. "Rangers: Selected Combat Operations in World War II; Rescue at Cabanatuan." Leavenworth Papers 11. U.S. Army Command and General Staff College. Accessed June 2012. www.4point2.org.

Kuehn, Bernard Julius Otto. "Japanese Activities." In *The Vault: Bernard Julius Otto Kuehn*, 137–48. FBI Records, file number 65–1574. January 5, 1942 (FBI Report date). Accessed October 2012. http://vault.fbi.gov.

Landsea, Chris. "Why Don't We Try to Destroy Tropical Cyclones by Nuking Them?" Hurricane Research Division, Atlantic Oceanographic and Meteorological Laboratory, National Oceanic and Atmospheric Administration. Accessed August 2013. www.aoml.noaa.gov.

La Rocca, Gerard A. Various commendations. Private collection of Gerard A. La Rocca.

Laurie, Clayton D. "Anzio 1944: The U.S. Army Campaigns of World War II." U.S. Army Center of Military History, U.S. Army. Accessed June 2012. www.history.army.mil.

"Lawrence Douglass Greene." Association of the 1st Battalion (Mechanized), 50th Infantry. Accessed March 2013. www.ichiban1.org.

Lethbridge, Cliff. "The Missile Ranges Takes Shape (1949–1958)." *The History of Cape Canaveral*. Spaceline.org. Accessed August 2013. www.spaceline.org.

Lokker, Clarence J. "Blue Monday." Ca. late 1930–early 1940s. Private collection of Edward Rowny.

Luelliot, Nowfel, and Danny O'Hara. "The Tiger and the Elephant, Viet Minh Strategies and Tactics." *Indo 1945–1954: From Haiphong to Dien Bien Phu*. Accessed July 2013. http://indochine54.free.fr.

Mabunga, Manuel. "Memorial Day 1994: A Brief Description of Our First Main Line of Defense at Mabatang, Bataan." Commemoration of Nininger Statue and Memorial, Fort Lauderdale, FL, May 30, 1994. Private collection of John Patterson.

MacArthur, Douglas. "MacArthur's Address to the Corps." MacArthur Foundation. May 12, 1962. Accessed October 15, 2013. http://www.west-point.org.

MacDonald, Charles B. "United States Army in World War II: The European Theater of Operations, the Siegfried Line Campaign." United States Army Center of Military History. 1963. Accessed August 2013. www.history.army.mil.

McDaniel, W. Thomas, Jr. *The Major: The Senior Officer in Charge Commanding Fellow Prisoners of War*. Xlibris Corporation, 2011.

Miltonberger, Butler B., and James A. Huston. "Counter-Counterattacks Mortain." In *134th Infantry Regiment: Combat History of World War II*, 78–89. Accessed January 2012. http://coulthart.com.

Murray, John F. T. "The Army-McCarthy Confrontation: A Worthy Campaign." 1995. Private collection of Sue Anne Murray Brown.

———. "An Oral History of Colonel John F. T. Murray." Interviews by Danny R. Ross and Earle Munns Jr. January 6, 1987. Private collection of John Murray Jr.

"NATO: Shifts at Shape." *Time*, July 13, 1953.

Niderost, Eric. "Baptism of Fire: Kasserine Pass, 1943." *Military Heritage Magazine*, Summer 2008. Repr. Military History Online. Accessed July 2013. www.militaryhistoryonline.

"Norden Bombsight." U.S. Centennial of Flight Commissions. Accessed September 2012. www.centennialofflight.gov.

"Normandy American Cemetery and Memorial." American Battle Monuments Commission. Accessed July 2013. www.abmc.gov.

Norton, John. Interview by Patricia T. Redmond. July 14, 2004. Veterans History Project. National Society of the Daughters of the American Revolution, Frederick, MD, Chapter. Private collection of John Norton Jr.

O'Donnell, Franklin. "Explorer I." Jet Propulsion Laboratory, California Institute of Technology. 2007. Accessed September 2012. www.jpl.nasa.gov.

Oland, Dwight D. "North Apennines: The U.S. Army Campaigns of World War II." U.S. Army Center of Military History. Accessed August 2013. www.history.army.mil.

"Operation Husky: The Invasion of Sicily, July 1943." Second World War Experience Centre. Accessed August 2013. www.war-experience.org.

Operation Sandstone: Sixth, Seventh and Eighth Atomic Bomb Test Eniwetok Atoll Marshall Islands. Narrated by Carey Wilson. Atomic Energy Commission, Lookout Mountain Laboratory, United State Air Force. Hollywood: Metro-Goldwyn Mayer, 1948.

Osborn, Alex F. "Creative Collaboration by Groups." Extract from *Applied Imagination, Principals and Procedures of Creative Problem-Solving*. New York: Scribner's Sons, 1953. Private collection of Herbert Stern.

Patterson, Michael Robert. "Arlington National Cemetery: Where Valor Proudly Sleeps." Various biographies accessed 2011–13. http://arlingtoncemetery.net/.

"Portable Flame Throwers (German)." Intelligence Bulletin 2, no. 8 (1944). Lone Sentry. Accessed August 2013. www.lonesentry.com.

Powell, Edwin L. "The History of Army Aviation, Senior Officers Debriefing Program." Interview by Bryce R. Kramer and Ralph J. Powell. March 18, 1978. Annapolis, MD. U.S. Army Military History Institute. Private collection of Douglas Powell.

———. Interview by Dr. Lynn L. Sims. December 10, 1982. Annapolis, MD. Private collection of Douglas Powell.

———. "The Picnic." Believed to be first published in Fleet Landing retirement community newsletter, n.d. Private collection of Douglas Powell.

———. "The True Story of the Kasserine Pass." Believed to be first published in Fleet Landing retirement community newsletter, n.d. Private collection of Douglas Powell.

"Radio Navigation: 'Flying the Beam.'" *Time and Navigation*. Smithsonian. Accessed July 2013. http://timeandnavigation.si.edu.

Ramey, Roger M. Commendation memo to Major Gerard A. La Rocca, Air Task

Unit 7.4.2, June 4, 1948, from Headquarters, Air Task Group 7.4 (Prov), San Francisco, California. From the private collection of La Rocca.

Ramsey, N. F. "History of Delivery Program Prior to the Establishment of Project A." *History of Project A*. September 27, 1945. Accessed June 2012. www .alternatewars.com.

"Ranger History: World War II Ranger Battalions." SpecialOperations.com. Accessed June 2012. www.specialoperations.com.

Reed, Wilson R., and June Reed. "Standardization at NATO: Additional Information for Wilson Reed." March 10, 2012. Private collection of June Reed.

Ritter, László, *War on Tito's Yugoslavia? The Hungarian Army in Early Cold War Soviet Strategy*. Edited by László Ritter, Christian Nuenlist, and Anna Locher. Parallel History Project on Cooperative Security. February 2005. Accessed August 2013. www.janeliunas.lt.

Roosevelt, Franklin D. *Graduation Address at United States Military Academy*. West Point, New York. June 12, 1939. Accessed October 15, 2013. http://www .presidency.ucsb.edu/.

Rowny, Edward L. *Smokey Joe and the General*. Edited by Anne Kazel-Wilcox. CreateSpace Independent Publishing Platform, Amazon.com, 2013.

Salmon, Andrew. "January 1968: Assassins Storm Seoul; US Spyship Seized." *Korea Times*, January 24, 2010. Accessed August 2012. www.koreatimes.co.kr.

Schlosser, Jim. "Man Honors Father He Never Knew." *Geborener Deutscher* 11, no. 4, (1999). Accessed March 2013. http://wmlgage.com.

Shapira, Ian. "Barbara Robbins: A Slain CIA Secretary's Life and Death." *Washington Post*, May 6, 2012. Accessed May 2012. http://articles. washingtonpost.com.

Skowronek, Col. Paul George. "United States-Soviet Military Liaison in Germany since 1976." PhD diss., University of Colorado, Boulder, 1976.

Stern, Herbert. "325th Field Artillery Battalion, 84th Infantry Division Artillery." June 16, 2007. World War II summary of battalion operations from the private collection of the author.

———. "Comments on Joint Advanced Study Group, 26 June 1961." Memorandum for Director, Joint Staff. Private collection of Herbert Stern.

Stoy, Tim. "The Other Side of the Hill: How the German High Command Viewed the Fighting at Bennwihr; Sigolsheim and Hill 351 in Alsace, December 1944." January 2010, The Dragon, Fifteenth Infantry Regiment. Private collection of Henry Bodson.

Strausbaugh, Leo V. "The 6th Ranger Battalion: Strausbaugh Remembers." Descendants of WWII Rangers. Accessed March 2012. www.wwiirangers.com.

Sublette, Carey. "Nuclear Weapons Frequently Asked Questions." Nuclear Weapon Archive. Version 2.13: May 15, 1997. Accessed November 2012. http: //nuclearweaponarchive.org.

Thomas, C., J. Goetz, J. Stuart, and J. Klemm. "Analysis of Radiation Exposure for Naval Personnel at Operation Sandstone." Science Applications International Corporation. August 15, 1983. Accessed April 2013. www.dtra.mil.

"Timeline." *USO Entertainment*. www.uso.org. Accessed August 2013.

Trueman, Chris. "The Battle of Guadalcanal." *History Learning Site*. Accessed July 2013. www.historylearningsite.co.uk.

———. "Operation Dragoon." *History Learning Site*. Accessed July 2013. www .historylearningsite.co.uk.

Truman, Harry S. "Remarks to the President's Advisory Commission on Universal Training." American President Project. December 20, 1946. Accessed August 2012. www.presidency.ucsb.edu.

United News. "Japanese Sign Final Surrender!" United Newsreel Corporation, 1945.

Universal-International News. "Atlas in Orbit: Radio Ike's Message of Peace to the World." Commentator Fred Maness. December 22, 1958.

USAFFE (United States Army Forces in the Far East). "Battle of Abucay, 9–23 January 1942, USAFFE and Japanese Units and Respective Commanders Involved." Map provided to John Patterson, nephew of Alexander Nininger, by Manuel Mabunga, with legend added by Mabunga. Private collection of John Patterson.

"U.S. Army, 1st Logistical Command." Brochure covering Vietnam, ca. 1968–70. Private collection of Walter Woolwine.

U.S. Army, 1st Logistical Command, Information Office. "A Talk with the CG." Special issue, *Dynamo* (1970): 1–5. Private collection of Walter Woolwine.

"U.S. Army Divisions in World War II." *History Shots: Wall Graphics*. Accessed August 2013. www.historyshots.com.

USMA Class of 1941. *Blacker, Bolder and Gayer: The Silver Anniversary Yearbook of the Class of '41*. American Yearbook Company, 1966.

———. *Gold '41: Commemorating the Fiftieth Anniversary of the USMA Class of 1941*. Marceline, MO: Walsworth, 1990.

U.S. Military Academy. *Howitzer*. West Point, NY: USMA, 1941.

———. *Official Register of the Officers and Cadets*. United States Military Academy Printing Office, 1940.

"V-2 Rocket." White Sands Missile Range. Accessed May 2013. www.wsmr.army. mil.

"V-2 Rocket Components." White Sands Missile Range. Accessed August 2013. http://www.wsmr.army.mil.

Watson, Mark S. "Air-Assault Unit Seen Bold Move." *Baltimore Sun*, November 17, 1963. Private collection of Edward Rowny.

Weist, Dwight, announcer. "82nd Division in Victory Parade." RKO-Pathe News. January 12, 1946. Accessed April 2012. www.criticalpast.com.

Whitman, John W. *Bataan: Our Last Ditch*. New York: Hippocrene Books, 1990.

"World: How Tough Is a Hero?" *Time*, February 9, 1942.

"The X-1 Research Airplane." *NASA—Dryden History—Historic Aircraft—X-1*. NASA. October 9, 2008. Accessed August 2013. www.nasa.gov.

INDEX OF FORMATIONS AND UNITS

In World War II or post-war occupation duties, unless otherwise noted

INDEX OF NAMES AND SUBJECTS